Cisco ISP Essentials

Barry Raveendran Greene, Philip Smith

Cisco Press

Cisco Press
201 West 103rd Street
Indianapolis, IN 46290 USA

Cisco ISP Essentials

Barry Raveendran Green, Philip Smith

Copyright © 2002 Cisco Systems, Inc.

Published by:
Cisco Press
201 West 103rd Street
Indianapolis, IN 46290 USA

Printed in the United States of America 1 2 3 4 5 6 7 8 9 0

First Printing April 2002

Library of Congress Cataloging-in-Publication Number: 2001090435

ISBN: 1-58705-041-2

Warning and Disclaimer

This book is designed to provide information about best common practices for Internet service providers (ISPs). Every effort has been made to make this book as complete and as accurate as possible, but no warranty or fitness is implied.

The information is provided on an "as is" basis. The authors, Cisco Press, and Cisco Systems, Inc., shall have neither liability nor responsibility to any person or entity with respect to any loss or damages arising from the information contained in this book or from the use of the discs or programs that may accompany it.

The opinions expressed in this book belong to the author and are not necessarily those of Cisco Systems, Inc.

Feedback Information

At Cisco Press, our goal is to create in-depth technical books of the highest quality and value. Each book is crafted with care and precision, undergoing rigorous development that involves the unique expertise of members from the professional technical community.

Readers' feedback is a natural continuation of this process. If you have any comments regarding how we could improve the quality of this book, or otherwise alter it to better suit your needs, you can contact us through e-mail at feedback@ciscopress.com. Please make sure to include the book title and ISBN in your message.

We greatly appreciate your assistance.

Trademark Acknowledgments

All terms mentioned in this book that are known to be trademarks or service marks have been appropriately capitalized. Cisco Press or Cisco Systems, Inc., cannot attest to the accuracy of this information. Use of a term in this book should not be regarded as affecting the validity of any trademark or service mark.

Publisher	John Wait
Editor-In-Chief	John Kane
Cisco Systems Program Management	Michael Hakkert
	Tom Geitner
	William Warren
Acquisitions Editor	Amy Lewis
Production Manager	Patrick Kanouse
Development Manager	Howard Jones
Project Editor	San Dee Phillips
Copy Editor	Krista Hansing
Technical Editors	Brian Morgan and Bill Wagner
Team Coordinator	Tammi Ross
Book Designer	Gina Rexrode
Cover Designer	Louisa Klucznik
Production Team	Octal Publishing, Inc.
Indexer	Tim Wright

CISCO SYSTEMS

Corporate Headquarters
Cisco Systems, Inc.
170 West Tasman Drive
San Jose, CA 95134-1706
USA
http://www.cisco.com
Tel: 408 526-4000
    800 553-NETS (6387)
Fax: 408 526-4100

European Headquarters
Cisco Systems Europe
11 Rue Camille Desmoulins
92782 Issy-les-Moulineaux
Cedex 9
France
http://www-europe.cisco.com
Tel: 33 1 58 04 60 00
Fax: 33 1 58 04 61 00

Americas Headquarters
Cisco Systems, Inc.
170 West Tasman Drive
San Jose, CA 95134-1706
USA
http://www.cisco.com
Tel: 408 526-7660
Fax: 408 527-0883

Asia Pacific Headquarters
Cisco Systems Australia,
Pty., Ltd
Level 17, 99 Walker Street
North Sydney
NSW 2059 Australia
http://www.cisco.com
Tel: +61 2 8448 7100
Fax: +61 2 9957 4350

Cisco Systems has more than 200 offices in the following countries. Addresses, phone numbers, and fax numbers are listed on the Cisco Web site at www.cisco.com/go/offices

Argentina • Australia • Austria • Belgium • Brazil • Bulgaria • Canada • Chile • China • Colombia • Costa Rica • Croatia • Czech Republic • Denmark • Dubai, UAE • Finland • France • Germany • Greece • Hong Kong Hungary • India • Indonesia • Ireland • Israel • Italy • Japan • Korea • Luxembourg • Malaysia • Mexico The Netherlands • New Zealand • Norway • Peru • Philippines • Poland • Portugal • Puerto Rico • Romania Russia • Saudi Arabia • Scotland • Singapore • Slovakia • Slovenia • South Africa • Spain • Sweden Switzerland • Taiwan • Thailand • Turkey • Ukraine • United Kingdom • United States • Venezuela • Vietnam Zimbabwe

Copyright © 2000, Cisco Systems, Inc. All rights reserved. Access Registrar, AccessPath, Are You Ready, ATM Director, Browse with Me, CCDA, CCDE, CCDP, CCIE, CCNA, CCNP, CCSI, CD-PAC, *CiscoLink*, the Cisco Net*Works* logo, the Cisco Powered Network logo, Cisco Systems Networking Academy, Fast Step, FireRunner, Follow Me Browsing, FormShare, GigaStack, IGX, Intelligence in the Optical Core, Internet Quotient, IP/VC, iQ Breakthrough, iQ Expertise, iQ FastTrack, iQuick Study, iQ Readiness Scorecard, The iQ Logo, Kernel Proxy, MGX, Natural Network Viewer, Network Registrar, the Networkers logo, *Packet*, PIX, Point and Click Internetworking, Policy Builder, RateMUX, ReyMaster, ReyView, ScriptShare, Secure Script, Shop with Me, SlideCast, SMARTnet, SVX, TrafficDirector, TransPath, VlanDirector, Voice LAN, Wavelength Router, Workgroup Director, and Workgroup Stack are trademarks of Cisco Systems, Inc.; Changing the Way We Work, Live, Play, and Learn, Empowering the Internet Generation, are service marks of Cisco Systems, Inc.; and Aironet, ASIST, BPX, Catalyst, Cisco, the Cisco Certified Internetwork Expert Logo, Cisco IOS, the Cisco IOS logo, Cisco Press, Cisco Systems, Cisco Systems Capital, the Cisco Systems logo, Collision Free, Enterprise/Solver, EtherChannel, EtherSwitch, FastHub, FastLink, FastPAD, IOS, IP/TV, IPX, LightStream, LightSwitch, MICA, NetRanger, Post-Routing, Pre-Routing, Registrar, StrataView Plus, Stratm, SwitchProbe, TeleRouter, are registered trademarks of Cisco Systems, Inc. or its affiliates in the U.S. and certain other countries.

All other brands, names, or trademarks mentioned in this document or Web site are the property of their respective owners. The use of the word partner does not imply a partnership relationship between Cisco and any other company. (0010R)

About the Authors

Barry Raveendran Greene is a Senior Consultant in the Internet Architectures Group of Consulting Engineering, Office of the CTO, Cisco Systems. Cisco's CTO Consulting group assist ISPs throughout the world to scale, grow, and expand their networks. The assistance is delivered through consulting, developing new features, working new standards (IETF and other groups), and pushing forward Best Common Practices (BCPs) to the Internet community. Barry's current topics of interests are ISP Operations and Security as well as developing the features, functionality, and techniques to enhance an ISP's success.

Barry has been with Cisco since 1996, traveling to all parts of the world helping ISPs and telcos build the Internet. He is a former board member for the Asia Pacific Internet Association (APIA), co-creator for the APRICOT Conferences, Program Committee Member for ITU's Telecom 99, and facilitator for the creation of several Internet eXchange Points (IXPs) in Asia and Pacific. Barry is the co-coordinator for Cisco's ISP Workshop Program, which is designed to empower engineering talent in ISPs all over the world.

Mr. Greene has over 22 years experience in systems integration, security, operations, maintenance, management, and training on a variety of computer, internetworking, and telecommunications technologies. Before Cisco Systems, Barry was Deputy Director Planning and Operations for Singapore Telecom's SingNet Internet Service and the Singapore Telecom Internet Exchange (STIX); Network Engineer and Systems Integrator at Johns Hopkins University/ Applied Physics Lab (JHU/APL), Network Engineer and Systems Integrator Science Application International Corporation (SAIC), and a veteran of the United States Air Force.

Philip Smith is a Consulting Engineer in the Internet Architectures Group of Consulting Engineering, Office of the CTO, Cisco Systems. His role includes providing consultation and advice to ISPs primarily in the Asia Pacific region and also with other providers around the world. He concentrates specifically on network strategies, design, technology, and operations, as well as configuration, scaling, and training. He plays or has played a major role in training ISP engineers, co-founding the Cisco ISP/IXP Workshop programme, and providing ISP training and tutorials at many networking events around the world, including NANOG, RIPE, APNIC, ISOC, and APRICOT conferences. His other key interests include IPv6, BGP, IGPs, and network performance and data analysis.

Philip has been with Cisco since January 1998. Since joining, he has been working to promote and develop the Internet in the entire Asia Pacific region and has been actively involved in bringing the Internet to some countries in the region. He is a member of the APRICOT Executive Committee (the region's annual ISP operational and technology conference) as well as its Programme Committee, co-chair of APOPS (the region's ISP operational forum), and chair of two of APNIC's special interest groups (SIG)—the Routing SIG and the Exchange Point SIG. He also has a particular research interest in the growth of the Internet and provides a detailed daily analysis of the routing table as seen in the Asia Pacific to the general operator community worldwide.

Prior to joining Cisco, he spent five years at PIPEX (now part of UUNET's global ISP business), the UK's first commercial ISP, where he was Head of Network Engineering. As is common with startups in a rapidly growing marketplace, Philip gained deep experience in all of the engineering roles in an ISP, from support engineer, network operations, engineering, and development, before assuming responsibility for the entire UK network operation. He was one of the first engineers working in the commercial Internet in the UK, and he helped establish the LINX Internet Exchange Point in London and played a key role in building the modern Internet in Europe.

Philip is a Doctor of Philosophy and has a First Class Honours Degree in Physics. A native of Scotland, he now lives in Brisbane, Australia.

About the Technical Reviewers

Bill Wagner works as a Cisco Certified Systems Instructor (CCSI). He has over 22 years of computer programming and data communication experience. He has worked for corporations and companies such as Independent Computer Consultants, Numerax, McGraw-Hill/Numerax, and Standard and Poors. His teaching experience started with the Chubb Institute, Protocol Interface, Inc., and Geotrain. Bill is also a technical editor for numerous other Cisco Press titles.

Brian Morgan, CCIE #4865, CCSI, is the Director of Data Network Engineering at Allegiance Telecom, Inc. He's been in the networking industry for over 12 years. Prior to working at Allegiance, Brian was an Instructor/Consultant teaching ICND, BSCN, BSCI, CATM, CVOICE, and BCRAN. Brian is a co-author of Cisco Press's *CCNP Remote Access Exam Certification Guide* and technical editor of numerous other Cisco Press titles.

Acknowledgments

This book started life as a small whitepaper called "IOS Essentials," an attempt to document the various configuration and operational best practices which ISPs were using on their Cisco networking equipment. This whitepaper has, over the last few years, grown through several versions into this book, *Cisco ISP Essentials*.

We would like to thank the numerous friends and colleagues in the industry who have contributed to both the whitepaper and this book. Many have contributed their own text, made numerous suggestions, contributions, and clarifications, and also have provided their own deep real world operational experience with the Internet. Their willingness to help others *do the right thing* is one of the reasons for the Internet's success.

We'd also like to thank Howard Jones, our Development Editor, for the help and support he has given us. Thanks are also due to Amy Lewis and John Kane of Cisco Press for encouraging us and supporting us to make this book possible.

Barry Raveendran Greene and Philip Smith

Contents at a Glance

Table of Contents

Introduction

The Internet economy has played a significant part in the world economy since the mid 1990s. For many years prior, the Internet was the domain of U.S. academic research and defense internetworking, and a few entrepreneurs around the world who believed that a TCP/IP-based wide-area network (WAN) would be a viable alternative to the private wire networks that businesses were using to communicate with each other. The many ISP engineers who learned their skills in that period look on those early pioneering days at the end of the 1980s and early 1990s as something special. Work was invariably hard, and technology challenges were seemingly insurmountable when compared with the relative ease of use and configuration these days. But the sense of competition was more a friendly rivalry and partnership to make the fledgling Internet a fun place to be.

This pioneering spirit, and the desire of the Internet community to make the Internet a success, has resulted in the Internet becoming the major part of our lives at the start of the 21st century. It's now a huge commercial network, very competitive, with many players, small and large, from all over the world, heavily involved in its infrastructure. More people are taking part in the Internet every day, both end users with their first computer connecting to the World Wide Web, and new ISPs anxious to become part of a very significant growth industry. Furthermore, the few remaining countries in the world without an Internet connection are investigating connecting up and examining the advantages being networked will offer their local economies.

As the Internet has grown in our day-to-day consciousness, so have textbooks aspiring to help newcomers find the proverbial pot of gold: books ranging from beginner guides to designing web pages, to explaining what the Internet is, to describing the business process, to becoming a successful ISP. However, there has been precious little that describes the configuration concepts and tricks of the trade that ISP network engineers use in their daily lives—there is an argument which says, "We have been too busy fixing the potholes in the Internet superhighway to actually spend time writing down what we do."

Motivation

The inspiration for this book has come from three sources. The first is Cisco IOS Software. Cisco has been part of the Internet since the Internet started, building one of the first devices to move IP packets across a WAN. Over the years, IOS has grown from being a fairly basic piece of software to a highly sophisticated, feature rich, and extremely powerful router control suite. A tremendous range of features has been built into the IOS. This extensive feature set is excellent for public network ISPs, giving their network engineers a large number of options and capabilities that can be designed into the network.

While a huge number of features may be desirable, IOS also poses a problem—network engineers busy running their networks have a difficult time keeping up with all the new IOS features. Many engineers, even experienced network engineers, do not know how, when, and where to deploy the various features in their network.

This book highlights many of the key IOS features in everyday use in the major ISP backbones of the world. Judicious study and implementation of the IOS pearls contained in this book will help to prevent problems, increase security, improve performance, and ensure the operational stability of the Internet.

The second source of inspiration for writing this book is that there is no complete reference text for newcomers to the industry to take router products and build an ISP network from them. There is a great deal of documentation about network design practices, discussing ISP business practices, configuring the various routing protocols, and all the higher level services that ride on the Internet. Such texts as *Internet Routing Architectures,* Second Edition, and the *ISP Survival Guide* have helped many ISPs deal with scaling their backbones and getting the most from their ISP businesses. But when a newcomer is faced with a blue/green metal cased box fresh out of its packing box, a CD-ROM with all the documentation for this piece of equipment, there is the sinking feeling of "what happens now?" The intention of this book is to guide both newcomers and experienced network engineers through the optimal configuration of that blue/green box and its parent network, to integrate it effectively and securely into an ISP network, and to be part of the Internet backbone.

The final source of inspiration has already been touched on in this introduction: We all have been too busy working to write down what we are doing. Our daily working lives include outreach to new providers, helping existing providers make their networks better, and so on. There is much repetition of concepts which are obvious, but not documented in a general text. The "IOS Essentials Whitepaper" started this all off, documenting special Cisco IOS features that were in use almost exclusively in the ISP industry. Many friends and colleagues in the industry have encouraged us to write a book based around the whitepaper, putting our experiences and knowledge gained in the industry since the early 1990s down on paper so that others can benefit.

Intended Audience

The recommendations we make in this book focus on ISPs. The recommendations are not intended for other types of networks, whether private Internets or enterprise networks connecting to the Internet, although we are sure that some of the ideas and suggestions we make here could be applied successfully to such networks as well.

Engineers working for ISPs will benefit most from this text. (All engineers will benefit, be they engineers working in the ISPs Network Operations Center, working in the Customer Help Desk, or working on the core backbone itself.) All branches of an ISP engineering function will be exposed to the issues and concepts covered in this book, and we hope that this will be a valuable reference for everyone. The final chapter also has some relevance to the more business-orientated side of the ISP. Quite often, in our experience, planning a network is not treated quite as seriously as it should be. Planning is a joint effort between network engineers and business managers to ensure the best compromise between network design and the funding available to pay for it.

Organization

There are five chapters as well as several appendixes aimed to give the reader further information, tips, and templates relating to what has been covered in the paper. These chapters cover the following topics:

Chapter 1: Software and Router Management: Introduces the reader to Cisco IOS, the image trains designed specifically for ISPs, and how to manage these on the router. This chapter also covers router management, including configuration management, the command-line interface, and handling the status information, which the router can make available to its operators.

Chapter 2: General Features: Introduces the various miscellaneous features an ISP requires to organize on the router prior to dealing with routing protocols and network security. These features include the loopback interface, interface configuration good practices, CEF, and NetFlow.

Chapter 3: Routing Protocols: Covers the major issues facing ISPs with the configuration and feature set available with the major routing protocols. These include HSRP, IGP design, and the extensive feature set now available with the BGP implementation in Cisco IOS.

Chapter 4: Security: Covers the current major security features and support on the router, and gives an extensive discussion on the feature set available for defeating DoS attacks, which are so prevalent on the Internet today. Topics covered include router access, routing protocol security, and network security. Features discussed include applications of Unicast RPF and CAR.

Chapter 5: Operational Practices: The final chapter covers how the previous four chapters mesh together to help build an ISP backbone. The text concentrates on working through the typical processes used for building an ISP backbone, all the way from network design and layout, to positioning and implementing higher level services.

Appendixes: The appendixes provide additional reference material or examples to supplement the content of each chapter. Included here are route flap damping configurations, an extensive list of popular network management and monitoring tools in use, plus a working sample configuration of a simple ISP network using the IOS principles covered in this book.

The book is best read in order, because each chapter assumes knowledge of the content covered in previous chapters. Experienced engineers might be quite happy dipping into the text as they see fit. The style of the book is intended to allow both experts and beginners to feel at ease with the content.

Further Information

This book does not set out to summarize the rather copious documentation and other excellent materials Cisco has made available to the general public as well as to its customers. The book is based upon the "IOS Essentials Whitepaper," where we have collected preliminary documentation of features as they are released, or we have written our own explanation, as no documentation existed at all. Quite often Cisco's own documentation has followed much later than its first appearance in "IOS Essentials."

Along with this book, the authors are maintaining a web site with whitepaper updates to the contents of this book—http://www.ispbook.com. The web site http://www.cisco.com/public/cons/isp also contains other reference materials that may be useful for ISPs.

Where topics are not apparently covered in sufficient technical depth, the reader is encouraged to consult the following reference sources:

- Cisco System's Documentation (available to the general public on Cisco's website at http://www.cisco.com/univercd/) or on the CD-ROM that comes with each router.

- Cisco.com.

- Local Cisco Systems' support channels.

- Public discussion lists. The list that focuses specifically on ISPs that use Cisco Systems equipment is cisco-nsp hosted by Jared Mauch. cisco-nsp is a mailing list which has been created specifically for ISPs to discuss Cisco Systems products and their use. To subscribe, send an e-mail to: majordomo@puck.nether.net with a message body containing: *subscribe cisco-nsp*

## CHAPTER 1

Software and Router Management

This chapter covers many of the basic questions that ISPs ask when they are first faced with setting up routers for their Internet business. Although documentation shipped with any item of equipment provides a very comprehensive description of setup processes, more experienced ISPs usually have developed a methodology for how new hardware is deployed on a living backbone. Often the vendor's well-intentioned startup process for new users becomes more of a hindrance or inconvenience in these situations. This chapter does not provide an alternative to the recommendations, but it suggests what ISPs should consider as the initial configuration phase for their network equipment and the processes that they should follow during their business operation.

The first portion of the chapter covers the Cisco IOS Software and some of the ISP industry's current practices for choosing and deploying the software. This includes which version of operating system software the routers should use, how to get the chosen version on to the equipment, and the various strategies for management of the router operating software and configuration.

The second portion of the chapter covers aspects of router management. The user interface to Cisco routers has always been through a command-line interface (CLI). Back in the early days of IOS Software, this was of a very functional design—these days many features have been added, making it as flexible as many of the modern shells available on UNIX systems. Also covered are features of router management, including best practices for capturing logging information, applying time synchronization, using the Simple Network Management Protocol (SNMP), using http access rather than the CLI, and dealing with software crashes.

Which Cisco IOS Software Version Should I Be Using?

ISPs and NSPs operate in an environment of constant change, exponential growth, and unpredictable threats to the stability of their backbone. The last thing an Internet backbone engineer needs is buggy or unstable code on routers. As in any commercial-grade service providing infrastructure, the equipment forming that infrastructure requires stable operating software. The ISP space, however, also demands software that will give market leadership when it comes to new features. Herein is the difference between enterprise businesses and

Internet service provision: The former demands stability above all else and will change only when necessitated; typical software refresh cycles for enterprise networks are measured in years.

The other key differentiator between enterprise and ISP businesses is that ISPs expect to use the Internet for communication with their software vendors, for accessing new images, speaking to the technical assistance center, or communicating directly with the development engineers. This divergence from the traditional model of the software development and implementation process implied that ISPs require an IOS Software code train specific to their needs.

Midway through the life of the 10.3 software train, a team of Cisco engineers devoted to working with ISP-specific features created a branch of IOS Software that catered specifically for ISPs' requirements. The key characteristics were an IP-centric code base, stability, quick bug fixes, easy access to the key development engineers, and rapid feature additions. The so-called "isp-geeks" software started life as an unofficial ISP software issue, but with the arrival of the 11.1 software train, it had matured and developed into a release system specifically targeted to ISPs. 11.1CA was used to deliver new ISP-only features months before these appeared anywhere else—and 11.1CC was the successor to 11.1CA, used to deliver the now widely deployed CEF functionality. As IOS Software becomes more feature-rich, this ISP software train concept has been further developed and enhanced, and it now provides a well-developed and stable platform for all ISPs.

Along with the development of specific IOS Software images for ISPs, the Service Provider feature set was added to all Cisco IOS Software released. This software is based on the IP-only image but with additional features for ISPs. Such software can be recognized by the "-p-" in the image name. This image is usually all that any ISP needs to run. These images cannot be ordered at time of router purchase, but they can be downloaded from Cisco.com before deployment of the router in service. For example, a 7200 ordered by an ISP might come with the c7200-i-mz.120-6 image—this image should be replaced with the Service Provider equivalent, c7200-p-mz.120-6. These Service Provider "-p-" images are built for all supported router platforms, unlike the more limited platform support available on the ISP release trains.

At the time of writing, our recommended IOS Software branches for ISPs are the following:

- **12.0S**—Supporting the 7200, RSP7000, 7500, and 12000 series routers
- **12.0**—Supporting 2500, 2600, 3600, and 4000/4x00 series routers[1]
- **12.1**—Supporting the new hardware platforms not supported by 12.0 (such as 3660)

Releases 11.1CC and 11.2GS are no longer recommended for ISP backbones because they do not support the current generation of hardware in use, nor will they be enhanced to support new hardware or software features. For example, 11.1CC has gained no new features since 11.1(26)CC. Releases prior to 12.0 are now coming to the end of their life. Although

support new hardware or software features. For example, 11.1CC has gained no new features since 11.1(26)CC. Releases prior to 12.0 are now coming to the end of their life. Although they are still supported by Cisco, they will not gain any new features. Migration from these old releases should be part of the ongoing upgrade planning process in all ISP networks at the moment.

In addition to these software releases, other specialized versions are available, and of course, there are newer developments than those listed previously.

- **12.0ST** is a version of 12.0S enhanced to include some of the features of 12.0T, specifically aimed at those ISPs deploying MPLS-based virtual private networks.

- **12.2** and **12.2T** are the successor developments of 12.1 and 12.1T. At the time of this writing, these two release trains were just made available, and we don't recommend their use in an ISP network unless they have unique features not available in the recommended trains. For example, 12.2T sees the first release of a Cisco TAC–supported IPv6 software.

In the future, there will be other IOS Software releases following those mentioned here. Consult the Product Bulletin page on Cisco.com for up-to-date information. The online supplements to this book will list the current recommendations for ISPs.

NOTE Cisco Systems' most up-to-date recommendations on which IOS Software branch an ISP should be using are on the Product Bulletin page, available at Cisco.com, at http://www.cisco.com/warp/public/cc/general/bulletin/index.shtml.

Where to Get Information on Release 12.0S

Release 12.0S is now available from Cisco.com's Software Library, at http://cco.cisco.com/kobayashi/sw-center/sw-ios.shtml. The following URLs have some additional details on the features included in 12.0S, migration options, and how to download the software:

Cisco IOS Software Release 12.0S new features: http://www.cisco.com/warp/public/cc/pd/iosw/iore/iomjre12/prodlit/934_pb.htm

Cisco IOS Software Release 12.0S ordering procedures and platform hardware support: http://www.cisco.com/warp/public/cc/pd/iosw/iore/iomjre12/prodlit/935_pb.htm

Cisco IOS Software release notes for Release 12.0S: http://www.cisco.com/univercd/cc/td/doc/product/software/ios120/relnote/7000fam/rn120s.htm

Cisco IOS Software release 12.0S migration guide: http://www.cisco.com/warp/public/cc/pd/iosw/iore/iomjre12/prodlit/940_pb.htm

Further Reference on IOS Software Releases

Figures 1-1 and 1-2 provide a visual map of IOS Software releases up to 12.1—they also show how the different versions and trains interrelate. This has been and still is an often-asked question in the ISP arena and other marketplaces in which Cisco is present—these visual roadmaps have been created to show the interrelation of the different IOS Software versions. The current up-to-date roadmap can be seen at http://www.cisco.com/warp/public/620/roadmap.shtml. Consult the following URLs on Cisco.com for more detailed and up-to-date information on IOS Software release structure:

Cisco IOS Software releases: http://www.cisco.com/warp/public/732/Releases/

Types of Cisco IOS Software releases: http://www.cisco.com/warp/customer/cc/pd/iosw/iore/prodlit/537_pp.htm

Release designations defined—software lifecycle definitions: http://www.cisco.com/warp/customer/417/109.html

Software naming conventions for Cisco IOS Software: http://www.cisco.com/warp/customer/432/7.html

IOS Software reference guide: http://www.cisco.com/warp/public/620/1.html

IOS Software feature navigator, from the "Service and Support" page on Cisco.com: http://www.cisco.com/cgi-bin/Support/FeatureNav/FN.pl

Figure 1-1 *Cisco IOS Software Roadmap up to Release 12.1*

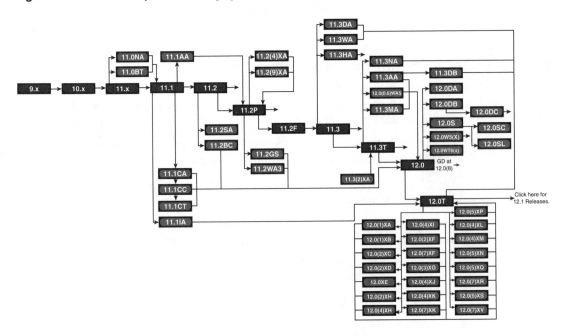

Figure 1-2   *IOS Software Roadmap from 12.1 Onward*

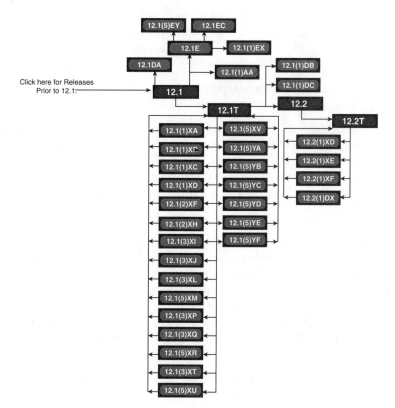

IOS Software Management

Most router platforms used in ISP backbone networks have very flexible RAM and Flash memory configurations. For private, enterprise, or campus networks, the number of changes required in software, new features, or even the network infrastructure is small. The Internet is changing and growing daily, and a common mistake by new ISPs is to underspecify the equipment that they purchase. This should not be taken as a recommendation to buy what might seem like unneeded memory. It is recognition of the fact that having to upgrade a router every few months because "unforeseen" growth in the Internet causes disruption to the network and can potentially affect the reliability of hardware. Many Internet engineers support the notion that the more often humans touch a piece of hardware, the less reliable that hardware becomes.

Flash Memory

The Flash memory on a router is where the IOS Software images are stored. When a new router is purchased, it has the IOS Software image specified at the time of ordering installed in Flash. Flash memory usually is built into the router, and some platforms have expansion slots where PCMCIA Flash cards or Flash disks can be installed.

It is good practice to supplement the built-in Flash with another area of Flash memory. This can be done in at least two ways:

1 Partition the built-in Flash memory. This can be done using the configuration command. For example, the following command will partition the Flash into two areas of 8 MB each (assuming 16 MB of installed Flash memory and also assuming that the hardware supports this type of partitioning):

```
partition flash 2 8 8
```

2 Install a Flash card or Flash disk in one or both of the external flash slots.

Having more than one Flash memory area ensures that the router IOS Software image can be upgraded without affecting the existing image. For example, if there is room for only one image in Flash and it is the image that the router is running, the existing image needs to be removed before a new one can be installed. What would happen, say, if the router crashed during the image upgrade? Recovery is possible with the boot image, but this is significantly more difficult than if proper precautions were taken. By copying the new image into the other area of Flash memory, the ISP ensures that the network functionality is minimally affected in the event of a crash or other unforeseen problems during image upgrade.

The new image in the second area of Flash memory easily can be selected, as shown in the following example for the 7500 series routers:

```
boot system flash slot1:rsp-pv-mz.120-5.S
boot system flash slot0:rsp-pv-mz.111-25.CC
boot system flash
```

This tells the router to boot rsp-pv-mz.120-5.S from slot1 Flash first. If that image cannot be found or the Flash card is not in slot1, the router looks for rsp-pv-mz.111-25.CC in slot0. If that image cannot be found, the router boot software looks for the first image in any of the system Flash.

Consider this example, on the 36x0 series routers, where the main 16 MB Flash has been partitioned:

```
boot system flash flash:1:c3640-p-mz.120-5.S
boot system flash flash:2:c3640-p-mz.112-19.P
boot system flash
```

This tells the router to boot c3640-p-mz.120-5.S from the first Flash partition. If the router cannot find that image, it will look for c3640-p-mz.112-19.P in the second Flash partition. Failing that, it looks for the first usable IOS Software image in Flash memory.

This type of arrangement ensures that, in the event of image corruption, a problem with the operating image, or a router crash, some backup image always is available on the router. Proper precautions ensure minimal network downtime during maintenance periods or emergency occasions. Downloading a new image during a network down situation with customers and management exerting pressure is unnecessary extra stress that easily could have been avoided with a little precaution.

Common practice is for ISPs to leave the known working image on one of the Flash cards or Flash partitions of the router. If deployment of a new release (which has passed tests in the lab environment) exhibits some problem or defect later in operation, it is easy to backtrack to the old image.

Finally, it makes no commercial or operational sense to skimp on the amount of Flash memory. As more of the features requested by ISPs are added to IOS Software, the image grows larger. Sizing Flash to the current image size is a false economy because, more than likely, in the near future a larger image with new features might require Flash memory larger than what has been installed in the router.

System Memory

Another common practice among the Tier 1 and Tier 2 ISPs in all regions of the world is maximizing the memory on every router. Cisco recommends the necessary amount of memory required to run each IOS Software image. Downloading a new image from Cisco.com includes a question asking users if they are fully aware of the memory requirements for the chosen image. Ignore the minimum recommendations at your peril!

For example, at the time of this writing, it is recognized that 128 MB of memory is the minimum requirement to operate a router carrying the full Internet routing table. Any ISP requesting IOS Software release 12.0S is required to acknowledge this fact. IOS Software release 12.0S will still operate inside 32 MB of memory on a 7200 router and will carry the majority of the Internet routes with 64 MB of memory (with minimal configuration and all features turned off). For example, the BGP algorithms will use more memory if it is available to improve their efficiency. Skimping on memory means affecting the performance of the routers and the end result, which the customer experiences.

Many ISPs now simply specify maximum memory when they purchase new routing hardware. They recognize that sending an engineer to remove processor cards costs money through downtime, extra human resources, and potential service disruption, and it shortens the lifetime of the equipment through the human interaction. "Fit and forget" is the norm among many of the largest ISPs today.

When and How to Upgrade

Several ISPs upgrade their router software almost every time Cisco releases a new image. This is recognized by most industry operators as being bad practice. The only time that any

ISP should be upgrading software is when it is required to fix bugs, support new hardware, or implement new software features. In many other industries, changing core operating software is seen as a major event not to be undertaken lightly. Yet for some reason, some ISPs seem to think that a fortnightly upgrade is good practice.

Based on what most Tier 1 and Tier 2 ISPs now do, software upgrades are carried out only when they are required. Extensive testing is carried out in the test lab (how many ISPs have a test network that looks like one of their PoPs, or a portion of their network?). Deployment happens only after extensive testing, and even then new images are implemented with caution on a quieter part of the network. For example, the software versions in one PoP might be updated and left running for a week or a fortnight to check for any issues; after this initial deployment phase, the rest of the network will be upgraded.

Caution is of paramount importance on a commercial-grade network. Even when upgrades are carried out, remember the recommendations discussed in this section. IOS Software makes it easier by giving backout paths through alternative images. Never attempt an upgrade without being aware of potential side effects from unforeseen problems, never attempt an upgrade without a backout plan, and never attempt an upgrade without having read the release notes that come with the software release. It also helps to read the release notes for all intermediate releases because that will give the engineer good information about what has changed in the software over the release cycle.

Another practice implemented by most Tier 1 and Tier 2 ISPs is to minimize the number of different versions of IOS Software images running on their network's routers. This is almost always done for administrative and management reasons. Apart from reducing the number of potential interoperability issues due to bugs and new features, it is easier to train operations staff on the features and differences between a few images than it is to train them on the differences among many images. Typically ISPs aim to run no more than two different IOS Software releases. One image is the old release; the other is the one on which they are doing the blanket upgrade on the backbone. Upgrades tend to be phased, not carried out en masse overnight. If the ISPs have access equipment, such as the AS5x00 series, or cable/ xDSL aggregation devices, they will deploy different IOS Software images on these devices. But again, if one dial box needs to be upgraded, ISPs tend to upgrade them all to ensure a consistent IOS Software release on that network.

A typical software version strategy is something like the following:

- **Core/backbone network**—One software release (xxxx-p-mz.120-17.S1) runs on all backbone routers. The software on these routers probably is changed every six months or even less frequently. The Internet core carries only IP packets, and rarely are new features or capabilities added. Well-run Internet cores often have routers with uptimes exceeding six months, sometimes even over one year.

- **Distribution and leased-line aggregation layer**—One software release runs on all routers. This tends to be the part of the network that customers connect to, so often new features and newly deployed connection services demand a more frequent software update cycle.

- **Dial access layer**—A common software release is run on all access platforms. As with the previous example, a more frequent cycle might be necessary. Some ISPs build new infrastructure for new services, so when infrastructure is unchanging, it makes little sense to upgrade software. Some dialup networks that we have had experience with have had hardware running the same software image for several years.

- **VPN access layer**—A common software release is run on all platforms. This example is included because it is the current fashion in the industry. Often ISPs use bleeding-edge software and hardware to deliver VPN services, and frequent upgrades for new features can be necessary from time to time. Again, the usual rule applies: Don't change it unless new features are necessary; it saves the customers from going through pain.

Some of the bigger ISPs have weekly software strategy meetings, with the aim to ensure consistency across the company business for software deployed on the backbone. New software has to be approved across the engineering and operations management, and then it is deployed only after fairly intensive proof testing in the lab. Software version consistency monitored by the ISP's NOC, often through automatic or cron-based tools that log into all the routers and other equipment and grab the version number of the running software and the contents of the router's Flash memory.

Finally, adopting some strategy is strongly recommended. Having no strategy usually means that in times of crisis during network problems, the operations engineers will resort to a random walk through different software versions in the desperate hope that something might work to stabilize a network problem. Having strong control over software versions will mean that diagnosing network problems can be achieved more easily.

Copying New Images to Flash Memory

Copying a new image into Flash memory in itself isn't a complicated process, but there are a few good practice points to be aware of. The most important point is to re-emphasize that leaving a backout image somewhere on the router is good practice and plain common sense. So many network outages have been prolonged because a new router image failed and the ISP didn't leave a backout image on the device.

New images should be loaded into Flash during maintenance periods, not when the router is live carrying a full traffic load. Although the activity of copying an image to Flash won't impact the router's operation, it is advisable to avoid enhancing the possibility of an accident while the network is in production. At least an operational error during a maintenance period won't cause customer anger because customers were expecting downtime during the maintenance period (assuming that the customers were informed in the first place, another key point that several ISPs seem to forget!).

Basically two ways exist for copying images to and from the router Flash. Using TFTP is the more traditional way and has been part of IOS Software for a very long time. FTP support was added with the arrival of 12.0 software; this is somewhat more efficient and flexible than using TFTP, and it does not have TFTP's 16 MB file size restriction.

Copying Using TFTP

The commands to copy software into Flash memory have been refined in releases from 12.0, making the mechanics of getting software to and from the router simpler and more consistent in style. The **copy** command has been enhanced to support a URL appearance covering all system devices in a consistent format, as in this example:

```
beta7200#copy tftp ?
  bootflash:      Copy to bootflash: file system
  disk0:          Copy to disk0: file system
  disk1:          Copy to disk1: file system
  flash:          Copy to flash: file system
  ftp:            Copy to ftp: file system
  lex:            Copy to lex: file system
  null:           Copy to null: file system
  nvram:          Copy to nvram: file system
  rcp:            Copy to rcp: file system
  running-config  Update (merge with) current system configuration
  slot0:          Copy to slot0: file system
  slot1:          Copy to slot1: file system
  startup-config  Copy to startup configuration
  system:         Copy to system: file system
  tftp:           Copy to tftp: file system
beta7200#copy tftp
```

This is somewhat improved over the rather inconsistent and platform-dependent format used in previous releases.

Before copying the image to Flash, make sure that the Flash has enough space for the new image. Preferably install two Flash devices or partition the existing Flash device, as has been described previously. Use **cd**, **delete**, **erase**, and **squeeze** (depending on platform) to clear enough space on the Flash file system. Make sure that the partition/Flash holding the currently running image is not touched. If there is any problem with the upgrade, a backout path is available. And don't forget to set up the ***boot system xxxxx*** IOS Software configuration command so that the router is told to boot the currently running image.

When the flash partition is ready, a **copy** command can be issued to copy the new IOS Software image from the remote device (which could be any of those listed previously) to the partition. An example of the **copy** command follows:

```
beta7200#copy tftp slot1:
Address or name of remote host []? noc1
Source filename []? 12.0S/c7200-p-mz.120-6.S
Destination filename [c7200-p-mz.120-6.S]?
Accessing tftp://noc1/12.0S/c7200-p-mz.120-6.S...
Loading 12.0S/c7200-p-mz.120-6.S from 192.168.3.1 (via Serial3/1):
!!!!!!!!!!!!!!!!!!!!!!!!!!!!!!!!!!!!!!!!!!!!!!!!!!!!!!!!!!!!!!!!!!!!!!!!!!!!!!!!!!!!!!!!
!!!!!!!!!!!!!!!!!!!!!!!!!!!!!!!!!!!!!!!!!!!!!!!!!!!!!!!!!!!!!!!!!!!!!!!!!!!!!!!!!!!!!
```

```
[OK - 5708964/11417600 bytes]

5708964 bytes copied in 330.224 secs (17299 bytes/sec)
beta7200#
```

This will copy the image c7200-p-mz.120-6.S from the tftp server to the Flash device in slot1. The command also can be shortened to this, which will achieve the same thing:

```
beta7200#copy tftp://noc1/12.0S/c7200-p-mz.120-6.S slot1:
Destination filename [c7200-p-mz.120-6.S]?
…etc…
```

Notice that the router will attempt to work out the filename from the URL string entered— this can be helpful and can save typing.

Copying Using FTP

FTP client support has been added in 12.0 images of IOS Software. TFTP has well-known limitations, with the 16 MB file size becoming an issue with some of the larger full-featured IOS Software images now being made available. The FTP client allows for FTPing images to and from an FTP server. The options for and the capabilities of the **ftp** command are the same as for the **tftp** command described previously.

The following is an example of a software download directly from Cisco's FTP site— something that cannot be done with TFTP (the password has been replaced by XXX in the example):

```
7206-AboveNet-SJ2#copy ftp://bgreene:XXX@ftp.cisco.com slot0:
Source filename []? /cisco/ios/12.0/12.0.9S/7200/c7200-k3p-mz.120-9.S.bin
Destination filename [c7200-k3p-mz.120-9.S.bin]?
Accessing ftp://bgreene:XXX@ftp.cisco.com //cisco/ios/12.0/12.0.9S/7200/c7200-k3p-
mz.120-9.S.bin...Translating "ftp.cisco.com"...domain server (207.126.96.162) [OK]

Loading /cisco/ios/12.0/12.0.9S/7200/c7200-k3p-mz.120-9.S.bin
```

As ISPs have gained experience with using FTP, it has very much become the preferred method of putting images and other information onto the router. We encourage you to look at this method, if you have not already done so, and adopt it as current practice from here on.

WARNING   It's important to be aware that on the 2500 series routers the image runs from Flash, so a reload of the router to run the BOOTROM image is required to upgrade. The BOOTROM image does not support FTP copies of the IOS Software image onto the router, even though it is possible to enter the command sequences listed previously—the BOOTROM attempts to upload the image using TFTP, its only supported functionality.

Reloading the Routers

When the image has been successfully loaded by either the TFTP or FTP method and has been verified, set up the router to boot the new image (use the **no boot system** and **boot system** commands described previously). It is also a good idea to configure another **boot system** command pointing to the backup image (as in the example in the earlier section).

The standard way of implementing new software on the router is to use the **reload** command—this simply reboots the router. Use the command with caution—doing so outside a maintenance slot will attract customer anger because of the potential number of minutes of downtime experienced.

If desirable, the router even can be configured to do a timed/delayed reboot sometime in the future. Use that feature with care, though; it is perfectly feasible to do timed reboots on several routers and completely break a portion of the ISP network! We have seen several cases of planned software upgrades go wrong because the ISP made a configuration error and the resulting phased timed reload gradually pulled the network over—without the ISP's operations staff being able to do anything about it. A guideline rule is that it is acceptable to do timed reloads at the edge of a network, but core devices, by their nature, are critical for the operational integrity of the backbone and should be handled appropriately with direct input from the operations team.

The **reload** command has three options that many ISPs find useful. Examples of their use are shown in Table 1-1.

Table 1-1   **reload** *Command Examples*

beta7200# reload at 17:05 Reload scheduled for 17:05:00 AEST Mon Jul 16 2001 (in 5 hours and 10 minutes)	Reboots the router at 17:05 local time on the router. Notice the detailed confirmation.
Proceed with reload? [confirm]	Shows a message and the prompt to confirm.
beta7200# reload in 180 Reload scheduled for 16:10:35 AEST Mon Jul 16 2001 (in 3 hours)	Reboots the router in 180 minutes. Again, notice the detailed confirmation message and the prompt to confirm.
Proceed with reload? [confirm]	Shows a message and the prompt to confirm.
beta7200# reload cancel	Cancels a previously set up reload.

Don't forget that the **reload cancel** command can be used to undo any timed reload—if a timed and phased reload of several routers has been set up and must be backed out of, ensure that there is sufficient good access to each router (preferably with out-of-band management) so that the **cancel** command can be implemented without panicking.

Also notice that when a timed reload has been set up on the router, using a **show version** command or simply logging into the router will show that a timed reload has been set up—for example:

```
[philip@pfs-pc philip]$ telnet beta7200
Trying 192.168.4.130...
Connected to eth1-0.beta7200 (192.168.4.130).
Escape character is '^]'.

User Access Verification

Username: philip
Password:

Reload scheduled for 17:05:00 AEST Mon Jul 16 2001 (in 1 hour and 4 minutes)
beta7200>
```

When the new image has been booted successfully, it should be put through acceptance tests during the maintenance slot (these tests could be as simple as asking, "Does the routing work?") and then should be monitored during operation. Don't delete the previous image—you know that it works, so if it is left on the other Flash partition, a back out path is available in case of future problems. The old image can be deleted after a decision has been made to further upgrade the IOS Software. The benefit of configuring two Flash devices/partitions is clear to see—ease of maintenance!

WARNING   Upgrade a router only when there are bug fixes or when new hardware support or new software features are required. Otherwise, do not touch that router! "If it isn't broken, don't fix it!"

Configuration Management

The following section discusses some of the configuration-management features on the router. This includes how to handle the configuration in the NVRAM, how to use the TFTP and FTP server functions on the router, and some of the shortcuts available at the CLI.

NVRAM, TFTPserver, and FTPserver

The onboard router NVRAM is used to store the router's active configuration. Most ISPs keep an off-router copy of this configuration, too. In the unlikely event that the configuration is lost on the router, they can quickly recover the system with the off-router backup. There are several options for off-router backup of the running configuration:

- Write configuration to a TFTP server using the **write net** command. (In IOS Software release 12.0 and more recent software, the **write net** command has been superseded with the more sophisticated copy function. The equivalent command is **copy running tftp:**.)

- Configurations saved by an operator's **write net** command are kept under automated revision control. Combined with TACACS+ authentication (see later), it is possible to track who has changed what and when. This is important for accountability and configuration backout in case of problems.

- An automated (for example, UNIX cron) job collects the configuration from the router every few hours or so. The collected copy is kept under revision control. Changes can be flagged to the network-monitoring system, to the NOC, or to the operations engineers. Some public domain tools are available to do this; the best known and most popular is RANCID (Really Awesome New Cisco conflg Differ), at http://www.shrubbery.net/rancid/.

- Router configurations are built from a master configuration database. The running configuration is only a copy, with the master configuration kept off-router. Any updates to the running configuration are made by altering the master files (under revision control); the new master configuration then is implemented during maintenance periods.

NOTE   See Chapter 2, "General Features," for a discussion on loopback interfaces and for best practices for configuring the router for TFTP services.

The IOS Software command prompts to save the configuration are given in the following examples. The syntax has been significantly changed starting with IOS Software release 12.0, mainly to make the commands used to transfer configuration files and IOS Software between operator/NOC and the router more consistent. The IOS Software command before release 12.0 is given in the following example:

```
alpha7200#write network
Remote host []? noc-pc
Name of configuration file to write [alpha7200-confg]?
Write file router2-confg on host 192.168.3.1? [confirm]
Building configuration...

Writing alpha7200-confg !!! [OK]
alpha7200#
```

From release 12.0 onward, the command to do the same thing is **copy**, as given in the following example:

```
beta7200#copy running tftp:
Remote host[]? noc-pc
Destination filename [beta7200-confg]?
Write file tftp://noc-pc/beta7200-confg? [confirm]
!!! [OK]
beta7200#
```

NOTE	The **write network** command still is supported in release 12.0, although it might be withdrawn in a future release.

Since release 12.0, FTP also can be used to copy configurations to an FTP server. This provides more security for the configurations because the FTP server requires a username/password. Cisco provides two ways of to provide the username/password to the FTP client.

The first way puts the username and password as part of the IOS Software configuration. With service password-encryption turned on, the FTP password would be stored with encryption type 7:

```
ip ftp source-interface Loopback 0
ip ftp username user
ip ftp password quake
```

This allows the FTP command to transparently insert the username/password when connection to the FTP server.

```
Excalibur#copy running-config ftp:
Address or name of remote host []? 1.13.13.13
Destination filename [excalabur-confg]?
Writing excalabur-confg !!
3803 bytes copied in 3.848 secs (1267 bytes/sec)
Excalibur#
```

The alternative is to include the username/password in a standard URL format:

```
Excalibur#copy running-config ftp://user:quake@1.13.13.13
Address or name of remote host [1.13.13.13]?
Destination filename [excalabur-confg]?
Writing excalabur-confg !!
3800 bytes copied in 4.152 secs (950 bytes/sec)
Excalibur#
```

Large Configurations

When the NVRAM is not large enough to store the router configuration, there is an option that allows the configuration to be compressed (using a gzip-like compression algorithm):

```
service compress-config
```

Use this only if there is a requirement to do so. If the existing NVRAM can hold the configuration uncompressed, do not use this feature. Some ISPs have extremely large configurations, and this feature was introduced to assist them.

If the router configuration has become very large, it is worth checking whether some of the newer IOS Software features can be used. One example is to use prefix lists instead of access lists; the former is more space-efficient in NVRAM and also is more efficient in operation.

Command-Line Interface

The IOS Software CLI is the traditional (and favored) way of interacting with the router to enter and change configuration and to monitor the router's operation. This section describes the ISP operator's use of the CLI; it is also possible to use a web browser to interact with and configure the router. Use of the HTTP server is briefly covered later in the chapter.

The CLI is now very well documented in the Cisco UniverCD documentation set, at http://www.cisco.com/univercd/cc/td/doc/product/software/ios120/12cgcr/fun_r/ index.htm. However, a few tips and tricks that are regularly used by ISPs are worth mentioning here.

Editing Keys

Several keys are very useful as shortcuts for editing the IOS Software configuration. Although these are covered in detail in the IOS Software release 12.0 documentation set, it is useful to point out those used most commonly, shown in Table 1-2.

Table 1-2   *Common Editing Shortcuts*

Key	Function
Tab	Completes the command being typed in. This saves typing effort and is especially useful when the operator is still learning the IOS Software command set.
?	Lists the available commands starting with the characters entered so far.
Up/down arrow	Allows the operator to scroll up and down through the history buffer.
Ctrl-A	Moves the cursor to the beginning of the line.
Ctrl-E	Moves the cursor to the end of the command line.
Ctrl-K	Deletes all characters from the cursor to the end of the command line.
Ctrl-W	Deletes the word to the left of the cursor.
Ctrl-X	Deletes all characters from the cursor to the beginning of the command line.
Esc-B	Moves the cursor back one word.
Esc-F	Moves the cursor forward one word.

The complete list of commands can be found in the IOS Software documentation: http://www.cisco.com/univercd/cc/td/doc/product/software/ios120/12cgcr/fun_r/ frprt1/frui.htm.

CLI String Search

After a considerable number of requests from ISPs, a UNIX grep-like function (pattern search) has been introduced as a new feature in IOS Software from releases 11.1CC and 12.0. It allows operators to search for common expressions in configuration and other terminal output. Again, only salient points are covered here because the IOS Software documentation now gives more detailed information at http://www.cisco.com/univercd/cc/td/doc/product/software/ios120/120newft/120t/120t1/cliparse.htm.

The function is invoked by using a vertical bar "|", like the UNIX **pipe** command:

```
beta7200#show configuration | ?
  begin    Begin with the line that matches
  exclude  Exclude lines that match
  include  Include lines that match
beta7200#show configuration _
```

Following one of these three options, the operator should enter a regular expression to get a pattern match on the configuration, as in the preceding example. The regular expressions can be single or multiple characters or a more complex construction, in a similar style to UNIX regular expressions.

```
Defiant#show running-config | begin router bgp
router bgp 200
 no synchronization
 neighbor 4.1.2.1 remote-as 300
 neighbor 4.1.2.1 description Link to Excalabur
 neighbor 4.1.2.1 send-community
 neighbor 4.1.2.1 version 4
 neighbor 4.1.2.1 soft-reconfiguration inbound
 neighbor 4.1.2.1 route-map Community1 out
 maximum-paths 2
 --More--
```

During the display of configuration or file contents, the screen pager —More— will appear if the output is longer than the current terminal length setting. It is possible to do a regular expression search at this prompt, too. The / key matches the **begin** keyword; the - key means exclude, and the + key means to include.

Finally, in enable mode it is possible to use the **more** command to display file contents. Regular expressions (as in the preceding example) can be used with **more**. The options available with **more** follow in this example:

```
beta7200#more ?
  /ascii      Display binary files in ascii
  /binary     Force display to hex/text format
  /ebcdic     Display binary files in ebcdic
  bootflash:  File to display
  disk0:      File to display
  disk1:      File to display
  flash:      File to display
  ftp:        File to display
  null:       File to display
  nvram:      File to display
  rcp:        File to display
```

```
slot0:      File to display
slot1:      File to display
system:     File to display
tftp:       File to display
beta7200#
```

By using the | after the **more** command and its option, it is possible to search within the file for the strings of interest in the same way as discussed previously.

Detailed Logging

Keeping logs is a common and accepted operational practice. Interface status, security alerts, environmental conditions, CPU process hog, and many other events on the router can be captured and analyzed with UNIX syslog. IOS Software has the capability of doing UNIX logging to a UNIX syslog server. The router syslog format is compatible with BSD UNIX syslog (found as part of most UNIX and Linux systems deployed today). Table 1-3 shows a typical logging configuration for ISPs.

Table 1-3   *A Typical Logging Configuration*

no logging console	Don't send logs to the router console
logging buffered 16384	16 KB history buffer on router
logging trap debugging	Catch debugging level traps (in other words, everything)
logging facility local7	Syslog facility on syslog server
logging 169.223.32.1	IP address of your first syslog server
logging 169.223.45.8	IP address of your second syslog server

To set up the syslog daemon on a UNIX system, include a line such as the following in the file /etc/syslog.conf:

```
local7.debugging     /var/log/cisco.log
```

It is considered good practice to reserve a syslog facility on the UNIX log host for each type of network device. So, for example, backbone routers can use **local7**, access servers can use **local5**, TACACS+ can use **local3**, and so on. An example of a working syslog configuration file is given here:

```
# Log all kernel messages to the console.
kern.*                                          /var/log/kern.log

# Log everything apart from the specific entries given after this line
*.debug;kern.none;mail.none;authpriv.none;local7.none\
        local5.none;local4.none;local3.none    /var/log/messages

# The authpriv file has restricted access.
authpriv.*                                      /var/log/secure

# Log all the mail messages in one place.
mail.*                                          /var/log/maillog
```

```
# Everybody gets emergency messages.
*.emerg                                                          *

# Save mail and news errors of level err and higher in a special file.
uucp,news.crit                                          /var/log/spooler

# Cisco Access server log
local7.*                                                /var/log/cisco-core-log

# Cisco Access server log
local5.*                                                /var/log/cisco-access-log

# NetFlowLog
local4.*                                                /var/log/netflowlog

# TACACS+
local3.*                                                /var/log/tacacs+

# Save boot messages to boot.log
local1.*                                                /var/log/boot.log
```

Putting all the logs in one huge file simply makes system management hard and makes debugging problems by searching the log file next to impossible. More modern UNIX platforms require network support in the syslog daemon to be enabled by a runtime option (network support now is disabled by default, to avoid security problems). Check that you see the **-r** in the syslog command line, as in the following example, when you list the process on a UNIX system (the example is for Red Hat Linux):

```
pfs-pc$ ps ax | grep syslog
  496 ?         S       0:04 syslogd -r
20853 pts/5     S       0:00 grep syslog
pfs-pc$
```

When collecting logging information, it is important not to forget to parse the logs for any useful or network critical information. It is also essential to remember to rotate the logs on a daily or weekly basis. Some commercial UNIX systems have this available as part of the distribution. In Linux, the log rotation can be configured in /etc/logrotate.conf—consult the Linux man pages for more information. It's also possible to configure how many old copies are retained, and some ISPs have modified the log rotation scripts to archive logs that have expired out of rotation. (Indeed, some business and accounting requirements state that evidence of transactions or operations must be stored for several years—in this case, system logs often are archived on CD-ROM or other high-density storage medium.)

By default, log messages are not time-stamped. If the routers are configured for UNIX logging, you will want detailed time stamps of for each log entry:

```
service timestamps debug datetime localtime show-timezone msec
service timestamps log datetime localtime show-timezone msec
```

This will produce a syslog message that looks something like the following:

```
Jul 27 15:53:23.235 AEST: %SYS-5-CONFIG_I: Configured from console by philip on
console
```

The command-line options in the **timestamps** command are as follows:

- **debug**—All debug information is time-stamped.
- **log**—All log information is time-stamped.
- **datetime**—The date and time are included in the syslog message.
- **localtime**—The local time (instead of UTC) is used in the log message.
- **show-timezone**—The time zone defined on the router is included. (This is useful if the network crosses multiple time zones.)
- **msec**—Time accuracy is expressed as milliseconds, which is useful if NTP is configured.

By default, a syslog message contains the IP address of the interface that it uses to leave the router. You can require all syslog messages to contain the same IP address, regardless of which interface they use. Many ISPs use the loopback IP address. This keeps their syslogs consistent and allows them to enhance the security of their syslog server host (by the use of TCP wrappers or router filters, for example). To configure syslog to use the loopback as source IP address, enter this configuration command:

```
logging source-interface loopback0
```

NOTE   See Chapter 2 for a discussion on loopback interfaces, best practices for configuring the log hosts for syslog services, and so on.

Another command to consider is the **no logging console** command. Sometimes logging generates a tremendous amount of traffic on the console port. Of course, this happens just when you really need to connect to the console port to troubleshoot what is causing the tremendous surge of messages. Therefore, it is good practice to turn off console logging to keep the console port free for maintenance. A common ISP strategy is to use the router vty ports (with Telnet or Secure Shell) for day-to-day administration and then to restrict the console port for emergency uses only. Often this is aided or enforced by connecting the console to the out-of-band management in place at the ISP's point of presence.

In review, with all the options used, a typical ISP logging configuration would look like the following:

```
service timestamps debug datetime msec localtime show-timezone
service timestamps log datetime msec localtime show-timezone
!
no logging console
logging buffered 16384
logging trap debugging
logging facility local7
logging 169.223.32.1
logging 169.223.45.8
logging source-interface loopback0
!
```

Syslog Topologies

ISPs use one of two syslog topologies in their networks. The first is a traditional centralized syslog infrastructure that has the syslog servers in a central location supporting all the logging flows from the network devices in the network (see Figure 1-3). This is located in one of the ISP's major data centers or the ISP's NOC. The advantage with this topology is that all the raw syslog data is quickly available in one location. The disadvantage of this topology is one of scaling the amount of syslog data coming to one location and the possibility of losing log information sent across long distances of the network during times of congestion.

Figure 1-3   *Tailing a Centralized Syslog File for a Cisco Router*

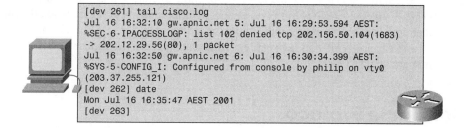

```
[dev 261] tail cisco.log
Jul 16 16:32:10 gw.apnic.net 5: Jul 16 16:29:53.594 AEST:
%SEC-6-IPACCESSLOGP: list 102 denied tcp 202.156.50.104(1683)
-> 202.12.29.56(80), 1 packet
Jul 16 16:32:50 gw.apnic.net 6: Jul 16 16:30:34.399 AEST:
%SYS-5-CONFIG_I: Configured from console by philip on vty0
(203.37.255.121)
[dev 262] date
Mon Jul 16 16:35:47 AEST 2001
[dev 263]
```

The second topology is a distributed topology. Syslog servers are pushed out to the edges of the network or are spread across several data centers. For example, each major PoP would have a syslog server for all the devices in the PoP. Syslog data is either preprocessed on the remote server or pulled from the distributed servers to centralize the server for processing. This topology is more scalable for larger networks and is less likely to be impacted by network congestion or other problems in the backbone.

Either of these two topologies (and other topologies) will work. What is important is that the syslog information is collected and actually used to maintain your network.

Analyzing Syslog Data

Configuring the routers to export syslog data is one step. The next step is to store the data, analyze it, and use it in day-to-day operations. Interface status, security alerts, and debugging problems are some of the most common events that ISPs monitor from the collected syslog data (an example of the output from the collected syslog data is in Figure 1-3). Some use custom-written Perl scripts to create simple reports. Others use more sophisticated software to analyze the syslog data and create HTML reports, graphs, and charts.

Table 1-4 is a list of known available software that analyzes syslog data. Even if you are going to write your own scripts, it's worth checking out the commercial packages to see what can be done with syslog data.

Table 1-4   *Software That Analyzes Syslog Data*

Cisco Resource Manager	http://www.cisco.com/warp/public/cc/pd/wr2k/rsmn/index.shtml
Private I	http://www.opensystems.com/index.asp
Crystal Reports	http://www.seagatesoftware.com/crystalreports/
Netforensics	http://www.netforensics.com/

One item to remember with the ISP's syslog infrastructure is this: *Time synchronization is critical!* To compare logs from two routers in different parts of the network, the time on them must be synchronized with that on the syslog server. Hence, the ISP must take the effort to deploy NTP in its network, ensuring that the entire network and systems infrastructure are in time sync.

Network Time Protocol

Time synchronization across the ISP's network is one of those least talked about yet critical pieces of the network. Without some mechanism to ensure that all devices in the network are synchronized to exactly the same time source, functions such as accounting, event logging, fault analysis, security incident response, and network management would not be possible on more than one network device. Whenever an ISP's system or network engineer needs to compare two logs from two different systems, each system needs a frame of reference to match the logs. That frame of reference is synchronized time.

The Network Time Protocol (NTP) is probably the most overlooked configuration feature on an ISP's network. NTP is a hierarchical protocol designed to synchronize the clocks on a network of computing and communication equipment. It is a dynamic, stable, redundant protocol used to keep time synchronized between network devices to a granularity of 1 ms. First defined in RFC 958, NTP has since been modified to add more redundancy and security. Other RFCs for time synchronization include the following:

- RFC 1128, "Measured Performance of the Network Time Protocol in the Internet System," 1989
- RFC 1129, "Internet Time Synchronization: The Network Time Protocol," 1989
- RFC 1165, "Network Time Protocol (NTP) over the OSI Remote Operations Service," 1990
- RFC 1305, "Network Time Protocol (Version 3) Specification," 1992 (draft standard)
- RFC 2030, "Simple Network Time Protocol (SNTP) Version 4 for IPv4, IPv6, and OSI," 1996 (informational)

An NTP network usually gets its time from an authoritative time source, such as a radio clock, a global positioning system (GPS) device, or an atomic clock attached to a time server. NTP then distributes this time across the network. NTP is hierarchical, with different time servers maintaining authority levels. The highest authority is Stratum 1. Levels of authority then descend from 2 to a maximum of 16. NTP is extremely efficient; no more than one packet per minute is necessary to synchronize two machines to within a millisecond of one another.

NTP Architecture[2]

In the NTP model, a number of primary reference sources, synchronized by wire, GPS, or radio to national standards, are connected to widely accessible resources, such as backbone gateways, and are operated as primary time servers. NTP provides a protocol to pass timekeeping information from these servers to other time servers from the Internet and to cross-check clocks and correct errors arising from equipment or propagation failures. Local-net hosts or gateways, acting as secondary time servers, use NTP to communicate with one or more of the primary servers. To reduce the protocol overhead, the secondary servers distribute time to the remaining local-net hosts. For reliability, selected hosts are equipped with less accurate (and less expensive) radio clocks. These hosts are used for backup in case of failure of the primary or secondary servers or the communication paths between them.

The NTP "network" consists of a multiple redundant hierarchy of servers and clients, with each level in the hierarchy identified by a stratum number. This number specifies the accuracy of each server, with the topmost level (primary servers) assigned as 1 and each level downward (secondary servers) in the hierarchy assigned as one greater than the preceding level. Stratum 1 is populated with hosts with bus or serial interfaces to reliable sources of time, such as radio clocks, GPS satellite timing receivers, or atomic clocks. Stratum 2 servers might be company or campus servers that obtain time from some number of primary servers over Internet paths and provide time to many local clients. The Stratum 2 servers can be configured to peer with each other, comparing clocks and generating a synchronized time value.

NTP performs well over the nondeterministic path lengths of packet-switched networks because it makes robust estimates of three key variables in the relationship between a client and a time server. These three variables are network delay, dispersion of time packet exchanges (a measure of maximum clock error between the two hosts), and clock offset (the correction to apply to a client's clock to synchronize it). Clock synchronization at the 10 ms level over long-distance (2000 km) WANs and at the 1 ms level for LANs is routinely achieved.

There is no provision for peer discovery or virtual-circuit management in NTP. Data integrity is provided by the IP and UDP checksums. No flow-control or retransmission facilities are provided or necessary. Duplicate detection is inherent in the processing algorithms.

NTP uses a system call on the local host to skew the local system clock by a small amount to keep the clock synchronized. If the local clock exceeds the "correct" time by a preset threshold, NTP uses a system call to make a step adjustment of the local clock.

NTP is careful to avoid synchronizing to a system whose time might not be accurate. It avoids doing so in two ways. First, NTP will never synchronize to a system that is not itself synchronized. Second, NTP compares the time reported by several systems and will not synchronize with a system whose time is significantly different from the others, even if its stratum is lower.

Client/Server Models and Association Modes

NTP servers can associate with each other in a number of modes. The mode of each server in the pair indicates the behavior that the other server can expect from it. An association is formed when two peers exchange messages and one or both of them create and maintain an instantiation of the protocol machine. The association can operate in one of several modes: server, client, peer, and broadcast/multicast. The modes further are classified as active and passive. In active modes, the host continues to send NTP messages regardless of the reachability or stratum of its peer. In passive modes, the host sends NTP messages only as long as its peer is reachable and operating at a stratum level less than or equal to the host; otherwise, the peer association is dissolved.

- **Server mode**—By operating in server mode, a host (usually a LAN time server) announces its willingness to synchronize, but not to be synchronized by a peer. This type of association ordinarily is created upon arrival of a client request message and exists only to reply to that request; after that, the association is dissolved. Server mode is a passive mode.

- **Client mode**—By operating in client mode, the host (usually a LAN workstation) announces its willingness to be synchronized by but not to synchronize the peer. A host operating in client mode sends periodic messages regardless of the reachability or stratum of its peer. Client mode is an active mode.

- **Peer mode**—By operating in peer mode (also called *symmetric* mode), a host announces its willingness to synchronize and be synchronized by other peers. Peers can be configured as active (symmetric-active) or passive (symmetric-passive).

- **Broadcast/multicast mode**—By operating in broadcast or multicast mode, the host (usually a LAN time server operating on a high-speed broadcast medium) announces its willingness to synchronize all of the peers, but not to be synchronized by any of them. Broadcast mode requires a broadcast server on the same subnet, while multicast mode requires support for IP multicast on the client machine as well as connectivity through the MBONE to a multicast server. Broadcast and multicast modes are active modes.

Normally, one peer operates in an active mode (symmetric-active, client, or broadcast/ multicast modes), while the other operates in a passive mode (symmetric-passive or server modes), often without previous configuration. However, both peers can be configured to operate in the symmetric-active mode. An error condition results when both peers operate in the same mode, except for the case of symmetric-active mode. In this case, each peer ignores messages from the other so that previous associations, if any, will be demobilized due to reachability failure.

Implementing NTP on an ISP's Routers

The time kept on a machine is a critical resource, so we strongly recommend that you use the security features of NTP to avoid the accidental or malicious setting of an incorrect time. Two mechanisms are available: an access list–based restriction scheme and an encrypted authentication mechanism. The following example highlights both NTP security options.

Cisco's implementation of NTP does not support Stratum 1 service; in other words, it is not possible to connect a router running IOS Software directly to a radio or atomic clock. It is recommended that time service for your network be derived from the public NTP servers available in the Internet. If the network is isolated from the Internet, Cisco's implementation of NTP allows a system to be configured so that it acts as though it is synchronized with NTP, when, in fact, it has determined the time using other means. Other systems then synchronize to that system with NTP. The command to set up a router in this way is

```
ntp master 1
```

This tells the router that it is the master time source and is running at Stratum 1.

The following example is an NTP configuration on a router getting a Stratum 2 server connection from 192.36.143.150 and peering with 169.223.50.14. The peered IP addresses are the loopback addresses on each router. Each router is using the loopback as the source. This makes security easier (note the access list).

```
clock timezone SST 8
!
access-list 5 permit 192.36.143.150
access-list 5 permit 169.223.50.14
access-list 5 deny any
!
ntp authentication-key 1234 md5 104D000A0618 7
ntp authenticate
ntp trusted-key 1234
ntp source Loopback0
ntp access-group peer 5
ntp update-calendar
ntp server 192.36.143.150
ntp peer 169.223.50.14
!
```

NTP Deployment Examples

ISPs use several designs to deploy NTP on their backbones. It is hard to recommend a best current practice, but this section lists a few examples:

- **Flat peer structure**—All the routers peer with each other, with a few geographically separate routers configured to point to external systems. From experience, this is very stable, but convergence of time will be longer with each new member of the NTP mesh. The larger the mesh is, the longer it takes for time to converge.

- **Hierarchy**—The BGP route reflector hierarchy is copied for the NTP hierarchy. Core routers (route reflectors) have a client/server relationship with external time sources, the reflector clients have a client/server relationship with the core routers, the customer routers have a client/server relationship with the reflector clients, and so on down the tree. Hierarchy is proven to scale well. A simple hierarchy that matches the routing topology provides consistency, stability, and scalability—hence, it is our favorite technique.

- **Star**—Here all the ISP routers have a client/server relationship with a few time servers in the ISP's backbone. The dedicated time servers are the center of the *star*. The dedicated time servers are usually UNIX systems synchronized with external time sources or their own GPS receiver. This setup also is reported to be very stable.

Undoubtedly there are other possibilities, too. The main aim is to go for stability because time synchronization is a key tool within the ISP backbone.

NTP in a PoP (Example)

Devices in an ISP PoP do not need to be part of the backbone NTP mesh. Instead, the devices in the PoP (routers, NAS, switches, and workstations) use the two core *PoP gateway* routers as the NTP servers for the PoP. All devices will use both routers as NTP sources, simplifying the NTP configuration and decreasing the NTP convergence time in the PoP.

As can be seen in Figure 1-4, devices in a PoP all need time synchronization. Accounting on the RADIUS server needs to be synchronized with the NAS equipment, which needs to be synchronized with the syslog server, which needs to be synchronized with the access routers, which needs to be synchronized with the NetFlow collectors, and so on. Having all devices use the same two servers (one primary, one backup) ensures time synchronization among all devices.

Figure 1-4   *Typical Internet PoP Built for Redundancy and Reliability Using the Core Routers as NTP Servers*

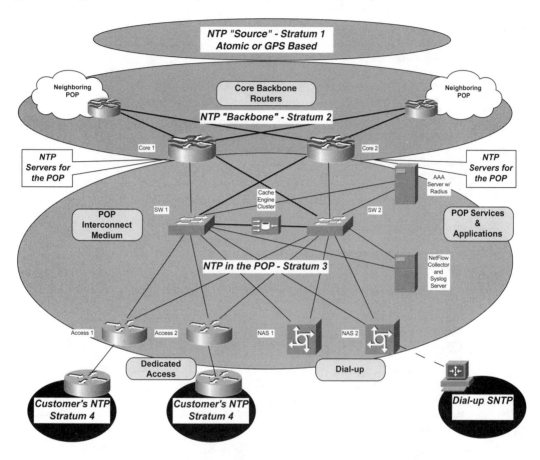

Configuration is simplified with only two servers. For example, NAS 1, a Cisco 3640 with 96 built-in modems, would have a configuration highlighted in Example 1-2. PoP gateway routers Core 1 and Core 2 have two configuration options. First, each device in the PoP can be manually configured with an **ntp peer** command. Even though the peer commands open the gateway routers to have the capability to allow synchronization, the **ntp server** commands on the PoP devices will make this unlikely. Yet, there is always the chance of maintenance-induced trouble (MIT)—misconfiguration on the PoP gateway or on one of the PoP network devices. Therefore, a second option offers more protection. This second option uses the **ntp access-group** command to limit what can query, serve, and be an NTP peer. Examples 1-1 and 1-2 demonstrate how the **ntp access-group** command is used to add an extra layer of security for all the NTP peers on the ISP's backbone while allowing a general access list to cover all the devices in the PoP. If the ISP is following a logical addressing plan, the whole PoP will be assigned one block of IP addresses for all the infrastructure and loopback addresses. This makes the **ntp access-group serve-only** ACL easier to create, with one ACL covering the entire PoP.

Example 1-1   *NTP Configuration for the PoP Gateway Routers*

```
! PoP Gateway Router
!
ntp authentication-key 4235 md5 ISPWorkshop
ntp authenticate
ntp trusted-key 4235
!
! Lock NTP source to the uplink
!
ntp source Loopback0
ntp update-calendar
!
! List of NTP Peers - Adding an additional Security Layer
!
ntp access-group peer 99
!
! Allow PoP Devices to use this router as an NTP Server
ntp access-group serve-only 42
!
! Loopback Addresses of the Backbone Routers
ntp peer 200.200.1.1
ntp peer 200.200.1.2
ntp peer 200.200.1.3
ntp peer 200.200.1.4
!
```

Example 1-2   *NTP Devices in the PoP*

```
! PoP Devices
!
ntp authentication-key 4235 md5 ISPWorkshop
ntp authenticate
!
ntp trusted-key 4235
!
! Lock NTP source to the uplink
ntp source Loopback0
ntp update-calendar
!
! IP Addresses to Routers Core 1 and Core 2
ntp server 192.135.248.249
ntp server 192.135.248.250
!
```

Further NTP References

Table 1-5 shows some URLs with further pointers to NTP information, software, and hardware.

Table 1-5   *Useful NTP URLs*

Network Time Protocol (NTP) Master Clock for the U.S.	http://tycho.usno.navy.mil/
Datum Inc, Bancomm Timing Division	http://www.datum.com/
True Time, Inc.	http://www.truetime.com
The Time Web Server (Time Sync), by Dave Mills	http://www.eecis.udel.edu/~ntp/
Coetanian Systems Time Synchronization Server 100	http://www.coetanian.com/tss/tss100.htm

Simple Network Management Protocol

Keeping data on the health of an ISP's network is critical to its survival as a business. For example, an ISP must know the load on its backbone circuits and the load on its customer circuits. It also needs to keep track of the packets lost on routers at various points of the network. And it needs to be aware of long-term trends on the overall growth of the network. SNMP can collect and process all of this data—hence, it is a very critical utility for network engineers.

Given the wide range of freeware, shareware, and commercially available SNMP tools, all ISPs should be capable of collecting SNMP data, processing it, graphing it, and analyzing it for proper traffic engineering. Appendix E, "Traffic Engineering Tools," lists pointers to various software and tools on the Net.

Remember that SNMP, especially version 1, has very weak security! If SNMP will not be used, turn it off! On the other hand, ensure that sufficient configuration information is present to control the use of SNMP so that it doesn't become a security risk. Most importantly, never leave a configuration that includes "public" or "private" as the community string—these strings are so well known and are common defaults on hardware shipping from so many vendors that they are open invitations to abuse, filters or not.

SNMP in Read-Only Mode

If SNMP is used in a read-only scenario, ensure that it is set up with appropriate access controls. The following is an example:

```
!
access-list 98 permit 215.17.34.1
access-list 98 permit 215.17.1.1
access-list 98 deny   any
```

```
!
snmp-server community 5nmc02m RO 98
snmp-server trap-source Loopback0
snmp-server trap-authentication
snmp-server enable traps config
snmp-server enable traps envmon
snmp-server enable traps bgp
snmp-server enable traps frame-relay
snmp-server contact Barry Raveendran Greene [bgreene@cisco.com]
snmp-server location Core Router #1 in City Y
snmp-server host 215.17.34.1 5nmc02m
snmp-server host 215.17.1.1 5nmc02m
snmp-server tftp-server-list 98
!
```

Note the application of **access-list 98**. The community string **5nmc02m** is not encrypted, hence the need to use an access list to control access. This is too often forgotten, and if the community string is known outside the ISP, it can easily lead to the compromise of a router. In fact, some scripts available on the Internet allow script kiddies[3] to probe a router and crack the community name. Unless *both* SNMP is set up to send a trap on community name authentication failure *and* the SNMP management device is configured to react to the authentication failure trap, the script kiddies most likely will discover the community name.

ISPs always should remember that accepting SNMP only from known good IP addresses does not guarantee their security. Unless the ISP has some very serious antispoofing measures in place, it cannot completely rely on IP addresses for the primary security of any system. IP addresses frequently are spoofed, so layered security in which the system relies on several mechanisms has proven to be more effective.

The **snmp-server host** configuration lists the hosts to which SNMP information is sent— if there is no means of collecting SNMP traps, don't configure **snmp-server host**, saving CPU cycles and network bandwidth. ISPs should ensure that the **snmp-server host** is configured to receive and respond to SNMP traps. For example, a Perl script on a PC running UNIX or Linux with UCD SNMP[4] could receive an SNMP environmental trap relating to high router internal temperature, e-mail it to the NOC alias, send an alphanumeric page to the on-duty engineer, and open a trouble ticket.

SNMP can be set up with more than one community, with a different access list. This is quite useful, say, if different groups in the company require different SNMP access to the router, or if a transit ISP offers SNMP read access to its ISP customers on its aggregation router. An example might look like the following:

```
!
access-list 97 permit 220.3.20.1
access-list 97 deny    any
!
access-list 98 permit 215.17.34.1
access-list 98 permit 215.17.1.1
access-list 98 deny    any
!
snmp-server community 5nmc02m RO 98
snmp-server community 1spxs RO 97
!
```

SNMP in Read-Write Mode

If SNMP will be used in read-write mode, think very carefully about the configuration and why there is a requirement to do this. Configuration errors in this scenario could leave the router very vulnerable.

If possible, put an ACL at the edge of your network to prevent outside parties from probing your network with SNMP. Many publicly and commercially available tools will scan *any* network on the Internet with SNMP. This could map out your entire network or discover a device that has had SNMP left open

---

Recommendation   In short, our recommendation is not to use SNMP in read-write mode on any ISP router—the operational risks more than outweigh any advantages.

SNMP and Commercial Network Management Software

One thing to be aware of is that some commercial network management software likes to take over the network by doing autodiscovery of devices on the backbone. Many ISP engineers don't approve of this style of network management and tend to build their own tools that are suitable for monitoring the backbone. For those ISPs that rely on commercial packages, such as HP OpenView, it is worth remembering and understanding the impact that the autodiscovery function has. Autodiscovery fits very nicely into a campus network where the network operators have little control over the backbone and what is added to it. However, the network operations staff should be in control of an ISP backbone, and all additions and removals from the backbone should be premeditated.

One example follows. An ISP was using a commercial package to monitor its backbone and was being severely troubled by very high CPU utilization. After a lot of research, it was discovered that the autodiscovery function of the management system was downloading the entire routing table from each of the routers. This ISP, of course, was carrying all 80 KB prefixes that were present at the time. Given the CPU hit dealing with a full BGP routing table, it is little wonder that an SNMP poll of the routing table was causing high CPU usage. The workaround was the following SNMPv2 configuration:

```
snmp-server view cutdown internet included
snmp-server view cutdown ipRouteTable excluded
snmp-server view cutdown ipNetToMediaTable excluded
snmp-server view cutdown at excluded
snmp-server community public view cutdown RO
```

For routers that run IOS Software releases that don't take the preceding object names, the following will also achieve the same result:

```
snmp-server view cutdown internet included
snmp-server view cutdown ip.21 excluded
snmp-server view cutdown ip.22 excluded
snmp-server view cutdown mib-2.3 excluded
snmp-server community public view cutdown RO
```

This basically stops the router from responding to SNMP queries regarding the routing and ARP tables.

HTTP Server

The HTTP server is a new feature in 11.1CC and 12.0 software that, when configured and enabled, allows the network operator to view and configure the router through a convenient and easy-to-use web interface (with common browsers such as Netscape or Internet Explorer). This is intended as an alternative to the CLI described earlier in this chapter, mainly aimed at customers who would prefer to "point and click" their way through configuring network equipment.

Because most ISPs have been using the CLI for many years, very few (if any) actually use the HTTP server capability. It is worth checking that the HTTP server has not been enabled by default, or in error, or during system installation. This configuration command will ensure that the server is not running:

```
no ip http server
```

If there is a need to configure the HTTP server because web-based configuration of the router is desired, we strongly advise that the server be configured with the appropriate security—for example,

```
ip http server
ip http port 8765           ! use a non-standard port
ip http authentication aaa  ! use the AAA authentication method which has
                            ! been configured
ip http access-class <1-99> ! access-list to protect the HTTP port
```

Notice the suggestion of a nonstandard port. This adds a little obscurity to the web server on the router, making potential attack a little more difficult. Also notice the access list used and the authentication type (AAA is discussed in the section on router security). This ensures that only the permitted administrative users of the router get access to the device from the authorized IP address range.

Recommendation	In short, our recommendation is not to use the HTTP server on any ISP router or switch—the operational risk far outweighs any advantage.

Core Dumps

A core dump facility has been part of IOS Software for several years and many software releases. The core dump facility operates like the UNIX variant—when a program crashes, the memory image is stored in a core file. When a router crashes, a copy of the core memory is kept. Before the memory is erased upon reboot, the router can be set up to copy the core dump out to a UNIX server. An account (FTP, TFTP, or RCP) and sufficient disk space (equal to the amount of memory on the router per dump) needs to be set up and allocated.

Here is an example using FTP:

```
ip ftp source-interface Loopback0
ip ftp username cisco
ip ftp password 7 045802150C2E
!
exception protocol ftp
exception dump 169.223.32.1
!
```

Note the use of the loopback interface as a source interface. It is recommended that access to the cisco account be made as secure as possible. For example, do not send core dumps to the same FTP server as the one used to provide generic anonymous or user FTP accounts. Use a wrapper for the FTP daemon, and make sure that only the loopback interfaces are listed in any system filter lists.

Be aware that RCP is inherently insecure and that its use cannot be recommended over a public network. Also, TFTP core dumps (which are the default in IOS Software) support system memory sizes only up to 16 MB. Generally, it is recommended that FTP core dumps be configured whatever the situation or router hardware configuration is.

More detailed information for configuring core dumps on a Cisco IOS Software–based system is located on the Cisco Documentation CD. It is publicly available on the Cisco.com site at http://www.cisco.com/univercd/cc/td/doc/cisintwk/itg_v1/tr19aa.htm. It includes information needed to troubleshoot problems using the **core dump** and **show stacks** commands.

Conclusion

This chapter has described some of the management issues that ISPs should consider for the installation and operation of their network equipment. It has worked through more or less in chronological order the basic steps that an ISP should take before deploying a new piece of equipment. These steps include determining which version of operating system software to choose for the routers, getting the chosen version on to the equipment, and employing the various strategies for management of the router operating software and configuration. Frequently used features of the CLI were introduced as well.

The chapter concluded with some basic features of router management, including best practices for capturing logging information, configuring time synchronization, using SNMP, using HTTP access, and dealing with crashes.

Endnotes

[1] Yes, there are many ISPs in the world whose entire backbone is built on 2500s!

[2] This section was written for Cisco's DNS/DHCP Manager. Sections of the documentation on NTP have been included here. The complete document can be found at http://www. cisco.com/univercd/cc/td/doc/product/iaabu/cddm/cddm111/adguide/ntp.htm

[3] Script kiddies are amateur crackers who use scripts to break into and cause damage to networks and systems on the Internet.

[4] CMU SNMP has not been updated in a while, and the project was taken over by UCD. However, in October 2000, the project was moved over to SourceForge and renamed NET-SNMP. It has been substantially improved and modified over the original CMU and UCD versions. It is by far the best and most configurable system—and it's free! Visit http://net-snmp.sourceforge.net/ for the NET-SNMP project home page.

## CHAPTER 2

General Features

This chapter covers general features that ISPs should consider for their routers and network implementations. Most are good design practices and don't leverage particular unique Cisco IOS Software features, but each demonstrates how IOS Software can aid the smooth operation of an ISP's business. Many of the features discussed here are described in the context of the ISP software covered in Chapter 1, "Software and Router Management."

The importance of the loopback interface should never be overlooked, especially for general operations and management of the router. Indeed, it is surprising how few ISPs make use of this time-saving resource. The chapter continues with a discussion on how to configure router interfaces and check their status.

Following the discussion of basic management configuration is an introduction to the CEF and NetFlow capabilities that ISPs should be using on their routers. The chapter finishes with a brief look at Nagle before discussing the importance of the DNS in an ISP's operation.

IOS Software and Loopback Interfaces

The use of the loopback interface is mentioned in many instances throughout this book. Although this is not a feature unique to IOS Software, there are many and considerable advantages in making full use of the capability that the loopback interface allows. This section brings together all the occasions where the loopback interface is mentioned throughout the book and describes how they can be useful to the ISP network engineer.

Motivation for Using the Loopback Interface

ISPs endeavor to minimize the unnecessary overhead present in their networks. This unnecessary overhead can be the number of networks carried in the IGP, the number of skilled engineering staff to operate the network, or even network security. The utilization of one feature, the loopback interface on the router, goes a long way to help with each of the three scenarios mentioned here.

Control of the size of the IGP is attended to by summarization of point-to-point addresses at PoP or regional boundaries, the use of IP unnumbered on static WAN interfaces, and a carefully designed network addressing plan. ISP network security is of paramount importance, and any techniques that make the management simpler are usually welcomed. For example, when routers access core servers, ISPs apply filters or access lists to these servers so that the risk of compromise from the outside is reduced. The loopback interface is helpful here as well.

It is very common to assign all the IP addresses used for loopback interfaces from one address block. For example, an ISP with around 200 routers in a network might assign a /24 network (253 usable addresses) for addressing the loopback interface on each router. If this is done, all dependent systems can be configured to permit this address range to access the particular function concerned, whether it is security, unnumbered WAN links, or the iBGP mesh. Some examples of the use of the loopback interface in the ISP environment follow in the rest of this section.

BGP Update Source

In the following example, the iBGP mesh is built using the loopback interface on each router. The loopback doesn't ever disappear, which results in a more stable iBGP, even if the underlying physical connectivity is less than reliable.

```
hostname gateway1
!
interface loopback 0
  ip address 215.17.1.34 255.255.255.255
!
router bgp 200
  neighbor 215.17.1.35 remote-as 200
  neighbor 215.17.1.35 update-source loopback 0
  neighbor 215.17.1.36 remote-as 200
  neighbor 215.17.1.36 update-source loopback 0
!
```

Router ID

If a loopback interface is configured on the router, its IP address is used as the router ID. This is important for ensuring stability and predictability in the operation of the ISP's network.

OSPF chooses the designated router (DR) on a LAN as the device that has the highest IP address. If routers are added or removed from the LAN, or if a router gains an interface with a higher address than that of the existing DR, the DR likely will change if the DR or backup designated router (BDR) fails. This generally is undesirable in an ISP network because ISPs prefer to have the DR and BDR routers established deterministically. This change in DR and BDR can be avoided by ensuring that the loopback interface is configured and in use on all routers on the LAN.

The loopback interface is used for the BGP router ID. If the loopback isn't configured, BGP uses the highest IP address on the router. Again, because of the ever-changing nature of an ISP network, this value can change, possibly resulting in operational confusion. Configuring and using a loopback interface ensures stability.

NOTE   If the router has two or more loopback interfaces configured, the router ID is the highest IP address of the configured loopback interfaces at the time of booting the router.

Exception Dumps by FTP

Cisco routers can be configured to dump core memory to an FTP server as part of the diagnostic and debugging process. However, this core dump should be to a system not running a public FTP server, but one heavily protected by filters (TCP Wrapper even) that allow only the routers access. If the loopback interface address is used as source address from the router and is part of one address block, the filter is very easy to configure. A 200-router network with 200 disparate IP addresses makes for a very large filter list on the FTP server. Examine the following example IOS Software configuration:

```
ip ftp source-interface Loopback0
ip ftp username cisco
ip ftp password 7 045802150C2E
exception protocol ftp
exception dump 169.223.32.1
```

TFTP Server Access

TFTP is the most common tool for uploading and downloading configurations. The TFTP server's security is critical, which means that you should always use security tools with IP source addresses. IOS Software allows TFTP to be configured to use specific IP interfaces address. This allows a fixed ACL on the TFTP server based on a fixed address on the router (for example, the loopback interface).

```
ip tftp source-interface Loopback0
```

SNMP Server Access

If SNMP is used in the network, the loopback interface again can be brought into use for security access issues. If SNMP traffic from the router is sourced from its loopback interface, it is easy to protect the SNMP management station in the NOC. A sample IOS Software configuration follows:

```
access-list 98 permit 215.17.34.1
access-list 98 permit 215.17.1.1
access-list 98 deny    any
```

```
!
snmp-server community 5nmc02m RO 98
snmp-server trap-source Loopback0
snmp-server trap-authentication
snmp-server host 215.17.34.1 5nmc02m
snmp-server host 215.17.1.1 5nmc02m
```

TACACS/RADIUS Server Source Interface

Most ISPs use TACACS+ or RADIUS for user authentication. Very few define accounts on the router itself because this offers more opportunity for the system to be compromised. A well-protected TACACS+ server accessed only from the router's loopback interface address block offers more security of user and enable accounts. A sample configuration for standard and enable passwords follows:

```
aaa new-model
aaa authentication login default tacacs+ enable
aaa authentication enable default tacacs+ enable
aaa accounting exec start-stop tacacs+
!
ip tacacs source-interface Loopback0
tacacs-server host 215.17.1.2
tacacs-server host 215.17.34.10
tacacs-server key CKr3t#
!
```

When using RADIUS, either for user administrative access to the router or for dial user authentication and accounting, the router configuration to support loopback interfaces as the source address for RADIUS packets originating from the router looks like this:

```
radius-server host 215.17.1.2 auth-port 1645 acct-port 1646
radius-server host 215.17.34.10 auth-port 1645 acct-port 1646
ip radius source-interface Loopback0
!
```

NetFlow Flow Export

Exporting traffic that flows from the router to a NetFlow Collector for traffic analysis or billing purposes is quite common. Using the loopback interface as the source address for all exported traffic flows from the router allows for more precise and less costly filtering at or near the server. A configuration example follows:

```
ip flow-export destination 215.17.13.1 9996
ip flow-export source Loopback0
ip flow-export version 5 origin-as
!
interface Fddi0/0/0
 description FDDI link to IXP
 ip address 215.18.1.10 255.255.255.0
 ip route-cache flow
 ip route-cache distributed
 no keepalive
!
```

Interface FDDI0/0/0 has been configured to capture flow records. The router has been configured to export Version 5–style flow records to the host at IP address 215.17.13.1 on UDP port 9996, with the source address being the router's loopback interface.

NTP Source Interface

NTP is the means of keeping the clocks on all the routers on the network synchronized to within a few milliseconds. If the loopback interface is used as the source interface between NTP speakers, it makes filtering and authentication somewhat easier to maintain. Most ISPs want to permit their customers to synchronize only with their time servers, not everyone else in the world. Look at the following configuration example:

```
clock timezone SST 8
!
access-list 5 permit 192.36.143.150
access-list 5 permit 169.223.50.14
!
ntp authentication-key 1234 md5 104D000A0618 7
ntp authenticate
ntp trusted-key 1234
ntp source Loopback0
ntp access-group peer 5
ntp update-calendar
ntp peer 192.36.143.150
ntp peer 169.223.50.14
!
```

Syslog Source Interface

Syslog servers also require careful protection on ISP backbones. Most ISPs prefer to see only their own systems' syslog messages, not anything from the outside world. Denial-of-service attacks on syslog devices are not unknown, either. Protecting the syslog server is again made easier if the known source of syslog messages comes from a well-defined set of address space—for example, that used by the loopback interfaces on the routers. See the following configuration example:

```
logging buffered 16384
logging trap debugging
logging source-interface Loopback0
logging facility local7
logging 169.223.32.1
!
```

Telnet to the Router

This might seem to be an odd example in a document dedicated to IOS Software essentials. However, remember that a loopback interface on a router never changes its state and rarely has any need to change its IP address. Physical interfaces can be physically swapped out or renumbered, and address ranges can change, but the loopback interface will always be there.

So, if the DNS is set up so that the router name maps to the loopback interface address, there is one less change to worry about during operational and configuration changes elsewhere in the ISP backbone. ISP backbones are continuously developing entities. Here's an example from the DNS forward and reverse zone files:

```
; net.galaxy zone file
net.galaxy.      IN       SOA      ns.net.galaxy. hostmaster.net.galaxy. (
                                   1998072901 ; version == date(YYYYMMDD)+serial
                                   10800      ; Refresh (3 hours)
                                   900        ; Retry (15 minutes)
                                   172800     ; Expire (48 hours)
                                   43200 )    ; Minimum (12 hours)
                 IN       NS       ns0.net.galaxy.
                 IN       NS       ns1.net.galaxy.
                 IN       MX       10 mail0.net.galaxy.
                 IN       MX       20 mail1.net.galaxy.
;
localhost        IN       A        127.0.0.1
gateway1         IN       A        215.17.1.1
gateway2         IN       A        215.17.1.2
gateway3         IN       A        215.17.1.3
;
;etc etc

; 1.17.215.in-addr.arpa zone file
;
1.17.215.in-addr.arpa.   IN       SOA      ns.net.galaxy. hostmaster.net.galaxy. (
                                   1998072901 ; version == date(YYYYMMDD)+serial
                                   10800      ; Refresh (3 hours)
                                   900        ; Retry (15 minutes)
                                   172800     ; Expire (48 hours)
                                   43200 )    ; Minimum (12 hours)
IN       NS       ns0.net.galaxy.
                 IN       NS       ns1.net.galaxy.
1                IN       PTR      gateway1.net.galaxy.
2                IN       PTR      gateway2.net.galaxy.
3                IN       PTR      gateway3.net.galaxy.
;
;etc etc
```

On the router, set the Telnet source to the loopback interface:

```
ip telnet source-interface Loopback0
```

RCMD to the Router

RCMD requires the operator to have the UNIX rlogin/rsh clients to enable access to the router. Some ISPs use RCMD for grabbing interface statistics, uploading or downloading router configurations, or taking a snapshot of the routing table. The router can be configured so that RCMD connections use the loopback interface as the source address of all packets leaving the router:

```
ip rcmd source-interface Loopback0
```

Interface Configuration

Configuring interfaces involves more than simply plugging in the cable and activating the interface with the IOS Software command **no shutdown**. Attention should be applied to details such as whether it is a WAN or a LAN, whether a routing protocol is running across the interface, addressing and masks to be used, and operator information.

description

Use the **description** interface command to document details such as the circuit bandwidth, the customer name, the database entry mnemonic, the circuit number that the circuit supplier gave you, and the cable number. This sounds like overkill, especially if there is a customer database within the ISP organization. However, it is very easy to pick up all the relevant details from the router **show interface** command if and when an engineer needs to be onsite, when an engineer is away from the database system, or when the database is unavailable. There can never be too little documentation, and documentation such as this ensures that reconstructing configurations and diagnosing problems are made considerably easier.

bandwidth

Don't forget the **bandwidth** interface command. It is used by interior routing protocols to decide optimum routing, and it is especially important to set this command properly in the case of backbone links using only a portion of the available bandwidth support by the interface. For example, a serial interface (Serial0/0) on a router supports speeds up to 4 Mbps but has a default bandwidth setting of 1.5 Mbps. If the backbone has different size links from 64 Kbps to 4 Mbps and the **bandwidth** command is not used, the interior routing protocol will assume that all the links have the same cost and will calculate optimum paths accordingly—and this could be less than ideal.

On customer links, it might seem that this setting is superfluous because an interior routing protocol is never run over a link to a customer. However, it provides very useful online documentation for what the circuit bandwidth is. Furthermore, the bandwidth on the circuit is used to calculate the interface load variable—some ISPs monitor their customer interfaces loading by SNMP polls so that they can get advance warning of problems or congestion, or to proactively inform customers of necessary upgrades. (Some ISPs look at the load variable; other ISPs look at the five-minute average, inbound and outbound. If you monitor the load variable, you need to set the bandwidth so that it matches the true circuit bandwidth, not the default configured on the router.)

ip unnumbered

Traditionally ISPs have used IP addresses for the point-to-point links on leased-line circuits to customers. Indeed, several years ago, before the advent of CIDR, it was not uncommon to see a /26 or even a /24 used for simple point-to-point link addresses. With the advent of CIDR, /30 networks have been used instead (/30 is a block of four addresses, two of which can be used for physical interfaces). However, this led to problems because IGPs of some of the larger ISPs were starting to carry several thousand networks, affecting convergence time and resulting in an administrative and documentation nightmare.

To avoid problems with large numbers of /30s floating around the ISP's internal routing protocol, and to avoid the problems of keeping internal documentation consistent with network deployment (especially true in larger ISPs), many are now using unnumbered point-to-point links.

An *unnumbered* point-to-point link is one requiring no IP addresses. The configuration is such that traffic destined for one network from another simply is pointed at the serial interface concerned. **ip unnumbered** is an essential feature applicable to point-to-point interfaces such as Serial, HSSI, POS, and so on. It enables the use of a fixed link (usually from ISP to customer) without consuming the usual /30 of address space, thereby keeping the number of networks routed by the IGP low. The **ip unnumbered** directive specifies that the point-to-point link should use an address of another interface on the router, typically a LAN or more usually a loopback interface. Any networks that must be routed to the customer are pointed at the serial interface rather than the remote address of the point-to-point link, as would be done in normal instances.

Caveats

ISPs need to consider some situations before implementing an IP unnumbered system for their customer point-to-point connections. These are considerations only—bear in mind that many ISPs have used IP unnumbered for several years, mainly so that they can control the size of the IGP running in their backbone network.

- **Pinging the customer**—Many ISPs use monitoring systems that use **ping** to check the status of the leased line (customer connectivity). Even if the customer unplugs the LAN, an alarm will not be raised on the ISPs management system. This is because the customer router still knows that the LAN IP address is configured on the system and is "useable." As long as the IP address is configured on the LAN, there will be no reachability issues with using **ip unnumbered**.

- **Routing protocols**—If a routing protocol needs to be run over this link, it is operationally much easier to use IP addresses. Don't use **ip unnumbered** if the customer is peering with you using BGP across the link or if the link is an internal backbone link. Simply use a network with a /30 address mask. (Routing will work over unnumbered links, but the extra management and operational complexity probably outweighs the small address space advantage gained.)

- **Loopback interfaces on the customer's router**—These offer no advantage to addressing the **ping** problem, and they unnecessarily consume address space (not to mention adding complexity to the customer router configuration).

ip unnumbered Configuration Example

Using the preceding configuration commands, a typical configuration on the ISP's router would be as follows:

```
interface loopback 0
  description Loopback interface on Gateway Router 2
  ip address 215.17.3.1 255.255.255.255
  no ip redirects
  no ip directed-broadcast
  no ip proxy-arp
!
interface Serial 5/0
  description 128K HDLC link to Galaxy Publications Ltd [galpub1] WT50314E R5-0
  bandwidth 128
  ip unnumbered loopback 0
  no ip redirects
  no ip directed-broadcast
  no ip proxy-arp
!
ip route 215.34.10.0 255.255.252.0 Serial 5/0
```

The customer router configuration would look something like this:

```
interface Ethernet 0
  description Galaxy Publications LAN
  ip address 215.34.10.1 255.255.252.0
  no ip redirects
  no ip directed-broadcast
  no ip proxy-arp
!
interface Serial 0
  description 128K HDLC link to Galaxy Internet Inc WT50314E  C0
  bandwidth 128
  ip unnumbered ethernet 0
  no ip redirects
  no ip directed-broadcast
  no ip proxy-arp
!
ip route 0.0.0.0 0.0.0.0 Serial 0
```

In this example, the regional or local registry has allocated the customer the network block 215.34.10.0/22. This is routed to the customer site with the static route pointing to Serial 5/0. The customer router simply needs a default route pointing to its serial interface to ensure a connection.

With this configuration, there are no /30s from point-to-point links present in the IGP, and the ISP does not need to document the link address or keep a table/database up-to-date. It all makes for easier configuration as well as easier operation of the ISP's business.

Note the contents of the description field. This example has included the following:

bandwidth of the circuit	**128K**
encapsulation	**HDLC**
name of the company	**Galaxy Publications Ltd**

continues

database mnemonic in the ISP's internal database	**[galpub1]**
telco's circuit ID	**WT50314E**
cable number	**R5-0**

All of these are online documentation, seemingly superfluous, but very necessary to ensure smooth and efficient operations. All the information pertinent to the customer's connection from the cabling to the IP values is contained in the interface configuration. If the ISP's database is down or unavailable, any debug information required by operators or engineers can be found on the router itself.

Interface Status Checking

Some useful hidden IOS Software commands enable the operator to check the status of the interfaces in IOS Software. Three useful commands are **show interface switching**, **show interface stats**, and **show idb**.

show interface switching

The IOS Software command **show interface switching** provides useful information about the switching status of the router's interfaces, either on an individual interface basis or over the whole router. The full command format is **show interface** [*int n/n*] **switching**, where an optional argument is the specific interface in question. Command completion cannot be used for **switching**—it needs to be typed in up to and including the second *i*. Sample output might look like the following:

```
gw>show interface FastEthernet 1/0 switching
FastEthernet1/0 Production LAN
          Throttle count          0
       Drops     RP               0         SP              0
   SPD Flushes   Fast             0         SSE             0
   SPD Aggress   Fast             0
   SPD Priority  Inputs        2421         Drops           0

        Protocol       Path   Pkts In    Chars In    Pkts Out   Chars Out
          Other     Process         0           0       74633     4477980
          Cache misses             0
                       Fast         0           0       31653     2957994
                  Auton/SSE         0           0           0           0
            IP     Process   5339594   516613071     5622371   851165330
          Cache misses       5391487
                       Fast 256289350 1125491757  257803747  2058541849
                  Auton/SSE         0           0           0           0
           ARP     Process     16919     1015300       34270     2056200
          Cache misses             0
                       Fast         0           0           0           0
                  Auton/SSE         0           0           0           0
           CDP     Process     12449     4083272       12440     4142520
          Cache misses             0
                       Fast         0           0           0           0
                  Auton/SSE         0           0           0           0
gw>
```

This sample output shows SPD[1] activity, as well as other activity on that particular interface on the router. Note the references to autonomous/SSE switching—this is applicable only to the Cisco 7000 series with Silicon Switch Engine only (a product that is now discontinued but was a significant part of the Internet core in the mid-1990s). Fast switching refers to all packets that have not been process-switched, which would include Optimum switching, NetFlow, and CEF.

show interface stats

The IOS Software command **show interface stats** is the second useful command to show interface status. It shows the number of packets and characters inbound and outbound on an individual router interface or all of them. The full command format is **show interface** [*int n/n*] **stats**, where an optional argument is the specific interface in question. Command completion cannot be used for **stats**—at least *st* needs to be typed in at the command prompt. Sample output might look like this:

```
gw>show interface stats
Interface FastEthernet0/0 is disabled

FastEthernet1/0
          Switching path    Pkts In    Chars In    Pkts Out   Chars Out
              Processor      5371378   521946816     5746126   862068168
            Route cache    256413200  1149405512   257960291  2072462774
                  Total    261784578  1671352328   263706417  2934530942
gw>
```

As for interface switching, the output differentiates between packets that go via the processor and those that have been processed via the route cache. This is useful to determine the level of process switching taking place on the router.

On a router that supports distributed switching (for example, 7500 with VIP interfaces), the output will look like the following:

```
gw>show interface stats
FastEthernet0/1/0
          Switching path    Pkts In    Chars In    Pkts Out   Chars Out
              Processor       207745    14075132      270885    21915788
            Route cache            0           0           0           0
      Distributed cache          93        9729           0           0
                  Total      207838    14084861      270885    21915788
```

Notice that packets that have been processed via the distributed cache are counted separately from those handled via the central route cache and the processor.

show IDB

Each interface on the router has an associated interface descriptor block allocated to it. In the early days, each physical interface mapped to one IDB, and routers generally could support up to 300 IDBs (for example, the Cisco AGS+).

However, with the increasing numbers of new connection services, and with ATM and Frame Relay providing large numbers of subinterfaces, routers have had to scale to supporting several thousand IDBs. **show IDB** recently has become a visible command in IOS Software (CSCds89322); it allows ISPs to find out how many IDBs are configured on the router:

```
gw#show idb
24 SW IDBs allocated (2368 bytes each)

21 HW IDBs allocated (4040 bytes each)
HWIDB#1    1    FastEthernet0/0 (HW IFINDEX, Ether)
HWIDB#2    2    FastEthernet1/0 (HW IFINDEX, Ether)
HWIDB#3    3    Serial2/0 (HW IFINDEX, Serial)
HWIDB#4    4    Serial2/1 (HW IFINDEX, Serial)
HWIDB#5    5    Serial2/2 (HW IFINDEX, Serial)
HWIDB#6    6    Serial2/3 (HW IFINDEX, Serial)
HWIDB#7    7    FastEthernet3/0 (HW IFINDEX, Ether)
HWIDB#8    8    FastEthernet5/0 (HW IFINDEX, Ether)
HWIDB#9    20   Dialer0 (HW IFINDEX, Serial)
HWIDB#10   21   Loopback0 (HW IFINDEX)

gw#
```

To find out how many IDBs are supported on different router platforms, consult Cisco.com documentation—for example, http://www.cisco.com/warp/public/63/idb_limit.html. Although most smaller router platforms still support only 300 IDBs at maximum, some of the larger platforms can go as high as 10,000 (7200/12.2T release). These values might change as future enhancements are made to Cisco IOS Software.

Cisco Express Forwarding

CEF is now the recommended forwarding/switching path for Cisco routers in an ISP environment. CEF adds increased performance, scalability, and resilience, and enables new functionality over the older optimum switching. Details on the operation and functionality of CEF are now covered in detail by the IOS Software documentation and in several whitepapers describing CEF (see references in the "Technical Reference and Recommended Reading" section at the end of this book).

Implementation is simple with either of the following commands (depending on the platform):

```
ip cef
ip cef-distributed
```

The key issue for ISPs is ensuring that CEF is turned on. On most platforms, CEF is *not* turned on by default, so ISP engineers need to ensure that CEF is turned on. Table 2-1 provides a list of the default CEF configurations for various Cisco platforms. ISPs should check their configuration scripts to ensure that CEF/dCEF is turned on, especially for the 7200-based edge platforms such as uBR, 6400, and 5800 NAS.

Table 2-1   *Default Configuration for CEF on Various Platforms*

On This Platform...	The Default Is...
2600/3600	CEF is not enabled.
4500/4700	CEF is not enabled.
7000 series with RSP 7000	CEF is not enabled.
7200	CEF is not enabled.
7500	CEF is enabled, but distributed CEF is not.
7600 OSR	CEF is enabled.
12000 GSR	Distributed CEF is enabled.

CEF will be discussed in more depth in Chapter 4, "Security." One of the best security tools available for an ISP is Unicast Reverse Path Forwarding. This requires CEF to be activated on the router because the reverse path check is dependent on the FIB table, which is part of the CEF process.

NetFlow

Enabling NetFlow on routers provides network administrators with access to packet flow information from their network. Exported NetFlow data can be used for a variety of purposes, including security monitoring, network management, capacity planning (as in Figure 2-1), customer billing, and Internet traffic flow analysis.

NetFlow is available on all router platforms from the 2600 series upward from the 12.0 software release onward. It was first introduced in 11.1CC on the 7200 and 7500 platforms. It can be enabled on a per-interface basis on the routers, as in the following example:

```
interface serial 5/0
 ip route-cache flow
 !
```

If CEF is not configured on the router, this turns off the existing switching path on the router and enables NetFlow switching (basically modified optimum switching). If CEF is configured on the router, NetFlow simply becomes a "flow information gatherer" and feature accelerator—CEF remains operational as the underlying switching process.

NetFlow Feature Acceleration

NetFlow feature acceleration works for a limited set of features that can take advantage of flow process short cuts. NFFA reserves space in the flow cache for state information belonging to features converted to use the flow acceleration. The features can then attach per-flow state to the cache entry, using NetFlow as a quick way to access information that is flow-based. For example, NetFlow policy routing (NPR) uses flow acceleration to eliminate route-map checks on a per-packet basis. NetFlow feature acceleration is turned on with the following command:

```
ip flow-cache feature-accelerate
```

As of 12.0(11)S, the following features have been converted to work with NetFlow feature acceleration:

- Numbered access lists
- Named access lists
- IP accounting
- Crypto decrypt
- Crypto encrypt
- Policy routing
- WCCP redirection

Figure 2-1 *Netflow in Its Capacity-Planning Role*

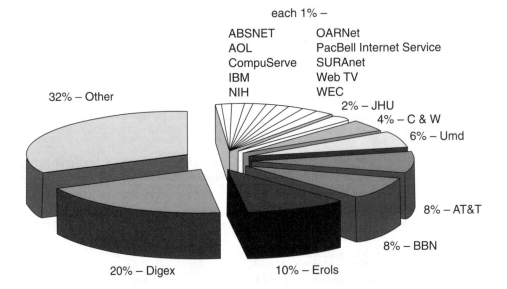

Public Routers 1, 2, 3 Month of September Outbound Traffic

NetFlow Statistics—Basics

To view NetFlow information on the router, simply enter the command **show ip cache flow**. This displays the current flow cache on the terminal screen (see Example 2-1).

Example 2-1   *Sample Output from Displaying Flow Information on a NetFlow-Enabled Router*

```
gw>sh ip cache flow
IP packet size distribution (410772243 total packets):
   1-32   64    96   128   160   192   224   256   288   320   352   384   416   448   480
   .000 .168 .384 .102 .160 .107 .019 .005 .003 .001 .001 .000 .000 .000 .003

   512   544   576  1024  1536  2048  2560  3072  3584  4096  4608
   .001 .000 .035 .000 .003 .000 .000 .000 .000 .000 .000

IP Flow Switching Cache, 4456704 bytes
  15074 active, 50462 inactive, 125120769 added
  369493980 ager polls, 0 flow alloc failures
  last clearing of statistics 4d05h
Protocol          Total    Flows   Packets Bytes   Packets Active(Sec) Idle(Sec)
--------          Flows     /Sec   /Flow  /Pkt    /Sec   /Flow      /Flow
TCP-Telnet          605      0.0      44    52      0.0     8.1        9.1
TCP-FTP            3494      0.0      22    64      0.2     9.4       12.9
TCP-FTPD           4104      0.0     757   376      8.4    34.9        5.7
TCP-WWW          845158      2.3      16   281     39.1     4.5        6.8
TCP-SMTP          87119      0.2      10   201      2.5     4.2       13.1
TCP-X                59      0.0       2    68      0.0     0.4       12.0
TCP-BGP           62074      0.1       5   255      0.9     9.6       18.5
TCP-NNTP              5      0.0       3    48      0.0     8.8       19.6
TCP-Frag              2      0.0       2    40      0.0     0.1       21.2
TCP-other      11879955     32.3       5   141    174.2     2.5        7.5
UDP-DNS        70078211    191.0       3    90    586.3     4.8       19.1
UDP-NTP           31804      0.0       1    72      0.0     0.0       19.0
UDP-TFTP            327      0.0       3   153      0.0     4.8       19.2
UDP-Frag              9      0.0       4   311      0.0    22.5       18.2
UDP-other      41601240    113.4       2   157    301.3     4.1       19.1
ICMP             498404      1.3       4   170      5.7    10.7       19.0
IGMP                  2      0.0     113   551      0.0     6.8       19.8
IP-other          20236      0.0       4   299      0.2    12.7       18.7
Total:        125112808    341.1       3   126   1119.2     4.4       17.9

SrcIf        SrcIPaddress    DstIf        DstIPaddress      Pr SrcP DstP  Pkts
Se2/0        207.69.200.110  Fa1/0        203.37.255.121    11 2245 0035     1
Fa1/0        203.37.255.121  Se2/0        207.69.200.110    11 0035 2245     1
Fa1/0        203.37.255.97   Se2/0        169.229.128.130   11 0035 0C1C     1
Se2/0        169.229.128.130 Fa1/0        203.37.255.97     11 0C1C 0035     1
Se2/0        195.28.226.121  Fa1/0        203.37.255.97     11 0408 0035     1
Fa1/0        203.37.255.97   Se2/0        195.28.226.121    11 0035 0408     1
Fa1/0        203.37.255.97   Se2/0        163.21.134.2      11 0035 0035     2
Se2/0        202.103.229.40  Fa1/0        203.37.255.97     11 0A6B 0035   248
Se2/0        163.21.134.7    Fa1/0        203.37.255.97     11 0035 0035     4
```

continues

Example 2-1 *Sample Output from Displaying Flow Information on a NetFlow-Enabled Router (Continued)*

```
Fa1/0       203.37.255.97   Se2/0   163.21.134.7     11 0035 0035     4
Fa1/0       203.37.255.97   Se2/0   202.103.229.40   11 0035 0A6B   248
Se2/0       163.21.134.2    Fa1/0   203.37.255.97    11 0035 0035     2
Se2/0       63.87.170.77    Fa1/0   203.37.255.97    11 B034 0035     2
Fa1/0       203.37.255.97   Se2/0   63.87.170.77     11 0035 B034     2
```

The first part of the output displays the packet size distribution of the traffic flowing *into* the interfaces that NetFlow is configured on. The next portion of the output displays the flows, packet size, activity, and so on for the flows per well-known protocol. The final section displays the source and destination interfaces/addresses/ports for the currently active traffic flows.

It is also possible to export this collected data to a system that will collect the data, allowing the ISP to carry out further analysis. Public-domain software is available (cflowd from Caida and NetFlowMet from the University of Auckland, for example), as well as fully featured and supported commercial products, such as Cisco's NetFlow Collector and Analyzer packages.

NetFlow Data Export

The greatest benefits of NetFlow are found when its data is exported to collection systems and then are analyzed and processed. Cisco has adopted a broad approach to facilitate this activity. These include donations for freeware collection/analysis software, Cisco's own commercial software, tools for others to create their own software, and partnerships with companies that make commercial-grade billing systems based on NetFlow export.

To export the data, the following configuration commands are required:

```
ip flow-export version 5 [origin-as|peer-as]
ip flow-export destination x.x.x.x udp-port
ip flow-export source Loopback0
```

The first command line sets the export version to 5 (basically this includes BGP information such as AS number) and has options to include **origin-as** or **peer-as** in the exported records. Most ISPs use the **origin-as** option because that will record the origin AS of the prefix originating the flow. This has become a frequently asked question on the CAIDA cflowd list, with ISPs forgetting the **origin-as** option and then not understanding why so many of their exported records have an origin of AS 0.

The second command line configures the IP address of the destination system, the NetFlow collector system, and the UDP port that the collector is listening on. Most ISPs use high UDP ports, such as 9999 or in the 60,000s. Note that because the flow records use UDP, it is important to design the infrastructure so that the flow collector is not too far away from the originating router. Some ISPs that use NetFlow for billing purposes build a separate management network simply to support this function.

The third command line originates all the flow traffic using the IP address of the loopback interface. This makes the cflowd configuration file easier to construct for several routers because most ISPs number their router loopbacks out of one contiguous block.

To determine the status of the flow export, it is possible to check on the router to see what has been sent. Obviously the collector system should be checked as well—cflowd, for example, has extensive instructions on how to debug any flow export problems. An example of the usage of the IOS Software command follows:

```
gw>sh ip flow export
Flow export is enabled
  Exporting flows to 220.19.51.35 (9998)
  Exporting using source interface Loopback0
  Version 5 flow records, origin-as
  264038749 flows exported in 8801292 udp datagrams
  0 flows failed due to lack of export packet
  6079835 export packets were sent up to process level
  0 export packets were punted to the RP
  0 export packets were dropped due to no fib
  0 export packets were dropped due to adjacency issues
  0 export packets were dropped due to fragmentation failures
  0 export packets were dropped due to encapsulation fixup failures
```

A new feature as of Cisco IOS Software release 12.0(5)S is NetFlow aggregation, in which summarization/aggregation of the flow records is carried out on the router before the data is exported to the collecting system. The aim is to reduce the amount of data going across the network from router to flow collector, thereby improving the reliability of the collecting system. Flow aggregation is enabled by the following commands:

```
ip flow-aggregation cache as|destination-prefix|prefix|protocol-port|source-prefix
   enabled
   export destination x.x.x.x UDP-port
```

Subcommands required include **enabled**, which switches on the flow aggregation, and **export destination**, which lists the host that will gather the aggregated records. The collector host needs to support NetFlow Type 8 records to be capable of reading the aggregated information.

Turn On Nagle

The Nagle congestion-control algorithm is something that many ISPs turn on to improve the performance of their Telnet sessions to and from the router. When using a standard TCP implementation to send keystrokes between machines, TCP tends to send one packet for each keystroke typed. On larger networks, many small packets use up bandwidth and contribute to congestion.

John Nagle's algorithm (RFC 896) helps alleviate the small-packet problem in TCP. In general, it works this way: The first character typed after connection establishment is sent in a single packet, but TCP holds any additional characters typed until the receiver acknowledges the previous packet. The second, larger packet is sent, and additional typed characters are saved until the acknowledgment comes back. The effect is to accumulate characters into larger chunks and pace them out to the network at a rate matching the round-trip time of the given connection. This method is usually good for all TCP-based traffic and helps when connectivity to the router is poor or congested or the router itself is busier than normal. However, do not use the **service nagle** command if you have XRemote users on X Window sessions or sourcing voice over IP traffic or other real-time traffic from the router—performance will become very poor.

The IOS Software command to enable Nagle follows:

```
service nagle
```

NOTE	Without **service nagle** on a Cisco router, each character in a Telnet session is a separate CPU interrupt. Hence, a command such as **show tech** will force a large number of CPU interrupts, impacting the performance of the router. From a Cisco point of view, the Nagle service not only helps to optimize the Telnet session but also lessens the load on the router.

DNS and Routers

The DNS might be an unusual topic to put into a book covering ISP network essentials and Cisco IOS Software best practices. However, it is one of the most overlooked systems topics in the ISP industry—yet it is probably the most important part of the public visibility of the network to get right. If the DNS does not work, the public thinks that the network is broken—many newspaper headlines in the last few years have displayed such apocryphal headlines simply because of operational errors or problems with the DNS.

An ISP network engineer must pay attention to two aspects of the DNS. The first is the business of putting all the name-to-address-to-name mappings in the system so that routers can be recognized by their English-language names rather than by four boring decimal numbers separated by dots. Humans aren't good at remembering the latter. The second aspect is to actually enable support for the DNS in the routers themselves. This section covers only the router aspect—Chapter 5, "Operational Practices," describes configuration and placement of the DNS systems throughout the ISP backbone.

Mapping IP Addresses to Names

Mapping domain names to IP addresses and vice versa is one of those commonly overlooked areas in a new ISP's operations. Doing a trace from Australia across the backbones in the United States to a site in the United Kingdom gives you something like Example 2-3.

Example 2-2 *Example Traceroute Across the Internet from Australia to the United Kingdom*

```
traceroute to k.root-servers.net (193.0.14.129), 30 hops max, 38 byte packets
 1  fe5-0.gw.apnic.net (202.12.29.190) 0.707 ms  0.534 ms  0.497 ms
 2  Serial1-0-3.cha8.Brisbane.telstra.net (139.130.64.97) 5.999 ms 5.131 ms
    6.155 ms
 3  GigabitEthernet5-1.cha-core4.Brisbane.telstra.net (203.50.51.1) 6.148 ms
    4.972 ms  4.537 ms
 4  Pos2-0.chw-core2.Sydney.telstra.net (203.50.6.225) 19.355 ms 18.595 ms
    19.797 ms
 5  Pos4-0.exi-core1.Melbourne.telstra.net (203.50.6.18) 32.120 ms 32.968 ms
    32.544 ms
 6  Pos5-0.way-core4.Adelaide.telstra.net (203.50.6.162) 50.088 ms 46.171 ms
    44.896 ms
 7  Pos6-0.wel-core3.Perth.telstra.net (203.50.6.194) 88.296 ms 75.545 ms
    83.527 ms
 8  GigabitEthernet4-0.wel-gw1.Perth.telstra.net (203.50.113.18) 78.172 ms
    76.116 ms  75.851 ms
 9  Pos1-0.paix1.PaloAlto.net.reach.com (203.50.126.30) 305.915 ms 309.617 ms
     314.994 ms
10  fe0.pao0.verio.net (198.32.176.47) 308.744 ms 304.431 ms 304.230 ms
11  p4-6-0-0.r02.mclnva02.us.bb.verio.net (129.250.2.246) 380.061 ms 380.639 ms
    380.292 ms
12  p16-0-0-0.r01.mclnva02.us.bb.verio.net (129.250.5.253) 384.100 ms 384.124 ms
384.382 ms
13  p4-7-2-0.r00.nycmny06.us.bb.verio.net (129.250.3.181) 390.487 ms 390.300 ms
    396.328 ms
14  p4-0-2-0.r01.nycmny06.us.bb.verio.net (129.250.3.130) 390.196 ms 384.921 ms
    385.245 ms
15  gxn.d3-1-0-1.r01.nycmny06.us.bb.verio.net (129.250.16.198) 321.844 ms
    319.204 ms 319.252 ms
16  se6-1-0-llb-x-ny2.NY1.core.rtr.xara.net (194.143.164.45) 325.706 ms 320.925 ms
    320.557 ms
17  se5-1-llb-ny1.HU1.core.rtr.xara.net (194.143.164.97) 325.264 ms 322.578 ms
    321.049 ms
18  po2-0-llb-hu1.TH30.core.rtr.xara.net (194.143.164.189) 389.618 ms 390.177 ms
    388.401 ms
19  gb11-0-0-llb-x-many.TH1.core.rtr.uk.xo.net (194.143.163.130) 398.421 ms
    388.459 ms 390.471 ms
20  fa0-0.gxn-linx.transit1.linx.net (195.66.248.33) 388.834 ms 391.937 ms
    389.687 ms
21  k.root-servers.net (193.0.14.129) 387.544 ms 391.093 ms 387.059 ms
```

Notice that each router IP address has a corresponding DNS entry. These very descriptive DNS names help Internet users and operators understand what is happening with their connections and which route the outbound traffic is taking. The descriptive names are an invaluable aid to troubleshooting problems on the net.

Table 2-2 shows some examples of descriptive DNS formats used by various ISPs.

Table 2-2 *DNS Formats*

ISP	Example Use of the DNS
C&W	bordercore4-hssi0-0.SanFrancisco.cw.net
BBN Planet	p2-0.paloalto-nbr2.bbnplanet.net
Concert	core1-h1-0-0.uk1.concert.net
Sprint	sl-bb6-dc-1-1-0-T3.sprintlink.net
DIGEX	sjc4-core5-pos4-1.atlas.digex.net
Verio	p0-0-0.cr1.mtvwca.pacific.verio.net
IIJ	otemachi5.iij.net
Qwest	sfo-core-03.inet.qwest.net
Telstra BigPond	Pos5-0-0.cha-core2.Brisbane.telstra.net
UUNET	ATM2-0.BR1.NYC5.ALTER.NET
Teleglobe	if-8-0.core1.NewYork.Teleglobe.net
VSNL	E3-VSB1-LVSB.Bbone.vsnl.net.in
KDD Internet	gsr-ote3.kddnet.ad.jp
ChinaNet	p-10-1-0-r1-s-bjbj-1.cn.net

DNS Resolver in IOS Software

You can specify a default domain name that the Cisco IOS Software will use to complete domain name requests for functions such as Telnet, TFTP, and other instances of name completion (for example, **ip ospf domain-lookup**). You can specify either a single domain name or a list of domain names. Any IP host name that does not contain a domain name will have the domain name that you specify appended to it before being added to the host table.

```
ip domain-name name
ip domain-list name
```

It is also advisable to include a name server for the router to resolve the DNS request:

```
ip name-server server-address1 [[server-address2]...server-address6]
```

Remember that the current practice on the Internet is to quote at least two DNS resolvers. The reason is the same as for any other situation: redundancy. If one DNS server disappears, the other one can take over. When both are there, the router will look up the servers in a round-robin fashion for each request.

Conclusion

This chapter covered the important steps necessary for an ISP to set up its initial router configuration correctly. It discussed the importance of the loopback interface, how to configure interfaces, as well as how to set up CEF and NetFlow. Nagle also was covered, and the chapter concluded with a discussion on how an ISP uses DNS for the network backbone infrastructure.

Combining this chapter with Chapter 1, the ISP now should have a workable router configuration ready for configuring routing protocols and the security features necessary for any ISP backbone.

Endnotes

[1] SPD is discussed in detail in Chapter 3, "Routing Protocols."

## CHAPTER 3

Routing Protocols

The book so far has concentrated on getting the core equipment in the ISP backbone up to a state in which it can be introduced safely into the larger network and the Internet. This chapter introduces the major routing protocols and some of the most useful features in those routing protocols that are available for ISPs.

Most of this chapter's content covers BGP, the Border Gateway Protocol used by ISP networks to pass routing information between each other. In fact, BGP has grown to be more than just a routing protocol used by network border routers—BGP is now the mechanism for transporting noninfrastructure prefixes and routing information around the ISP's backbone. The first part of this chapter discusses initial setup of the router, interior routing protocols, and the Hot Standby Routing Protocol (HSRP), a Cisco feature designed to make the dual homing of hosting networks failsafe and redundant.

This chapter assumes that the ISP engineer has a working understanding of the core routing protocols used in the Internet. If not, please refer to the online whitepapers or the publications listed in the "Technical References and Recommended Reading" section at the end of this book.

CIDR Features

All network devices connected to the Internet must be CIDR-compliant (documented in RFCs 1812 and 2644). Cisco routers running Cisco IOS Software versions earlier than Release 12.0 are made CIDR-compliant if these two commands are entered:

```
ip subnet-zero
ip classless
```

All Cisco routers connected to the Internet must have these commands turned on. IOS Software releases from 12.0 have these commands turned on by default, but it is still worthwhile to include them in any configuration template, just in case any operator removes the defaults.

It makes good sense in the ISP operations world never to rely on any equipment vendor's defaults and instead to be very clear what the requirements for your own backbone are. Defaults are for enterprise and other networks, not the specialized and public ISP backbones. (See the section titled "BGP Features and Commands" for BGP requirements.)

Note that the terms *subnet* and *supernet* do not make much sense in the classless Internet (RFC 1812). Unfortunately, these terms are still widely in use:

- *Subnet* sometimes is used to refer to a prefix that shares the same initial network portion as another prefix but has a larger mask. (For example, 192.168.1.128/26 still is called a subnet of 192.168.1.0/24 because the first 24 bits are shared between the two routes.) We prefer the term *subprefix* to refer to such a network.

- *Supernet* sometimes is used to refer to the aggregate of two prefixes that are bit-wise neighbors. (For example, 192.168.8.0/24 can be combined with 192.168.9.0/24 to form the aggregate [or supernet] 192.168.8.0/23.) We prefer the term *aggregate* to refer to such a network.

IP Classless

The command **ip classless** in Cisco IOS Software affects how the router looks up routes in the IP routing table when it is trying to route an IP packet. It changes the route lookup from using the old classful method to using classless rules, even for classful routing protocols that still might be running on the router.

The Old Classful Route Lookup Rules

The old behavior of a Cisco router is to assume that it knows about all the routes/subnetworks of a directly attached network. It will do a classful route lookup to determine a match and then check for subnets. For example, when the router receives a packet, the network portion of the destination address is compared to the routing table for a match. If there is a match, the subnets listed for that classful network are examined. If a match is found, the packet is forwarded. If no match is found, the packet is dropped and an ICMP Destination Unreachable message is returned. This is true even if a default route exists in the IP routing table because the router assumes that it knows about all routes for that classful network.

Consider the situation if a packet arrives with destination address 192.168.1.200 and the routing table has only the subnet 192.168.1.0/26 in it. The router will attempt to look for 192.168.1.0/24 (the parent Class C network of the destination address) and forward to that network's origin. If that Class C address does not exist in the routing table and a subnet of the Class C address covering 192.168.1.200 does not exist in the routing table, the router will drop the packet.

The Classful Route Lookup Rules

The **ip classless** command has changed the old behavior for all routing protocols configured on the router. The router ignores the class of the destination address and directly compares the network portion of the destination address with all its known routes. If no match is found, the packet is forwarded to the default route, if one exists; otherwise, it is dropped. This latter action is required for any router connected to the Internet.

Repeating the previous example but using the default classless rules, if a packet arrives for host 192.168.1.200 and the routing table has only the network 192.168.1.0/26, the router will drop the packet unless a default route has been configured on the router. This is the expected behavior since the Internet became classless in 1994.

The Zero IP Subnet

The command **ip subnet-zero** tells the router that the zero subnet is a legitimate subnet of the classful network being configured on the router. For example, if the Class C network 129.168.128.0 is subdivided into eight subnets, each would have a /27 mask for the zero subnet, 192.168.128.0/27, through to the seventh subnet, 192.168.128.224/27.

The first and last subnets of a classful network historically were not used because of the potential confusion between these and the network/broadcast address of that classful network. Consider this example:

    192.168.128.20   192.168.128.00001010
    255.255.255.224   255.255.255.11100000

The first 3 bits of the final octet are 0, indicating the zero subnet or 192.168.128.0. However, the Class C network 192.168.128.0 is written in the same way, giving rise to possible confusion on the router and some older TCP/IP stacks. So the zero subnet cannot be assigned to an interface in this case.

Nowadays in the classless Internet, 192.168.128.0/27 is simply another network with no possibility of confusion with 192.168.128.0/24. Note that misconfiguration of the network mask on a host on the 192.168.128.0/27 subnet results in the possibility of confusion if the network address 192.168.128.0 is used, but this is a configuration error on the part of the user, not a consequence of the addressing scheme as in the case of the classful system.

Also, IP stacks on virtually all systems connected to the Internet support classless IP and, therefore, allow the use of the zero subnet for addressing purposes. Configuring **ip subnet-zero** on the router allows the zero subnet to be used on router interfaces.

More information on the zero subnet can be found in the Cisco.com Technical Note at http://www.cisco.com/warp/public/105/40.html.

Selective Packet Discard

When a link goes into a saturated state, the router will drop packets. The problem is that the router will drop any type of packets, including routing protocol packets. Selective Packet Discard (SPD) attempts to drop nonrouting packets instead of routing packets when the link is overloaded.

The basic idea behind SPD is this: If you mark all BGP and IGP packets as being "important" and prefer these packets over others, you should process a larger percentage of the packets that will allow routing and, consequently, keep the BGP and IGP sessions stable.

SPD can be configured as follows. Some of these commands are hidden from the Cisco IOS Software configuration helper but are well known to the ISP community. (Note the difference between the 11.1CC and 12.0 release versions of the commands.)

The following command turns on SPD. The **no** version of the command turns off SPD. The default is on for IOS Software versions 12.0 and later.

```
[no] ip spd enable     ! for 11.1CC
[no] spd enable        ! for 12.0+
```

The default value is 100. It is also possible to specify how many high-precedence packets you will queue over the normal input hold queue limit. This is to reserve room for incoming high-precedence packets. The command to do this is as follows:

```
ip spd headroom        ! for 11.1CC
spd headroom           ! for 12.0+
```

It is also possible to set lower and upper IP process-level queue thresholds for SPD. With SSE-based SPD, lower-precedence packets randomly are dropped when the queue size hits the minimum threshold. The drop probability increases linearly with the queue size until the maximum threshold is reached, at which point all lower-precedence packets are dropped. For regular SPD, lower-precedence packets are dropped when the queue size reaches the minimum threshold. Defaults are 50 and 75, respectively. These default values were not based on real-life experience at the time they were chosen, so they might need some tuning. The command to set the threshold levels is as follows:

```
[no] ip spd queue [min-threshold | max-threshold] <n>
```

The **show ip spd** exec command also shows the current SPD mode, the current and max size of the IP process-level input queue, and the available headroom. SPD mode is one of disabled, normal, random drop, or full drop. High-precedence packets go to the priority queue. A sample output from the router follows:

```
alpha#show ip spd
Current mode: normal.
Queue min/max thresholds: 73/74, Headroom: 100, Extended Headroom: 10
IP normal queue: 0, priority queue: 0.
SPD special drop mode: none
alpha#
```

show interface switching has some extra information, too, when SPD is turned on:

```
gmajor#show interface ethernet 3/0 switching
Ethernet3/0 CORE BACKBONE
         Throttle count        0
         Drops        RP       0        SP           0
    SPD Flushes      Fast      0        SSE     542019

    SPD Aggress      Fast      0
    SPD Priority   Inputs  88141        Drops        0
```

SPD flushes separate the route processor and switch processor flushes, and SPD Priority lists the priority packets received and dropped as the result of exceeding the headroom threshold.

Note that **switching** is a hidden option for the **show interface** command and must be entered in full to be recognized by the command parser.

SPD is activated by default on all IOS Software releases from 12.0; it is recommended that its configuration be left in the default state unless you understand what you are doing. Some ISPs have gained extra benefits by modifying SPD parameters; however, most simply leave the default configuration. 11.1CC and 11.1CA supported SPD as an option, and if those releases still are being used, it is best that SPD be switched on as indicated here.

Hot Standby Routing Protocol

A new feature in recent versions of IOS Software is the Hot Standby Routing Protocol (HSRP, described in the informational RFC 2281—see http://www.ietf.org/rfc/rfc2281.txt). This feature is especially useful on LANs within the ISP's backbone—for example, for network servers, non-Cisco access servers, and hosted servers.

The motivation for this protocol is to support the need for a default gateway on LAN networks when two gateway routers are providing connectivity to the wider network and the Internet. Routers tend to support the full set of routing protocols. Most computer workstations run variants of UNIX or Windows, for which there is either no or minimally functional routing software. Configuring something such as the public-domain software GATED or the vendor's own software to perform a dynamic routing function is usually an unnecessary and unwieldy compromise. The easiest and best solution is to configure a static default route on the workstation or server and use HSRP.

Figure 3-1 shows a typical LAN with two routers used to connect to the ISP backbone. To implement HSRP, the configuration required for these two routers looks something like the following:

```
Router 1:
interface ethernet 0/0
 description Server LAN
 ip address 169.223.10.1 255.255.255.0
 standby 10 ip 169.223.10.254
!
```

```
Router 2:
interface ethernet 0/0
 description Service LAN
 ip address 169.223.10.2 255.255.255.0
 standby 10 priority 150
 standby 10 preempt
 standby 10 ip 169.223.10.254
 !
```

Figure 3-1   *Dual-Gateway LAN*

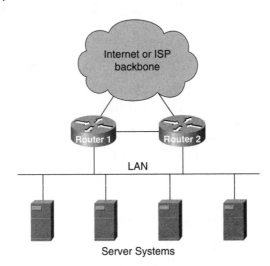

Server Systems

The two routers have their LAN IP addresses conventionally defined in the preceding configuration. However, another IP address has been defined in the command line **standby 10 ip 169.223.10.254**. This address is the address of the virtual default gateway defined on the LAN. All the systems on the LAN, apart from Router 1 and Router 2, use this address as the "default route." Router 2 has a standby priority of 150, higher than the default of 100. Therefore, Router 2 will be the default gateway at all times unless it is unavailable (that is, down). The **preempt** directive tells Router 1 and Router 2 that Router 2 should be used as the default gateway whenever possible. For example, if Router 2 were temporarily out of service, it would take over from Router 1 when it is returned to normal operation.

A potential issue here is that all the outbound traffic goes through Router 2; whereas, inbound traffic may be shared between the two. Some ISPs like to share outbound traffic between the two routers; this is achieved by setting up two standby groups as in the following example:

```
Router 1:
interface ethernet 0/0
 description Server LAN
 ip address 169.223.10.1 255.255.255.0
 standby 10 ip 169.223.10.254
```

```
  standby 11 priority 150
  standby 11 preempt
  standby 11 ip 169.223.10.253
 !

Router 2:
interface ethernet 0/0
  description Service LAN
  ip address 169.223.10.2 255.255.255.0
  standby 10 priority 150
  standby 10 preempt
  standby 10 ip 169.223.10.254
  standby 11 ip 169.223.10.253
 !
```

With this configuration on the two routers, the ISP sets the default route configuration on its servers so that traffic is shared between the two virtual default gateways. A good first starting point is to configure half of the servers to point to 169.223.10.254 and the remaining servers to point to 169.223.10.253. If finer load balancing is required, the ISP simply changes which default gateway the server has configured on it. If one link fails, the other router will take over all traffic until the failed router returns to normal operation.

HSRP more recently has been enhanced to include the capability to monitor the state of the uplinks from the gateway routers. So, for example, if the links connecting Router 1 and Router 2 in Figure 3-1 were serial connections to other PoPs, HSRP can be configured to monitor those links and "fail" one router if its uplink goes down. The sample configuration for this might be the following, where Serial 0/0 on Router 1 and Serial 3/1 on Router 2 are tracked for their status:

```
Router 1:
interface ethernet 0/0
  description Server LAN
  ip address 169.223.10.1 255.255.255.0
  standby 10 ip 169.223.10.254
  standby 10 track Serial 0/0
  standby 11 priority 150
  standby 11 preempt
  standby 11 ip 169.223.10.253
  standby 11 track Serial 0/0
 !

Router 2:
interface ethernet 0/0
  description Service LAN
  ip address 169.223.10.2 255.255.255.0
  standby 10 priority 150
  standby 10 preempt
  standby 10 ip 169.223.10.254
  standby 10 track Serial 3/1
  standby 11 ip 169.223.10.253
  standby 11 track Serial 3/1
 !
```

If either goes down because of a link failure or a remote end failure, the router will remove itself from availability, resulting in failover to the other router in the standby group.

IP Source Routing

The Cisco IOS Software examines IP header options on every packet. It supports the IP header options Strict Source Route, Loose Source Route, Record Route, and Time Stamp, which are defined in RFC 791. If the software finds a packet with one of these options enabled, it performs the appropriate action. If it finds a packet with an invalid option, it sends an ICMP Parameter Problem message to the source of the packet and discards the packet.

IP has a feature known as *source routing* that allows the source IP host to specify a route through the IP network. Source routing is specified as an option in the IP header. If source routing is specified, the software forwards the packet according to the specified source route. The default is to perform source routing.

Some ISPs do not want their customers to have access to source routing, so it is turned off at the customer edge. You can do this is with the following generic command:

```
no ip source-route
```

Some ISPs like to have source routing available to troubleshoot problems in their own networks and neighboring networks, especially when routing has broken inside one of those networks. Other ISPs require source routing to be turned on when peering with ISPs. An example of using traceroute with source routing enabled on the intermediate networks follows. The ISP is checking the path from 192.121.154.170 to www.sprint.net. The **-g** option specifies that traceroute should do the probe as though packets are coming from the 192.121.154.170 source address. Notice the **!S** in Step 18—this states that that host (router) is blocking IP source routing.

```
Unix% /usr/local/bin/traceroute -g 192.121.154.170 www.sprint.net
traceroute to www.sprint.net (208.27.196.10), 30 hops max, 40 byte packets
 1  fe0-1-0.hr1.cbg1.gbb.uk.uu.net (158.43.128.192)  1.294 ms  0.703 ms  0.539 ms
 2  pos0-0.cr1.cbg1.gbb.uk.uu.net (158.43.129.129)  0.748 ms  0.993 ms  0.747 ms
 3  pos0-0.cr2.cbg1.gbb.uk.uu.net (158.43.129.133)  1.586 ms  1.146 ms 2.145 ms
 4  pos0-2.cr2.lnd6.gbb.uk.uu.net (158.43.254.2)  4.43 ms  4.143 ms  3.731 ms
 5  ge2-0.cr1.lnd6.gbb.uk.uu.net (158.43.254.65)  4.395 ms  4.044 ms  4.148 ms
 6  POS11-0-0.GW2.LND1.Alter.Net (146.188.5.41)  4.898 ms  10.705 ms  5.082 ms
 7  122.at-2-0-0.XR2.LND2.Alter.Net (146.188.15.170) 5.995 ms  6.179 ms  6.039 ms
 8  194.ATM1-0-0.HR2.LND1.Alter.Net (146.188.15.129) 12.422 ms 7.229 ms  6.018 ms
 9  146.188.13.165 (146.188.13.165)  7.4 ms  8.331 ms  8.376 ms
10  gblon802-ta-d5-1-0.ebone.net (192.121.154.113) 16.846 ms 15.647 ms 21.246 ms
11  gblon801-ta-p6-0-0.ebone.net (192.121.154.170) 21.513 ms  21.535 ms  21.871 ms
12  gblon304-tb-p0-1.ebone.net (195.158.226.233) 366.643 ms 358.076 ms 269.65 ms
13  usnyk106-tc-p0-3.ebone.net (195.158.229.17)  359.798 ms 204.034 ms 241.634 ms
14  sl-bb11-nyc-5-3.sprintlink.net (144.232.9.229) 380.835 ms 84.641 ms 96.338 ms
15  sl-bb10-nyc-9-0.sprintlink.net (144.232.7.1)  94.433 ms  90.512 ms  87.394 ms
16  sl-bb12-rly-7-0.sprintlink.net (144.232.9.226) 102.331 ms 88.533 ms 93.294 ms
17  sl-bb11-rly-8-0.sprintlink.net (144.232.7.213) 89.341 ms 103.678 ms 174.892 ms
18  sl-bb5-dc-4-0-0.sprintlink.net (144.232.7.166)  86.662 ms !S  88.132 ms !S *
```

WARNING	As a general rule of thumb, if you are not using IP source routing, you should turn it off. IP source routing is a well-known security vulnerability used in attacks against a system.

Configuring Routing Protocols

This section examines the most efficient and effective ways of configuring IGPs and BGP to give greatest scalability in IOS Software. An IGP is the interior gateway protocol and is the medium through which an ISP's backbone routers pass routing information about the ISP's infrastructure to each other. As will be mentioned several times in this book, the design goal for an IGP is to keep the number of prefixes in it as small as possible. All prefixes which do not belong to the ISP's infrastructure are put into BGP; these are the prefixes that need local, national, regional, or global visibility.

Essentially three IGPs are in use by ISPs today. These are the protocols Intermediate System-to-Intermediate System (IS-IS), Open Shortest Path First (OSPF), and Enhanced Internal Gateway Routing Protocol (EIGRP). The former are industry standards. IS-IS was developed by OSI (ISO 10589) and is now being enhanced by the IETF (RFC 1195 is a proposed standard) through the IS-IS Working Group. OSPF was developed by the IETF specifically for IP (RFC 1131) and has been much enhanced to the Internet standard described in RFC 2328. EIGRP is an enhancement of IGRP developed by Cisco in the late 1980s.

Only one EGP is used in the Internet. BGP Version 4 has been used since 1994 as the routing protocol for autonomous systems to exchange prefixes with each other. BGP4 is the classless version of BGP and has seen many enhancements over the last few years as the Internet grows ever larger.

Router ID

The router identifier in an IGP is chosen from the loopback interface of the router, if configured at the time the routing process is started. If more than one loopback interface is configured with an IP address, the router identifier is the highest of those IP addresses. If the loopback is not configured, the highest IP address configured on the router at the time the IGP was started is used. ISPs prefer stability, so the loopback interface usually is configured and active on most ISP routers.

The router ID also is used as the last step of the BGP path-selection process. There's another reason to ensure that the loopback interface is configured and has an IP address: If there is no loopback, the router ID is the highest IP address configured on the box at the time the

BGP process was started. (This is potentially problematic because, if the router is gaining more interfaces or more activated connections with IP addresses assigned to them, the router ID can potentially change if the router is rebooted or the BGP process is restarted.)

Choosing an IGP

A general discussion on the appropriate technical choice of IGPs for an ISP backbone is currently beyond the scope of this book. Many good comparisons have been done describing the pros and cons of the different IGPs. A commonly quoted example is the presentation by Dave Katz at the June 2000 NANOG (http://www.nanog.org/mtg-0006/katz.html) comparing IS-IS and OSPF.

The choice of IGP generally seems to be made on the basis of experience because technically there is little way to choose among the three for most practical purposes. Those engineers with a strong IS-IS background will always choose IS-IS. Those with a strong OSPF background will always choose OSPF. The rule of thumb seems to be that beginners to interior routing choose EIGRP because it is easy to get started. However, OSPF is a better choice because it forces good IGP design to ensure that the network will scale. And those who are very experienced tend to choose IS-IS on Cisco routers because it allows for better scaling with more configuration options than the other two IGPs.

Putting Prefixes into the IGP

At least three possible ways exist for inserting prefixes into the IGP. However, ISPs aim to find the most efficient method and the one that will give greatest scalability of their networks.

The **network** Statement

The most efficient, scalable, and safe method is to use the **network** statement to cover the infrastructure addresses that have an active IGP running over them or require them to be carried in the IGP. A sample configuration might be as follows:

```
!
interface loopback 0
 ip address 220.220.16.1 255.255.255.255
!
interface serial 0/0
 ip address 220.220.17.1 255.255.255.252
!
interface serial 1/0
 ip unnumbered loopback 0
```

```
!
router ospf 100
 network 220.220.16.1 0.0.0.0 area 0
 network 220.220.17.0 0.0.0.3 area 0
 passive-interface loopback 0
 passive-interface serial 1/0
 !
```

Notice the use of the **passive-interface** command to disable OSPF neighbor discovery on any interfaces that do not have connected neighbors or that don't need to run a routing protocol.

It is not good practice, and indeed is strongly discouraged, to redistribute anything into an interior routing protocol. This is rarely required.

redistribute connected into an IGP

Using the **redistribute connected** command injects the prefixes assigned to every connected interface into the IGP. Apart from creating an external network type, which, for example, in OSPF is carried across all areas, the router periodically must examine the Routing Information Base (RIB) to see if there are any changes to the connected state. This takes extra CPU cycles. Additionally, any link-state changes are passed into the IGP, something that might not be desirable, especially in the case of link addresses going to external connections. In the OSPF example, the external link-state change is heard over the whole network.

Another problem is that redistributing connected interfaces into an IGP covers all connected interfaces on a routing device. Some addresses might not be desirable in an IGP, so ISPs then would have to add a route map to apply an access-list filter to the redistribution process. This could cause something else to go wrong: Access lists can be deleted by accident, resulting in prefixes being leaked into the IGP. Again, this is undesirable.

The recommendation is to avoid using **redistribute connected** if at all possible. Many ISPs do use **redistribute connected subnets** *route-map* through their own experience and operational practices, but most new starters in the industry have built large successful networks without needing this type of redistribution.

redistribute static into an IGP

The **redistribute static** command injects all static routes into the IGP. Apart from creating an external network type, which, for example, in OSPF is carried across all areas, the router periodically must examine the RIB to see if there are any additions to or deletions from the static route configuration. This takes extra CPU cycles. And if the next hop to which the static route points disappears, the static route is withdrawn, with a resulting withdrawal from the IGP. (Of course, the recently introduced permanent static route is designed to work around this problem, but the problem is best avoided in the first place!)

The other problem with redistributing static routes into an IGP is that it covers all static routes configured on a routing device. Some prefixes might not be desirable in an IGP, resulting in a situation similar to that noted in the **redistributed connected** case.

The recommendation is to avoid using **redistribute connected** if at all possible. Very few ISPs use this type of redistribution because BGP is the favored protocol for carrying most address space chunks now.

IGP Summarization

It is good practice and aids scalability to ensure that summarization is implemented where it makes sense and whenever it is possible. IGPs work most efficiently with as few prefixes as possible in the routing protocol. Small IGPs converge more quickly, ensuring rapid network healing in case of link failures. Configuring summarization is different for each protocol—consult the IOS documentation on Cisco.com. For example, OSPF uses the **area <n> range** OSPF subcommand.

IGP Adjacency Change Logging

Neighbor state logging should be enabled in each IGP. This means that it becomes easier to find out about neighbor states, reasons for state changes, and so on. For each IGP, the IGP subcommand **log-adjacency-changes** enables logging. (Some older versions of IOS Software require the IGP to be specified as well—for example, **ospf log-adjacency-changes**.) By the time this book is published, the command will likely be enabled by default in IOS Software.

If logging is enabled, log messages are sent to wherever the logging output has been configured. For most ISPs, this would be a UNIX syslog server and the internal logging buffer held on the router—see the section "Detailed Logging" in Chapter 1, "Software and Router Management," for information on how to configure this on the router. The typical output would be similar to what follows; this example shows the activation of a neighbor adjacency with a router connected to serial3/2:

```
Nov 10 03:56:23.084 AEST: %OSPF-5-ADJCHG: Process 1, Nbr 192.168.2.2 on Serial3/2
from DOWN to INIT, Received Hello
Nov 10 03:56:32.620 AEST: %OSPF-5-ADJCHG: Process 1, Nbr 192.168.2.2 on Serial3/2
from INIT to 2WAY, 2-Way Received
Nov 10 03:56:32.620 AEST: %OSPF-5-ADJCHG: Process 1, Nbr 192.168.2.2 on Serial3/2
from 2WAY to EXSTART, AdjOK?
Nov 10 03:56:32.640 AEST: %OSPF-5-ADJCHG: Process 1, Nbr 192.168.2.2 on Serial3/2
from EXSTART to EXCHANGE, Negotiation Done
Nov 10 03:56:32.676 AEST: %OSPF-5-ADJCHG: Process 1, Nbr 192.168.2.2 on Serial3/2
from EXCHANGE to LOADING, Exchange Done
Nov 10 03:56:32.676 AEST: %OSPF-5-ADJCHG: Process 1, Nbr 192.168.2.2 on Serial3/2
from LOADING to FULL, Loading Done
```

This shows the detailed establishment of the OSPF neighbor relationship between two routers, going from the Hello state through 2WAY, Exchange-Start, and Loading to Full adjacency. Although this sort of detail might not always be required, it becomes very important when the ISPs are following the recommended practice of enabling authentication on the IGP between routers. (Neighbor authentication is covered in more detail in Chapter 4, "Security.")

Putting Prefixes into BGP

As with IGPs, there are at least three possible ways of inserting prefixes into BGP. These methods are discussed in the following three sections.

The **network** Statement

The safest method to use is one **network** statement per prefix that is to be injected into BGP. A sample configuration might be as follows:

```
interface loopback 0
 ip address 220.220.16.1 255.255.255.255
!
interface serial 1/0
 ip unnumbered loopback 0
!
router bgp 100
 no synchronization
 network 220.220.18.0 mask 255.255.252.0
!
ip route 220.220.18.0 255.255.252.0 serial 1/0
!
```

It is not good practice, and indeed it is strongly discouraged, to redistribute any interior routing protocol into BGP. It is never required, and in the past it has led to many serious accidents on the global Internet.

redistribute connected into BGP

Using the **redistribute connected** command injects the prefixes assigned to any connected interface into BGP. As with IGP, one disadvantage is that the router periodically must examine the RIB to see if there are any changes to the connected state, taking extra CPU cycles. Additionally, any link-state changes are passed into BGP, generating a route flap on the Internet routing table and wasting considerable CPU cycles on all routers in the Internet that have a view of this prefix.

Another problem is that redistributing connected interfaces into BGP covers *all* connected interfaces on a routing device. If some addresses aren't desirable in BGP, ISPs would need to add a route map to apply an access-list filter to the redistribution process. This could cause something else to go wrong—access lists can be deleted by accident, resulting in prefixes being leaked into BGP. Again, this is very undesirable.

The recommendation is to avoid using **redistribute connected** if at all possible. Very few ISPs use this type of redistribution because it rarely has any real use for BGP.

redistribute static into BGP

Using the **redistribute static** command injects all static routes into BGP. Again, the router periodically must examine the RIB to see if there are any additions to or deletions from the static route configuration. This takes extra CPU cycles. And if the next hop to where the static route points disappears, the static route is withdrawn, with a resulting withdrawal from BGP. A withdrawal from BGP results in a route flap, as mentioned previously. (As in the IGP case, the permanent static route is designed to work around this issue, but the problem is best avoided in the first place!)

Again, redistributing static routes into BGP covers all static routes configured on a routing device. Some prefixes (such as the RFC 1918 prefixes) might not desirable in BGP, so ISPs would add a route map to apply an access-list filter to the redistribution process. This can potentially lead to the situation discussed in the case of **redistribute connected**.

Some situations demand **redistribute static**, especially when communities are attached to the prefixes inserted into the BGP process. This appears to be the preferred process among ISPs because they find it easier to manage than applying a prefix matching the route map to individual **network** statements. The following example is very typical on a customer aggregation or edge device that sets a community of 65534:1234 on all the ISP's customer prefixes:

```
router bgp 65534
 redistribute static route-map static-to-bgp
 !
route-map static-to-bgp permit 5
  match ip address prefix-list netblock-to-bgp
  set community 65534:1234
  set origin igp
 !
ip prefix-list netblock-to-bgp permit 220.220.0.0/16 le 30
 !
ip route 220.220.1.32 255.255.255.224 serial 0/0
 !
```

There are dangers with this: The prefix list could be deleted, but the ISP must weigh this danger against the administrative inconvenience/overhead of setting communities and so on on a per-network-statement basis.

The recommendation is to try to avoid using **redistribute static** if at all possible and then use it only if the situation (such as the one described previously) really warrants it.

IGP Configuration Hints

ISPs should be aware of a few configuration hints when configuring IGPs for their backbones. When the decision between EIGRP, OSPF, and IS-IS has been made, the aim is to design the IGP for efficient operation, fast failover, and, most important, scalability.

Network Design

Many good documents are available on the Cisco.com Website to help with IGP design—detailed design is beyond the scope of this book. However, it is worth emphasizing the ISP engineer's well-known design tips:

- Three types of prefixes exist:
    - Access network prefixes
    - Infrastructure prefixes
    - External prefixes
- IGPs carry infrastructure prefixes only.
- Access network prefixes are not part of the infrastructure—use either **ip unnumbered** or BGP **next-hop-self** if at all possible.
- Customer prefixes are never carried in an IGP; BGP is designed for this.
- IGPs are kept small for best convergence speed; using a good address plan and summarization can help.
- iBGP and eBGP prefixes are never distributed into an IGP.
- IGP prefixes are never distributed into BGP.

Prefix Types

Many newcomers to the Internet industry react with surprise when the experienced engineers talk about the different types of prefixes present in an Internet backbone. It is very important to differentiate among access network prefixes, infrastructure prefixes used for the ISP's backbone, and external prefixes that cover the remaining uses.

Access Network Prefixes

Access network prefixes commonly are used in nonpermanent access networks. So customers connecting using cable, ADSL, PSTN, or ISDN dialup tend to be assigned address space on a dynamic basis. When they connect, PPP or DHCP is used to assign them an address for the duration of their session. When they terminate the connection, the address goes back into the pool.

Access network prefixes are not carried in the IGP. If they were carried in the IGP, then every time a customer connects to the network, one /32 address would be injected into the IGP, flooded through the IGP backbone or area, and causing a small CPU hit. This doesn't scale—yet many small ISPs do this without thinking. But imagine running this with a 10,000-port network—several hundred connections per second could bring the network to its knees. We have been involved in many critical network failures caused simply by announcing the entire dial address space as /32s into the backbone IGP.

The correct way to carry the access network is to inject the aggregate hosted by the aggregation server into the iBGP. Whether this means running iBGP on the aggregation server so that it can announce the prefix or running iBGP on the distribution layer and pointing appropriate static routes to the aggregation box is up to the ISP network in question. But this is the correct and scalable method employed by most ISPs.

Some ISPs sell services to dial customers that include a fixed /32 address, no matter where they connect in the network. Although these are attractive, the service is technically ill conceived and is very hard to deliver. ISPs that do offer these services tend to build a dial network that is gatewayed onto the core backbone. A separate IGP is used in the dial network, and it has no interaction with the core IGP. The dial network address range is injected into the ISP backbone using iBGP.

Infrastructure Prefixes

Infrastructure prefixes are the only set of prefixes that should appear in the ISP IGP. Infrastructure prefixes are the routers' loopback interface addresses and the point-to-point links connecting all the routers in the backbone. So it should be very easy to predict the size of the IGP—simply adding the number of routers to the number of discrete links will give the number.

External Prefixes

External prefixes account for all other prefix types not covered in this section. If the ISP is assigning address space to customers, these are external prefixes. If the ISP is hearing prefixes being announced from peers and customers by BGP, these are external prefixes.

All external prefixes should be carried in iBGP. They are announced to other autonomous systems using eBGP, if they are to be announced. They should never appear in the IGP.

Configuring OSPF

OSPF enforces a fairly rigid design for an ISP backbone. Area 0 is the backbone area and must exist if there are to be more than two OSPF areas in a network. Area 0 provides transit between the other areas, and every other area must be connected to it.

OSPF offers a multitude of area types, including backbone, regular, stub, totally stubby, and not so stubby areas. Most ISPs tend to use only backbone and regular areas; very few make use of OSPF inter-area summarization capabilities. The reason is that, these days, iBGP carries all the prefixes across an ISP backbone. All that OSPF carries are the loopbacks and the infrastructure addresses, and it is often desirable to see those across the entire backbone. Loopbacks do need to be visible across the backbone because the loopback is usually the iBGP next hop for most of the prefixes carried in the backbone. An iBGP next hop cannot be a default route created by OSPF or BGP.

Putting a prefix into OSPF is achieved simply by creating a **network** statement with the relevant network, inverse mask, and area to which the network should belong. So, to put 192.168.1.0/24 into OSPF, the command required is simply this

```
Router8(config-router)# network 192.168.1.0 0.0.0.255 area 0
```

This prefix cannot be put into OSPF unless it is physically attached to the router, so announcing 192.168.1.0/24 needs an interface to use an address out of this network block.

To find neighbors in OSPF, simply mark the required interface as being nonpassive. The IOS Software default is to assume that all interfaces are active. Because most ISP routers have large numbers of interfaces, and OSPF tends to run only on interfaces connected to other routers, it is really important to change OSPF's default behavior of searching for neighbors on every interface so that they all are marked as passive unless required. This is achieved by using the **passive-interface default** command. It is recommended that ISPs use this command by default in any configuration template that they create for their routers. Otherwise, large aggregation routers waste CPU sending OSPF hellos to nonexistent neighbors on all the interfaces that it has. (Worse, if customer networks are connected and their neighboring router is running OSPF, an adjacency might be established, wreaking havoc in the ISP backbone.)

A typical router configuration might look something like the following:

```
interface FastEthernet1/0
 description Ethernet backbone
 ip address 200.200.7.129 255.255.255.224
 no ip redirects
 no ip directed-broadcast
 no ip proxy-arp
 ip ospf message-digest-key 1 md5 7 01100F175804
 no ip mroute-cache
!
interface Serial1/0
 description 2 Mbps Link to Router8
 bandwidth 2000
 ip address 200.200.7.1 255.255.255.252
 no ip redirects
 no ip directed-broadcast
 no ip proxy-arp
 ip ospf message-digest-key 1 md5 7 01100F175804
 no ip mroute-cache
 no fair-queue
!
router ospf 100
 log-adjacency-changes                       ! log adjacency changes
 passive-interface default                   ! all interfaces are passive...
 no passive-interface FastEthernet 0/0       ! ...except these two
 no passive-interface Serial 1/0
 area 0 authentication message-digest        ! authentication
 network 200.200.7.254 0.0.0.0 area 0        ! network statements for those...
 network 200.200.7.0 0.0.0.3 area 0          ! ...prefixes which need to be...
 network 200.200.7.128 0.0.0.31 area 0       ! ...in OSPF.
!
ip ospf name-lookup                          ! DNS resolution for show commands
!
```

Notice the OSPF configuration, especially the neighbor authentication. This will be covered in Chapter 5, "Operational Practices." It is very important that authentication be used for all routing protocol neighbor relationships. Denial-of-service attacks on routing protocols are becoming more common as the more traditional avenues are being closed up.

If an area is not physically connected to the backbone area, OSPF provides a concept called a *virtual link*. ISPs sometimes need to use virtual links if their networks don't fall into the rigid layout required by OSPF. The virtual link is a bridge over an intermediate area, connecting the remote area to the backbone. A configuration sample from a router using two virtual links to connect to the core backbone follows:

```
router ospf 100
 log-adjacency-changes
 area 0 authentication message-digest              ! virtual link goes to Area0
 area 30 authentication message-digest
 area 30 virtual-link 222.222.7.224 message-digest-key 1 md5 7 13061E010803
 area 30 virtual-link 222.222.35.224 message-digest-key 1 md5 7 00071A150754
 area 40 authentication message-digest
 passive-interface default
 no passive-interface Serial 0/0
 no passive-interface Serial 0/1
 network 222.222.11.224 0.0.0.0 area 30
 network 222.222.17.0 0.0.0.3 area 30
 network 222.222.32.0 0.0.0.3 area 40
 !
```

The router physically connects Area 30 to Area 40 and requires a virtual link to two routers in Area 0 so that Area 40 can see the rest of the ISP's backbone.

Very little else is required for configuring OSPF. As long as the basic design rules are remembered, OSPF works well and scales very nicely. There is no real limit to the number of routers that can be in an area. However, it is worth being prudent and designing so that OSPF Area 0 is the backbone of the ISP network and the subareas are the distribution and access layers of the network. A typical configuration is to use Area 0 for the national backbone and for each PoP to have one area of its own. The more routers exist in an area, or the more areas a router is a member of, the more the CPU has to work. If the backbone is richly meshed or has unstable physical connections, it is better to have fewer routers in an area and fewer areas connected to one router.

Configuring IS-IS

IS-IS is quite similar to OSPF in many ways, and both use the same Dijkstra SPF algorithm for path calculation. Implementation is slightly different, though, and IS-IS support in IOS Software has benefited from many years of experience in the major ISP backbones in the United States.

IS-IS does not have an area concept like OSPF. Instead, it has two levels: Level 1 (areas) and Level 2 (the backbone). The IS-IS backbone is simply a contiguous collection of Level 2–capable routers linking Level 1 areas together. Most ISPs implement IS-IS using Level 2 only—they see little benefit in the extra complexity that running both Level 1 and Level 2 offers. A router can be in Level 1 only, Level 2 only, or both Level 1 and Level 2. IS-IS has a link-state database for Level 1 and also one for Level 2.

Another feature of IS-IS is that it does not use IP for transport. Instead, it relies on CLNS, a protocol that runs on the wire alongside IP. (For the security conscious, this makes IS-IS harder to attack because CLNS rarely is routed across the Internet.) To enable CLNS on a router, the global configuration command **clns routing** is required.

As with OSPF, IS-IS needs to carry only infrastructure addresses; this means the point-to-point links for the backbone networks and the loopback addresses of the network equipment. IS-IS automatically installs all connected interfaces into the routing protocol, so no **network** statements are required. Also, to make IS-IS find neighbors, simply activate IS-IS on a router interface and the neighbor will be found. This is much easier than handling the passive/no-passive interface and the **network** statement/mask as found in OSPF.

Because IS-IS is using CLNS, each router requires a number called an NSAP, a number that can be between 8 and 20 bytes large. Each NSAP must be unique across the backbone. NSAPs are set using the **net** statement under IS-IS. Although NSAPs are supposed to be officially allocated by OSI, most ISPs simply pick a number that works for them and use it. OSI protocols are not announced across the Internet, so there is no danger of a collision between NSAP addresses used in different ISPs.

The other thing to note when setting up a new IS-IS backbone is that wide metrics should be used. The original IS-IS used narrow metrics (6 bit), which allows only 63 different values. Wide metrics are 32 bit, obviously giving considerable more scope and flexibility. Wide metrics should be set as the default in any ISP template for IS-IS. IS-IS has a uniform value of 10 for the link cost; OSPF sets the link cost based on the bandwidth configured on the interface. So, to make different links have different costs, the IS-IS metric is configured manually. Having only 6 bits to play with is very restrictive, especially with the larger backbones, so the 32-bit metric makes more sense from the start.

A configuration example corresponding to the initial preceding OSPF example might be as follows:

```
clns routing
!
interface FastEthernet1/0
 description Ethernet backbone
 ip address 200.200.7.129 255.255.255.224
 ip router isis CORE                     ! activate IS-IS on this interface
 isis circuit-type level-2               ! Level 2 only
 no ip redirects
 no ip directed-broadcast
 no ip proxy-arp
 no ip mroute-cache
!
interface Serial1/0
 description 2 Mbps Link to Router8
 bandwidth 2000
```

```
      ip address 200.200.7.1 255.255.255.252
      ip router isis CORE                    ! activate IS-IS on this interface
      isis circuit-type level-2              ! Level 2 only
      no ip redirects
      no ip directed-broadcast
      no ip proxy-arp
      no ip mroute-cache
      no fair-queue
     !
    router isis CORE
      net 39.1234.0000.0000.0001.00
      is-type level-2-only
      metric-style wide
      log-adjacency-changes
     !
```

IS-IS has several other performance options that make it ideally suited for larger ISP backbones. These include the capability to reconfigure timer values for larger topologies, to leak Level 2 specifics into Level 1 areas, and to support mesh groups for NBMA clouds.

Configuring EIGRP

EIGRP also is used quite extensively in ISP backbones, finding favor with ISPs that have been required to support multiple protocols in the past. It's also accepted that EIGRP is probably the easiest routing protocol to get started with. It found favor (in the form of IGRP) with ISPs that didn't want to use IS-IS in the earlier days of the Internet when implementations of OSPF were still not mature enough for their needs.

EIGRP has no area concept—the network runs as one large IGP. EIGRP does support summarization like the other two IGPs; in our experience, many ISPs that use EIGRP make quite significant use of summarization across the backbone. It is quite common for the point-to-point links in each PoP to be addressed out of one block; the aggregate for that block then is announced as a summary along the links leading away from that PoP.

The same design goals are required for EIGRP. The IGP must be kept as small as possible, so only infrastructure prefixes should be injected into EIGRP. As with OSPF and IS-IS, the larger the IGP routing table is, the slower convergence becomes and the greater the likelihood of instability in the backbone becomes.

The configuration concepts are very similar to OSPF. The **network** statement is used to inject prefixes into EIGRP, and interfaces need to be marked as passive or not passive to disable or enable EIGRP sending routing updates on those interfaces. The preceding example implemented using EIGRP looks like the following:

```
    interface FastEthernet1/0
     description Ethernet backbone
     ip address 200.200.7.129 255.255.255.224
     no ip redirects
     no ip directed-broadcast
     no ip proxy-arp
     no ip mroute-cache
```

```
!
interface Serial1/0
 description 2 Mbps Link to Router8
 bandwidth 2000
 ip address 200.200.7.1 255.255.255.252
 no ip redirects
 no ip directed-broadcast
 no ip proxy-arp
 no ip mroute-cache
 ip summary-address eigrp 100 200.200.7.0 255.255.255.0
 no fair-queue
!
router eigrp 100
 passive-interface default                 ! all interfaces are passive...
 no passive-interface FastEthernet 0/0      ! ...except these two
 no passive-interface Serial 1/0
 no default-information out                 ! disallow distr of default info
 network 200.200.7.254 0.0.0.0 area 0       ! network statements for those...
 network 200.200.7.0 0.0.0.3 area 0         ! ...prefixes that need to be...
 network 200.200.7.128 0.0.0.31 area 0      ! ...in EIGRP.
 no auto-summary
 eigrp log-neighbor-changes                 ! log neighbor changes
!
```

EIGRP has autosummarization enabled by default—this should be disabled in an ISP backbone. Autosummary, like BGP, automatically summarizes any redistributed prefix to the classful boundary. Clearly, this is not required in an Internet environment that has been classless for many years. Also, the redistribution of default information should be disabled. There is rarely any need for this in an ISP backbone because exit paths usually are determined by the information carried in iBGP. EIGRP supports logging of neighbor changes in addition to logging of neighbor warnings. As with the other two IGPs, logging more information of problems is generally advisable in an ISP network.

The **summary-address** line in the previous configuration for serial1/0 announces 200.200.7.0/24 to the neighbor on that link rather than announcing any subnets. This leads to greater efficiencies in the operation of EIGRP and can help reduce the overall size of the backbone IGP routing table.

Design Summary

The three preceding subsections gave brief examples of configuring each of the three popular IGPs to operate in an ISP backbone. Questions often are asked about which IGP is better or which is easier to configure. Hopefully these examples have shown that there is little to choose when it comes to configuration, and the benefits in an ISP backbone usually come down to the scalability of each IGP and the familiarity that the operators have with them.

CAUTION   Be sure to remember this one important point: Keep the size of the IGP routing table as
small as possible!

If ISPs follow this caution, they will have no problem scaling the backbone. As a general
rule of thumb, an IGP with more than 5000 routing table entries will have trouble scaling
much further, will have trouble dealing with circuit breaks, and will demonstrate a significant slow down in convergence. This 5000 limit has proven true in our experience in the
networks that we have been involved in—it is independent of processor power and is more
representative of the typical backbone topologies used by medium-size ISPs today.

It is worth bearing in mind that the largest ISPs carry more than 5000 prefixes in their
backbones. However, this is achieved by very careful design and handcrafting of many of
the IGP parameters. Indeed, most of the largest backbones in the Internet today are using
IS-IS as the IGP, a testament to its long deployment, good scalability features, and the
operational experience gained since the late 1980s.

The BGP Path-Selection Process[1]

BGP routers typically receive multiple paths to the same destination. The BGP best-path
algorithm decides which is the best path to actually install in the IP routing table and,
therefore, the route to use for forwarding traffic. The following text summarizes this
algorithm.

For the purposes of understanding this algorithm, begin by assuming that all received paths
for particular prefix are arranged in a list, similar to the output of the **show ip bgp** *prefix*
command.

Some paths received by the router are not considered candidates for the best path. Such
paths typically do not have the valid flag in the output of **show ip bgp** *x.x.x.x*. It is important
to understand these cases before looking at the algorithm itself.

   1   Ignore paths marked as "not synchronized" in the output of **show ip bgp** *x.x.x.x*. If
       BGP synchronization is enabled—which is the current default in IOS Software—
       there must be a match for the prefix in the IP routing table for an internal (that is,
       iBGP) path to be considered a valid path. Most ISPs will want to disable
       synchronization using the **no synchronization** BGP subcommand.

   2   Ignore paths for which the NEXT_HOP is inaccessible. This is why it is important to
       have an IGP route to the NEXT_HOP associated with the path.

3 Ignore paths from an eBGP neighbor if the local AS appears in the AS path. Such paths are denied upon ingress into the router and are not even installed in the BGP RIB. The same applies to any path denied by routing policy implemented through access, prefix, AS path, or community lists, *unless* inbound soft reconfiguration is configured for the neighbor.

4 If **bgp bestpath enforce-first-as** is enabled and the UPDATE does not contain the AS of the neighbor as the first AS number in the AS_SEQUENCE, send a NOTIFICATION and close the session.

5 Ignore paths marked as "(received-only)" in the output of **show ip bgp** *x.x.x.x*. This path has been rejected by policy but has been stored by the router because soft-reconfiguration inbound has been configured for the neighbor sending the path.

6 Ignore paths with a next-hop metric marked as inaccessible.

The BGP Best-Path Algorithm for IOS Software

Assign the first valid path as the current best path. Now compare the best path with the next path in list, until the end of the list of valid paths is reached.

1 Prefer the path with the largest weight. Note that **weight** is a Cisco specific parameter, local to the router on which it is configured.

2 Prefer the path with the largest LOCAL_PREF.

3 Prefer the path that was locally originated through a **network** or **aggregate** BGP subcommand or through redistribution from an IGP.

4 Prefer locally sourced network/redistributed paths over locally generated aggregates.

5 Prefer the path with the shortest AS path.

   A. This step is skipped if **bgp bestpath as-path ignore** is configured.

   B. An AS_SET counts as one AS, no matter how many autonomous systems are in the set. The AS_CONFED_SEQUENCE is not included in the AS path length.

6 Prefer the path with the lowest origin type: IGP is lower than EGP, and EGP is lower than INCOMPLETE.

7 Prefer the path with the lowest MED.

   A. This comparison is done only if the first (that is, neighboring) AS is the same in the two paths; any confederation sub-autonomous systems are ignored. In other words, MEDs are compared only if the first AS in the AS_SEQUENCE is the same; any preceding AS_CONFED_SEQUENCE is ignored.

   B. If **bgp always-compare-med** is enabled, MEDs are compared for all paths. This knob needs to be enabled over the entire AS. Otherwise, routing loops could occur.

    C. If **bgp bestpath med confed** is enabled, MEDs are compared for all paths that consist only of AS_CONFED_SEQUENCE (that is, paths originated within the local confederation).

    D. Paths received with no MED are assigned a MED of 0, unless **bgp bestpath missing-is-worst** is enabled, in which case they effectively are considered to have (although not actually assigned) a MED of 4,294,967,295. Any route received from a neighbor with a MED of 4,294,967,295 will have the MED changed to 4,294,967,294 before insertion into the BGP table.

    E. BGP Deterministic MED (see the section "BGP Deterministic MED" later in this chapter) also can influence this step.

8 Prefer the eBGP over iBGP paths. Note that paths containing AS_CONFED_SEQUENCE are local to the confederation and, therefore, are treated as internal paths. There is no distinction between confederation external and confederation internal.

9 Prefer the path with the lowest IGP metric to the BGP next hop.

10 If **maximum-paths** N is enabled and there are multiple external/confederation-external paths from the same neighboring AS/sub-AS, then insert up to N most recently received paths in the IP routing table. This allows eBGP multipath load sharing. The maximum value of N is currently 6; the default value, with the knob disabled, is 1. The oldest received path is marked as the *best* path in the output of **show ip bgp** *x.x.x.x*, and the equivalent of **next-hop-self** is performed before forwarding this best path on to internal peers.

11 Prefer the path that was received first (that is, the oldest one).

    A. This step minimizes route flapping because a newer path will not displace an older one, even if it otherwise would be selected on account of the additional decision criteria below. It makes more sense to apply the additional decision steps only below to iBGP paths, to ensure a consistent best-path decision within the network and thereby avoid loops.

    B. This step is skipped if **bgp bestpath compare-routerid** is enabled.

    C. This step is skipped if the ROUTER_ID is the same because the routers were received from the same router.

    D. This step is skipped if there is no current best path. An example of losing the current best path occurs when the neighbor offering the path goes down.

12 Prefer the route coming from the BGP router with the lowest router ID. The router ID is the highest IP address on the router, with preference given to loopback interfaces if one or more are configured. It also can be set manually through **bgp router-id** *x.x.x.x*. Note that if a path contains route reflector attributes, the originator ID is substituted for the router ID in the path-selection process.

13 If the originator/router ID is the same, prefer the path with the minimum cluster ID length. This will be present in BGP route-reflector environments only, and it allows clients to peer with route reflectors/clients in other clusters. In this scenario, the client must be aware of the route reflector–specific BGP attributes.

14 Prefer the path coming from the lowest neighbor address. This is the IP address used in the BGP neighbor configuration, and it corresponds to the address that the remote peer uses in the TCP connection with the local router.

BGP Features and Commands

BGP is the heart of the Internet. It is the essential protocol that keeps it all glued together. Yet, because the only thing you can guarantee on the Internet is change, BGP needs consistent updates with new features and functionality to help ISPs manage and scale their networks. This section details some of the early documentation and configuration notes for ISP network engineers rather than being a replacement for the documentation at Cisco.com (http://www.cisco.com/univercd/home/home.htm).

We will cover these new features/commands briefly in this section. ISP engineers need to understand when to use these commands on their backbones. Hence, detailed examples on how these commands are used can be found in *Using the Border Gateway Protocol for Interdomain Routing* (http://www.cisco.com/univercd/cc/td/doc/cisintwk/ics/icsbgp4.htm).

Stable iBGP Configuration

An ISP's backbone should be built using an IGP to carry internal infrastructure addressing and using iBGP to carry access networks, customer networks, and Regional Registry–assigned aggregates. There is the obvious distinction in services and function, but, more important, IGPs converge faster than iBGP and respond to changes in conditions (physical link status) more quickly. This design is deployed by many ISPs.

A common error is to use IP addresses of Ethernet or FDDI interfaces as the remote peer addresses. There could be no issue when the remote address is active, but as soon as the interface goes down, the peering is torn down because the address is no longer reachable. Most ISP backbone designs have routers connected by at least two interfaces to the rest of the network. It would be unfortunate to have the iBGP peering go down if one WAN link had gone down when, in fact, the router is perfectly accessible through another connection. The design using two exit paths per router should be taken advantage of. This is done by using the loopback interface, a "real" interface but without any physical connectivity. The interface always exists, and it can be shut down only by the IOS Software **shutdown** command. Choosing the loopback interface and assigning it a host IP address (/32) guarantees a more stable iBGP, regardless of the underlying physical network issues taken care of by the IGP.

```
hostname gateway1
!
interface loopback 0
  ip address 215.17.1.34 255.255.255.255
!
router bgp 200
  neighbor 215.17.1.35 remote-as 200
  neighbor 215.17.1.35 description iBGP with CR2
  neighbor 215.17.1.35 update-source loopback 0
  neighbor 215.17.1.36 remote-as 200
  neighbor 215.17.1.36 description iBGP with CR3
  neighbor 215.17.1.36 update-source loopback 0
!
```

Routers 215.17.1.35 and 215.17.1.36 see the BGP updates coming from address 215.17.1.34 of gateway1. Likewise, gateway1 hears the BGP updates coming from 215.17.1.35 and 215.17.1.36 (loopback interfaces configured on those routers). This configuration is independent of the backbone infrastructure and is not dependent on the physical connectivity of the routers.

The loopback interfaces on an ISP network usually are addressed out of one block of address space, with each loopback address carried in the ISP's IGP as a /32 address. The reasons for assigning loopback interface addresses out of one block will become apparent later in this chapter.

Notice the use of the **description** command. This is new in IOS Software Releases 11.1CC and 12.0, allowing a description of the BGP peering to be entered into the router configuration. Its use is strongly encouraged because it makes understanding and debugging of configuration and operation so much easier.

Note that, for eBGP configuration, IP addresses of real interfaces generally are used. This is because no IGP is running between ISP backbones or autonomous systems. eBGP peering routers have no way of finding out about external networks, apart from the other end of a point-to-point WAN link that will be linking the two together.

BGP Autosummary

In IOS Software, autosummarization is turned on by default for all prefixes that are redistributed into BGP from other routing protocols. This feature automatically summarizes subprefixes to the classful network boundaries when crossing classful network boundaries. The Internet registries now are allocating from the former Class A space; an ISP today is more likely to be allocated a /18 IPv4 address from what used to be the Class A space. BGP's default behavior is to take that /18 and advertise a /8. Without the BGP command **no autosummary**, BGP autosummarizes the /18 into a /8. At the least, this will cause confusion on the Internet, but worse, it potentially will attract other ISPs' unroutable traffic to the local backbone, with due consequences on circuit and systems loading.

Here's an example: An ISP is allocated 24.10.0.0/18. The ISP suballocates this /18 for its customers. The ISP wants to advertise the /18 to the Internet. BGP's default behavior would be to automatically summarize the /18 into the classful boundary, 24.0.0.0/8, the old Class A address. The problem is that other ISPs are also getting /18 allocations from the IPv4 Registry.

In today's classless Internet world, in which the former Class A space is being efficiently suballocated, ISP and enterprise backbones that use BGP and redistribute prefixes from other routing protocols have to use **no auto-summary.**

It should be noted that redistribution into BGP for any ISP backbone is strongly discouraged! Therefore, ISPs that are not doing redistribution can safely omit the **no auto-summary** command. However, as with everything else, it is good practice to include the command; it prevents future accidents.

BGP Synchronization

The (historical) default in IOS Software is for BGP not to advertise a route until all routers within the AS have learned about the route through an IGP. In today's Internet, and certainly since the mid-1990s, ISPs have designed their networks so that the iBGP carries customer and Internet prefixes and the IGP carries the infrastructure addresses. It is very uncommon for a prefix to appear both because of an IGP and because of iBGP. So synchronization *must be turned off* for all ISP configurations. To do this, use this BGP configuration **no synchronization** command.

BGP Community Format

Many ISPs make extensive use of BGP communities for routing policy decision making. A BGP community tutorial is beyond the scope of this book, but ISP engineers should be aware of the two formats supported in IOS Software. The original format for a community number took the form of a 32-bit integer. More recently, the representation of a community was redefined in the Internet space as being two 16-bit integers separated by a colon, per the BGP standard. The first 16-bit number is accepted as being the ISP's AS (because community numbers are exportable between autonomous systems with the **send-community** BGP directive). The second 16-bit number is used to represent different policies that the ISP wants to implement. Note that some standard communities are defined as common or current practice; these are documented in RFC 1998.

The configuration command is this

```
ip bgp-community new-format
```

This command converts communities from looking something like 13107210 to a more human-friendly 200:10. It should be noted that BGP does not care which format is used internally; the field is still 32 bits total. This new format is purely for appearance and practicality purposes.

BGP Neighbor Shutdown

A new feature introduced into 11.1CC and 12.0 software is the capability to shut down a BGP peering without actually removing the configuration. Previously, the only way to disable a BGP peering was to delete the configuration from the router. This was very disruptive to the router's functioning, and it significantly increased the likelihood of making mistakes when reinstating the configuration at a later stage.

A neighboring peering is shut down with this command example:

```
router bgp 200
  neighbor 169.223.10.1 shutdown
```

To reinstate the peering when the problem or reason for shutdown has been removed, simply enter the opposite command:

```
router bgp 200
  no neighbor 169.223.10.1 shutdown
```

Notice that the command is **no neighbor 169.223.10.1 shutdown**, with the **no** coming first instead of the possibly more intuitive **neighbor 169.223.10.1 no shutdown**. Be very aware of this because it is possible to forget or mistype the **shutdown** portion of the command, thus deleting the whole BGP configuration for that neighbor.

All users of BGP are encouraged to use neighbor shutdown rather than deleting the configuration—it greatly enhances the ease and reliable operation of the network.

BGP Dynamic Reconfiguration

Two methods are available now to dynamically reset a BGP peering session without tearing down the entire peering. Normally, when an ISP requires changing the policy in a BGP peering, the peering itself has to be torn down so that the new policy can be implemented. For peerings exchanging a large number of routes in the Internet, this can be extremely disruptive, putting load on the CPU of both routers involved and resulting in a routing flap through the backbone as the ISP's network announcements are withdrawn and then reinstated.

The first and older method is soft reconfiguration; the second and strongly recommended method is route refresh. It is now considered best current practice for ISPs that have external BGP peerings to use dynamic reconfiguration. The impact on their networks, their customers' perceived service quality, and the Internet is too great without this feature. Consider the impact and effects in the following section discussing BGP route flap damping. Also, it is recommended to discourage all operations staff from doing a hard clear of BGP unless it is an absolute last resort.

Soft Reconfiguration

BGP soft reconfiguration capability was introduced in IOS Software Releases 11.1CC, 11.2P, and 12.0. With this feature enabled, after the policy changes have been made, the ISP simply can implement a soft reset of the peering without having to tear it down. To support soft reconfiguration on a peering, the router requires one extra configuration command, for example:

```
router bgp 200
  neighbor 215.17.3.1 remote-as 210
  neighbor 215.17.3.1 soft-reconfiguration in
  neighbor 215.17.3.1 route-map in-filter in
  neighbor 215.17.3.1 route-map out-filter out
  !
```

If the policy on the peering must be changed, the ISP makes the changes to the route-map configuration in the previous example and then simply issues the command **clear ip bgp neighbor 215.17.3.1 soft**. If only the inbound or outbound policy needs to be changed, the **clear** command can be supplemented with **in** or **out** directives.

Notice the preceding configuration. Soft reconfiguration is required only inbound; outbound does not need to be explicitly configured because, to make outbound policy configuration changes, the BGP process simply has to send an incremental update to its neighbor.

One caveat is that soft reconfiguration can require a lot more router memory because the router must store prefixes that it has received before the BGP inbound policy is implemented. If the inbound policy is complex or there are multiple peerings, it is possible that almost twice the amount of memory will be required by the BGP process than if soft reconfiguration was not configured.

Route Refresh

A new feature available from IOS Software Release 12.0(5)S is route refresh (documented in RFC 2918). The concept is similar to soft reconfiguration, but this is a capability shared between two BGP speakers (as opposed to soft reconfiguration, which is configured on the local router only) and it is negotiated automatically at the time the BGP session is brought up. To find out whether route refresh is supported, check the BGP neighbor using the following command:

```
alpha>sh ip bgp neighbors 192.168.4.130
BGP neighbor is 192.168.4.130, remote AS 2830, external link
  Index 1, Offset 0, Mask 0x2
   Community attribute sent to this neighbor
   BGP version 4, remote router ID 192.168.11.1
   BGP state = Established, table version = 207, up for 16w1d
   Last read 00:00:01, last send 00:00:08
   Hold time 30, keepalive interval 10 seconds
   Configured hold time is 30, keepalive interval is 10 seconds
   Default information originate
   Unicast default sent, multicast default not sent
   Neighbor NLRI negotiation:
     Configured for unicast routes only
     Peer negotiated unicast routes only
     Exchanging unicast routes only
   Received route refresh capability(new) from peer
   ^^^^^^^^^^^^^^^^^^^^^^^^^^^^^^^^^^^^^^^^^^^^^^^^^^
```

```
Minimum time between advertisement runs is 30 seconds
Received 1648106 messages, 0 notifications, 0 in queue
Sent 1648064 messages, 0 notifications, 0 in queue
Prefix advertised 125, suppressed 1, withdrawn 66
Route refresh request: received 0, sent 1
Connections established 2; dropped 1
Last reset 16w1d, due to Peer closed the session
Number of unicast/multicast prefixes received 3/0
```

The portion highlighted with ^^^^^^^^^^^^^^^ shows that the route refresh capability has been negotiated between the two BGP neighbors. The "(new)" in the **capability** statement indicates that the routers support the IANA-assigned route refresh capability code (which has a value of 2, described in RFC 2918) rather than the Cisco-specific code when the feature first was developed by Cisco (which would show up as "(old)"). (All the IANA-assigned BGP capability codes are listed at http://www.iana.org/assignments/capability-codes.)

If the local router requires a fresh view of the routing table, it can send a route-refresh request to the neighboring BGP peer. This would be required, for example, when the inbound routing policy has been changed. Upon receipt of the route-refresh request, the remote router would send its list of prefixes to the requesting router. The route refresh capability requires no extra memory on the local router. Where the capability exists between speakers, it is strongly recommended that this is chosen over soft reconfiguration (because the latter requires more memory to store the inbound prefixes received from the remote peer). To request a route refresh inbound, use this command:

```
clear ip bgp [neighbor] in
```

No other configuration is required. To reset the BGP session outbound using route refresh, simply use this command:

```
clear ip bgp [neighbor] out
```

BGP Route Reflectors and the BGP Cluster ID

One mechanism that is available for scaling the iBGP mesh is to set up a route reflector cluster-based system across the ISP backbone. A route-reflector cluster typically is made up of one or more routers as the reflector, with the remaining routers in the cluster configured as clients. These clients need to peer only with the reflector, not any other router in the iBGP mesh. A typical example is that shown in Figure 3-2.

However, most ISPs choose to implement clusters with two route reflectors, as in Figure 3-3. This gives them redundancy in the cluster if one route reflector fails.

Figure 3-2   *BGP Route-Reflector Cluster*

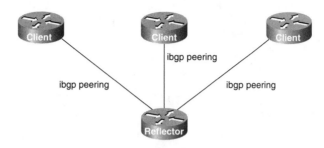

Figure 3-3   *BGP Route-Reflector Cluster with Two Route Reflectors*

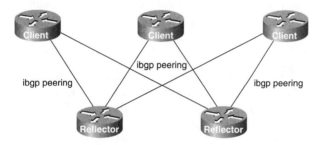

Network designers should be aware of some caveats when configuring route reflectors. As soon as a router is configured as a route reflector, it is assigned a cluster identifier automatically by the BGP process. This cluster ID is the BGP router ID, usually the loopback interface address of the router. The goal of a cluster ID is *only* to reduce the propagation of BGP updates between route reflectors when the same client uses multiple route reflectors. A route reflector will not accept an update coming from another route reflector that has the same ID (the ID is stored in the **cluster-list** attribute). This is because this update has been received already from the client (because the client peers with all route reflectors of the cluster).

Now, what if the cluster ID in both route reflectors isn't the same? In that case, a client connected to two route reflectors sends its update to both, and each route reflector sends this update to the other. The result is that they receive the same update twice. Now route reflectors act as BGP routers. When they discover that the update is exactly the same, they select just one (the one with the shortest cluster list) and propagate that one to other neighbors. There will be no routing loops because we are talking about *identical updates*: same net/mask, same next hop.

Some ISPs choose to change the default cluster ID to values that let them more easily identify regions/clusters in the backbone. And quite often they set the cluster ID of the route reflectors in each PoP to be the same value. They should do so only with the purpose of the cluster ID kept in mind:

- Each client *must* peer with both route reflectors. Failure to do so could result in routing loops.

- The physical path from the client to the route reflector must *not* be through another route reflector in the cluster. Failure to adhere to this will result in a routing black hole.

Is the overhead of one extra routing update worth sacrificing for an increased risk in routing black holes because of network topology?

Note the last point: It seems to be accepted wisdom and, indeed, is often documented that the cluster ID should be the same on both route reflectors in a cluster. This is potentially dangerous and could cause more problems than leaving the status quo. (One example might be the situation in which one reflector is physically reachable from the client only through the other reflector. The best path could be valid through the cluster ID but could be unreachable.)

Finally, there is little wrong with having overlapping route-reflector clusters, as shown in Figure 3-4. Many ISPs that have installed a route-reflector hierarchy across their backbones have done so very successfully simply using the default IOS Software values for the cluster ID. The early IOS Software restriction of a route-reflector client being able to belong to only one route reflector now has been removed, so setting up clients to be members of two clusters is common practice across the Internet. If in doubt, the question to ask is this: "Is the overhead of one extra routing update worth sacrificing for an increased risk in routing black holes because of network topology?" Network topology changes on a monthly or more frequent basis in an ISP backbone, so what might have been a perfect design on the first day potentially could become a liability later.

Figure 3-4 *Overlapping Route-Reflector Clusters*

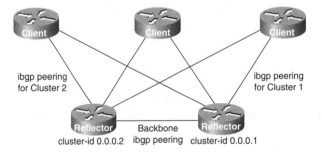

next-hop-self

The BGP command **next-hop-self** simply does as it suggests. The next-hop announcements from this router are set to the local router ID rather than the IP address of the origin of the prefix. To configure **next-hop-self**, use the following BGP configuration:

```
router bgp 200
 neighbor 215.17.3.1 remote-as 210
 neighbor 215.17.3.1 next-hop-self
 !
```

Two common implementation examples are given in the following sections. The first deals with external connections, such as those to other networks or Internet exchange points; the second deals with aggregation routers, in which customer links are terminated onto the ISP backbone.

External Connections

If a prefix is heard from an external network, the next hop is preserved throughout the IGP. However, setting **next-hop-self** on the border router that is distributing the eBGP prefix into iBGP means that the external prefix will receive the router ID (loopback interface IP address) of the border router rather than the external next hop.

Several ISPs choose to do this rather than transport the external point-to-point links across the backbone. ISPs with a large number of BGP customers or external private peers will use this mechanism—each peer potentially can add another /30 to the IGP across the backbone. Removing these extra /30s helps to keep the IGP table as small as possible.

This feature also is used especially by ISPs at exchange points to ensure consistency and reliability of connections across the exchange. Indeed, it is considered a strongly recommended practice because it stops the potentially fraudulent activity of stealing bandwidth at the exchange point. If the ISP is carrying the exchange-point LAN address across its backbone in the IGP (or in iBGP), then it is announcing reachability of the exchange across the entire network. So a peering customer (usually ISP) that is also present at the exchange point could send traffic to this ISP and have it successfully delivered to the exchange point using the ISP's infrastructure rather than his own poorer connection. A sample configuration using a GRE tunnel, which could be used by such a perpetrator, follows. Figure 3-5 gives a picture of how this might be done.

```
Router D:
interface tunnel 0
 ip address 221.0.1.1 255.255.255.252
 tunnel source 220.0.0.2
 tunnel destination 169.223.0.2
 !
 ip route 169.223.0.2 255.255.255.255 220.0.0.1
```

```
Router B:
interface tunnel 0
 ip address 221.0.1.2 255.255.255.252
 tunnel source 169.223.0.2
 tunnel destination 220.0.0.2
 !
 ip route 220.0.0.2 255.255.255.255 169.223.0.1
```

The GRE tunnel is used both to defeat reverse path forwarding checks that AS 109 may be carrying out and to hide the traffic from AS 109. Reverse path forwarding checks are covered in more detail in Chapter 4.

Figure 3-5   *GRE Tunnels at IXPs/NAPs*

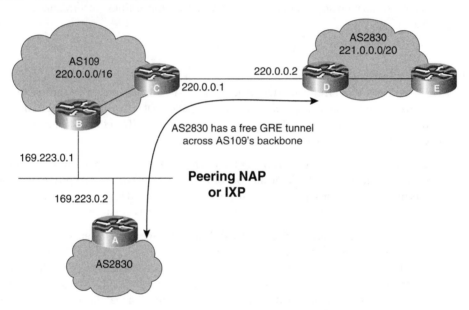

Hopefully, this section has demonstrated how important the **next-hop-self** BGP setting is. If the ISP in AS 109 had used **next-hop-self** for the IXP LAN rather than carrying 169.223.0/24 across its backbone, the customer in AS 2830 would not have been able to construct the GRE tunnel as pointing the static route from Router D to Router C. Router C would not know how to get to the 169.223.0/24 network, so all the traffic would have been dropped on the floor. The same goes for Router B: If Router B does not know how to get to the 220.0.0.0/30 point-to-point link, the tunnel again could not have been built. In fact, it is very common for an ISP router at an IXP to carry nothing more than the ISP's internal network prefixes, carrying a default route is equivalent to saying that the router knows how to get to the *entire* Internet.

Aggregation Routers

If a prefix is injected into the iBGP at a gateway router (the standard way of injecting a customer prefix into the iBGP), the next-hop address is the IP address of the point-to-point link between the gateway aggregation router and the customer. This means that the iBGP has a large number of next-hop addresses to resolve from the IGP (not bad in itself) and that the IGP will be larger, resulting in slower convergence and greater potential instability in case of instability or failures in the network.

The obvious solution to this is to use IP unnumbered. The next-hop address in that case will be the router ID. However, many ISPs that started off using IP addresses on point-to-point links have a lot of work to do to migrate to IP unnumbered on all their customer point-to-point connections. A quicker fix, which lets them scale the IGP but does not require undue haste (that is, panic!) in renumbering large numbers of customer interfaces is to set **next-hop-self** on the iBGP peers of the gateway router. The customer prefixes then will appear in the iBGP with the loopback address of the aggregation router, simplifying the route lookups and, more important, meaning that the IGP no longer has to carry all the point-to-point link addresses used for customer connections. (This also assumes that the point-to-point link addresses have been assigned in a block per router and are transported by the iBGP. If the point-to-point addresses are not in the iBGP, the customer point-to-point link will not be pingable, which could be an unacceptable situation for providers that monitor the state of their customer links.)

BGP Route Flap Damping

Route flap damping (introduced in Cisco IOS Software at Release 11.0) is a mechanism for minimizing the instability caused by route flapping. A route flap occurs when a BGP network prefix is withdrawn and reannounced; specifically, this happens when a BGP speaker hears a WITHDRAW followed by an UPDATE for a prefix. (A peering with an eBGP neighbor being reset does *not* count as a flap.) Whenever a network goes down, the rest of the Internet is told about it. Hence, BGP propagates this state change throughout the Internet (unless, of course, ISPs in the path do something to block this propagation through route filters or something similar).

If the state change is caused by faulty circuits (frequently going up and down) or from misconfigured routing (redistributing the IGP into the EGP), the Internet would experience several hundred BGP state changes a second. For every state change, BGP must allocate time to process the work and pass on the changes to all other BGP neighbors. This places unnecessary extra strain on the backbone routers recomputing best paths and propagating these changes. Hence, the tool to control and minimize the effect of route flaps is BGP damping.

Command Syntax

The following are the commands used to control route damping:

```
bgp dampening [[route-map map-name] | [half-life-time reuse-value suppress-value
maximum-suppress-time]]
```

- *half-life-time*—Has a range of 1 to 45 minutes; current default is 15 minutes.

- *reuse-value*—Has a range of 1 to 20,000; default is 750.

- *suppress-value*—Has a range of 1 to 20,000; default is 2000.

- *max-suppress-time*—Gives the maximum duration that a route can be suppressed. Its range is 1 to 255; the default is four times the half-life time (60 minutes).

- **show ip bgp dampened-paths**—Displays all the damped routes, with the time remaining to unsuppress. This is very useful for finding out which sites are having instability problems.

- **clear ip bgp dampening** [*address mask*]—Clears the damping related information. This also unsuppresses the suppressed routes and is a very useful tool when one of your customers calls about an unreachable network that has been suppressed.

A route map can be associated with BGP damping to selectively apply the damping parameters if certain criteria are found. Example selective damping criteria include matching on the following:

- A specific IP route

- An AS path

- A BGP community

Adjusting the damping timers becomes essential when administrators cannot afford to have a long outage for a specific route. BGP damping with route maps is a powerful tool to selectively penalize ill-behaved routes in a user-configurable and controlled manner.

Recommended route flap damping parameters for use in the Internet were combined in a document by the RIPE Routing Working Group (routing-wg@ripe.net) and are available at http://www.ripe.net/docs/ripe-229.html. These values are used by many European and U.S. ISPs and are based on the operational experienced gained in the industry. Detailed examples of BGP damping techniques with route maps can be found in the book *Internet Routing Architectures*, Second Edition, by Sam Halabi and Danny McPherson. However, it is very unusual for ISPs to use more than the default IOS Software setting or the settings contained in RIPE-229.

Implementation

For each flap, a penalty (1000) is applied to the route. For an attribute change, a penalty of 500 is applied to the route. As soon as the penalty exceeds the suppress limit, the advertisement of the route is suppressed. The penalty is exponentially decayed based on a preconfigured half-life time. When the penalty decreases below the reuse limit, it is unsuppressed. A pictorial description of flap damping is given in Figure 3-6.

Figure 3-6   *BGP Route Flap Damping*

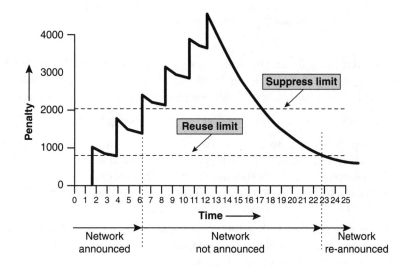

The routes external to an AS learned through iBGP will not be damped. This is to avoid the iBGP peers having higher penalty for routes external to the AS. It also ensures that only directly connected eBGP peers will have route flap damping applied to them, even though the configuration on the router is applied on a global basis.

Any route that flaps at a rate more than the half-life time eventually will be suppressed. The penalty is decayed at a granularity of 5 seconds, and the entries are unsuppressed with the granularity of 10 seconds. Furthermore, when the penalty is less than half of the reuse limit, the damping information is purged.

The maximum suppress time is the final important parameter used for configuring route flap damping. It is the maximum time that a prefix can be suppressed, and the other three parameters must be chosen accordingly. It is also a key parameter in the software implementation for flap damping (see RFC 2439 for a detailed discussion). If the half-life time is 15 minutes and the maximum suppress time is 60 minutes, the reuse limit is used to compute what the maximum possible penalty can be. All route-flap penalties cannot exceed this maximum value. It is most important for the suppress limit to be *less* than the maximum possible value that the route flap penalty can be; otherwise, no prefixes will be suppressed. Parameters chosen should be checked to ensure that they achieve the desired effect. (A maximum is set for the value of the penalty so that if a prefix is oscillating frequently, the resultant penalty attached to it doesn't generate a huge number and, therefore, become unlikely ever to be reused.) The mathematical equation might be as shown in Figure 3-7.

Figure 3-7 *Calculating the Maximum Possible Penalty*

$$\text{max-penalty} = \text{reuse-limit} \times 2^{\left(\frac{\text{max-suppress-time}}{\text{half-life}}\right)}$$

For the IOS Software default configuration of **bgp dampening 15 750 2000 60**, this would make the maximum possible penalty of 12,000. So, even if the prefix carries on flapping after the penalty has reached 12,000, the penalty will not be increased anymore.

These are some examples of good and bad flap-damping parameters:

- **bgp dampening 30 2000 3000 60**—These values are valid. The maximum suppress time is 60 minutes, the reuse limit is 2000, and the maximum possible penalty is 8000. A suppress limit of 3000 means that penalties easily can exceed the suppress limit. (A maximum possible penalty of 8000 decays to 4000 after one half-life [30 minutes] and to 2000 after two half-lives [60 minutes].)

- **bgp dampening 15 750 3000 45**—These values are valid. The maximum suppress time is 45 minutes, the reuse limit is 750, and the maximum possible penalty is 6000. The suppress limit of 3000 is easily reachable.

- **bgp dampening 15 500 2500 30**—These values are illegal and won't give rise to any prefixes being suppressed because of flaps. The maximum suppress time is 30 minutes, so to reach the reuse limit of 500 with a half-life time of 15 minutes, the penalty must reach 2000. However, the suppress limit has been set to 2500, so no prefixes will be suppressed.

- **bgp dampening 30 750 3000 60**—These values are valid but won't give rise to any prefixes being suppressed because of flaps. The maximum suppress time is 60 minutes, so to reach the reuse limit of 750 with a half-life time of 30 minutes, the suppress limit must be 3000. However, prefixes are suppressed only after the penalty reaches 3000. Because the penalty is adjusted every five seconds, the prefix will be suppressed only if an update arrives within five seconds of the withdrawal. This is extremely unlikely, so no prefixes will be suppressed with this example.

Designing Flap Damping Parameters

It is important to note that prefixes are suppressed only when they are heard from a neighbor and have a flap history and a penalty value that will cause them to be suppressed. A prefix attracts a penalty of 1000 when the WITHDRAW is heard from the neighboring eBGP peer. However, because the prefix has been withdrawn, it is not present in the BGP table apart from having a history entry, so it will not be damped. The penalty will decay, however.

When the prefix is reannounced by the neighbor, if the penalty is still above the suppress limit, the prefix will be suppressed. If the penalty is below the suppress limit, the prefix will not be suppressed. It is important to remember this when designing flap-damping parameters. The maximum possible penalty should be set considerably larger than the suppress limit; otherwise, there is the possibility of a slowly oscillating prefix not being suppressed as intended.

For example, **bgp dampening 30 751 3000 60** will generate a maximum possible penalty of 3004, which is only four higher than the suppress limit. The fastest that the prefix would reappear in the BGP table is one minute later the next time the BGP process runs, and that intervening time could have attracted around 100 points of decay, thereby bringing the penalty below 3000 and not causing any damping to happen. If **bgp dampening 30 800 3000 60** was used, the penalty would still be above 3000 and the prefix would be suppressed as intended.

BGP Flap Statistics

It is possible to monitor the flaps of all the paths that are flapping. The statistics will be lost when the route is not suppressed and stable for at least one half-life time. The display looks like the following:

```
cerdiwen#sh ip bgp neighbors 171.69.232.56 flap-statistics
BGP table version is 18, local router ID is 172.19.82.53
Status codes: s suppressed, d damped, h history, * valid, > best, i - internal
Origin codes: i - IGP, e - EGP, ? - incomplete

    Network          From          Flaps Duration Sup-time Path
*> 5.0.0.0          171.69.232.56  1     0:02:21           300
*> 6.0.0.0          171.69.232.56  2     0:03:21           300
```

The following are the new commands that display flap statistics:

- **show ip bgp flap-statistics**—Displays flap statistics for all the paths

- **show ip bgp flap-statistics regexp** [*regexp*]—Displays flap statistics for all paths that match the regular expression

- **show ip bgp flap-statistics filter-list** [*list*]—Displays flap statistics for all paths that pass the filter

- **show ip bgp flap-statistics** *x.x.x.x* [*m.m.m.m*]—Displays flap statistics for a single entry

- **show ip bgp flap-statistics** *x.x.x.x m.m.m.m* **longer-prefix**—Displays flap statistics for more specific entries

- **show ip bgp neighbor** *x.x.x.x* **flap-statistics**—Displays flap statistics for all paths from a neighbor

NOTE   Because we maintain information about only one path for a neighbor, the **show ip bgp flap-statistics** neighbor could show a different path for the same network layer reachability information (NLRI).

The following commands could be used to clear the flap statistics:

- **clear ip bgp flap-statistics**—Clears flap statistics for all routes
- **clear ip bgp flap-statistics regexp** [*reg*]—Clears flap statistics for all the paths that match the regular expression
- **clear ip bgp flap-statistics filter-list** [*list*]—Clears flap statistics for all the paths that pass the filter
- **clear ip bgp flap-statistics** *x.x.x.x* [*m.m.m.m*]—Clears flap statistics for a single entry
- **clear ip bgp** *x.x.x.x* **flap-statistics**—Clears flap statistics for all paths from a neighbor

BGP Neighbor Authentication

You can invoke MD5 authentication between two BGP peers. This feature must be configured with the same password on both BGP peers; otherwise, the connection between them will not be made. Invoking authentication causes the Cisco IOS Software to generate and check the MD5 digest of every segment sent on the TCP connection. If authentication is invoked and a segment fails authentication, a message appears on the console.

Configuring a password for a neighbor causes an existing session to be torn down and a new one to be established. If you specify a BGP peer group by using the **peer-group** *name* argument, all the members of the peer group will inherit the characteristic configured with this command. If a router has a password configured for a neighbor but the neighbor router does not, a message such as the following appears on the console while the routers attempt to establish a BGP session between them:

```
%TCP-6-BADAUTH: No MD5 digest from [peer's IP address]:
    11003 to [local router's IP address]:179
```

Similarly, if the two routers have different passwords configured, a message such as the following appears on the console:

```
%TCP-6-BADAUTH: Invalid MD5 digest from [peer's IP address]:
    11004 to [local router's IP address]:179
```

The following example specifies that the router and its BGP peer at 145.2.2.2 invoke MD5 authentication on the TCP connection between them:

```
router bgp 109
 neighbor 145.2.2.2 password v61ne0qkel33&
```

BGP MED Not Set

When an MED is not set on a route, Cisco IOS Software has always assumed that the MED is 0. Some other vendors have assumed that the MED is 4,294,967,295 ($2^{32} - 1$). This divergence can result in eBGP routing loops between Cisco routers and other vendors' routers. This confusion was the result of a lack of any definition in the BGP standard on what to do if a MED was not set. The most recent IETF decision regarding BGP MED assigns a value of infinity to the missing MED, making the route lacking the MED variable the least preferred. The default behavior of BGP routers running Cisco IOS Software is to treat routes without the MED attribute as having a MED of 0, making the route lacking the MED variable the most preferred. To configure the router to conform to the belated IETF standard, use this command (new in IOS Software Releases 12.0 and 12.1 but not in 12.0S):

```
router bgp 109
 bgp bestpath missing-as-worst
```

ISPs should seriously consider whether they need to implement this command, given the large deployment of routers in the Internet that are using the Cisco default. Implementing this command without considering the consequences will have just as serious of an impact as not being aware of the situation in the first place.

BGP Deterministic MED

If **bgp deterministic-med** is not enabled, the order in which routes are received could impact MED-based best-path decisions. This can occur when the same route is received from multiple autonomous systems or confederation sub-autonomous systems, with exactly the same path length and different MEDs.

For example, consider the following routes, received in the order shown:

- **A**—ASPATH 1, MED 100, internal, IGP metric to NEXT_HOP 10
- **B**—ASPATH 2, MED 150, internal, IGP metric to NEXT_HOP 5
- **C**—ASPATH 1, MED 200, external

If the paths were received in this order, a BGP-speaking router without deterministic MED configured would choose path B over path A because of a lower IGP metric to reach the NEXT_HOP (see Step 10 in the BGP path-selection process). It would then prefer path C to path B because it is external. However, path C has a higher MED than path A.

Enabling **bgp deterministic-med** removes any temporal dependency of MED-based best-path decisions. It ensures that correct MED comparison is made across all routes received from the same AS and that path A is chosen as the best path in the example. Note that if **bgp always-compare-med** is enabled, BGP MED decisions always will be deterministic.

Cisco strongly recommends enabling **bgp deterministic-med** in all new network deployments. ISP engineers also should consider retroactively installing this configuration but should make sure that there is no unforeseen operational impact in doing so.

Comparing Router IDs

As part of the standard path-selection process in IOS Software, the router does not switch between two eBGP paths based solely upon the router ID. Consider a situation in which a router hears two announcements of a particular prefix from two different neighbors. If the path-selection process determines that all attributes are identical apart from the router ID, it currently takes the path with the oldest entry in the routing table, not the entry with the lowest router ID. This choice was made to maintain stability in operational backbones over the last decade. However, it is actually counter to RFC 1771, which states that the router IDs always should be compared.

A new BGP option has been added (fully documented in CSCdr47086) from IOS Software Releases 12.0(11)S and 12.1(3) that makes the path-selection process compliant with the RFC:

```
bgp bestpath compare-routerid
```

This tells the BGP path-selection process to always compare router IDs at the appropriate stage. The IOS Software default remains unchanged.

BGP network Statement

A historical limitation was placed on the number of **network** statements that could be applied to the BGP configuration. In the early days of IOS Software, in which the average router had at most 30 interfaces, the limit of 200 **network** statements seemed a large number compared with the number of networks that such a router could originate. However, in the last five years or so, routers have grown through having hundreds of interfaces to the thousands of interfaces that we see on some of the platforms today. Obviously, 200 **network** statements is a severe limitation (and, unfortunately, has resulted in many ISPs heading down the path of redistributing prefixes from other routing protocols into BGP). CSCdj57631 removed the 200 **network** statement limit for BGP (as well as OSPF, RIP, and EIGRP) in late 1997 in IOS Software Releases 11.1CC and 11.3, and now it is recommended practice for all new deployments to use the **network** statement to inject prefixes into BGP.

Removing Private Autonomous Systems

Some ISPs use private autonomous systems within their networks (typically but not exclusively for customers who multihome onto the backbone). A new BGP option (CSCdi64489) prevents any private autonomous systems from being leaked to the Internet:

```
router bgp 109
 neighbor 145.2.2.2 remove-private-AS
```

If the BGP update has private autonomous systems[2] in the AS path, this option removes the private AS numbers. Note that it will not work if there are private and public autonomous systems in the AS path; thus, this option cannot be used when a network is using a private AS for its BGP yet is providing transit to the public Internet (this is considered a configuration error). Note that in the case of BGP confederations, the private AS will be removed as long as the private AS appears after (and outside) the confederation portion of the AS path. It should be noted that this command can be used only for eBGP peers; it has no effect on iBGP peers. Before the existence of this command, most ISPs used a combination of AS path access lists and proxy announcements to remove private autonomous systems. That process was clumsier and often prone to error. For this reason, **remove-private-AS** is strongly recommended to remove private autonomous systems from the public Internet, and it is recommended to be included as part of the default BGP configuration template on all new and current network deployments. The configuration template in Appendix B, "Cut-and-Paste Templates," includes this.

For reference and comparison purposes, the old method is shown here:

```
router bgp 109
 network 220.10.0.0 mask 255.255.224.0
 neighbor 145.2.2.2 filter-list 5 out
!
ip as-path access-list 5 deny ^(65534_)+$
!
ip route 220.10.0.0 255.255.224.0 null0 250
```

This configuration has the same effect as using one line **remove-private-AS** for the AS 65534 peer, but it is more prone to error by requiring a filter list and a static pull-up route to ensure that the /19 prefix appears in the routing table.

BGP local-as

A recent addition to BGP is the **local-as** neighbor option, which allows the AS number of the network to be changed for eBGP peerings. It isn't possible in IOS Software to configure BGP to run in more than one AS; the local AS feature provides a solution to this requirement.

Configuration

Router A is in AS 109, and Router B is in AS 159. However, when A peers with B, it uses AS 210 as its AS number. As far as B is concerned, it is peering with a router in AS 210. Operationally, this is equivalent to Router B peering with a router in AS 210, and that router peering with Router A in AS 109. The AS path for all prefixes learned from Router B as seen on Router A would be 210_159. AS 210 is inserted into the AS path sequence. The AS path for all prefixes learned from Router A by Router B would be 210_109.

Router A configuration:

```
router bgp 109
 neighbor 145.2.2.2 remote-as 159
 neighbor 145.2.2.2 local-as 210
```

Router B configuration:

```
router bgp 159
 neighbor 144.2.2.1 remote-as 210
```

local-as can be configured per eBGP peer or per peer group. It cannot be configured for individual members of a peer group. Also, **local-as** cannot be configured with the AS number of the BGP process of the local router, nor can it be configured with the AS number of the BGP process on the remote router. **local-as** cannot be used between two confederation eBGP peers, either—they must be true eBGP peers.

Motivation

The **local-as** feature most often is used and was requested by ISPs that are active in acquiring other ISPs. If an ISP purchases another ISP, a significant amount of work goes into renumbering the acquired ISP's backbone into the same AS number as that of the purchaser. However, in some situations the acquired ISP might have agreements with peers or a specific eBGP configuration that is hard to migrate to the new AS (for political or technical reasons, or both). The **local-as** option can make the peering router in AS 109 look as though it really is in AS 210, the ISP network that was purchased, until the political and technical issues with the interprovider peer can be sorted out.

BGP Neighbor Changes

It is possible to log neighbor state changes to a UNIX syslog server. This is extremely useful for most syslog-based monitoring systems because it gives early warning of problems with iBGP peers, and more especially external BGP neighbors. The logging is enabled by the following commands:

```
router bgp 109
 bgp log-neighbor-changes
```

Note that, as of IOS Software Releases 12.1(4) and 12.0(12)ST, the default action is to log all BGP neighbor changes (see DDTS CSCdm59903). At time of writing, the default was not yet included in IOS Software Release 12.0S.

Also note that, as of CSCdr54231, BGP notification messages are included when **bgp log-neighbor-changes** is configured. Before CSCdr54231, the only way to see these messages was to enable **debug ip bgp**, which was a bit limiting for most ISPs! This alteration has been included in IOS Software Releases from 12.0(10)S3, 12.1(3), and 11.1(34)CC.

Limiting the Number of Prefixes from a Neighbor

At times, either through configuration error or through a blatant attack on the Internet, the global default free routing table jumped to two to three times its size. This caused severe problems on sections of the Internet. The BGP neighbor command **maximum-prefix** was added to help networks safeguard against these sorts of problems. This command allows you to configure a maximum number of prefixes that a BGP router is allowed to receive from a peer. It adds another mechanism (in addition to distribute lists, filter lists, and route maps) to control prefixes received from a peer. When the number of received prefixes exceeds the maximum number configured, the router terminates the peering (by default). However, if the keyword **warning-only** is configured, the router instead only sends a log message but continues peering with the sender. If the peering is terminated, the peer stays down until the **clear ip bgp** command is issued.

In the following example, the maximum number of prefixes allowed from the neighbor at 129.140.6.6 is set to 150,000 (the global Internet route table was around 106,000 at the time of this writing):

```
router bgp 109
 network 131.108.0.0
 neighbor 129.140.6.6 maximum-prefix 150000
```

The **maximum-prefix** command sends log messages also, so any overrun can be trapped by a management system that monitors the router's syslog output. One message is sent when the number of prefixes received reaches the configured threshold value:

```
%BGP-4-MAXPFX: No. of unicast prefix received from 129.140.6.6 reaches 113021, max
150000
```

The default threshold is 75 percent. This value can be changed by specifying the threshold percentage in the **maximum-prefix** line. The following example sets the threshold to 95 percent:

```
router bgp 109
 bgp log-neighbor-changes
 neighbor 129.140.6.6 maximum-prefix 120000 95
```

Another message is sent when the number of prefixes received exceeds the maximum number of prefixes configured. Logging of neighbor changes is included for completeness in this example:

```
%BGP-3-MAXPFXEXCEED: No. of unicast prefix received from
129.140.6.6: 123411 exceed limit 120000
%BGP-5-ADJCHANGE: neighbor 129.140.6.6 Down - BGP Notification Sent
```

Limiting the AS Path Length from a Neighbor

Often ISPs are required to limit the length of the AS path that they receive from their peers, especially when trying to configure multihoming with good load sharing.

The hard way to do this is to use an AS path access list with a very long match string—for example, something like this

```
router bgp 109
 neighbor 192.168.1.1 remote-as 65534
 neighbor 192.168.1.1 filter-list 1 in
 !
 ip as-path access-list 1 permit ^[0-9]*_[0-9]*_[0-9]*
    _[0-9]*_[0-9]*_[0-9]*_[0-9]*_[0-9]*_[0-9]*_[0-9]+$
 !
```

This will permit all prefixes with an AS path less than or equal to 10 ASNs. However, this is quite ugly, and the problem is easier to solve with the **maxas-limit** command:

```
router bgp 109
 neighbor 192.168.1.1 remote-as 65534
 neighbor 192.168.1.1 maxas-limit 10
 !
```

This does almost the same thing. The main difference between the AS path filter example and the **maxas-limit** command is that, in the latter case, all received prefixes are included in the BGP table, but only those with an AS path length less than or equal to 10 ASNs are included in the BGP path-selection process. (At the time of this writing, **maxas-limit** is a hidden command.)

BGP fast-external-fallover

By default, if the physical connection to the eBGP neighbor goes down, the peering relationship is reset immediately. By adding the **no bgp fast-external-fallover** configuration, the peering is held open for the duration of the BGP keepalive timer. This configuration is desirable, if not essential, in the case of long-distance peering links or unreliable or long-latency connections to other autonomous systems, and when ISPs prefer stability over convergence speed in large networks.

```
router bgp 109
 no bgp fast-external-fallover
```

Note that the fast failover for external peers only applies to direct eBGP peerings. Those peerings using eBGP-multihop are not subjected to fast-external-fallover processes. Also note that fast-external-fallover does not apply to iBGP peerings.

WARNING   This configuration option should be used with care. It is recommended that **fast-external-fallover** be used only for links to an ISP's upstream provider or over unreliable links. Because the failover is slower, it is possible to blackhole routes for up to three minutes. This could prove problematic, for example, on a link to a multihomed customer, where peering might have suffered an unintentional reset because of human activity.

BGP Peer Group[3]

The major benefit of BGP peer groups is a reduction of resources (CPU load and memory) required in update generation. Peer groups also simplify BGP configuration.

With BGP peer groups, the routing table is walked only once per peer group, and updates are replicated to all other peer-group members that are in sync. Depending on the number of members, the number of prefixes in the table, and the number of prefixes advertised, this could significantly reduce the load. Thus, it is highly recommended that peers with identical outbound announcement policies be grouped into peer groups.

Requirements

All members of a peer group must share identical outbound announcement policies (for example, distribute lists, filter lists, and route maps), except for the originating default, which is handled on a per-peer basis even for peer-group members.

The inbound update policy can be customized for each individual member of a peer group.

A peer group must be either internal (with iBGP members) or external (with eBGP members). Members of an external peer group have different AS numbers.

Historical Limitations

Several limitations existed with BGP peer groups in older IOS Software versions:

- If used for clients of a route reflector, all the clients should be fully meshed.
- If used as an eBGP peer group, transit cannot be provided among the peer-group members.
- All the eBGP peer-group members should be from the same subnet to avoid nonconnected next-hop announcements.

Inconsistent routing would occur if these limitations were not followed. They have been removed starting with the following IOS Software versions: 11.1(18)CC, 11.3(4), and 12.0. Only the router on which the peer groups are defined needs to be upgraded to the new code.

Typical Peer Group Usage

ISP network engineers group BGP peers on a router into peer groups based on their outbound update policies. A list of peer groups commonly by ISPs follows:

- **Normal iBGP peer group**—For normal iBGP peers.
- **iBGP client peer group**—For reflection peers on a route reflector.
- **eBGP full routes**—For peers to receive full Internet routes.
- **eBGP customer routes**—For peers to receive routes from direct customers of the ISP only. Some members can be configured with **default-origination** to receive the default route as well as the customer routes.
- **eBGP default routes**—For peers to receive the default route and possibly a few other routes.

BGP Peer Group Examples

This example shows an iBGP peer group for a router inside an ISP's backbone:

```
router bgp 109
 neighbor internal peer-group
 neighbor internal remote-as 109
 neighbor internal update-source loopback 0
 neighbor internal send-community
 neighbor internal route-map send-domestic out
 neighbor internal filter-list 1 out
 neighbor 131.108.10.1 peer-group internal
 neighbor 131.108.20.1 peer-group internal
 neighbor 131.108.30.1 peer-group internal
 neighbor 131.108.30.1 filter-list 3 in
 !
```

This example shows an eBGP peer Group for a router peering with several ISPs, all with the same advertisement policies:

```
router bgp 109
 neighbor external-peer peer-group
 neighbor external send-community
 neighbor external-peer route-map set-metric out
 neighbor external-peer route-map filter-peer in
 neighbor 160.89.1.2 remote-as 200
 neighbor 160.89.1.2 peer-group external-peer
 neighbor 160.89.1.4 remote-as 300
 neighbor 160.89.1.4 peer-group external-peer
 !
```

The iBGP and eBGP configuration templates in Appendix B make use of peer groups as examples. It is recommended that you to try use peer groups wherever possible because the increased readability of the configuration and modest performance benefits for the router are worthwhile.

One important point to note is the interaction between route maps and peer groups. If a route map is applied inside a peer group, a route map applied to the actual peer is accepted by the parser but isn't actually used. In other words, the route map configured inside a peer group overrides the route map configured on the actual neighbor—for example:

```
router bgp 109
 neighbor external-peer peer-group
 neighbor external send-community
 neighbor external-peer route-map set-metric out
 neighbor external-peer route-map filter-peer in
 neighbor 160.89.1.2 remote-as 200
 neighbor 160.89.1.2 peer-group external-peer
 neighbor 160.89.1.2 route-map set-policy out
 !
```

The route map **set-policy** will be ignored in the previous configuration because the peer group route map **set-metric** will override it.

BGP Multipath

The BGP implementation in IOS Software supports three ways of load sharing over parallel circuits. Two of them are applicable to eBGP. eBGP multihop has been used in IOS Software for several years and is the common way of setting up an eBGP peering without using the directly connected peer addresses; the common use of this is for load sharing over parallel peering circuits. More recently, eBGP multipath was added to give an alternative mechanism for load sharing without some of the side effects experienced with eBGP multihop.

The third multipath feature is a very recent addition to IOS Software and is applicable to iBGP only. It allows load sharing over parallel paths within an ISP's network (independent of any load sharing available through the IGP).

eBGP Multipath

With IOS Software Release 11.1CC came a new BGP feature that allows more than one path to the same destination to be installed in the forwarding table. This feature, called eBGP multipath, is designed to allow ISPs to load-share over external circuits to eBGP neighbors.

When the border router has more than one path to the same external network, the BGP path-selection process makes a decision at Step 11, installing the oldest received path into the RIB. So only one of the external paths is used. eBGP multipath allows the router to install up to a maximum of six paths in the forwarding table. To enable this feature, configure **maximum-paths** under **router bgp** as follows:

```
router bgp 100
 maximum-paths 1-6
 !
```

Two or more eBGP paths are considered candidates for all multipath attributes (weight, localpref, AS-PATH [entire attribute, not just length]). Origin and MED are the same.

Care is required when using eBGP multipath. If the external peer or peers are carrying the full routing table, the local router supporting multipath will receive two full BGP feeds and will require sufficient memory to support this. This is why it is more normal for ISPs to use an eBGP-multihop configuration to support load sharing over parallel paths to an external peer.

eBGP Multihop

Consider this example. AS 100 connects to AS 200 using three parallel circuits between their two border routers. An eBGP multipath IOS Software configuration example is given here that will let the border router in AS 100 to load-share outbound traffic on the three circuits:

```
interface serial 1/0
 ip address 1.1.1.2 255.255.255.252
!
interface serial 1/1
 ip address 1.1.1.6 255.255.255.252
!
interface serial 1/2
 ip address 1.1.1.10 255.255.255.252
!
router bgp 100
 neighbor 1.1.1.1 remote-as 200
 neighbor 1.1.1.1 prefix-list AS200peer in
 neighbor 1.1.1.5 remote-as 200
 neighbor 1.1.1.5 prefix-list AS200peer in
 neighbor 1.1.1.9 remote-as 200
 neighbor 1.1.1.9 prefix-list AS200peer in
 maximum-paths 3
!
```

If AS 200 is delivering the full routing table, the AS 100 border router will require sufficient memory to support the three full views.

The equivalent configuration using eBGP multihop is more memory-efficient in the case of large routing tables being exchanged; it is given here:

```
interface loopback 0
 ip address 1.1.0.1 255.255.255.255
!
interface serial 1/0
 ip address 1.1.1.2 255.255.255.252
!
interface serial 1/1
 ip address 1.1.1.6 255.255.255.252
!
interface serial 1/2
 ip address 1.1.1.10 255.255.255.252
!
router bgp 100
 neighbor 1.1.1.255 remote-as 200
 neighbor 1.1.1.255 ebgp-multihop 2
 neighbor 1.1.1.255 update-source loopback 0
 neighbor 1.1.1.255 prefix-list AS200peer in
!
ip route 1.1.1.255 255.255.255.255 serial 1/0
ip route 1.1.1.255 255.255.255.255 serial 1/1
ip route 1.1.1.255 255.255.255.255 serial 1/2
!
```

Notice that the eBGP peering is set up between the loopback interfaces of the two routers. There is only one BGP session, so it is more efficient in router memory. Notice the **ebgp-multihop** configuration. Some ISPs allow 255 for the maximum number of intermediate hops; however, it is recommended that, to avoid potential problems with routing loops or black holes, the *multihop* parameter be set to the actual number of hops required between the two routers.

This example is the most common use of eBGP multihop. Some ISPs also use eBGP multihop for all their customer BGP connections. It is our experience that there is little to be gained by doing this because most ISPs have separate aggregation points for BGP customers and statically connected customers. Terminating customer BGP connections is usually minimal overhead compared with the backbone iBGP sessions present in most ISP networks.

iBGP Multipath

A new feature added to IOS Software Release 12.0ST allows iBGP to gain a multipath feature similar to what has been available for eBGP since 11.1CC.

When there are multiple border BGP routers with reachability information heard over eBGP, and if no local policy is applied, the border routers will choose their eBGP paths as best path. They advertise that best path inside the ISP network. So, from a pure core router's perspective, there can be multiple paths to the same destination, but only one path will be selected as the best and be used for forwarding. If the multiple paths are equidistant, it is sometimes desirable to use them for load balancing.

To enable this feature, configure **maximum-paths ibgp** under router BGP as follows:

```
router bgp 100
 maximum-paths ibgp 1-6
 !
```

Two or more iBGP paths are considered candidates for multipath if the following criteria are met:

- All attributes (weight, localpref, AS-PATH [entire attribute, not just length], Origin, MED, and IGP distance are the *same*.
- The next hops are different.

The best-path calculation continues until the last step of the BGP path-selection process, so the best path that is advertised will remain the same with and without this feature turned on. Out of the candidate multipaths, the best path is *always* inserted into the RIB. Other candidate multipaths are inserted depending on the number of paths allowed into the RIB through the **maximum-paths ibgp** command.

Applying Policy with BGP

The main differentiator between BGP and an IGP is that BGP can be used to apply policies to the exchange of routing information between two neighboring routers. This section considers the policy options available, from the introduction of prefix list filtering and the application of route maps, to the use of BGP policy accounting to characterize traffic flowing into and out of a network.

Using Prefix Lists in BGP Route Filtering[4]

The prefix list feature offers significant performance improvement (in terms of CPU consumed) over the access list in route filtering of routing protocols. It also provides for faster loading of large lists and support for incremental configuration. In addition, the command-line interface is much more intuitive. This feature is available in IOS Software versions from 11.1 (17)CC, 11.3(3), and 12.0.

According to one ISP that has done some in-depth performance testing of prefix lists and access lists, a 7507/RSP4 running 11.1(20)CC took more than 15 minutes to boot using extended ACLs for filtering BGP routes. The same test with prefix lists had the router booting and fully operational in less than 5 minutes. The configuration involved around 95,000 lines of ACL (or prefix lists) total for all neighbors, a configuration around 6 MB in total size. Given this type of experience, it is easy to see why most ISPs now are using prefix lists rather than ACLs for prefix filtering on their BGP peering sessions.

The prefix list preserves several key features of the access list:

- Configuration of either **permit** or **deny**
- Order dependency—first match wins
- Filtering on prefix length, both exact match and range match

However, prefix lists, or prefix lists in route maps, do not support packet filtering. This section presents the detailed configuration commands and several applications of the prefix list in route filtering.

Configuration Commands

Three configuration commands are related to the prefix list.

The following command can be used to delete a prefix list:

```
no ip prefix-list list-name
```

Here, *list-name* is the string identifier of a prefix list.

This next command can be used to add or delete a text description for a prefix list:

```
[no] ip prefix-list list-name description text
```

The following command can be used to configure or delete an entry of a prefix list:

```
[no] ip prefix-list list-name [seq seq-value] deny|permit \
    network /len [ge ge-value] [le le-value]
```

Several command attributes exist, as can be seen in the three preceding examples. These attributes have the following meanings:

- *list-name*—Mandatory. This is the string identifier of a prefix list.

- **seq** *seq-value*—Optional. This attribute can be used to specify the sequence number of an entry of a prefix list. By default, the entries of a prefix list would have sequence values of 5, 10, 15 and so on. In the absence of a specified sequence value, the entry would be assigned with a sequence number of (Current_Max+ 5).

Note   A prefix list is an ordered list, like an access list. Entries are evaluated in order of increasing sequence number. In the case of apparently conflicting entries for the same prefix, the one with the lowest sequence number is considered the real match. For example

```
ip prefix-list test permit 221.10.16.0/21
ip prefix-list test deny 221.10.16.0/21
```

contains an apparent conflict. However, the permit comes first, so the /21 network is allowed by the prefix list.

- **deny|permit**—Mandatory. The action is taken once a match is found.
- *network/len*—Mandatory. This is the prefix (that is, network and prefix length). Multiple policies (exact match or range match) with different sequence numbers can be configured for the same *network/len*.
- **ge** *ge-value*—Optional.
- **le** *le-value*—Optional.

Both **ge** and **le** are optional. They can be used to specify the range of the prefix length to be matched for prefixes that are more specific than *network/len*. An exact match is assumed when neither **ge** nor **le** is specified. The range is assumed to be from *ge-value* to 32 if only the **ge** attribute is specified. The range is assumed to be from **len** to *le-value* if only the **le** attribute is specified.

A specified *ge-value* or *le-value* must satisfy the following condition:

```
len < ge-value < le-value <= 32
```

Some configuration examples are given in Tables 3-1 and 3-2. They show how simple it is to set up a prefix list. It is left as an exercise to the reader to work out what the equivalent access list might be.

Table 3-1   *Specification of Exact Prefixes*

Desired Action	IOS Software Command
Deny the default route 0.0.0.0/0	**ip prefix-list abc deny 0.0.0.0/0**
Permit the prefix 35.0.0.0/8	**ip prefix-list abc permit 35.0.0.0/8**

Table 3-2 *Specification of Group of Prefixes*

In 192/8, accept up to /24	**ip prefix-list abc permit 192.0.0.0/8 le 24**
In 192/8, deny /25+	**ip prefix-list abc deny 192.0.0.0/8 ge 25**
In all address space, permit /8 – /24	**ip prefix-list abc permit 0.0.0.0/0 ge 8 le 24**
In all address space, deny /25+	**ip prefix-list abc deny 0.0.0.0/0 ge 25**
In 10/8, deny all	**ip prefix-list abc deny 10.0.0.0/8 le 32**
In 204.70.1/24, deny /25+	**ip prefix-list abc deny 204.70.1.0/24 ge 25**
Permit all	**ip prefix-list abc permit 0.0.0.0/0 le 32**

Incremental Configuration

A prefix list can be reconfigured incrementally; that is, an entry can be deleted or added individually. For example, to change a prefix list from the initial configuration to a new configuration, only the difference between the two needs to be deployed, as follows.

The initial configuration:

```
ip prefix-list abc deny 0.0.0.0/0 le 7
ip prefix-list abc deny 0.0.0.0/0 ge 25
ip prefix-list abc permit 35.0.0.0/8
ip prefix-list abc permit 204.70.0.0/15
```

The new configuration:

```
ip prefix-list abc deny 0.0.0.0/0 le 7
ip prefix-list abc deny 0.0.0.0/0 ge 25
ip prefix-list abc permit 35.0.0.0/8
ip prefix-list abc permit 198.0.0.0/8
```

The difference between the two configurations:

```
no ip prefix-list abc permit 204.70.0.0/15
ip prefix-list abc permit 198.0.0.0/8
```

The sequence number is used internally to identify the real match (the one with the lowest sequence number) when multiple prefix-list entries match a given prefix. It also can be used to insert an entry in a specific relative position (for example, a sequence number of 7). However, in most cases a prefix list can be structured so that there is no need to specify sequence numbers, and such an approach would make it easier to automate prefix-list generation, configuration difference generation, and deployment. The sequence numbers can be switched off so that they do not appear in the configuration by using this command:

```
no ip prefix-list sequence-number
```

How a Prefix List Match Works

The matching is similar to that of the access-list—more specifically:

* An empty prefix list permits all prefixes.

- An implicit **deny** is assumed if a given prefix does not match any entries of a prefix list.

- When multiple entries of a prefix list match a given prefix, the one with the smallest sequence is considered as the "real" match. In short, the first match wins!

Here is an example to illustrate the first match rule. Supposed that a prefix list is configured as follows:

```
ip prefix-list abc deny 10.0.0.0/8 le 32
ip prefix-list abc permit 0.0.0.0/0 le 32
```

Then the given prefix 10.1.0.0/16 would match both entries. However, the prefix will be denied because the first entry is the real match.

Consider this second example. Suppose that a prefix list is configured as follows:

```
ip prefix-list abc deny 0.0.0.0/0 le 32
ip prefix-list abc permit 10.0.0.0/8
```

The first line in the prefix list matches all prefixes, so all prefixes will be blocked in the prefix list's application, even though there is a following line permitting 10.0.0.0/8. Prefix lists are order sensitive when there is more than one possible match—the first match wins.

show and **clear** Commands

Table 3-3 gives a list of **show** and **clear** commands that can be used to control prefix lists and that give the operator more information about what is happening.

Table 3-3   **show** *and* **clear** *Commands*

IOS Software Command	Action
show ip prefix-list [detail|summary]	Displays information on all prefix lists
show ip prefix-list [detail|summary] [*name*]	Displays information for a prefix list
show ip prefix-list *name* **[seq** *seq-num*]	Displays the prefix list entry with the given sequence number
show ip prefix-list *name* *network/len*	Displays the policy associated with the node *network/len*
show ip prefix-list *name* *network/len* **longer**	Displays all entries of a prefix list that are more specific than the given *network/len*
show ip prefix-list *name* *network/len* **first-match**	Displays the entry of a prefix list that matches the given *network/len*
clear ip prefix-list [*name*] [*network/len*]	Resets the hit count of prefix list entries

Using Prefix Lists with BGP

The prefix list can be used as an alternative to the BGP **neighbor** *x.x.x.x* **distribute-list** command. The configuration of prefix lists and distribute lists for a BGP peer are mutually exclusive.

```
router bgp xxx
 neighbor x.x.x.x prefix-list name in|out
```

Using Prefix Lists in a Route Map

The prefix list can be used as an alternative to an access lists used in the command **match ip address|next-hop|route-source** *access-list* of a route map. The configurations of prefix lists and access lists are mutually exclusive within the same sequence of a route map.

```
route-map name permit|deny seq-num
 match ip address|next-hop|route-source prefix-list name [name ...]
```

Besides its application in BGP, route maps using prefix-lists can be used for route filtering, default origination, and redistribution in other routing protocols as well. For example, the following configuration can be used to conditionally originate a default route (0.0.0.0/0) when there exists a prefix 10.1.1.0/24 in the routing table:

```
ip prefix-list cond permit 10.1.1.0/24
!
route-map default-condition permit 10
 match ip address prefix-list cond
!
router rip
 default-information originate route-map default-condition
!
```

Using Prefix Lists in Other Routing Protocols

The prefix list can be used to filter inbound and outbound routing updates, as well as to control route redistribution between different routing protocols. Compared with using the access list, prefix list–based filtering offers the capability of prefix length filtering. As usual, access lists and prefix lists are mutually exclusive in one **distribute-list** command.

Inbound updates can be filtering on the prefix, the gateway, or both the prefix and the gateway:

```
router rip | igrp | eigrp
 distribute-list {prefix name1} | {gateway name2} |{prefix name1 gateway name2} in
 [interface]
```

Here, *name1* is the name of a prefix list to be applied to the prefix being updated, and *name2* is the name of a prefix list to be applied to the gateway (that is, the next hop) of a prefix being updated. The filtering also can be specified with a specific interface.

```
router rip | igrp | eigrp ...
 distribute-list prefix name1 out [routing_process | interface]
```

For example, in the following configuration, the RIP process will accept only prefixes with prefix length of /8 to /24:

```
router rip
 version 2
 network x.x.x.x
 distribute-list prefix max24 in
 !
ip prefix-list max24 seq 5 permit 0.0.0.0/0 ge 8 le 24
 !
```

Also, the following configuration will make RIP accept routing updates only from 192.1.1.1, besides filtering on prefix length:

```
router rip
 distribute-list prefix max24 gateway allowlist in
 !
ip prefix-list allowlist seq 5 permit 192.1.1.1/32
 !
```

BGP Filter Processing Order

When constructing BGP filters, most ISPs use prefix lists or distribute lists, AS path filters, and route maps to implement their filtering policies. It is important to realize that these lists are processed in a particular order—newer engineers sometimes are unaware of the standard IOS Software sequence. In the following, example the IOS Software configuration generator (NVGEN) has printed the configuration into the previous order:

```
router bgp 10
 neighbor 220.0.0.1 remote-as 11
 neighbor 220.0.0.1 prefix-list rfc1918-in in
 neighbor 220.0.0.1 prefix-list rfc1918-out out
 neighbor 220.0.0.1 route-map in-peer in
 neighbor 220.0.0.1 route-map out-peer out
 neighbor 220.0.0.1 filter-list 5 in
 neighbor 220.0.0.1 filter-list 6 out
```

Implementation order is different, though. For IOS Software Release 12.0S and all those before 12.0(5)T, it is the following:

```
router bgp 10
 neighbor 220.0.0.1 remote-as 11
 !
 ! actual implementation order: 12.0S and <=12.0T
 !
 neighbor 220.0.0.1 filter-list 5 in
 neighbor 220.0.0.1 route-map in-peer in
 neighbor 220.0.0.1 prefix-list rfc1918-in in
 !
 neighbor 220.0.0.1 prefix-list rfc1918-out out
 neighbor 220.0.0.1 filter-list 6 out
 neighbor 220.0.0.1 route-map out-peer out
 !
```

For inbound prefix announcements, the filter list is applied first, followed by the route map and finally by the prefix list (or distribute list—remember that prefix lists and distribute lists are mutually exclusive). For outbound prefix announcements, the order is partially reversed, with prefix lists being considered first, followed by filter lists, and finally by any route-map policy.

For IOS Software Release 12.0ST and all those releases from 12.1, the processing order has been changed to the following:

```
router bgp 10
 neighbor 220.0.0.1 remote-as 11
 !
 ! actual implementation order: 12.0ST and >=12.1
 !
 neighbor 220.0.0.1 filter-list 5 in
 neighbor 220.0.0.1 prefix-list rfc1918-in in
 neighbor 220.0.0.1 route-map in-peer in
 !
 neighbor 220.0.0.1 prefix-list rfc1918-out out
 neighbor 220.0.0.1 filter-list 6 out
 neighbor 220.0.0.1 route-map out-peer out
 !
```

Notice the difference between the two examples—route maps now are processed last in IOS Software Release 12.0ST and all releases from 12.1. This order is deemed more efficient for the router to process: Route maps often are used for policy implementations, and it makes little sense to implement policy on prefixes that later will be dropped by a prefix-list filter.

BGP Conditional Advertisement

Conditional advertisement of prefixes has been introduced into IOS Software Releases 11.1CC, 11.2, 12.0 and more recent versions, in an effort to contribute to the stability of large BGP-based networks (specifically, the Internet). Conditional advertisement usually is configured when an AS has at least two connections to another AS. The inter-AS peering routers watch the links between the autonomous systems. If one link fails, prefixes are advertised out of the other link. This allows ISPs to set up efficient and effective multihoming without leaking many subprefixes to the Internet, yet retain a good degree of backup in the case of uplink failure.

The configuration command is this

```
router bgp 109
 neighbor 129.140.6.6 remote-as 159
 neighbor 129.140.6.6 advertise-map announce non-exist-map monitor
 !
```

non-exist-map describes the prefix that will be monitored by the BGP router. The **advertise-map** statement describes the prefix that will be advertised when the prefix in **non-exist-map** has disappeared from the BGP table. The route maps named announce and monitor are standard IOS Software route maps and are used to configure the prefixes that will be part of the conditional advertisement process.

Conditional Advertisement Example

Consider the example depicted in Figure 3-8. This shows a dual-homed enterprise network (AS 300) that has received address space from its two upstream ISPs. It announces the 215.10.0.0/22 prefix to ISP 1 (AS 100) and the 202.9.64/23 prefix to ISP 2 (AS 200). These networks are part of the respective upstream ISPs address blocks, so all that the Internet sees are the two aggregates as originated by ISP 1 and ISP 2. This is the steady state situation.

Figure 3-8   *BGP Conditional Advertisement—Steady State*

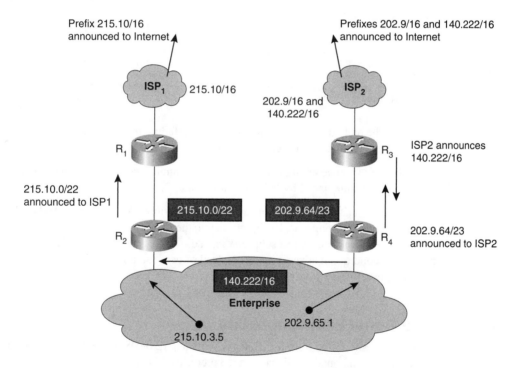

So that conditional advertisement can be used, ISP 2 needs to announce a prefix to the enterprise. In this example, it uses its own 140.222/16 address block; the Enterprise needs to run iBGP between its two border routers so that R2 has the 140.222/16 prefix in its BGP table. (It doesn't have to be ISP 2's /16 block—it can be any prefix agreed upon between the enterprise and upstream, as long as a prefix is announced.)

Consider now the case in which the link from the enterprise to ISP 2 fails. Because the link fails, the enterprise router R4 no longer hears the 140.222/16 announcement from ISP 2. R4's iBGP session with R2 no longer advertises this prefix, so R2 no longer hears 140.222/16. This is the required condition to activate the conditional advertisement—140.222/16 is no longer in R2's BGP table. R2 now starts advertising the 202.9.64/23 prefix to ISP 1 so that connectivity to that prefix is maintained during the failure of the link to ISP 2. The example after link failure is shown in Figure 3-8.

The configuration to achieve this is required only on Router 2 and is as follows:

```
! Router 2 configuration
router bgp 300
 neighbor <R1> remote-as 100
 neighbor <R1> advertise-map ISP2-subblock non-exist-map ISP2-backbone
 !
route-map ISP2-subblock permit 10
 match ip address 1                                ! ISP2-subblock-prefix
 !
route-map ISP2-backbone permit 10
 match ip address 2                                ! ISP2-backbone-prefix
 !
access-list 1 permit 202.9.64.0 0.0.1.255         ! ISP2-subblock-prefix
access-list 2 permit 140.222.0.0 0.0.255.255      ! ISP2-backbone-prefix
 !
```

Access list 1 is the prefix that will be announced during failure mode. Access list 2 describes the prefix that is monitored to detect whether a failure has happened.

Of course, Router 4 can be configured with a similar conditional advertisement statement, monitoring a prefix announced by ISP 1 toward Router 2.

In short, conditional advertisements ensure that a multihomed AS will have good backup/failure modes without having to leak subprefixes into the Internet routing table unnecessarily. Only in the case of link failure is a subprefix leaked—consider the effects of route flap damping using conditional advertisements instead of using standard BGP backup configuration (see Figure 3-9).

BGP Outbound Route Filter Capability

This new feature, supported from IOS Software Release 12.0(5)S onward, allows one BGP speaker to install its inbound locally configured prefix-list filter on the remote BGP speaking router. This is used especially to reduce the number of unwanted routing updates from the remote peer.

The remote BGP speaker applies the received prefix-list filter in addition to its locally configured outbound filters (if any), to constrain or filter its outbound routing updates to the neighbor. This mechanism can be used to avoid unwanted routing updates and thus help reduce resources required for routing update generation and processing.

Figure 3-9   *BGP Conditional Advertisement—Failure Mode*

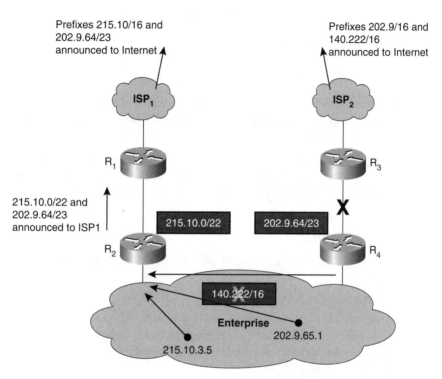

For example, prefix-list ORF can be used to address the issue of receiving unwanted full routes from multihomed BGP customers. The customer simply can enable this feature on a router and thus allow providers to manage the filtering of the route announcements. This avoids unwanted routing updates coming from the customer to the upstream ISP.

Currently the prefix-list ORF is implemented for IPv4 unicast only. Some points to note about the implementation are listed here:

- By default, the prefix-list ORF capability is not advertised to any neighbors.
- The capability cannot be advertised to a neighbor that is a peer group member.
- The prefix-list ORF is pushed over to the peer router immediately after the session is established if the local router has received the ORF capability and has configured an inbound prefix-list filter for the neighbor.

Configuration

The router configuration command is included in the following example:

```
router bgp Y
  neighbor x.x.x.x remote-as Z
  neighbor x.x.x.x description Peer router R2
  neighbor x.x.x.x capability prefix-filter
  neighbor x.x.x.x prefix-list FilterZ-in in
```

This command can be used to enable the advertisement of the prefix-list ORF capability to a neighbor. Using the **no neighbor** *x.x.x.x* **capability prefix-filter** command disables the prefix-list ORF capability.

When the BGP peering is established in this example, the router (R1) pushes its prefix list FilterZ-in over to its peer router x.x.x.x (R2). R2 receives the prefix-list filter and applies it to its outbound update to R1 (in addition to its local policy, if any is configured).

Pushing Out a Prefix-List ORF

The command to push out a prefix-list ORF and receive route refreshes from a neighbor is given here:

clear ip bgp *x.x.x.x* **in prefix-filter**

When the inbound prefix list changes (or is removed), this command can be used to push out the new prefix list and consequently receive route refreshes from the neighbor based on the new prefix list. The keyword **prefix-filter** is ignored if the prefix-list ORF capability has not been received from the neighbor.

Without the keyword **prefix-filter**, the command **clear ip bgp** *x.x.x.x* **in** simply performs the normal route refresh from the neighbor. It does not push out the current inbound prefix-list filter to the neighbor. The command is useful when inbound routing policies other than the prefix-list filter, such as the route map, changes.

Displaying Prefix-List ORF

The command to display the prefix-list ORF received from a neighbor is shown here:

show ip bgp neighbor *x.x.x.x* **received prefix-filter**

This displays the received prefix list. Changes to the output of **show ip bgp neighbor** *x.x.x.x* now include information about whether ORF is supported or available, as can be seen in the following snippet:

```
...
Prefixlist ORF
  Capability advertised; received
  Filter sent; received (25 entries)
...
```

BGP Policy Accounting

BGP policy accounting allows you to account for IP traffic differentially by assigning counters based on community list, AS number, or AS path on a per-input-interface basis. It is not, as the name might suggest, accounting based on any BGP policies that have been set, so it should not be confused with prefix filtering, route maps, or AS filters.

Using BGP policy accounting, you can account for traffic (and apply billing) according to the routes that specific traffic traverses. This way, for example, domestic, international, terrestrial, satellite, and other traffic can be identified and accounted for on a per-customer basis.

This feature takes advantage of BGP's table map capability to classify the prefixes that it puts into the routing table according to community lists, AS path, AS number, and so on. Based on those match criteria, this feature sets a bucket number (currently 1 to 8) of an accounting table that is associated with each interface. Each bucket thus represents a traffic classification.

This allows IP traffic to be accounted differentially by community list, AS number, and AS path per input interface.

Configuration

Specify communities into community lists (or define AS path lists and so on) that will classify traffic for accounting.

```
ip community-list 30 permit 100:190
ip community-list 40 permit 100:198
ip community-list 50 permit 100:197
ip community-list 60 permit 100:296
ip community-list 70 permit 100:201
!
```

Define a route map to match community lists, and set the appropriate bucket number:

```
route-map set_bucket permit 10
 match community 30
 set traffic-index 2                    ! ← Look here
!
route-map set_bucket permit 20
 match community 40
 set traffic-index 3
!
route-map set_bucket permit 30
 match community 50
 set traffic-index 4
!
route-map set_bucket permit 40
 match community 60
 set traffic-index 5
!
route-map set_bucket permit 50
 match community 70
 set traffic-index 6
```

Modify the bucket number when the IP routing table is updated with BGP learned routes:

```
router bgp 110
 table-map set_bucket                          ! ← Look here
 network 15.1.1.0 mask 255.255.255.0
 neighbor 14.1.1.1 remote-as 100
!

ip classless
ip bgp-community new-format
```

Enable the policy-accounting feature on the input interface connected to the customer:

```
interface POS7/0
 ip address 15.1.1.2 255.255.255.252
 no ip directed-broadcast
 bgp-policy accounting                         ! ← Look here
 no keepalive
 crc 32
 clock source internal
```

Each customer is connected to a separate input interface (this works on software interface descriptor blocks, so these can be subinterfaces) that has the previously displayed table of counters associated with it.

Displaying BGP Policy Accounting Status

To inspect which prefix is assigned which bucket and which communities, do the following:

```
Router#sh ip cef 196.240.5.0 detail
196.240.5.0/24, version 21, cached adjacency to POS7/2
0 packets, 0 bytes, traffic_index 4            ! ← Look Here
  via 14.1.1.1, 0 dependencies, recursive
    next hop 14.1.1.1, POS7/2 via 14.1.1.0/30
    valid cached adjacency

Router#sh ip bgp  196.240.5.0
BGP routing table entry for 196.240.5.0/24, version 2
Paths: (1 available, best #1)
  Not advertised to any peer
  100
    14.1.1.1 from 14.1.1.1 (32.32.32.32)
      Origin IGP, metric 0, localpref 100, valid, external, best
      Community: 100:197                       ! ← Look Here
```

To look at traffic statistics per interface, do this

```
LC-Slot7#sh cef interface traffic-statistics
:
POS7/0 is up (if_number 8)
Bucket        Packets          Bytes

    1              0              0
    2              0              0
```

```
3               50              5000
4              100             10000
5              100             10000
6               10              1000
7                0                 0
8                0                 0
```

Displaying BGP Policy Accounting Statistics

The statistics are stored in a table of packet/byte counters per input software interface (with the assumption that each customer is connected to an input software interface). You can display them with **show cef interface** *interface* **policy-statistics**. SNMP support will be added sometime in the near future.

The statistics actually are displayed per configured table map match category. Using a route map, you can match against configured community lists, AS paths, and so on, and you can set this to correspond to a specific bucket/index in the previously mentioned table.

Multiprotocol BGP[5]

RFC 2858 describes extensions to BGP designed to carry multiple network layer protocols (such as IPv6, IPX, Multicast, and so on). The extensions are backward compatible so that a router that supports the extensions can interoperate with a router that does not support the extensions (with the support of BGP capabilities as defined in RFC 2842). With the support of RFC 2858, it also can be seen that BGP can carry address families as defined in RFC 1700. Therefore, it is possible to exchange reachability information of more than one address family or sub-address family between two BGP neighbors. The term *address family* is used to refer to both address families (as in IPv6) and sub-address families (as in unicast or multicast).

With the need to introduce support for address families in BGP, it became clear that, to scale the IOS Software CLI, a complete redesign of the BGP configuration CLI was necessary. This section describes the changes made and gives examples comparing the old and new versions. It should be noted that the new CLI is available only in IOS Software Releases 12.0ST and 12.1 onward. IOS Software Releases 12.0, 12.0S, and older do not support the new CLI.

Motivation for a New CLI

Several motivations arose for rewriting the BGP CLI. These motivations and requirements include the following:

- The BGP session-related commands are common for all address families and should be configured only once to identify the neighbor.

- The topology and policy of each address family might be different.
- The inbound and outbound policies could be different for each address family.
- BGP router can be a route reflector for one address family but not for all.
- No additional overhead should be present if IPv4 unicast BGP is configured.
- Prefixes can be sourced (with a **network** statement or redistribution) within any address family independently.
- Peer group functionality should be maintained in the address family because that is relevant for update generation.
- The configuration should not result in repeating the commands.

Based on these requirements, the new command set available under **router bgp <as>** can be subdivided into three sections:

- **Commands global to the router**—These commands affect the operation of the BGP global to the box. Examples: **bgp deterministic-med** and **bgp cluster-id**.
- **Commands to identify the neighbors/peer groups**—These commands define the neighbor or peer group (which are accessible from the default routing table) by specifying the remote AS, eBGP multihop, update source, and so on. Examples: **neighbor** *x.x.x.x* **remote-as** and **neighbor** *x.x.x.x* **description**.
- **Commands per address family**—Two sets of commands can be applied to address families.
  - **Global to per address family**—These commands are neighbor-independent and allow the behavior of BGP to be changed for that specific address family. Prefixes to be sourced (using a **network** statement or redistribution) under this address family fit into this category. Examples: **network** *x.x.x.x*, **redistribute dvmrp**, and **bgp scan-time**.
  - **Per-neighbor/peer group**—These commands configure policy for the neighbors or peer groups with distribute lists, prefix lists, or route maps. The neighbors also can be configured as clients or can be added as members of a peer group. The neighbors need to be explicitly activated to exchange the multiprotocol BGP prefixes. Examples: **neighbor** *x.x.x.x* **filter-list**, **neighbor** *x.x.x.x* **route-map**, and **neighbor** *x.x.x.x* **activate**.

Command Group Organization

The commands listed in the first preceding group have no ambiguity, so they all can appear under the **router bgp <as>** definition. The commands listed in the second group have no ambiguity either, so they can follow the first group of commands under the main BGP definition (with the exception of VPNs). The commands listed in the third group can have potential ambiguity and thus are listed under a new address family submode:

```
router bgp <AS>
  address-family afi sub-afi
  ...
  exit-address-family
exit
```

A neighbor can have different route map or prefix list statements, one per address family.

For configuring IPv4 unicast BGP (vanilla BGP) policy for the neighbors, it is possible to configure them following the Group 2 commands. This is very similar to what is present in the old CLI. The address family IPv4 unicast is implicit. It is also possible to configure the IPv4 unicast BGP policy using the address family submode. In **show running-config**, address family IPv4 unicast is shown, and IPv4 unicast global (3a) and policy (3b) commands are listed within the mode. Under the address family submode, the commands of Group 3a, will appear first. These are commands that are global to this address family. Following the Group 3a commands are the commands of Group 3b. These commands implement the policy to the neighbors for that address family. Before any policy is defined to a neighbor under an address family, the following neighbor should be activated for that address family. The command to do that is as follows:

```
router bgp <AS>
  address-family afi sub-afi
    neighbor x.x.x.x activate
    ...
  exit-address-family
exit
```

The new configuration structure looks like this:

```
router bgp 1
  bgp deterministic-med                       -> Global
  bgp bestpath med confed                     -> Global
  neighbor ebgp peer-group                    -> Peer group defn, Global
  neighbor 1.1.1.1 remote-as 1                -> Neighbor defn, Global
  neighbor 2.2.2.2 remote-as 2                -> Neighbor defn, Global
  neighbor 3.3.3.3 remote-as 3                -> Neighbor defn, Global
  !
  address-family ipv4 unicast                 -> Address family IPv4 unicast
  bgp scan-time 45                            -> Global to IPv4 unicast
  aggregate-address 50.0.0.0 255.255.0.0      -> Global to IPv4 unicast
  neighbor ebgp activate                      -> Activate neighbor for IPv4 uni
  neighbor ebgp route-map ebgp-ucast-out out  -> Peer group IPv4 unicast policy
  neighbor 1.1.1.1 activate                   -> Activate neighbor for IPv4 uni
  neighbor 1.1.1.1 peer-group ebgp            -> Neighbor membership - IPv4 uni
  neighbor 1.1.1.1 route-map peer-ucast-in in -> Neighbor IPv4 unicast policy
  neighbor 2.2.2.2 activate                   -> Activate neighbor for IPv4 uni
  neighbor 2.2.2.2 route-reflector-client     -> RR client - IPv4-unicast
  neighbor 3.3.3.3 activate                   -> Activate neighbor for IPv4 uni
  neighbor 3.3.3.3 peer-group ebgp            -> Neighbor membership - IPv4 uni
```

```
!
address-family ipv4 multicast              -> Address family submode
network 100.0.0.0                          -> Global to IPv4 multicast
redistribute dvmrp route-map redist-map    -> Global to IPv4 multicast
neighbor ebgp activate                     -> Activate Neighbor for IPv4 mult
neighbor 1.1.1.1 peer-group ebgp           -> Neighbor membership - IPv4 mult
neighbor 1.1.1.1 route-map peer-mcast-in in -> Neighbor IPv4 multicast policy
neighbor 3.3.3.3 peer-group ebgp           -> Neighbor membership - IPv4 mult
exit-address-family
!
```

For more details on these commands, refer to the documentation on Cisco.com.

Comparison Between Old and New Styles

The following sections compare the old and new styles of BGP commands, specifically showing the improvements to the CLI when using the address family groupings mentioned previously.

activate

Old style: This command was not present in IOS Software Release 12.0S. The neighbor was activated for IPv4 BGP automatically. However, if the multiprotocol BGP were to be enabled, the **nlri** keyword in the **neighbor** command was used:

```
Router(config-router)#neighbor 1.2.3.4 remote-as 10 nlri unicast multicast
```

If the **nlri** keyword was not specified, the router exchanged IPv4 prefixes only. However, if the **nlri** keyword was specified with the **multicast** option only, only the IPv4 multicast session was activated. This way, only the unicast, or only the multicast, or both sessions could be activated.

Address family style: To enable an address family for the neighbor, the **activate** command is used in the router configuration or address family submode. The neighbors that are defined under the router configuration mode automatically are activated for IPv4. For all other address families, the neighbors must be activated explicitly. To deactivate a neighbor for an address family, use the **no** form of this command:

```
Router(config-router)#address-family ipv4 multicast
Router(config-router-af)# neighbor 1.2.3.4 activate
```

network

Old style: In the old-style CLI, the way to advertise a network over BGP or multiprotocol BGP was to use the **network** command. The command had an NLRI extension to specify whether the network was to be advertised over BGP or multiprotocol BGP or both. The absence of the **nlri** keyword implied IPv4 unicast BGP only—for example:

```
Router(config)#router bgp 10
Router(config-router)#network 1.0.0.0 mask 255.0.0.0 nlri unicast multicast
Router(config-router)#network 2.0.0.0 mask 255.0.0.0
Router(config-router)#network 3.0.0.0 mask 255.0.0.0 nlri multicast
```

Address family style: In this style, the presence of the address family submode obviates the need for the **nlri** keyword. To advertise a network over IPv4 BGP, the **network** command must be specified in router configuration mode. For the network to be advertised over the multiprotocol BGP session, the **network** command must specified under the IPv4 multicast address family submode.

The following advertises a network to all the neighbors in the IPv4 address family:

```
Router(config-router)#network 1.0.0.0 mask 255.0.0.0
Router(config-router)#network 2.0.0.0 mask 255.0.0.0
```

To advertise a network in the IPv4 multicast address family, do this

```
Router(config-router)#address-family ipv4 multicast
Router(config-router-af)#network 1.0.0.0 mask 255.0.0.0
Router(config-router-af)#network 3.0.0.0 mask 255.0.0.0
```

This way, networks can be advertised independently for the BGP and multiprotocol BGP sessions

Peer Groups

Old style: A peer group was defined in router configuration mode. To enable the peer group to exchange multiprotocol BGP prefixes, the **nlri** keyword was used. Using the **nlri** keyword, you could specify BGP or multiprotocol BGP. If the **nlri** keyword was not specified, it implied only IPv4 unicast BGP. The peer group members automatically inherited the unicast or multicast capability of the peer group.

```
Router(config)#router bgp 10
Router(config-router)#neighbor test peer-group nlri unicast multicast
Router(config-router)#neighbor 1.2.3.4 remote-as 20
Router(config-router)#neighbor 1.2.3.4 peer-group test
```

Address family style: The peer group is defined under router configuration mode. However because we have address family submodes, the need for the **nlri** keyword is obviated. The peer group or its members need to be activated in the IPv4 multicast address family to enable the exchange of multicast BGP prefixes. As with the **neighbor** command, a peer group and its members are activated by default for IPv4 BGP. This behavior can be overridden by the **no** form of the **activate** command.

```
Router(config)#router bgp 10
Router(config-router)#neighbor test peer-group
Router(config-router)#neighbor 1.2.3.4 remote-as 20
Router(config-router)#neighbor 1.2.3.4 peer-group test

Router(config-router)#address-family ipv4 multicast
Router(config-router-af)#neighbor test activate
Router(config-router-af)#neighbor 1.2.3.4 peer-group test
```

Route Maps

Old style: A single route map was used to specify policies for all address families. This route map then was applied either as the inbound or the outbound route of a peer or a peer group. Routing policies relating to the two address families that could be carried in the BGP session (IPv4 unicast and IPv4 multicast) were represented using a single route map by specifying the **match nlri** keyword on the route map paragraph. The **match nlri** clause in a route map had the following semantics:

```
match nlri multicast           -> Matches only multicast updates
match nlri multicast unicast   -> Matches any update (both unicast & multicast)
match nlri unicast or
(match nlri unspecified)        -> Matches only unicast updates.
```

The following example shows how to configure BGP so that any multicast routes from neighbor 1.1.1.1 will be accepted if they match access list 1:

```
router bgp 109
  neighbor 1.1.1.1 remote-as 1 nlri unicast multicast
  neighbor 1.1.1.1 route-map in filter-some-multicast
!
route-map filter-some-multicast
  match nlri multicast
  match ip address 1
!
```

Address family style: One of the important reasons for migrating configurations from the old mode to the address family mode is that routing policies expressed using the **match nlri** keyword in the paragraphs of the route map soon become unmanageable when complicated and differing policies have to be expressed for different address families. The new IOS Software versions must support more than two address families, which requires an elegant way of configuring policies for each address family. Having one route map for expressing all policies was seen to be inelegant and nonscalable. The introduction of a new parser mode for each address family facilitated the introduction of a new way of configuring policies on a per-AF basis—that is, simply use a route map statement for the neighbor under each of the address family modes. Not only can route maps be specified on a per-address-family basis, but all the filtering rules (prefix list, distribute list, and AS path filter list) can be too. With the new mode of configuring policies, the keyword **nlri** is not required; the parser would reject the occurrence of the **match nlri** clause in the route map paragraph.

The preceding example policy can be expressed in the address family style as follows:

```
router bgp 109
  neighbor 1.1.1.1 remote-as 1
  address-family ipv4 multicast
  neighbor 1.1.1.1 activate
  neighbor 1.1.1.1 route-map filter-some-multicast in
!
route-map filter-some-multicast permit 10
  match ip address 1
!
```

Redistribution

Old style: Redistribution is the process of importing routes from one routing protocol to another. When routes are redistributed into BGP using the **redistribute** statement, the BGP table (Loc-RIB, as specified in RFC 1771) into which the routes have to be redistributed must be specified. This BGP table can be either the unicast BGP table or the multicast BGP table. The old style of specifying the table into which a route must go used the **set nlri** clause in the redistribution route map. The **set nlri** clause in the redistribution route map has the following semantics:

```
set nlri multicast              -> redistributes the matching prefix to the
                                   multicast table.

set nlri unicast multicast      -> redistributes the matching prefix to
                                   both unicast and multicast tables.

set nlri unicast or             -> redistributes matching prefix to unicast
(set nlri unspecified)             table.
```

The following example shows how to configure redistribution in BGP so that all connected prefixes matching access list 1 in the routing table go into the multiprotocol BGP table:

```
router bgp 109
  redistribute connected route-map mbgp-source-map
!
route-map mbgp-source-map
  match ip address 1
  set nlri multicast
!
```

Address family style: With the introduction of address family mode, the address family mode under which the **redistribute** command is specified determines the table into which the redistributed prefixes are injected. So, if the **redistribute** statement is under the **address-family ipv4 multicast** mode, the redistributed prefixes gets into the multiprotocol BGP table, and so on. Hence, the old style redistribution configuration translates to the following in the address family style:

```
router bgp 109
!

  address-family ipv4 multicast
    redistribute connected route-map mbgp-source-map
```

```
!
route-map mbgp-source-map
  match ip address 1
  !
```

Note that with the introduction of the **redistribute** statement within the address family mode, the clause **set nlri** is not required and the parser rejects the presence of **set nlri** in the route map paragraph.

Route Reflector

Old style: In the old style CLI, a route reflector was specified for all address families and the route reflector reflected routes of all address families that it has negotiated with its clients. The route reflector knows that it must reflect routes from and to clients by specifying **route-reflector-client** for a particular neighbor or iBGP peer group. The following is an example in which the iBGP peer 1.1.1.1 is made a route-reflector client for both unicast and multicast IPv4 prefixes:

```
router bgp 109
  neighbor 1.1.1.1 remote-as 109 nlri unicast multicast
  neighbor 1.1.1.1 route-reflector-client
  !
```

Address family style: In the address family style of configuring router reflectors, the fact that a peer (or peer-group) is a route-reflector client is address family dependent; this means that it is configured in the address family mode. That is, just because a peer is a route-reflector client in IPv4 unicast mode does not make it automatically a route reflector client in the IPv4 multicast mode. This must be specified by configuring the client in the IPv4 multicast address family mode. Thus, the previous configuration, which makes 1.1.1.1 a client for both unicast and multicast client, can be expressed as follows:

```
router bgp 109
  neighbor 1.1.1.1 remote-as 109
  neighbor 1.1.1.1 route-reflector-client
  !
  address-family ipv4 multicast
  neighbor 1.1.1.1 activate
  neighbor 1.1.1.1 route-reflector-client
  !
```

This gives the operator flexibility to make a router the route reflector for only certain address families. As such, the route-reflector topologies for different address families can be different in the core.

Aggregation

Old style: In the old-style CLI, an multiprotocol BGP aggregate is configured the same way that you configure for unicast BGP using the **aggregate-address** command. The **aggregate-address** command was enhanced to specify whether the aggregate address should be applied to BGP or multiprotocol BGP using the **nlri** keyword in the **aggregate-address** command. The following is an example of generating aggregates in the multiprotocol BGP table:

```
router bgp 109
  aggregate-address 174.0.0.0 255.0.0.0 as-set nlri multicast
  !
```

The NLRI options that can be specified on an aggregate address command are **multicast**, **unicast multicast**, and **unicast**, which generates aggregates in the multiprotocol BGP table, both BGP and multiprotocol BGP tables, or just the BGP table, respectively. The absence of the **nlri** keyword in the **aggregate-address** command causes the aggregate to be generated in the unicast BGP table.

Address family style: The presence of individual modes for different address families eliminates the need for the **nlri** keyword in the **aggregate-address** command. The address family mode under which the aggregate is specified determines the table where the aggregated prefix should be generated. Hence, the previous aggregate can be generated in address family mode as follows:

```
router bgp 109
  address-family ipv4 multicast
  aggregate-address 174.0.0.0 255.0.0.0 as-set
  !
```

Upgrading to the New CLI

For a complete list of the commands available in the new CLI, consult the IOS Command documentation at Cisco.com. Upgrading the CLI requires installing an image that supports the reorganized BGP parser; these are 12.0ST and images from 12.1 onward. The existing BGP commands supported under the old CLI can be converted into the new style quite easily.

To have a smooth upgrade path, support has been added to parse the old 12.0S-style commands that had the **nlri** keyword. These commands are

- **neighbor**
- **network**
- **aggregate**
- **set** and **match nlri** in route maps

The only caveat is that the old style commands can be used as long as no new features need to be activated. In that event, the old style BGP commands need to be translated to the new style (discussed momentarily). When in the new mode, the old commands no longer will be accepted. In other words, the old (NLRI style) and the new (address family style) commands cannot be mixed in the same configuration. As the router parses the commands, it locks into a mode based on the first command that uniquely identifies a mode (for example, an **nlri** keyword or an address family keyword). After it is locked into a mode, the parser only accepts commands that are compatible with that mode.

To migrate to the new command set, the **bgp upgrade-cli** command must be entered in router configuration mode:

```
Router(conf-rout)#bgp upgrade-cli
```

This command translates the old configuration to the new one. A **write memory** must be done to save this configuration. (The **bgp upgrade-cli** command is not shown in the **show running-config**.)

Examples of the New CLI in Use

This section gives some examples of the revised CLI. They have been taken from real, live running configurations working in networks today.

The first example shows how BGP supporting IPv6 is configured. This router is a part of the 6BONE, the IPv6 experimental backbone:

```
!
router bgp 4608
 no synchronization
 no bgp default ipv4-unicast                    ! allow more than IPv4 uni
 bgp log-neighbor-changes
 bgp dampening
 neighbor UPSTREAMS peer-group
 neighbor iBGP-peers peer-group
 neighbor 2001:200:0:1805::2 remote-as 2500
 neighbor 3FFE:800::FFF9:0:0:9 remote-as 4554
 neighbor 3FFE:C00:E:11::1 remote-as 109
 neighbor 3FFE:C00:800F:FFFF::2 remote-as 4608
 !
 address-family ipv6                            ! set up IPv6 addr-family
 neighbor UPSTREAMS activate                    ! define UPSTREAMS
 neighbor UPSTREAMS send-community
 neighbor UPSTREAMS prefix-list block-my-sla in
 neighbor UPSTREAMS prefix-list announce-my-sla out
 neighbor iBGP-peers activate                   ! define iBGP peers
 neighbor iBGP-peers next-hop-self
 neighbor iBGP-peers send-community
 neighbor 2001:200:0:1805::2 peer-group UPSTREAMS
 neighbor 3FFE:800::FFF9:0:0:9 peer-group UPSTREAMS
 neighbor 3FFE:C00:E:11::1 peer-group UPSTREAMS
 neighbor 3FFE:C00:800F:FFFF::2 peer-group iBGP-peers
 network 3FFE:C00:800F::/48
 exit-address-family
 !
```

Notice how the configuration is separated into distinct parts. This router could support IPv4 BGP peering as well if the organization chose to do this. All that is configured here is IPv6 support, so the IPv6-specific commands are included under the IPv6 address family. Note the **activate** directive—this is needed to activate any peering inside an address family.

The second example is a simple MPLS/VPN example taken from the Cisco Systems' ISP Workshop program. Two VPNs have been set up across the ISP backbone; the ISP backbone is made up of three P routers and three PE routers. The P routers form the ISP core, and the PE routers deal with the VPN. This configuration is from one of the PE routers at the edge of the ISP network (PE stands for "provider edge"). The two BGP peerings are with the other two PE routers configured in this network. The P routers take no part in the iBGP configuration required for the VPN.

```
!
router bgp 100
 no synchronization
 neighbor 200.200.0.12 remote-as 100
 neighbor 200.200.0.12 update-source Loopback0
 neighbor 200.200.0.13 remote-as 100
 neighbor 200.200.0.13 update-source Loopback0
 no auto-summary
 !
 address-family ipv4 vrf VPN1                    ! define VPN1 and its addresses
 no auto-summary
 no synchronization
 network 172.16.1.0 mask 255.255.255.0
 network 172.16.2.0 mask 255.255.255.252
 exit-address-family
 !
 address-family ipv4 vrf VPN2                    ! define VPN2 and its addresses
 no auto-summary
 no synchronization
 network 172.16.1.0 mask 255.255.255.0
 network 172.16.2.0 mask 255.255.255.252
 exit-address-family
 !
 address-family vpnv4                            ! now set up the VPN address-fam
 neighbor 200.200.0.12 activate
 neighbor 200.200.0.12 send-community extended
 neighbor 200.200.0.13 activate
 neighbor 200.200.0.13 send-community extended
 no auto-summary
 exit-address-family
 !
```

Notice again how the configuration is neatly separated, making it much easier to read and understand. With the old-style CLI, it would have been very hard to configure this.

Summary

This chapter covered the major routing protocol features that ISPs need to consider for their backbone networks. It discussed general routing features that the router requires, covered the basic background for using IGPs and BGP, and showed the good design practices for implementing IGPs. The chapter then considered the ISP-friendly features of BGP in considerable detail. Most of these features are new or recent additions to IOS Software and warrant in-depth discussion. The chapter also looked at the policy features available for BGP in IOS Software and a mechanism for doing IP traffic accounting using BGP attributes. The chapter finished by looking at the new CLI available for BGP, designed to support multiple address families.

Endnotes

[1] This section originally was written by Mark Turner (markt@cisco.com) and can be found on Cisco.com at http://www.cisco.com/warp/public/459/25.shtml.

[2] Private autonomous systems are those AS numbers between 64512 and 65534. AS 65535 is reserved by IANA.

[3] Thanks to Enke Chen for providing most of the text describing BGP peer groups.

[4] The core of this section is by Bruce R. Babcock (bbabcock@cisco.com) and Enke Chen.

[5] This section is based on the address family release notes originally written by Srihari Ramachandra.

## CHAPTER 4

Security

This chapter on Cisco IOS Software security features assumes that the ISP engineer has a working grasp of the fundamentals of system security. If not, the materials listed in the reference section should be reviewed first to help gain an understanding of some of the fundamentals. It is also important to note that the following sections are intended to supplement, not replace, Cisco documentation. It is assumed that the ISP engineer will read such documentation in parallel with this chapter.

This chapter describes tools that all ISPs should consider for their overall security architectures. Most of these tools are passive tools. When configured, they will help prevent security problems from happening and make it more difficult to cause mischief on an ISP's network.

The chapter is split into several sections. These cover ISP security in general, the process of securing the router, the routing protocol, and the network. After this, the chapter looks in more detail at how to implement the unicast reverse path forwarding (RPF) check and how to use Committed Access Rate (CAR) to deal with attacks in progress. The chapter concludes with a brief discussion on how to approach ISP security and how to react to incidents underway. The various sections are titled as follows:

- Securing the Router
- Securing the Routing Protocol
- Securing the Network
- Unicast RPF
- Using CAR to Counter DoS Attacks
- Reacting to Security Incidents

Subdividing the text in this way supports the formation of a clear strategy for an ISP to work on to minimize the effects of a security incident.

Securing an enterprise network from Internet threats is easy when compared with the problems of security facing an ISP. When an enterprise network connects to the Internet, there is essentially one Internet security problem—protecting your network from outside intrusion. To achieve Internet security objectives, an enterprise must balance trade-offs with connectivity, accessibility, performance, and security.

An ISP's security concerns are much broader. The ISP business is all about transparent, cost-effective, and high-performance Internet connectivity. Security measures will affect the ISP's network operation, yet security threats are real and need to be protected against. ISPs are very visible targets for malicious, vindictive, and criminal attacks, so they must protect themselves, help protect their customers, and minimize the risk of their customers becoming problems to others on the Internet (see Figure 4-1).

Figure 4-1 *An ISP's Security Threats Come from All Directions*

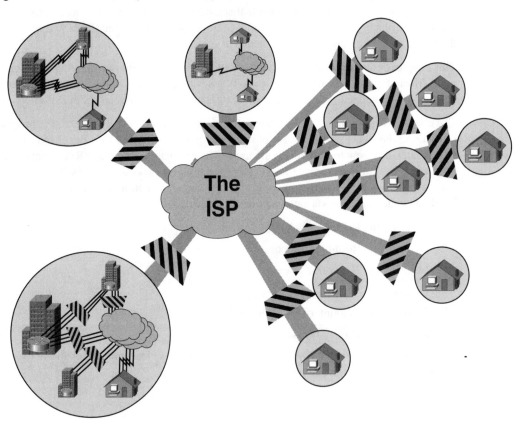

NOTE	No network is ever fully *secure* or *protected*. There is always a risk factor, especially for ISPs whose job it is to move other people's packets across their networks (other people's packets are customers' packets). What ISPs can expect to have are tools to build *resistance*. ISPs need to resist attacks and intrusion attempts to their networks, resisting long enough for internal security-reaction procedures to be activated to track the incident and apply countermeasures. The tools described in this chapter help to build *resistance* and *security*.

Securing the Router

Ensuring that each device on the network is as secure as possible is one of the first security tasks. This means that the mode of access, features/services turned on, and the configuration on the router all need to be reviewed from a mind-set of security. Simple security principles such as "if you are not using it, do not turn it on" can be applied to routers and switches just as easily as they can be applied to a UNIX server. Issues with how people gain access to the network devices and how that access is audited need to be considered as well. In today's Internet, attacks directed at the network device itself are a real threat; hence, tools to help ride out the direct attack must be considered. Securing the router/switch is the first thing that needs to be completed before any tools used to defend the network are implemented. Otherwise, the router/switch becomes the back door or Achilles' heel of the network.

Unneeded or Risky Global Services

Many of the built-in services in IOS Software are not needed in an ISP backbone environment. These features should be turned off in your default configuration. Turn them on only if there are explicit requirements.

```
no ip finger
no service pad
no service udp-small-servers
no service tcp-small-servers
no ip bootp server
```

Some of these services will be preconfigured in IOS Software (depending on the release) and can be turned off by default, but ISPs should ensure that they are explicitly turned off in the master configuration files.

The whitepaper/field alert "Defining Strategies to Protect Against UDP Diagnostic Port Denial-of-Service Attacks" describes the security risk and provides pointers to public discussion on the ISP Operations forums. This whitepaper is posted at http://www.cisco.com/warp/public/707/3.html and is visible to the general public (in other words, no Cisco.com login is required).

The services that should not be used are described in more detail here. For supplementary information, refer to the IOS Software documentation.

- **no ip finger** disables the process that listens for finger requests from remote hosts. Only ISP personnel normally access the backbone routers, and there are other and better means of tracking who is logged in. Besides, finger is a known security risk in the Internet because it divulges detailed information on people logged into a system. (In IOS Software releases earlier than 12.0, this command was **no service finger**.)

- **service pad** is not required. It refers back to the days of X.25 networking; in recent versions of IOS Software, **no service pad** has become the default.

- The small TCP and UDP servers are those with port numbers below 20. Typical services include echo and discard ports, with the former echoing all packets sent to it and the latter throwing away all packets sent to it. If they are enabled and active, they could be used to carry out successful DoS attacks—their use will divert CPU resources away from other processes, which will cause problems for the connected networks and Internet service dependent on that router.

- The bootp service provides support for systems that find their configuration using the bootp process. This commonly is used in LANs (X terminals commonly use bootp, for example) and never on the WAN. It should be disabled.

Unneeded or Risky Interface Services

Some IP features are great for campus LANs but do not make sense on an ISP backbone. Abuse of these functions by "cyberpunks" increases the ISP's security risk. All interfaces on an ISP's backbone router should have the following configured by *default*:

```
no ip redirects
no ip directed-broadcast
no ip proxy-arp
```

An explanation for each of these interface commands follows:

- **no ip redirects** means that the router will not send redirect messages if the IOS Software is forced to resend a packet through the same interface on which it was received.

- **no ip directed-broadcast** means that the translation of directed broadcast to physical broadcasts is disabled. If enabled, a broadcast to a particular network could be directed at a router interface, producing effects that could be undesirable and potentially harmful. An example of the ill effects of directed broadcasts being enabled is the so-called smurf attack. For more information about smurf, see Craig Huegen's smurf Web site at http://www.pentics.net/. Since IOS Software 12.0, **no ip directed-broadcast** has become the default on all router interfaces.

- **no ip proxy-arp** disables the proxy ARP function. Proxy ARP is defined in RFC 1027 and is used by the router to help hosts with no routing capability determine the MAC addresses of hosts on other networks or subnets. For example, if the router receives an ARP request for a host that is not on the same interface as the ARP request sender, and if the router has all of its routes to that host through other interfaces, it generates a proxy ARP reply packet giving its own local MAC address. The host that sent the ARP request then sends its packets to the router, which forwards them to the intended host. This is basically the router saying that it knows how to get to the host being requested by the ARP request sender. This configuration could be undesirable on an ISP backbone because ISP networks carry explicit routing information for all destinations on the Internet. Relying on proxy ARP could result in an Internet backbone router carrying a huge MAC address table, potentially hindering the router's performance.

Cisco Discovery Protocol

The Cisco Discovery Protocol (CDP) is used for some network-management functions on mainly campus LANs (although it often is used on smaller office LANs). It allows any system on a directly connected segment to discover that the equipment is manufactured by Cisco (a router, switch, and so on) and to determine information such as the model number and the software version running. This is very useful in some instances, but it does not make very much sense on an ISP's backbone because the ISP should be completely aware of what is installed and what software versions are running!

The information available from CDP does not threaten security, as such, but attackers could use CDP as an intelligence tool. Known bugs are targeted through the discovery of the specific version of software on the network device. As can be seen in Example 4-1, CDP easily highlights the specific IOS Software version on the router.

Example 4-1 *Information That Can Be Gained from CDP*

```
Defiant#show cdp neighbors detail
-------------------------
Device ID: Excalabur
Entry address(es):
  IP address: 4.1.2.1
Platform: cisco RSP2,  Capabilities: Router
Interface: FastEthernet1/1,  Port ID (outgoing port): FastEthernet4/1/0
Holdtime : 154 sec

Version :
Cisco Internetwork Operating System Software
IOS (tm) RSP Software (RSP-K3PV-M), Version 12.0(9.5)S, EARLY DEPLOYMENT MAINTENANCE
INTERIM SOFTWARE
Copyright (c) 1986-2000 by cisco Systems, Inc.
Compiled Fri 03-Mar-00 19:28 by htseng

Defiant#
```

CDP can be disabled using this global command:

```
no cdp run
```

If CDP is required on an ISP's network, it is possible to leave CDP running but disable the protocol on a per-interface basis. This interface configuration command disables CDP on a particular interface:

```
no cdp enable
```

It is strongly recommended that CDP be disabled on all public-facing interfaces, whether those face exchange points, upstream ISP, or even customers.

Note that CDP is enabled by default on 11.1CA, 11.1CC, and more recent software.

Login Banners

Much overlooked, but important in the age of the commercial ISP, is the **banner login** command. This feature is part of the **banner** command set, which displays text when users connect to the router. **banner login** displays text when a user first initiates a Telnet session to the router. It might seem trivial, but a lack of a banner is as effective a security device as a banner telling connected sessions that only those that are authorized are permitted to connect. Some ISPs are using banners with message content similar to the one that follows. Any ISP should consider whether its interest is served best by including a banner with an official warning or nothing at all. It is good practice not to identify too much about the system itself in the banner. (Things such as "joes-router" might not be such a good idea because they could give a hint about the user/owner of the system and any user IDs or passwords on it.)

```
banner login ^

Authorized access only

This system is the property of Galactic Internet

Disconnect IMMEDIATELY if you are not an authorized user!

Contact noc@net.galaxy +99 876 543210 for help.

^
```

Another type of banner available is the exec banner, displayed at the time a user has successfully authenticated and logged in. There are several other examples of the banner command, as can be seen in the following router output:

```
alpha7200(config)#banner ?
  LINE     c banner-text c, where 'c' is a delimiting character
  exec     Set EXEC process creation banner
  incoming Set incoming terminal line banner
  login    Set login banner
  motd     Set Message of the Day banner

alpha7200(config)#banner
```

For example, a note to all engineering staff on a backbone router after they have logged into the router might be as follows:

```
banner exec ^

PLEASE NOTE - THIS ROUTER SHOULD NOT HAVE A DEFAULT ROUTE!

It is used to connect paying peers. These 'customers' should not be able to
default to us.

The configuration of this router is NON-STANDARD

Contact Network Engineering +99 876 543234 for more information.

^
```

Use enable secret

Use the **enable secret** password in lieu of the **enable password** command. The encryption algorithm Type 7 used in **enable password** and **service password-encryption** is reversible. The **enable secret** command provides better security by storing the enable password using a nonreversible cryptographic function. The added layer of security encryption that it provides is useful in environments where the password crosses the network or is stored on a TFTP server.

```
service password-encryption
enable secret [removed]
no enable password
```

CAUTION   Do not remove the **enable password** as in the previous example if the boot ROMs or boot image of the router does not support the **enable secret** configuration. The use of **enable secret** is supported in IOS Software Release 11.0 and later. With an older boot ROM and **no enable password**, it is possible to gain access to the router without supplying any password if the router ends up running the boot image because of some network problem or malfunction. A network's first line of defense is the routers used, and anyone wanting to compromise a network more than likely will start with the router rather than any system behind that router (where configurations might be stored).

Almost all passwords and other authentication strings in Cisco IOS Software configuration files are encrypted using the weak, reversible scheme used for user passwords. To determine which scheme has been used to encrypt a specific password, check the digit preceding the encrypted string in the configuration file. If that digit is a 7, the password has been encrypted using the weak algorithm. If the digit is a 5, the password has been hashed using the stronger MD5 algorithm. Even though **enable secret** is used for the enable password, do not forget

service password-encryption so that the remaining passwords are stored in the configuration with Type 7 encryption rather than in plain text. Weak encryption is better than none at all.

For example, in the following configuration command, the **enable secret** command has been hashed with MD5:

```
enable secret 5 $1$iUjJ$cDZ03KKGh7mHfX2RSbDqP.
```

In this command, however, the password has been encrypted using the weak reversible algorithm:

```
username jbash password 7 07362E590E1B1C041B1E124C0A2F2E206832752E1A01134D
```

Because several versions of code have been designed to break the weak encryption on a Cisco router, ISPs are strongly encouraged to use other strategies for passwords that are not protected by strong encryption. Cisco IOS Software supports Kerberos, TACACS+, and RADIUS authentication architectures, so the option is open to use AAA to access the router instead of having usernames on the router itself.

The ident Feature

Identification (ident) support allows you to query a Transmission Control Protocol (TCP) port for identification. This feature enables an insecure protocol, described in RFC 1413, to report the identity of a client initiating a TCP connection and a host responding to the connection. Figure 4-2 gives an example of the communication process between client and server and shows how ident fits in as the "authorization" function. No attempt is made to protect against unauthorized queries. This command should be enabled only if the consequences and the advantages in the local situation are understood.

```
ip ident
```

Some ISP backbone engineers like ident. Others do not. New ISP engineers are recommended to look into ident, read the RFC, try it, and see if it fits as a security tool on the backbone. ident is not supported in the 12.0S family but might be supported in 12.2S.

Figure 4-2   *Overview of ident Protocol*

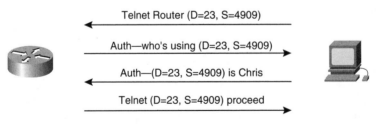

Telnet Router (D=23, S=4909)

Auth—who's using (D=23, S=4909)

Auth—(D=23, S=4909) is Chris

Telnet (D=23, S=4909) proceed

RFC 1413: Identification Protocol

"The information returned by this protocol is at most as trustworthy as the host providing it..."

SNMP Security

At the time of writing, even with the additional encryption added with SNMPv3, most ISPs still use SNMPv1. The apparent reason that no one has moved to SNMPv3 is that the risk assessment has never outweighed the key encryption coordination required for SNMPv3's full capabilities. The perceived weak security in SNMPv1 depends on four interlinked configurations that minimize the security risk:

- **Read-only access**—ISPs never configure SNMP with write access. All SNMP is configured for read only. This reduces the risk of intelligence gathering (someone reading SNMP MIBs) and DoS against SNMP (flooding the SNMP port with packets).

- **Access list protecting SNMP**—Access lists require that the source packet of the SNMP request match the ACL. Together with read-only access, these two steps make it extremely difficult for someone to do blind probes into SNMP[2]. If the person knows the SNMP community, a spoofed packet can get through the ACL and can trigger SNMP activity. Yet, because SNMP is only in read-only mode, the value of that activity is limited.

Note   In a blind probe, someone sends spoofed source packets to get through an ACL and does not expect a response back. The attacker is guessing that the information sent will trigger an event or security loophole.

- **Complex community names**—Community names, like any access password, can be guessed. Because a community does not name passwords (that is, you do not have to type them in to connect), long, complex, and mixed-character community names can be used. For example, an SNMP community name of cisco is much easier to guess than a complex community name of 123$#Cisco#$456. This complexity makes SNMP communities more resistant to guessing. Combining read-only access, ACLs, and complex community names provides a high degree of resistance to attack.

- **SNMP authentication failure trap**—Some ISPs add a check to the three steps used to protect SNMPv1. They do this through the SNMP authentication failure trap. When configured, SNMPv1 sends an authentication failure trap whenever a packet with an incorrect community string is received. So, if someone is spoofing the ACL and trying to guess the SNMP community, SNMP will send authentication traps to an SNMP trap server. The server that receives the authentication failure traps then can take the additional step of alerting the operations or security team that a number of SNMP authentication failures are happening on a specific device.

Used together, these four techniques are the primary defense used by most ISPs today. As SNMPv3 becomes more widely deployed, it is expected that a fifth technique of MD5 authentication will be added to the system of features used to protect SNMP.

Using the trap-source loopback 0

ISP best common practices (BCPs) has SNMP use the network device's loopback interface as the source and destination addresses for all SNMP traffic. SNMP server security is easier to manage if the SNMP traps originating from the network device use the loopback interface. This allows SNMP traps to pass packet filters protecting the SNMP servers even when there is a topology change on the network. Otherwise, SNMP traps use the source address of the interface in which the trap leaves the network device. For example, if a network device has two paths to get to the SNMP server—interfaces Serial1 and Serial3—and the path through Serial3 goes down, SNMP trap packets leaving interface Serial1 will use Serial1's IP address as the source. This means that the packet filters protecting the SNMP servers will need to have source address entries for both Serial1 and Serial3. Alternatively, if the SNMP traps use the loopback interface's address as the source, it does not matter which interface the packets exit; they will always have the same source address.

Originating SNMP trap sources to use the loopback interface is achieved with the following command:

```
snmp-server trap-source loopback 0
```

Router Access: Controlling Who Can Get into the Router

Access to routers to carry out administrative functions can be achieved either physically through the console port or remotely through a virtual terminal (VTY). The next few subsections discuss the principles and minimum secure configurations that should be used for access to the network device.

Principles

The VTY ports on the router are intended as the primary means of access to the device. The console port generally is used only for last-resort access, with the common setup being that the console is plugged into a "console server" that gives the ISP what is known as *out-of-band* access. Most versions of IOS Software have support for five VTY ports on the router—these ports are the most common way of accessing the device, are accessible across the network, and support multiple protocols. ISPs commonly use Telnet, with support for Secure Shell (SSH) added from IOS Software Releases 12.0S and 12.1T.

The following configuration guidelines are common sense but still are worth touching upon:

- Use access control lists (ACLs) to restrict Telnet connections to those from source networks that you trust. This is not foolproof, but it adds a layer of difficulty. It is also recommended that you include *antispoofing* filters on the edge of your network to prevent spoof attempts from outside your network.

- Implement *username/password* pairs instead of the traditional VTY password-only technique of logging into a router. Using both a username and a password increases the level of effort need to use brute force to crack the password. Ideally, an AAA protocol (RADIUS, TACACS+, or Kerberos) should be used. If an AAA protocol is used, the username/password pair can be used as a backup in case the AAA servers are not working or are not accessible.

- Include shorter inactivity timeouts. The inactivity timeout minimizes some of the risk when the careless operator leaves his terminal logged into the router.

Each of these will be examined in more detail in the following sections.

VTY and Console Port Timeouts

By default, the timeout applied to all connections to the VTY, console, and AUX ports on a router is 10 minutes. This timeout is controlled by the **exec-timeout** command, as in this example:

```
line con 0
 exec-timeout 5 0
line aux 0
 exec-timeout 10 0
line vty 0 4
 exec-timeout 5 0
!
```

Here the router has been told to disconnect console port and VTY connections that have been idle for more than 5 minutes and 0 seconds. The auxiliary port timeout has been set to 10 minutes.

Notice that setting the idle timeout to 0 means that the session will be left connected indefinitely. This generally is regarded as bad practice because it will hog the few available ports on the router and could cause maintenance access problems in case of emergencies.

Furthermore, enabling TCP keepalives on incoming connections ensures that any sessions left hanging by a remote system crash or disconnection will not block or use up the available router VTY ports. The following configuration command will ensure that sessions are not left hanging:

```
service tcp-keepalives-in
```

Access Lists on the VTY Ports

It is important to secure the VTY ports used for Telnet access with a standard ACL. By default, there are no access controls on any of the VTY ports. If this is left this way and a password is applied[1] to the VTY port, the router will be wide open to anyone who attempts a brute-force crack against the password. The following configuration with **access-list 3** is typical of a better approach:

```
aaa new-model
aaa authentication login Cisco-Lab local
!
username Cisco1 password 7 11041811051B13
!
access-list 3 permit 215.17.1.0 0.0.0.255
access-list 3 permit 215.17.34.0 0.0.0.255
access-list 3 deny    any
!
line vty 0 4
 access-class 3 in
 exec-timeout 5 0
 transport input telnet ssh
 transport output none
 transport preferred none
 login authentication Cisco-Lab
 history size 256
!
```

access-list 3 defines the networks 215.17.1/24 and 215.17.34/24 as the only ones with access to these VTYs (these networks could be the administration or NOC networks at two locations, for example). In the preceding example, a timeout of 5 minutes is applied to the interface. The second field is for seconds for finer granularity. ISPs generally pick the best timeout values according to experience and the operating environment. Also, all unnecessary transports are removed; users of VTYs require only character access to the router, nothing else. (Other available transports such as pad, rlogin, and V120 are not required on an ISP backbone router.) It is good practice to configure necessary transports on a per-interface-application basis—dialup users require only IP transport, for example. In this case, only Telnet has been permitted to the VTY port, and no outbound connections are permitted.

If the router supports more than five VTYs, do not forget them! IP-only software (-i- and -p- code releases) support only five, but other feature sets can support 64 or as many as 1024 VTYs. Be sure to apply access lists to all of them, if they are configured. The command **line vty 0 4** covers the first five VTY ports. To find out how many VTYs the router will support, enter the following command in configuration mode:

```
beta7200(config)#line vty 0 ?
   <1-4>  Last Line number
   <cr>
beta7200(config)#line vty 0 _
```

The router will print the last two lines, listing the VTY range supported. It then will give you the configure command prompt. Use this to ensure that all the VTYs on the router actually are protected by an access list.

access-list 3 provides simple protection. An ACL that will provide more detailed auditing is

```
access-list 199 permit tcp 215.17.1.0 0.0.0.255 any log
access-list 199 permit tcp 215.17.34.0 0.0.0.255 any log
access-list 199 deny   tcp any any range 0 65535 log
access-list 199 deny   ip any any log
```

This extended ACL (xACL) does everything that **access-list 3** does, but in addition, TCP and IP connections are logged to the syslog file. The advantage with this xACL is that attempts to scan or break into the router are logged with the TCP/IP information (that is, the source address) of the perpetrator. Both valid and unauthorized attempts are logged, and this is one way to check whether people are attempting a brute-force break-in to the router. On the syslog server, the log file can be analyzed for abnormal login attempts—see the following example:

```
Dec 28 17:29:34.917: %SEC-6-IPACCESSLOGP: list 199 permitted tcp 144.254.193.62(1749)
-> 0.0.0.0(23), 1 packet
```

VTY Access and SSH[2]

Before IOS Software Releases 12.0S and 12.1T, the only method really used to access the VTY ports was Telnet. rlogin has been used by some ISPs, especially for executing one-off commands, but the protocol is insecure and can't be recommended for any public network. SSH version 1 support now has been added, giving ISPs greater flexibility and some security when accessing their equipment across the Internet. SSH will form an encrypted tunnel between the client and the IOS Software SSH server. Because this tunnel is formed before any authentication is required, the authentication process between the user and the router is encrypted. This provides password confidentiality as they are transmitted between the client and the router, as well as confidentiality of the entire session.

The SSH tunnel provides remote terminal (VTY) access to the IOS Software. Any of the authentication methods used within IOS Software can be applied to the VTYs. This includes local passwords, TACACS+, and RADIUS. Username/password combinations, either local or through an AAA (TACACS+ or RADIUS), are a prerequisite to SSH working in IOS Software.

Before SSH can be configured, the router needs to be running a cryptographic image that supports SSH. The standard ISP (-p-) images do not have SSH support because the U.S. government restricts the export of 3DES. The cryptographic images are made available on Cisco.com after an approval application has been submitted. The approval application form can be found at http://www.cisco.com/cgi-bin/Software/Crypto/crypto_main.pl. After the application has been approved, permission will be granted to download the necessary images.

When the appropriate cryptographic image is running, SSH needs to be set up on the router. The following sequence of configuration commands gives an example of how this can be achieved:

```
beta7200(config)#crypto key generate rsa
beta7200(config)#exit
beta7200#write terminal
```

Select a key size of at least 1024 bits. Saving the configuration is necessary for the key to be saved and activated. After this, add **ssh** as the input transport on the VTYs:

```
line vty 0 4
 transport input telnet ssh
```

When this configuration has been completed, it is possible to use SSH to access the router. If the IOS Software image supporting DES is being used, the SSH client on the operator's system needs to support DES (most SSH clients have this disabled by default because it no longer is considered very secure). This could require the client to be recompiled (if this is an option).

NOTE   A username/password pair must be configured on the router before SSH access will work. However, it is strongly recommended that AAA be used to authenticate users (discussed later) because this is the preferred way of securing the router.

The following is the UNIX command to connect to the router beta7200 using SSH with the username philip.

```
ssh beta7200 -l philip
```

Since IOS Software Release 12.0(6)S (CSCdr82377), SSH can be used in reverse Telnet mode as well when connecting to out-of-band access routers. For example, the following command will connect to VTY port 16 using SSH:

```
ssh router telnet 10.0.0.1 2016
```

SSH will terminate on the out-of-band access router and then connect through reverse Telnet into the console connected to the device. SSH also can be used in batch commands:

```
ssh -x -t -c [des|3des] -l username ipaddr "show ip cache addr mask verbose flow"
```

In Release 12.0(9)S (CSCdp73127), an SSH client[3] was added to IOS Software. This allows an engineer to use SSH to get into a router and then use SSH from that router to hop to another router. It is common for backbone engineers to go from one router to another while in the midst of troubleshooting. The SSH client allows backbone engineers to use the same troubleshooting techniques without loss of capability.

The command syntax for the IOS Software SSH client is as follows:

```
ssh [-l userid] [-c des|3des] [-o numberofpasswdprompts n] [-p portnum]
ipaddr\hostname [IOS command]
```

The details of the command syntax are

- **-l** *userid* is the user to log in as on the remote machine. The default is the current user ID.

- **-c des|3des** specifies the cipher to use for encrypting the session. 3DES is encrypt-decrypt-encrypt with three different keys. The default is 3DES if this algorithm is included in the image; otherwise, the default is DES.

- **-o** specifies other options. There is only one currently, and that is *numberofpasswd prompts n*, which specifies the number of password prompts before ending the attempted session. The server also limits the number of attempts to 5, so it is useless to set this value larger than 5. Therefore, the range is set at 1 to 5 and the default is 3, which is also the IOS Software server default.

- **-p** *portnum* specifies the port to connect to on the remote host. The default is 22.

- *ipaddr\hostname* is the remote machine IP address or host name.

- *IOS command* is an IOS Software exec command enclosed in quotation marks. This will be executed on connection, and the connection will be terminated when the command has completed.

User Authentication

It is good practice to register each individual user with a separate user ID. If a generic account is set up, it is easier for it to fall into the wrong hands, and there is virtually no accountability. This results in abuse of access and potential malfunction of the network. In addition, if the default password-only login is used, it becomes very easy to use a brute-force crack utility to get the password. A username/password pair makes brute-force techniques harder but not impossible.

This example shows one way of configuring user IDs. It is practical for networks of a few routers, but it does not scale and it suffers from the weak Type 7 encryption. (This encryption type should be avoided but is given here for completeness.)

Start by configuring the following on the router:

```
username joe password 7 045802150C2E
username jim password 7 0317B21895FE
!
line vty 0 4
  login local
!
```

That changes the login prompt sequence from this

```
Password:
```

to this

```
Username:
Password:
```

Here, the username requested is from those listed previous. Each user will have to supply the password upon request.

At the time of this writing, MD5-style encryption was added to the **username** configuration command in some versions of IOS Software, so it is now possible to store username/ password pairs on the router to be certain that the passwords will not be reverse-engineered. The configuration looks like the following:

```
username joe secret 5 $1$j6Ac$3KarJszBV3VMaL/2Nio3E.
username jim secret 5 $1$LPV2$QO4NwAudy0/4AHHHQHvWj0
!
line vty 0 4
  login local
!
```

Although this adds security to the passwords stored on the router, we still recommend using a network-based authentication system, as described in the next section.

Using AAA to Secure the Router

The preferred and recommended method of securing access to the router is to use an AAA protocol such as TACACS+, RADIUS, or Kerberos. Here the usernames and passwords for all the users who have access to the routers are held at a central location, off the router. This has several advantages:

- Recall that the encryption method 7 is reversible. Anyone who has access to the router configuration potentially could work out the password and gain access to the system.

- If there is a new user or a user leaves the ISP, it is easy to change the password database once. Changing it on many different routers becomes a considerable task.

- Passwords are held in UNIX encrypted format on the central AAA server. The algorithm for UNIX password encryption is not reversible and thus is more secure.

- All accesses are logged to the AAA server. In fact, some AAA software will allow all actions on the router to be logged.

Commercial Cisco ACS software is available for Windows NT and Sun Solaris systems. A freely available TACACS+ server for UNIX platforms is provided on Cisco's engineering FTP site at ftp://ftp-eng.cisco.com/pub/tacacs/tac_plus.F4.0.4.alpha.tar.Z. This can be compiled and built on virtually all UNIX systems—in fact, many ISPs have integrated this into their own authentication processes.

On the router, a typical TACACS+ configuration would be as follows:

```
!
aaa new-model
aaa authentication login default tacacs+ enable
aaa authentication enable default tacacs+ enable
aaa accounting exec default start-stop tacacs+
!
ip tacacs source-interface Loopback0
tacacs-server host 221.17.1.2
tacacs-server host 221.17.34.10
tacacs-server key CKr3t#
!
```

To explain these commands, the **authentication login** states that TACACS+ should be used for login authentication. If the TACACS+ servers are not reachable, the local enable secret password is used. The **authentication enable** command states that TACACS+ should be used to authenticate the use of the **enable** command. The enable password should be taken from the TACACS+ server before using the local enable secret password.

Note the use of the loopback interface as the source of TACACS+ requests (reasons as in previous examples) and the use of two TACACS+ servers for redundancy and resilience.

If the router is running an IOS Software version that does not support TACACS+ (pre-11.0), it is strongly advised that it be upgraded to at least version 11.0 because the more recent software has more features appropriate to ISPs, as discussed in this chapter.

If the ISP engineering operations team does decide to store some local usernames and passwords on the router, using the new **username** *name* **secret** *secret* option, the configuration might look something like the following:

```
!
aaa new-model
aaa authentication login default tacacs+ local enable
aaa authentication enable default tacacs+ enable
aaa accounting exec default start-stop tacacs+
!
username joe secret 5 $1$j6Ac$3KarJszBV3VMaL/2Nio3E.
username jim secret 5 $1$LPV2$QO4NwAudy0/4AHHHQHvWj0
!
ip tacacs source-interface Loopback0
tacacs-server host 221.17.1.2
tacacs-server host 221.17.34.10
tacacs-server key CKr3t#
!
```

Note the **local** in the **authentication login** line. If the TACACS+ server is unavailable, the router will expect either of two local accounts joe or jim to be used for the login and authentication.

Router Command Auditing

Suppose that it has been a bad day at the office. You have had to fire an engineer on the operations team. It was a rough experience, with words exchanged. You have briefed your team, and people are starting to change things on the network, removing the ex-employee's access. Suddenly alarms trigger on all sorts of equipment in the NOC. A network-wide outage is spreading fast. Is it an attack? Is it a routing protocol collapse? What is happening? Devices are failing throughout the network, and customer lines are ringing off the hook. Someone from your team uses the out-of-band access to get into one of the affected switches. Horror! The entire configuration has been erased along with the software image. Other switches and routers are checked—they also have their configurations erased and software images erased. It is sabotage! You know who did it, but how are you going to prove it!

Yes, sabotage from disgruntled employees has happened in the past and will happen again. The two primary advantages of using TACACS+—centralized account control and command auditing—should provide enough motivation for ISPs to protect themselves from situations such as this one. With centralized control, the employee's account can be removed before he is given notice. If the employee had back-door access through another account, any commands run on the switches and routers would be audited, providing records that can be used in a court of law. In fact, from a security point of view, AAA should be viewed as authentication, authorization, and auditing—which, of course, is one of the strengths that TACACS+ has over RADIUS in the security domain.

AAA on the router and a TACACS+ server can be configured to track all commands or a limited set of commands typed into the router. AAA command accounting provides information about the exec shell commands for a specified privilege level that are being executed on a router. Each command accounting record includes a list of the commands executed for that privilege level, as well as the date and time that each command was executed and the user who executed it.

The following example shows the information contained in a TACACS+ command accounting record for privilege level 1:

```
Wed Jun 25 03:46:47 1997        172.16.25.15    fgeorge   tty3    5622329430/4327528
stop    task_id=3       service=shell   priv-lvl=1      cmd=show version <cr>
Wed Jun 25 03:46:58 1997        172.16.25.15    fgeorge   tty3    5622329430/4327528
stop    task_id=4       service=shell   priv-lvl=1    cmd=show interfaces Ethernet
0 <cr>
Wed Jun 25 03:47:03 1997        172.16.25.15    fgeorge   tty3    5622329430/4327528
stop    task_id=5       service=shell   priv-lvl=1      cmd=show ip route <cr>
```

The following example shows the information contained in a TACACS+ command accounting record for privilege level 15:

```
Wed Jun 25 03:47:17 1997        172.16.25.15    fgeorge   tty3    5622329430/4327528
stop    task_id=6       service=shell   priv-lvl=15   cmd=configure terminal <cr>
Wed Jun 25 03:47:21 1997        172.16.25.15    fgeorge   tty3    5622329430/4327528
stop    task_id=7       service=shell   priv-lvl=15   cmd=interface Serial 0 <cr>
Wed Jun 25 03:47:29 1997        172.16.25.15    fgeorge   tty3    5622329430/4327528
stop    task_id=8       service=shell   priv-lvl=15    cmd=ip address 1.1.1.1
255.255.255.0 <cr>
```

The next example, shown in Figure 4-3, is taken from the Cisco Secure AAA Server and demonstrates the advantage of command auditing. The display on the Cisco Secure software product is a simple summary of what was happening, at what time, and from where.

Figure 4-3   *Command Auditing on the Router Through Cisco Secure and TACACS+*

bgreene	NOC	enable <cr>	0	shell	tty0	4	210.210.51.224
bgreene	NOC	exit <cr>	0	shell	tty0	5	210.210.51.224
bgreene	NOC	no aaa accounting exe Worksho	0	shell	tty0	6	210.210.51.224
bgreene	NOC	exit <cr>	0	shell	tty0	8	210.210.51.224
pfs	NOC	enable <cr>	0	shell	tty0	11	210.210.51.224
pfs	NOC	exit <cr>	0	shell	tty0	12	210.210.51.224
bgreene	NOC	enable <cr>	0	shell	tty0	14	210.210.51.224
bgreene	NOC	show accounting <cr>	15	shell	tty0	16	210.210.51.224
bgreene	NOC	write terminal <cr>	15	shell	tty0	17	210.210.51.224
bgreene	NOC	configure <cr>	15	shell	tty0	18	210.210.51.224
bgreene	NOC	exit <cr>	0	shell	tty0	20	210.210.51.224
bgreene	NOC	write terminal <cr>	15	shell	tty0	21	210.210.51.224
bgreene	NOC	configure <cr>	15	shell	tty0	22	210.210.51.224
bgreene	NOC	aaa new-model <cr>	15	shell	tty0	23	210.210.51.224
bgreene	NOC	aaa authorization commands 0 de	15	shell	tty0	24	210.210.51.224
bgreene	NOC	exit <cr>	0	shell	tty0	25	210.210.51.224
bgreene	NOC	ping <cr>	15	shell	tty0	32	210.210.51.224
bgreene	NOC	show running-config <cr>	15	shell	tty66	35	210.210.51.224
bgreene	NOC	router ospf 210 <cr>	15	shell	tty66	45	210.210.51.224
bgreene	NOC	debug ip ospf events <cr>	15	shell	tty66	46	210.210.51.224

Configuration control and audit of who has done what and when on the routers is the key objective for using AAA command accounting on an ISP's backbone.

```
aaa new-model
aaa authentication login default tacacs+ enable
aaa authentication enable default tacacs+ enable
aaa accounting command 15 start-stop tacacs+
aaa accounting exec start-stop tacacs+
!
ip tacacs source-interface Loopback0
tacacs-server host 215.17.1.2
tacacs-server host 215.17.34.10
tacacs-server key CKr3t#
```

NOTE	When command accounting is enabled, all commands (that is, keystrokes) sent to the router in enable mode are logged in the accounting file on the accounting host. Be aware that, when changing sensitive configurations on the router, these changes are recorded in the accounting host log file. One example is where the last resort password (enable secret) is changed during an online session on the router; the new password will be recorded in full in the accounting file. Of course, the recommended way to change such a last-resort password is to use TFTP to copy the necessary configuration (including the first line disabling the accounting command and the last line reenabling it again!) from a TFTP server and never to make such changes live on the router.

One-Time Password

One advantage of ensuring that the ISP's operations team uses TACACS+ to access to the network's infrastructure is that one-time password (OTP) techniques can be used to provide an additional layer of security. The common approach usually is to use a smart card in the possession of the individual being authenticated. That individual enters a personal identification number (PIN) into the smart card. The smart card returns a time-sensitive password that can be used as the authentication password (see Figure 4-4). This password can be used only once, preventing password sniffing.

Figure 4-4   *OTP Systems Are Used in ISP Operations*

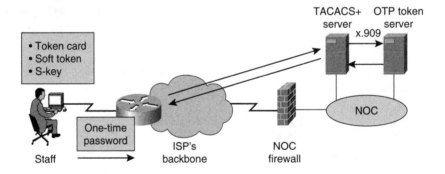

OTP techniques prevent an attacker from guessing a user's password through brute force. Because the password returned by the OTP card is valid only once and for only a specific window of time, forced password guessing is practically impossible (besides the fact that AAA systems such as TACACS+ will deactivate a user's account with too many failed login attempts). OTP systems also minimize the problems of staff writing down their passwords.

It is natural human behavior to write down complex passwords in case they are forgotten. You see people putting passwords on a file in a laptop, in a planner, in a PDA, on a desk, or at a desk at home. Each of these memory aides could be stolen or broken into, opening the risk of someone using that password as a way to break into the network. OTP systems force the individual to remember one password for the OTP card and then use it repeatedly. If the individual does not have the card, he cannot get a password and won't be able to get into the system.

The combination of ACL, TACACS+, SSH, and OTP combines to provide a strong security system to protect an ISP's network infrastructure.

What OTP Systems Are Supported?

Several third-party OTP systems are supported by Cisco's commercial TACACS+ server (CiscoSecure ACS) at the time of this writing. CiscoSecure ACS v2.3 for Windows NT supports token card servers from the following:

- Security Dynamics
- Axent Technologies
- Safeword (Secure Computing)
- CRYPTOCard (included)

CiscoSecure ACS v2.2 for UNIX supports token card servers from the following:

- CRYPTOCard (included)
- Secure Computing
- Security Dynamics

Due diligence is recommended. Hence, check the latest documentation on www.cisco.com for the most current list of supported OTP systems.

OTP Configuration Hints

OTP logins result in traffic to TACACS+ server, to the OTP service, back to the TACACS+ server, and then to the network device. Hence, the network device should be configured with a minimum 10-second TACACS+ timeout setting:

```
tacacs+ timeout 10
```

The default TACACS+ timeout setting of 1 second will cause OTP logins to fail a large percentage of the time.

For complete and detailed information on OTP configuration with CiscoSecure ACS, check the online documentation at www.cisco.com. Look for the chapter titled "Token Server

Support" (http://www.cisco.com/univercd/cc/td/doc/product/access/acs_soft/cs_unx/csu23ug/9_token.htm).

Managing ICMP Unreachables from the Router

The ICMP Destination Unreachable messages are key messages used to determine the state of the network. ICMP Unreachables are responses sent by a router/host/switch whenever the destination host address, protocol unreachable, or destination networks are not listed in the forward table (FIB) or services by the device. ICMP Unreachables are a normal function of the TCP/IP protocol suite. Yet, this normal state has been exploited to overload network devices, specifically sending packets that would require the device to respond with volumes of ICMP Unreachable messages.

As of DDTS CSCdr46528, Cisco has rationalized handling of ICMP Unreachables so that they are managed as close to the interface as possible. On distributed routing architectures (platforms such as the 7500, 7600, 10000, and 12000), the line card (LC) or versatile interface processor (VIP) handles the ICMP Unreachable replies. This isolates any ICMP Unreachable overload DoS/DDoS attacks to the LC/VIP, freeing the route processor (RP) from unnecessary burden.

In addition to this architectural theme, Cisco provides two features that ISPs should consider to limit the effects of an ICMP Unreachable DoS/DDoS attack on a router. These are the ICMP Unreachable rate-limiting feature and the **no ip unreachables** interface command.

ICMP Unreachable Rate Limiting

DDTS CSCdp28161 added an ICMP Unreachable rate-limiting feature in IOS Software Release 12.0(8)S. This feature is turned on by default and is not seen in the CLI unless the default rate limit is changed. This feature rate limits the router's responses to ICMP Unreachable messages leaving the router. The objective is to keep the router from being overwhelmed with an ICMP Unreachable overload (that is, a DoS attack against the router). By default, the router rate limits ICMP Unreachables to one per 500 milliseconds. Before IOS Software Release 12.0(8)S, this was not configurable. Now many ISPs can set the routers to respond to one ICMP Unreachable every 2000 ms, providing greater resistance to an ICMP Unreachable overload.

A new global command is introduced to control the ICMP Unreachable rate. This command is hidden unless the defaults are changed. The default is to have one ICMP Unreachable message per 500 ms.

```
ip icmp rate-limit unreachable [DF] 1-4294967295
no ip icmp rate-limit unreachable [DF]
```

The DF option rate limits the ICMP Unreachable message with code 4, fragmentation needed, and DF set.

Consultation with several ISPs resulted in the recommendation that ISPs should set this rate limit to one every two seconds. For example, the following example sets the rate of the ICMP Unreachable to one message per 2000 ms with DF set:

```
ip icmp rate-limit unreachable DF 2000
```

No IP Unreachables

For a long time, Cisco routers had the configuration capability to turn off ICMP Unreachable response. This was done with the interface command **no ip unreachables**. Whether this is done is an operational decision of the ISP—some do and some do not. The router requirements RFC (RFC1812) says that each device should respond with ICMP Unreachables, but when a network operator experiences an attack against a router, RFC niceties get left behind.

What can be recommended or considered is that **no ip unreachables** be applied to the special interfaces used on ISP routers: Loopback and Null0. For example, many ISPs use static routes to Null0 for their entire CIDR block to lock up their BGP advertisements. This Null0 route can be exploited by an ICMP Unreachable attack on the part of the CIDR block that has yet to be allocated and activated. By default, the router responds with ICMP Unreachable messages (rate limited to one per 500 ms) on the unallocated/activated part of the static to Null0. Turning off ICMP Unreachables prevents this from happening, blackholing the packets at that router.

```
interface Null0
 no ip unreachables
 !
ip route dest-to-drop mask Null0
```

NOTE   A recent audit around IOS Software Releases 12.0(16)S and 12.1(6)E ensured that the **no ip unreachables** command works on all line cards and routers. Previously this was not the case for several line cards, requiring fixes to be put in place.

Building a New Router or Switch

This final part of the router security section gives a demonstration of how an ISP engineer should go about deploying a new IP device on an ISP backbone. There is a proper, sensible, well-defined process for doing this—and not just one that involves plugging it in, switching it on, and then figuring out what to do, as is done by far too many ISP engineers today.

The Process

The process that should be followed goes something like the following steps. The technique is used by several ISPs and is part of the Cisco Systems ISP Workshops that have been running in many parts of the world for the previous several years.

1 **Switch on**—Make sure that the router is not connected to any LAN or WAN. Connect the console port to the computer or terminal server device, and then power up. When the new router asks to enter configuration mode, answer **no** to get to the **Router>** command prompt. Enter enable mode. (The quick-start configuration guide is great for new users to Cisco routers but is somewhat pointless for an ISP that is going to copy customized templates onto the device after it is securely connected to the LAN.)

2 **Set the router host name**—This is so that you know what you are typing on and what you are trying to configure. In the daily life of a busy engineer, being diverted briefly to another issue while in the middle of configuring the router and then coming back and not knowing what you are working on, can be a security risk or can cause disaster on the ISP backbone by configuring the wrong device.

3 **Set passwords**—This means setting an **enable secret**, putting a password on all the VTY ports on the router, and enabling **service password-encryption**. Obviously, configuring a network-based authentication system makes no sense at the moment because there is no network connected!

4 **Disable unnecessary services**—Remove global and per-interface services that should not be present on a ISP's router. This includes HTTPD and CDP if they are running by default.

5 **Set banners**—Set any login banners that are required for the VTYs or other ports of the router.

6 **Configure access lists**—Access lists for protecting the VTY ports should be configured on the router. Assuming that SNMP is disabled at this stage, an access list to protect the SNMP service on the router is not required. The VTY access list should allow connections from the NOC or management systems, nothing more. Access lists for any interfaces that will be brought live to complete the configuration also should be installed. Most new routers have a single LAN connection activated so that the rest of the configuration can be installed. This is usually all that is required at this stage.

7 **Now plug into the network**—Only at this stage has the router been sufficiently secured so that it can be connected to the network. The VTYs are protected to allow only permitted IP addresses, and the LAN/WAN interface is protected so that only permitted IP addresses can connect to the router. Minimal routing can be configured, whether this is part of the ISP's IGP process or a simple static route for default gateway.

8 **Configure TACACS+**—Now that the network connection has been activated, the network-based authentication system can be activated. Don't forget to remove any locally added username/password pairs and any passwords that have been added to the router VTY ports. Don't forget to log off and log on again to check that the configuration actually works.

9 **Configure NTP and logging**—Time synchronization should be configured, along with syslogging on the router. This is so that log messages of any issues can be captured on the log hosts, to keep a full record of what is happening on the router.

10 **Configure SNMP**—Many ISPs use tools such as MRTG, so now is the time to configure SNMP access and any necessary access lists to support secure access to the SNMP function.

11 **Configure remaining interfaces**—Any other interfaces that are required for the router's operation now should be configured.

12 **Configure routing protocols**—Now is the time to introduce an IGP (if not already configured earlier) and iBGP, if required.

13 **Finished!**—Use a network security tool such as SAINT to check the security of the router. In the absence of any such tools, ask colleagues to check the configuration for completeness, or run a diff against the configuration of a similarly configured router running successfully in the network.

These hints apply to routers and switches. Note that although some of them could be release-dependent, it is worth spending time to analyze what the software release will and will not support, and to make allowances in the previous checklist for those points.

Full Example

The following is a full example of a secure configuration template put together from all the techniques described so far:

```
service password-encryption
service tcp-keepalives-in
!
aaa new-model
aaa authentication login default tacacs+ enable
aaa authentication login Cisco-Lab local enable
aaa authentication enable default tacacs+ enable
aaa accounting exec default start-stop tacacs+
!
username Cisco1 password 7 11041811051B13
enable secret <removed>
!
access-list 199 permit tcp 221.17.1.0 0.0.0.255 any
access-list 199 permit tcp 221.17.34.0 0.0.0.255 any
```

```
access-list 199 deny   tcp any any range 0 65535 log
access-list 199 deny   ip any any log
!
ip tacacs source-interface Loopback0
tacacs-server host 221.17.1.2
tacacs-server host 221.17.34.10
tacacs-server key CKr3t#
!
line vty 0 4
 access-class 199 in
 exec-timeout 5 0
 transport input telnet ssh
 transport output none
 transport preferred none
 login authentication Cisco-Lab
 history size 256
!
```

Securing the Routing Protocol

How do you know that the routing updates from one of your internal backbone routers really came from a neighboring router on your backbone? You do not—unless neighbor authentication is used. Theoretically, routing information can be spoofed and injected into an ISP's backbone. The horror of seeing a normal 110,000-entry routing table jump to 200,000 or 500,000 entries—and then seeing these propagate all over the Internet—has been quietly talked about in the halls of Internet operations meetings. ISPs are strongly encouraged to prevent their routers from receiving fraudulent route updates by protecting the routing protocol updates.

Cisco IOS Software has several tools to help protect the routing protocols from intentional or unintentional attacks. The primary mechanism for protecting route protocol updates is router authentication. MD5 is a valuable tool that will validate the authentication of a routing update. The second tool is extended ACLs. ACLs should be used strategically throughout the network to validate the source/destination address of packets headed for the IGP and EGP ports. ACLs make it more difficult for DoS/DDoS attacks to target the routing protocol. Finally, specific commands and BCPs in the routing protocols help protect them from attack. For example, BGP's **maximum-prefix** command alerts the operators and optionally shuts down the BGP session whenever the maximum prefix limit is reached. This protects the router from being overwhelmed by the number of updates or having its memory completely consumed, potentially crashing the router. This section reviews these tools and techniques so that ISP engineers will have a better understanding of how to protect their routing protocols.

Authenticating Routing Protocol Updates

Neighbor router authentication is part of an ISP's total security plan. This section describes what neighbor router authentication is, how it works, and why it should be used to increase overall network security. Documentation details can be found at http://www.cisco.com/ univercd/cc/td/doc/product/software/ios122/122cgcr/fsecur_c/fothersf/scfroutr.htm.

Benefits of Neighbor Authentication

When configured, neighbor authentication occurs whenever routing updates are exchanged between neighbor routers. This authentication ensures that a router receives reliable routing information from a trusted source. Without neighbor authentication, unauthorized or deliberately malicious routing updates could compromise the security of your network traffic. A security compromise could occur if an unfriendly party diverts or analyzes your network traffic. For example, an unauthorized router could send a fictitious routing update to convince your router to send traffic to an incorrect destination. This diverted traffic could be analyzed to learn confidential information of your organization or merely could be used to disrupt your organization's capability to effectively communicate using the network. Neighbor authentication prevents any such fraudulent route updates from being received by your router.

Protocols That Use Neighbor Authentication

Neighbor authentication can be configured for the following routing protocols:

- Border Gateway Protocol (BGP)
- DRP Server Agent
- Intermediate System-to-Intermediate System (IS-IS)
- IP Enhanced Interior Gateway Routing Protocol (EIGRP)
- Open Shortest Path First (OSPF)
- Routing Information Protocol Version 2 (RIPv2)

When to Configure Neighbor Authentication

You should configure any router for neighbor authentication if that router meets all of these conditions:

- The router uses any of the routing protocols previously mentioned.
- It is conceivable that the router might receive a false route update.
- If the router received a false route update, your network might be compromised.
- If you configure a router for neighbor authentication, you also need to configure the neighbor router for neighbor authentication.

How Neighbor Authentication Works

When neighbor authentication has been configured on a router, the router authenticates the source of each routing update packet that it receives. This is accomplished by the exchange of an authenticating key (sometimes referred to as a password) that is known to both the sending and the receiving routers (as shown in Figure 4-5). Two types of neighbor authentication are used: plain-text authentication and Message Digest Algorithm Version 5 (MD5) authentication. Both forms work in the same way, with the exception that MD5 sends a "message digest" instead of the authenticating key itself. The message digest is created using the key and a message, but the key itself is not sent, preventing it from being read while it is being transmitted. Plain-text authentication sends the authenticating key itself over the wire.

Figure 4-5 *Router Authentication*

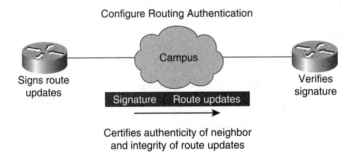

Configure Routing Authentication

NOTE   Plain-text authentication is not recommended for use as part of your security strategy. Its primary use is to avoid accidental changes to the routing infrastructure. Using MD5 authentication, however, is a recommended security practice.

CAUTION   As with all keys, passwords, and other security secrets, it is imperative that you closely guard the keys used in neighbor authentication. The security benefits of this feature rely upon all authenticating keys being kept confidential. Also, when performing router-management tasks through SNMP, do not ignore the risk associated with sending keys using nonencrypted SNMP.

Plain-Text Authentication

Each participating neighbor router must share an authenticating key. This key is specified on each router during configuration. Multiple keys can be specified with some protocols;

each key must be identified by a key number. In general, when a routing update is sent, the following authentication sequence occurs:

Step 1   A router sends a routing update with a key and the corresponding key number to the neighbor router. For protocols that can have only one key, the key number is always 0.

Step 2   The receiving (neighbor) router checks the received key against the same key stored in its own memory.

Step 3   If the two keys match, the receiving router accepts the routing update packet. If the two keys did not match, the routing update packet is rejected.

MD5 Authentication

MD5 authentication works similarly to plain-text authentication, except that the key is never sent over the wire. Instead, the router uses the MD5 algorithm to produce a "message digest" of the key (also called a "hash"). The message digest then is sent instead of the key itself. This ensures that nobody can eavesdrop on the line and learn keys during transmission. An example of the sequence involved in generating the hash is displayed in Figure 4-6 (for the originating router) and Figure 4-7 (for the destination router). These protocols use MD5 authentication:

- OSPF
- RIP Version 2
- BGP
- EIGRP
- IS-IS

Figure 4-6 *How Routing Protocol Authentication Operates—Originating Router*

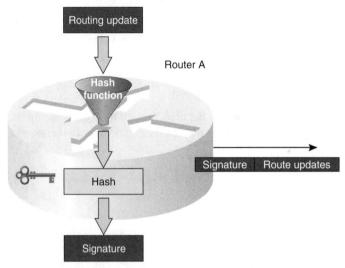

Signature = Encrypted hash of routing update

Figure 4-7 *How Routing Protocol Authentication Operates—Destination Router*

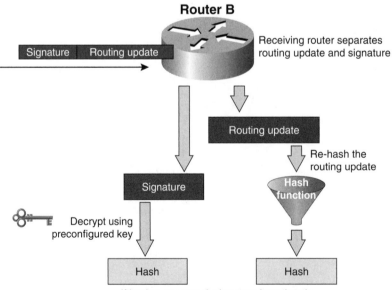

Routing Protocol Authentication Summary

The following are some examples of how router authentication is configured in OSPF, IS-IS, and BGP.

OSPF:

```
interface ethernet1
 ip address 10.1.1.1 255.255.255.0
 ip ospf message-digest-key 100 md5 cisco
 !
router ospf 1
 network 10.1.1.0 0.0.0.255 area 0
 area 0 authentication message-digest
```

IS-IS:

```
interface ethernet0
 ip address 10.1.1.1 255.255.255.0
 ip router isis
 isis password cisco level-2
```

BGP:

```
router bgp 200
 no synchronization
 neighbor 4.1.2.1 remote-as 300
 neighbor 4.1.2.1 description Link to Excalabur
 neighbor 4.1.2.1 send-community
 neighbor 4.1.2.1 version 4
 neighbor 4.1.2.1 soft-reconfiguration inbound
 neighbor 4.1.2.1 route-map Community1 out
 neighbor 4.1.2.1 password cisco
```

Securing the Network

The next step in ISP security is building resistance to attacks and intrusions into the network. For an ISP, this can be divided into three major areas:

- **Route filtering**—Controlling which routes are advertised and received from sources outside your autonomous system (AS)

- **Packet filtering**—Ensuring that packets that enter the network are valid and have a source address matching the origin

- **Rate limiting**—Limiting the amount of some types of traffic (such as ICMP) that has no valid reason to consume huge chunks of bandwidth

Each technique is considered in turn in the following sections.

Egress and Ingress Filtering

Egress and ingress filtering are a critical part of an ISP's router-configuration strategy. These terms are relative to the network ingress/egress filtering are applied:

- *Ingress filtering* applies filters to traffic coming into a network from outside (see Figure 4-8). This can be from an ISP's customers or traffic from the Internet at large.

- *Egress filtering* applies a filter for all traffic leaving an ISP's networks (see Figure 4-9). It is applied to information leaving the network to the Internet or customer networks.

Be mindful that these terms are relative to the specific network's point of view. For example, ISP B's egress traffic is ISP A's ingress traffic.

Ingress/egress filters help protect an ISP's resources and its customers' networks, allows it to enforce policy, and minimizes the risk of being the network chosen by hackers to launch an attack on other networks. ISPs are strongly encouraged to develop strategies using egress and ingress filtering to protect themselves from their customers and the Internet at large. By protecting themselves, the ISPs are working toward protecting the Internet in general.

BCP 38/RFC 2827, "Network Ingress Filtering: Defeating Denial-of-Service Attacks Which employ IP Source Address Spoofing" (by P. Ferguson and D. Senie, May 2000, http://www.ietf.org/rfc/rfc2827.txt) provides general guidelines for all ISPs on ingress and egress filtering. The Internet community now considers this document best current practice, and all ISPs should follow its recommendations.

Route Filtering

Route filtering removes specific routes from routing protocol advertisements. From the context of the Internet, route filtering is applied to the BGP ingress and egress advertisements with an ISP's customers and peers. In today's Internet, route filtering is done to meet two objectives. The first objective is to keep specific networks that should not be advertised on the net from propagating to other networks. For example, RFC 1918 addresses (which documents private address space), the host subnet (127.0.0.0/8), and multicast addresses (if multicast BGP is not used) should be filtered from an ISP's ingress and egress advertisements.[4] The second objective is to filter smaller network advertisements out of larger CIDR blocks. Some ISPs leak out a more specific route from a larger CIDR block (sometimes intentionally for operational reasons, but more often accidentally or through lack of knowledge). These leaks increase the rate of growth of the Internet Route Table. To discourage route leaking, some ISPs route filter on the prefix boundaries of the Regional Internet Registry's (RIR's) minimal IPv4 allocation block.[5] The ISPs that do this often are referred to as net police—hence, the name of this type of routing filter is called net police filtering. Examples of a routing filter to keep unregistered blocks out and net police filtering are provided in this section.

Figure 4-8   *Ingress Filtering*

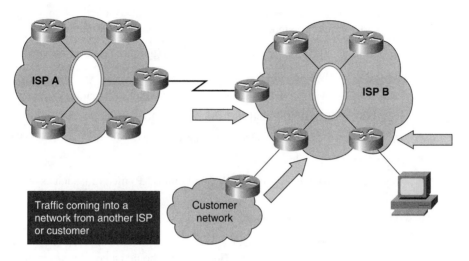

Figure 4-9   *Egress Filtering*

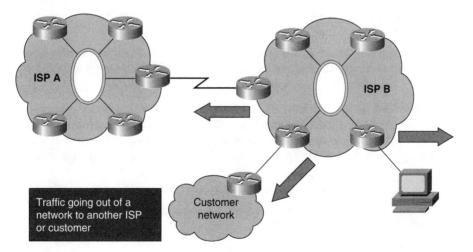

Networks That Should Not Be Advertised on the Internet

As mentioned earlier, some networks are reserved for special functions on the Internet. These networks should not appear in the Internet Route Table; examples are

- 0.0.0.0/0 and 0.0.0.0/8—Default and network 0 (unique and now historical properties)
- 127.0.0.0/8—Host loopback
- 192.0.2.0/24—TEST-NET generally used for examples in vendor documentation
- 10.0.0.0/8, 172.16.0.0/12, and 192.168.0.0/16—RFC 1918 private addresses
- 169.254.0.0/16—End-node autoconfiguration network in the absence of DHCP
- Any advertisements less than /24
- Any network from an Internet eXchange Point (IXP) medium, such as the Ethernet segment

These last two could be controversial:

- A /24 (the historical Class C address) has been the smallest block of IPv4 addresses ever allocated from an IP registry. Hence, there should be no advertisements less than a /24 on the Internet. Yet, for whatever reason, networks below /24 do appear in the Internet Route Table. So it is up to the ISP to decide whether to filter them.
- Filtering the IP networks of the IXPs is an option that many ISPs select. IXPs generally are not accustomed to providing transit to the Internet, so the IXP LAN does not need global visibility. For this reason, many ISPs filter these prefixes on the ingress and egress.

In his Internet Draft, Bill Manning has documented the networks that have special uses in the Internet. The current version is http://www.ietf.org/internet-drafts/draft-manning-dsua-07.txt at the time of this writing.[6]

The following is a list of some of the US IXP networks in ACL format.[7] Anyone who wants to implement this should first check that these are still valid IXP network blocks and should be prepared to put in the effort to maintain them. Also, it might be worth extending this list to include all the exchange points in the world (www.ep.net), a potentially harder job.

```
! MAE-East primary IP block
access-list 150 deny   ip 192.41.177.0 0.0.0.255 0.0.0.0 255.255.255.0
!
! MAE-East secondary IP block
access-list 150 deny   ip 198.32.186.0 0.0.0.255 0.0.0.0 255.255.255.0
!
! MFS Portion of MAE-West
access-list 150 deny   ip 198.32.136.0 0.0.0.255 0.0.0.0 255.255.255.0
!
! NASA/AMES - NASA Portion of MAE-West
access-list 150 deny   ip 198.32.184.0 0.0.0.255 0.0.0.0 255.255.255.0
!
! Ameritech Advanced Data Services - AADS
access-list 150 deny   ip 198.32.130.0 0.0.0.255 0.0.0.0 255.255.255.0
!
```

```
! Digital's Palo Alto Internet eXchange - PAIX
access-list 150 deny    ip 198.32.176.0 0.0.0.255 0.0.0.0 255.255.255.0
!
! Sprint NAP - Pennsauken
access-list 150 deny    ip 192.157.69.0 0.0.0.255 0.0.0.0 255.255.255.0
!
! Pac*Bell NAP
access-list 150 deny    ip 198.32.128.0 0.0.0.255 0.0.0.0 255.255.255.0
!
! MAE-LA
access-list 150 deny    ip 198.32.146.0 0.0.0.255 0.0.0.0 255.255.255.0
!
! MAE-Dallas
access-list 150 deny    ip 198.32.138.0 0.0.0.255 0.0.0.0 255.255.255.0
!
! MAE-Houston
access-list 150 deny    ip 198.32.150.0 0.0.0.255 0.0.0.0 255.255.255.0
!
```

As discussed in Chapter 3, "Routing Protocols," the use of BGP distribute list is considered deprecated by many ISPs. The newer BGP prefix lists are significantly quicker to load into the router and offer greater usability. They are also somewhat easier to configure (using natural network/prefix length representation) and use names rather than numbers, making it easier to keep track of the different filters on the router (named access lists also use names but have no performance advantage over standard access lists.)

Here is an example configuration and filter using a BGP prefix list:

```
router bgp 200
 no synchronization
 neighbor 220.220.4.1 remote-as 210
 neighbor 220.220.4.1 version 4
 neighbor 220.220.4.1 prefix-list rfc1918-sua in
 neighbor 220.220.4.1 prefix-list rfc1918-sua out
 neighbor 222.222.8.1 remote-as 220
 neighbor 222.222.8.1 version 4
 neighbor 222.222.8.1 prefix-list rfc1918-sua in
 neighbor 222.222.8.1 prefix-list rfc1918-sua out
 no auto-summary
!
ip prefix-list rfc1918-sua deny    0.0.0.0/0              ! Default
ip prefix-list rfc1918-sua deny    0.0.0.0/8 le 32        ! Network Zero
ip prefix-list rfc1918-sua deny    10.0.0.0/8 le 32       ! RFC1918
ip prefix-list rfc1918-sua deny    127.0.0.0/8 le 32      ! Hostnet
ip prefix-list rfc1918-sua deny    169.254.0.0/16 le 32   ! Non-DHCP Autoconf
ip prefix-list rfc1918-sua deny    172.16.0.0/12 le 32    ! RFC1918
ip prefix-list rfc1918-sua deny    192.0.2.0/24 le 32     ! TESTNET
ip prefix-list rfc1918-sua deny    192.168.0.0/16 le 32   ! RFC1918
ip prefix-list rfc1918-sua deny    224.0.0.0/3 le 32      ! Multicast
ip prefix-list rfc1918-sua deny    0.0.0.0/0 ge 25        ! prefixes >/24
ip prefix-list rfc1918-sua permit 0.0.0.0/0 le 32         ! Everything Else
!
```

Effects of CIDR-ization

One of the most critical issues that could threaten the stability of the Internet is the size of the global Internet Route Table. The table's growth influences scalability, increases operational/capital cost, and has posed a security risk to the Internet. For a variety of reasons, ISPs throughout the world have injected all sorts of networks into the Internet, ranging from /8s (old Class A's) to /32s (host routes). The result is rapid growth of the Internet Route Table.

Classless interdomain routing (CIDR) has had a noticeable and significant impact on the growth of the table. CIDR is a combination of revised IPv4 allocation policies (for instance, today's norm of provider-based addressing), updates to routing protocols (RIPv2, OSPF, IS-IS, and BGP), and new address-aggregation techniques to ensure that only the large allocated blocks of addresses get advertised into the global Internet Route Table. The impact of CIDR moved the growth rate from an exponential curve to linear growth.

Even though the introduction of CIDR did have an effect, it did not have as long term an effect as many providers and industry observers hoped it would. The linear growth rate was still fairly steep. Some operators on the Internet began to feel that the real problem was lazy ISPs that either did not care or did not know how to do proper aggregation. Two approaches were tried to encourage ISPs to do the right thing. The first approach was to post of the Internet CIDR Report to the core operational mailing lists weekly. The second approach was to implement filters on the routes announced by each ISP, basically accepting only the major allocated CIDR blocks and no more specifics. Both approaches are in use today and are items that all ISPs need to be aware of and consider.

The CIDR Report from Tony Bates (tbates@cisco.com) is a weekly analysis of the rate of growth of the Internet Route Table. The report, sent to all the major operations' mailing lists, provides the name of ISPs injecting the most prefixes, aggregated and unaggregated. Everyone saw who was causing the growth and then could apply peer pressure to have the corrections made. Figure 4-10 (the up-to-date version of this graph can be seen at http://www.telstra.net/ops/bgp) shows the growth of the Internet Route Table. Between late 1995 and 1998, peer pressure helped to stabilize the growth, and indeed helped slow down the growth rate, by late 1998, as can be seen in Figure 4-10. As newer routers with faster processors and more memory capacity were deployed, ISPs became less concerned with the growth in the routing table and hence lost interest in providing or accepting peer pressure. The CIDR reports are interesting but are losing their earlier impact, and they arguably are no longer serving their original function.

The following is a list of sites collecting data on the Internet Route Table:

> Tony Bates's Daily CIDR Report:
> http://www.employees.org:80/~tbates/cidr-report.html

> Philip Smith's Daily Routing Analysis:
> http://www.apnic.net/stats/bgp/

> Geoff Huston's BGP Table Data:
> http://www.telstra.net/ops/bgp/bgp-active.html

Figure 4-10 *BGP Route Table (November 15, 2001) from Telstra's AS 1221 Point of View*

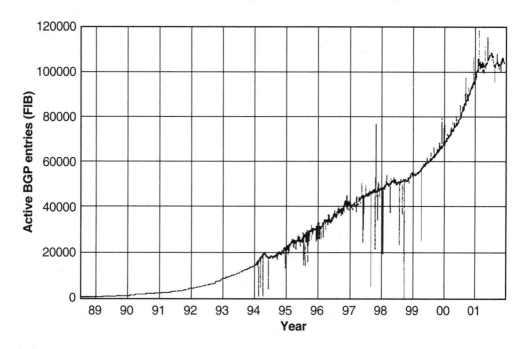

The second approach to encouraging ISPs to use proper aggregation was to install inbound prefix filters on route announcements. Sean Doran (smd@clock.org) was one of the first to notice and act on the fact that the new CIDR-based allocation policies from the three RIRs were not affecting the ISPs' announcements to the Internet. In Sean's words,

> What triggered the filter was the observation that the blocks freshly allocated by all three registries were very poorly aggregated. More annoyingly, those allocated to Sprint's principal peers (most notably Internet MCI) demonstrated the worst aggregation; in one case, a /14 was announced almost exclusively as prefixes no shorter than 19 bits.[8]

In essence, CIDR was not being implemented as originally intended. Sprint placed one of the first filters that enforced the RIR's default allocation size (see Table 4-1). This filter blocked any announcement from any ISP that was longer than its allocated address block. For example, if an ISP was allocated a /19 from RIPE NCC's 62/8 CIDR block, this is all that should be announced to the Internet. The RIPE NCC had published its minimum allocation size, so Sprint could construct a filter that would accept only a /19 or less from 62/8. So a /18 would pass the filter, but a /20, /21, /22, /23, /24, and so on would not pass.

The operational effects of these filters have been variable. Several ISPs joined Sprint in implementing such filters. All three RIRs have assisted the ISP community by publishing their default allocation sizes for all of their CIDR blocks (see Table 4-1 for a list of URLs).

Today, all three RIRs have a minimal allocation size of /20 on their new CIDR blocks, making it potentially easier for any ISP to filter on the registry allocation sizes if desired.

Table 4-1 shows where to get the list information on each RIR's minimal allocation size for each of the macro address blocks.

Table 4-1   *URLs to the RIR's Default Allocation Sizes*

APNIC	http://www.apnic.net/docs/add-manage-policy.html#6.9
ARIN	http://www.arin.net/regserv/IPStats.html
RIPE NCC	ftp://ftp.ripe.net/ripe/docs/ripe-211.txt

Do Net Police Filters Help Secure a Network?

In some incidents on the Internet, a rogue router (intentionally or unintentionally) has deaggregated the address blocks and started advertising lots of small, more specific networks. In one incident, the Internet Route Table grew from 50K routes to more than 120K routes over a period of several minutes. ISP security people have been mindful that this sort of attack is theoretically feasible. Yet it also has been proven that the net police filter is a deterrent to this sort of attack. For this attack to work, a router attached to the Internet and speaking BGP must take a large CIDR block (say, a /19) and advertise many more specifics (say, all possible /32s—8192 networks). A net police filter ensuring that a /19 or less (e.g., /18) would pass the filter and that all other more specifics would be dropped. The result is that the attack would have minimal effect on the ISP with the net police filter, while other ISPs without the net police filter would get a huge influx of new announcements, overloading the memory of their routers and potentially creating chaos on the net.

NOTE   Depending on the number of routes advertised, there might be additional load on the BGP process as it drops all these unwanted networks. Also, if BGP soft reconfiguration is turned on, each of the dropped networks still would get saved.

Negative Impact of Net Police Filters

The major downside, if not complete showstopper, for implementing net police filters on a network is their impact on legitimate multihoming. This is especially felt in developing parts of the Internet where new ISPs have received their first allocation from the regional registry and have a basic requirement to be multihomed as part of their business. Their /20 network block is all they have; if they subdivide this, they fall foul of the net police filters that that have been put in place. It is for this reason that many ISP operators outside the United States frown upon the concept. Many hours have been wasted trying to make multihoming work, only to be thwarted by net police filters implemented by an ISP in the United States.

As with all multihoming scenarios, the ISP always should announce its network block. This ensures connectivity to the Internet. However, announcing two /21s, the first step to basic inbound load sharing of traffic, will be impacted by their upstreams implementing RIR minimum allocation-size filters. Encountering any situation like this will require cooperation of upstream ISPs, or, in the worst case, considering moving custom elsewhere.

Creating Your Own Net Police Filter

ISPs that want to create their own net police filters are strongly encouraged to do the following:

- **Consider the impact**—Shutting the door doesn't make the storm go away—it shuts out everything, good and bad.

- **Maintain an accurate list**—Consult each of the RIR's published CIDR blocks for the default allocations. Ensure that you have an up-to-date list, and create a process for validating your filter with future updates of the RIR's list.

- **Consult with colleagues**—Consult with your peers about the list. If possible, compare what others have done with what you want to accomplish.

- **Publish policy**—A Web page with the filter policy is extremely helpful. Refer to the NANOG list of filter policies as an example (http://www.nanog.org/filter.html). Also put a comment in your AS object.

- **Keep it up-to-date!**—This is the most important part—and often the hardest to do. Be sensitive to complaints, especially about reachability from your customers or their customers—without them, you have no business.

The following is just one example of a net police filter. ISPs can use this as a starting point but are strongly encouraged to verify that everything in the list will work in their environments.

```
!
!! RIPE
ip prefix-list FILTER permit 62.0.0.0/8 ge 9 le 20
ip prefix-list FILTER permit 80.0.0.0/7 ge 9 le 20
ip prefix-list FILTER permit 193.0.0.0/8 ge 9 le 20
ip prefix-list FILTER permit 194.0.0.0/7 ge 9 le 20
ip prefix-list FILTER permit 212.0.0.0/7 ge 9 le 20
ip prefix-list FILTER permit 217.0.0.0/8 ge 9 le 20
!
!! APNIC
ip prefix-list FILTER permit 61.0.0.0/8 ge 9 le 20
ip prefix-list FILTER permit 202.0.0.0/7 ge 9 le 20
ip prefix-list FILTER permit 210.0.0.0/7 ge 9 le 20
ip prefix-list FILTER permit 218.0.0.0/7 ge 9 le 20
ip prefix-list FILTER permit 220.0.0.0/8 ge 9 le 20
!
!! ARIN
ip prefix-list FILTER permit 24.0.0.0/8 ge 9 le 20
ip prefix-list FILTER permit 63.0.0.0/8 ge 9 le 20
ip prefix-list FILTER permit 64.0.0.0/6 ge 9 le 20
```

```
ip prefix-list FILTER permit 68.0.0.0/8 ge 9 le 20
ip prefix-list FILTER permit 199.0.0.0/8 ge 9 le 20
ip prefix-list FILTER permit 200.0.0.0/8 ge 9 le 20
ip prefix-list FILTER permit 204.0.0.0/6 ge 9 le 20
ip prefix-list FILTER permit 208.0.0.0/7 ge 9 le 20
ip prefix-list FILTER permit 216.0.0.0/8 ge 9 le 20
!
!! General - Filter anything greater then /24
ip prefix-list FILTER deny  0.0.0.0/0 ge 25
!
!! Other filters...
```

Notice that only announcements of prefix sizes between /9 and /20 are permitted. No registry will allocate the entire /8 block to one ISP (at least, not so far), so a /8 announcement shouldn't be seen from these blocks. Likewise, because a /20 is the minimum allocation by the registries, nothing smaller should be seen. Some ISPs argue that the preceding ranges should be /9 through /21 or /22, to allow the possibility of implementing multihoming for the smaller ISPs. Providers that are implementing these filters should consider what they reasonably want to permit in their network.

Packet Filtering

DoS attacks, spoofing, and other forms of attacks are on the increase on the Internet. Many of these attacks can be thwarted through the judicious use of ingress (packets originating from your network) and egress (packets arriving from the Internet) packet filtering. In packet filtering, the router or switch inspects the packet's source or destination information and either passes or drops a packet based on a rule set. IP addresses and port numbers are the most common information used in the rule set.

NOTE   This section covers the simple case of single-homed downstream customers. More thought is required when applying packet filtering for ISPs that are multihomed. For example, when the customer ISP's link to your network goes down, you will see packets from that network coming from "the Internet." Also be aware that a multihomed customer might require special routing to implement load sharing; in that case, you will again see that ISP's traffic coming from "the Internet."

Cisco has several ways of inspecting and dropping packets:

- **ACLs**—An access list is used to match on the source/destination IP address, the protocol, or TOS to drop a packet.
- **Black-hole filtering (forwarding to Null0)**—The forward table routes the packet based on destination IP address to the adjacency Null0, dropping the packet.
- **Unicast RPF**—An MTRIE lookup into the FIB is done based on the source IP address. If the source IP address does not match the information in the forward table, the packet is dropped.

Note	An MTRIE is a storage mechanism made up of nodes and leaves, used in CEF.

- **Committed Access Rate (CAR)**—When the committed rate is set to 0, all packets are dropped. CAR can match packets based on ACLs or MTRIE lookups into the FIB's QoS-ID field.

Each of these packet-dropping techniques has various packet-per-second (PPS) performance impacts. Like any security tool, risks need to be weighed against the benefits.

NOTE	A performance impact could affect the forwarding speed of the router when many filters are applied. Cisco's newer switching technologies help minimize the performance impact. Turbo ACLs (compiled access lists) are available from IOS Software Release 12.0(6)S and give superior performance for access lists more than 10 entries long. Due care and consideration should be taken whenever the access list starts getting beyond 50 entries. However, it should be stated that trading a few microseconds of IP forwarding speed for the safety of minimizing the impact of DoS attacks could prove to be worthwhile.

Access Control Lists: General Sequential-Based ACLs

ACLs are the first option for a lot of organizations looking to enforce policy and provide a layer of security. At the same time, ACLs have the greatest scaling, performance, and security risk. Generally, traditional ACLs are processed sequentially (see Figure 4-11). Any router processing a packet through an ACL looks for a match on a list of ACL entries; each line of the ACL must be checked until there is a match. If the ACL is an extended version, the IP payload, ports, and application also must be checked sequentially (see Figure 4-12). Because many policy and security filters are ACLs with a lot of **deny** statements (see Example 4-2), a very long ACL increases the packet latency and consumes more CPU cycles.

NOTE	The general principle of ACLs and the processing involved are issues for all routers, not just Cisco routers. Cisco has tools such as NetFlow and Optimum switching that increase the performance of the ACL checks, yet even these have their limits.

Example 4-2 *Standard Access List with Lots of* **deny** *Statements*

```
access-list 25 deny 165.21.10.10
access-list 25 deny 171.68 34.1
access-list 25 deny 192.34.5.10

.
. many deny entries
.
access-list 25 deny 141.43.10.100
access-list 25 permit all
```

Figure 4-11 *Standard Access List—Incoming Packets*

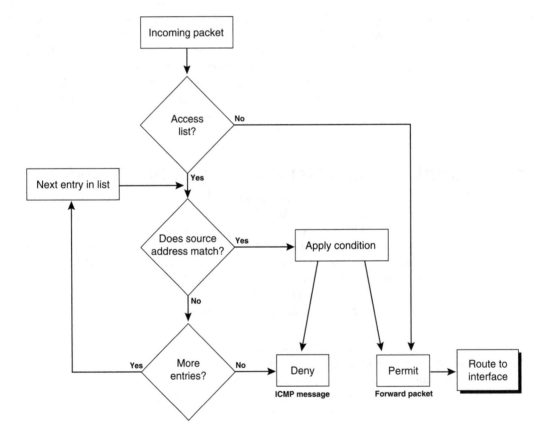

As the length of the policy filter increases, the burden on the processing power of the router reaches a point at which it is at 99 percent CPU utilization. Added to this is the 100 percent to 200 percent growth rate of the Internet. This means that as the PPS load on the router increases from the natural growth of the network, the CPU load and packet latency from ACL processing also increase, affecting the overall end-to-end bandwidth performance. To keep the ACL a relevant tool on the Internet, improvements need to be added to allow ACLs to scale. Faster processors, distributed processing, dedicated ASIC/TCAMs, and special flow-based switching technologies have been added to various Cisco products to allow ACLs to continue to keep pace with the Internet's growth. Yet, while keeping pace with the growth of the Internet, it is understood that sequential ACLs have limitations. One way around these limitations is to use a new way to process packets through an ACL: Turbo ACLs.

Figure 4-12 *Extended ACLs—Logical Flow for Every Packet*

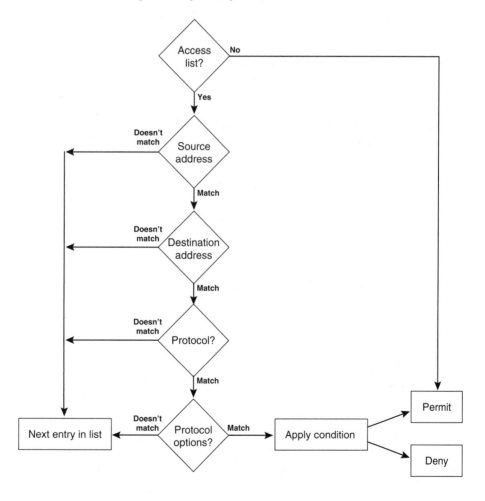

Access Control Lists: Turbo ACLs

Turbo ACLs use a technique that takes a standard or extended ACL, creates a set of data tables, and compiles them for runtime processing. For this reason, Turbo ACLs also are referred to as *compiled ACLs*. Turbo ACLs do not change the "first match wins" characteristic of all ACLs. Instead, they reduce the number of CPU operations to find a match, allowing for larger ACLs to be used without an increase in packet latency. This provides ISPs with a tool to allow large ACLs without a significant performance impact on the router.

As seen in Figure 4-13, when a Turbo ACL is activated in a router, it takes the standard ACL input, creates tables based on the ACLs entries, and compiles the tables to allow an arrayed match. The result is that a match is achieved in five steps, no matter what the size of the ACL is. This also means that a Turbo ACL's advantages become clear only when the ACL is longer than five entries. So ACLs with 3 or 5 lines would outperform Turbo ACLs, but Turbo ACLs with 300 to 500 lines would outperform sequentially searched ACLs. Figure 4-14 shows the result of one study on the performance difference between sequential ACLs and Turbo ACLs. As the length of the ACL increases, the time that it takes a sequential ACL to match increases (assuming a last-line match). Turbo ACLs provide consistency throughout the length of the ACL. The limit in the length of a Turbo ACL has more to do with the hardware performance envelope; memory, TCAM size, ASIC size, buffering, and CPU cycles are all factors that limit the maximum size of a Turbo ACL.

Figure 4-13 *Turbo ACLs: Processing Takes Five Steps, Regardless of Size*

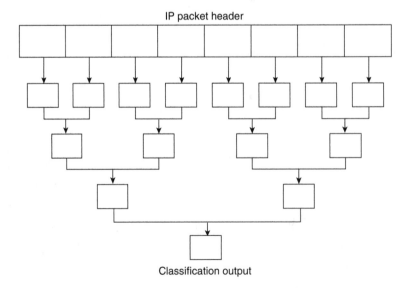

Figure 4-14 *Turbo ACL Performance Consistency*

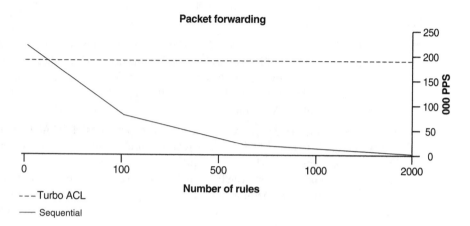

Turbo ACL Configuration Details and References

To activate Turbo ACLs in a Cisco router, the following global command is used:

```
access-list compiled
```

This applies Turbo ACLs to *all* ACLs on the router, no matter what their size is. Turbo ACLs were introduced in IOS Software Release 12.0(6)S. Keyword searches on Cisco.com or http://www.cisco.com/univercd/cc/td/doc/product/software/ios120/120newft/120limit/120s/120s6/turboacl.htm will provide configuration information on Turbo ACLs.

Full details of how Turbo ACLs work were given by author Andrew McRae (amcrae@cisco.com), in the paper "High-Speed Packet Classification," presented at the Australian UNIX Users Group national conference in September 1999 (http://www.employees.org/~amcrae/papers/packet_class/).

ASIC-Based ACLs

As the bandwidth and PPS rates increased, hardware vendors started to consider other packet-filtering technologies. Until quite recently, all packet filtering was done in software based around a CPU. This could be a centrally switched architecture (such as a Cisco 72XX) or a distributed switch architecture with line cards that were CPU-based (such as a Cisco 75XX with VIP cards, a Cisco 76XX with flex WAN cards, or a Cisco 12XXX with Engine 0 line cards). The alternative to doing packet filtering in software loaded on a CPU is to microcode the ACL onto an ASIC.

ASIC-based ACLs use the strengths of specifically designed hardware to accelerate the resolution of an ACL. Some ASICs could be mission-specific, with ACLs added as a supplement (for example, Salsa on the Cisco 12000's Engine 1 line cards). Other ASICs are very specific and are optimized just for ACL lookup (for example, TCAMs on the Cisco 7600 and future products). The impact is that ACLs in ASIC have different performance characteristics than ACLs processed by general software on a CPU:

- The first difference is performance, which shows a dramatic improvement. For some, it is an increase in the rate of PPS but is impacted by the depth of the ACL (as mentioned earlier, the depth of an ACL impacts the performance of some ACLs, taking longer to reach a match). Others show no PPS impact, allowing full switching up to the maximum depth of the ACL (this is 15,000 lines in a 7600's TCAM).

- The second characteristic difference is that some capabilities of the ACL are limited. For example, ASIC-based ACLs usually require a precompilation on the router before it is loaded into the ASIC. This precompilation happens behind the scenes after an ACL has been updated. However, by compiling the ACL, some per-ACE information is lost. For example, an operator can get the aggregate counters on most ASIC-based ACLs but cannot get the per-ACE counters (ACE stands for access control entry, a single line in an access control list).

- Finally, ASIC-based ACLs have an ACE depth limit. Software-based ACLs can rely on shared memory of a line card or a route processor, but hardware-based ACLs are restricted to the memory design size of the ASIC. Therefore, the number of ACEs in a software-based ACL potentially can be very large: whereas, the size of the hardware ACE potentially is limited. This puts a max limit on the number of line (ACEs) that an ACL can handle. For some ASICs, this number is low—the 12000's Engine 2 PSA ASIC can up to 448 ACEs. For other ASICs, it is high—the 7600's TCAM can go up to 15,000 ACEs.

Taken together, these ASIC-based ACL characteristics offer the operator new strengths but also new limitations. (It is a common security principle that no new level of security comes without new limitation.) Operators need to be mindful of these limitations as they use ACLs in their system of applying policy and security through their networks.

Salsa ACLs in the Cisco 12000 Engine 1 Line Card

The Salsa ASIC is a specialized chip that assists the line card's CPU in packet-processing (features) and route-lookup (forwarding) functions. Ingress (input) ACLs are the key packet-processing feature that the ASIC optimizes. By doing the input ACL lookup as it does route lookup, the Salsa ASIC frees up the line card's CPU, allowing for considerably faster packet processing. Because this is only a first-generation implementation of ACLs in ASICs, some limitations still exist:

- Only ingress ACLs are supported.

- Subinterfaces (such as VLANs or Frame Relay) are not supported.

- Salsa uses the shared memory of the line card, so there are no hard maximum limits to the number of ACE entries. Salsa support for ACLs is enabled by the configuration command **access-list hardware salsa**.

If this command is not in the configuration, ACLs will still work, but they will be evaluated on the line card's CPU and thus the line card will show much slower packet-forwarding performance than would have been possible with the ASIC-based ACLs.

PSA ACLs in the Cisco 12000 Engine 2 Line Card

The Cisco 12000's Engine 2 line card took the approach of using the spare capacity in the PSA forwarding ASIC to apply ACLs. Specific microcode needs to be loaded when the *hardware-based* ACL is applied to the PSA. The result is significant PPS performance, with ACL depth determined to be acceptable for most ISP operations (around 128 lines of ACE with 448-line capability). Although there is a PPS advantage with this implementation, there are also limitations. If these limitations are exceeded, the line card is designed to move the ACL's function out of the PSA forwarding ASIC into the line card's CPU, impacting the potential forwarding rate. Check with the latest GSR product documentation for these limitations. (The limitations usually evolve around max ACE limits versus dCEF table size.)

When a PSA ACL is applied to a router, it is enabled by default. The general IOS Software command **no access list hardware psa** can be used to disable this feature.

Using ACLs for Egress Packet Filtering: Preventing Transmission of Invalid IP Addresses

Egress packet filtering ensures that the packets that you send out to other networks (ISPs or customers) are valid. It can be applied either on the gateway (upstream—peering routers) or on the customer edge. By filtering packets on your routers that connect your network to the Internet (see Figure 4-15), you can permit only packets with valid source IP addresses to leave your network and get into the Internet. For example, if your network consists of network 165.21.0.0 and your router connects to your ISP using a serial 0/1 interface, you can apply the access list as follows:

```
access-list 110 permit ip 165.21.0.0 0.0.255.255 any
access-list 110 deny ip any any log
!
interface serial 0/1
 description Upstream Connection to ISP A
 ip access-group 110 out
!
```

The last line of the access list determines whether there is any traffic with an invalid source address entering the Internet. If there are any matches, they will be logged. It is not crucial to have this line, but it helps locate the source and extent of the possible attacks.

Figure 4-15 *Egress Packet Filtering on the Upstream Gateway Router*

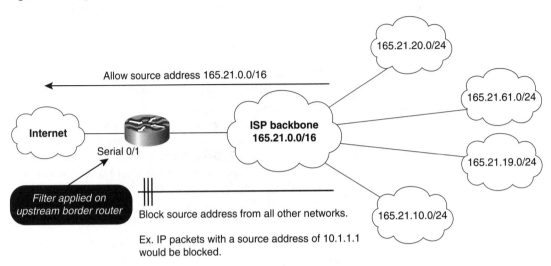

Some ISPs consider the option of egress filtering on the customer edge of their networks (see Figure 4-16). In this case, the objective is to ensure that packets bound for the customer do not have a source IP address within the range of addresses allocated by the ISP to the customer. For example, a packet with a destination address of 165.21.10.1 should not have a source address of 165.21.10.1. These are spoofed packets and should be dropped. The following is an example of an egress packet-filter ACL on the customer's interface:

```
access-list 121 deny ip 165.21.0.0 0.0.255.255 any
access-list 121 permit ip any any log
!
interface serial 1/1/1.3
 description T1 Link to Customer Acme Computer systems
 ip access-group 121 out
!
```

The key factor that limits this technique is the magnitude of the implementation. ISPs with 10,000 business customers do not see the benefits gained by managing 10,000 ACLs, especially when the customer is encouraged to implement ingress filtering on its gateway router.

Figure 4-16 *Egress Packet Filtering on the Customer Edge*

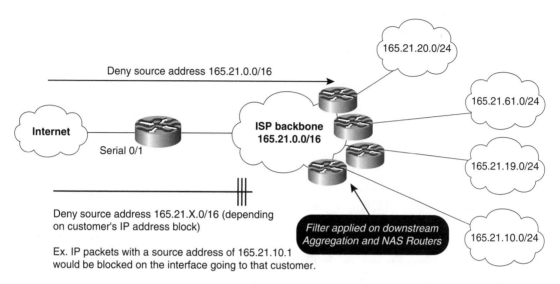

Using ACLs for Ingress Packet Filtering: Preventing Reception of Invalid IP Addresses

Ingress packet filtering validates the packets from the outside world (ISPs and customers) into and across your network. For an ISP, the outside world is any place outside the ISP's control. Obviously, packets from other ISPs are from the outside world and are not to be implicitly trusted. This also means that packets from an ISP's customers are from the outside world. Just because a network is a customer of an ISP does not make it a trusted network.

For ISPs that provide service to end networks, we highly recommend the validation of incoming packets from clients. This can be accomplished by the use of inbound packet filters on your border routers. Figure 4-17 is an example in which an ISP has one gateway to its upstream network. Customers with a network number of 165.21.10.0/24 should not see any packets coming from the Internet with 165.21.10.1 as the source address. These packets are attempts at spoofing and should be dropped. The following example shows a sample filter for network 165.21.0.0 with filters for private and rogue routes:

```
access-list 111 deny ip host 0.0.0.0 any log
access-list 111 deny ip 127.0.0.0 0.255.255.255 any log
access-list 111 deny ip 10.0.0.0 0.255.255.255 any log
access-list 111 deny ip 172.16.0.0 0.15.255.255 any log
```

```
access-list 111 deny ip 192.168.0.0 0.0.255.255 any log
access-list 111 deny ip 165.21.0.0 0.0.255.255 any log
access-list 111 permit ip any any
!
interface serial 1/0
 ip access-group 111 in
!
```

Figure 4-17 *Ingress Packet Filtering on the Upstream Gateway Router*

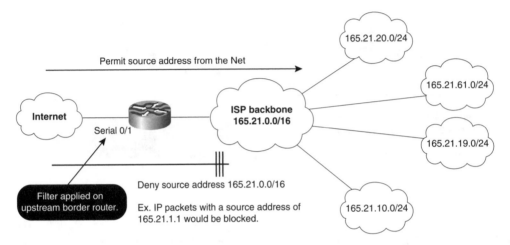

All the antispoofing, private address, and rogue filters have **any log** matches. It is not crucial to have this line, but it helps locate the source and extent of the possible probes or attacks. Figure 4-18 provides an illustration of ingress filtering on the upstream gateway router.

Figure 4-18 *Ingress Packet Filtering on the ISP/Customer Edge (IETF BCP Recommendation)*

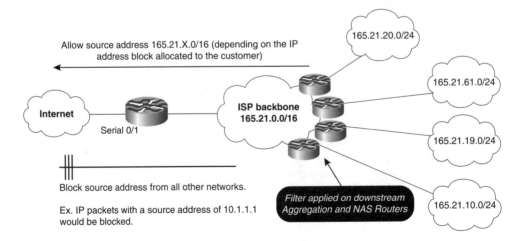

Although the example just given will work for all customers connecting to the Internet and many small- to medium-size ISPs, it is in addition to what is recommended in BCP 38/RFC 2827 "Network Ingress Filtering: Defeating Denial-of-Service Attacks Which Employ IP Source Address Spoofing," by P. Ferguson and D. Senie. BCP 38 recommends ingress filtering on the ISP/customer edge of the network. This filtering ensures that a source address of a packet matches the IP address block allocated to the customer. For example, a customer who has been allocated an IP address block of 165.21.10.0/24 should not send any packets with a source address of 192.168.1.1. The following is the example of an ingress packet-filtering ACL for the customer:

```
access-list 122 permit ip 165.21.0.0 0.0.255.255 any
access-list 122 deny ip any any log
!
interface serial 1/1/1.3
 description T1 Link to Customer Acme Computer systems
 ip access-group 121 in
!
```

Notice that the ACL is one line long and permits only authorized packets. The second line of the ACL, **deny ip any any log**, is optional. The one- or two-line ACL is easier to implement. The second **deny any** line is optional, but it does capture the packets that are denied and logs them in the router's syslog. The objective is to log packets that are in violation of the access list, allowing for the detection of compromised systems.

The limitation of this technique arises when there are thousands of leased-line customers; how is it possible to manage thousands of ACLs in a manner that is scalable for the router, for customer support personnel, and for the engineering staff running the network? The answer is not to use the access list technique, but to use unicast RPF, which is discussed in depth later in this chapter.

Black-Hole Routing as a Packet Filter (Forwarding to Null0)

Another way of implementing destination-based packet filtering on a router is to create a specific list of static host routes and point them to the pseudo-interface **Null0**. This technique commonly is referred to as black-hole routing. Null0 is a pseudo-interface, which functions similarly to the null devices available on most operating systems. This interface is always up and can never forward or receive traffic. Although Null0 is a pseudo-interface, within CEF it is not a *valid* interface. Hence, whenever a route is pointed to Null0, it will be dropped through CEF and dCEF's forwarding process with no processor overhead.

The null interface provides an alternative method of filtering traffic. You can avoid the overhead involved with using access lists by directing undesired network traffic to the null interface. The following example configures a null interface for IP route 127.0.0.0/16 and the specific host 171.68.10.1 (subnet mask 255.255.255.255):

```
interface Null0
 no icmp unreachables
 !
ip route 127.0.0.0 255.0.0.0 null 0
ip route 171.68.10.1 255.255.255.255 null 0
```

The **no icmp unreachables** command is used to prevent unnecessary replies whenever traffic is passed to the Null0 interface. Note that rate limiting should be applied to the icmp-unreachables option so that the router CPU does not get bogged down dealing with responses to discarded traffic. Consensus from ISPs using icmp-unreachables recommends the following configuration:

```
ip icmp rate-limit unreachable DF 2000
 !
interface Null0
 no icmp unreachables
 !
```

This rate-limits the icmp-unreachables response to one every two seconds, with the DF bit set (the IOS Software default is 500 ms).

Figure 4-19 gives a graphic example of how this black-list filtering technique works, comparing the packet paths with using an access list. By using the black-hole routing technique to implement black-list filtering (no pun intended), the strength of the router is utilized to drop packets bound for forbidden sites. A router's primary function is to forward packets, not filter packets. The black-hole routing technique uses the packet-forwarding power to drop all packets bound for sites on the black list.

Figure 4-19 *Using Static Host Routes to Null0 for Black-List Filtering*

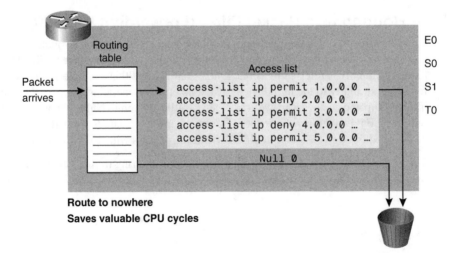

Two main drawbacks to this technique exist. First, access to all services at a given site must be restricted. The attraction of extended ACLs is the fine granularity given to filter at the application level. Black-hole routing does not have this granularity. It filters access for all packets bound to a specific host or subnet. Second, it is hard to bypass the black-hole routing technique. Any organization that wants to bypass the black list actually must find a way to bypass the filtering router's forwarding table. Compensating for either limitation is a nontrivial task.

BCP 38 Using Unicast RPF[10]

BCP 38/RFC 2827 provides a proactive step to prevent problems caused by packets with malformed or forged IP source addresses passing through a router. It is a wonderful security concept and will prevent many security problems on today's Internet. However, ISPs still have not widely adopted BCP 38, mostly because of concerns about scalability and the impact of the technique on the management of their routers.

Consider an ISP that would like to do BCP 38 with ACLs but is aggregating 10,000 leased-line customers onto its backbone. This means that 10,000 separate ACLs need to be created, maintained, and updated as new addresses are allocated to the ISP. Now consider an ISP with 100,000 leased-line customers, 500,000 leased-line customers, and so on. You can easily see the scalability problem posed when trying to implement BCP 38. Even scripted as part of configuration-management tools, implementing BCP 38 using ACLs adds scalability burdens for an overworked ISP operations and deployment team. Some way to automatically perform the BCP 38 check without the headache of ACLs is needed. This is where unicast reverse path forwarding (uRPF) provides the perfect solution.

uRPF originally was created to automatically achieve the BCP 38 packet filtering without the headaches of ACLs. It is a one-line interface configuration that can be placed in an ISP's deployment scripts. Hence, any installation engineer can apply BCP 38 filtering as soon as the leased line is installed to the site of the new customer. No ACLs, no need to maintain ACLs, and no need to change ACLs whenever new prefixes are allocated to the customer.

Background

uRPF is a CEF feature that uses the information in the FIB to automatically perform the BCP 38 checks. The original strict mode uRPF was designed for the customer/ISP edge of the network (see Figure 4-20). The objective was to design a feature that can easily be automated in the customer provisioning system, scale as new addresses blocks are allocated to the customer, and work with the MTRIE-based CEF switching. uRPF meets these objectives, even when the customers are multihomed to one or more upstream ISPs. Originally implemented in IOS Software 11.1(17)CC (available from March 1998), it has since been implemented throughout the IOS Software code train and works on routers from the largest to the smallest. Deployment of uRPF ranges from a small enterprise network using it to enhance a site's security to the largest Tier 1 ISPs in business today. uRPF is the proven and scalable ISP security tool for BCP 38/RFC 2827 deployment, eliminating excuses that ISPs have used in the past for not deploying ingress packet filtering on customers. It is accepted by many security experts that completely implementing uRPF checks on the edge of the Internet (where end sites connect to the ISPs) would eliminate a significant portion of the miscreant behavior on the Internet today.

Figure 4-20 *Original uRPF Deployment Was on the Customer/ISP Edge*

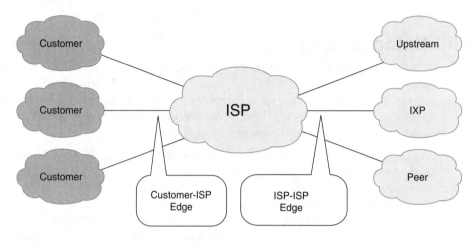

How uRPF Works: Strict Mode uRPF

When uRPF is enabled on an interface, the router verifies that all packets received on that interface have a source address that is reachable through that interface. This "look backward" capability is available only when CEF is enabled because the lookup relies on the presence of the FIB. uRPF ensures that there is a reverse-path route to the input interface of the packet. If there is a reverse-path route, the packet is forwarded as normal. If there is not a reverse-path route, the packet is dropped.

When a packet is received by a router's interface with uRPF, the following occurs:

1   uRPF does an MTRIE lookup on the source address in the FIB. It pulls up the next-hop and adjacency information from the source address's MTRIE.

2   The information from the MTRIE lookup is used to validate the packet's return path through the inbound interface. This is referred to as a FIB + adjacency check or a strict mode uRPF check.

3   If the FIB + adjacency check on the source matches, the packet continues forwarding through the router (see Figure 4-21).

4   If the FIB + adjacency check does not match, the packet enters the drop sequence (see Figure 4-22). These are packets whose source addresses do not match the information in the FIB.

5 If an uRPF ACL is applied, the packet is processed through that feature ACL before final dropping. This ACL could be configured to overrule the uRPF check and pass the packet.[11]

6 CEF table (FIB) lookup is carried out for packet forwarding, passing packets that match the FIB + adjacency check or dropping packets that are spoofed sources.

Figure 4-21 *uRPF Validating IP Source Addresses*

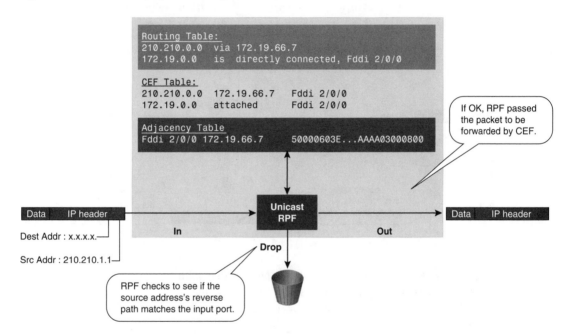

For example, if a customer sends a packet with the source address of 210.210.1.1 from interface FDDI 2/0/0, RPF checks the FIB to see if 210.210.1.1 has a path to FDDI 2/0/0. On the other hand, if a packet with a source address 144.64.21.1 arrives on FDDI 2/0/0, it would not match the information in the FIB glued to the FDDI 2/0/0 adjacency. The FIB has prefix 210.210.0.0/16 as the only prefix glued to the FDDI 2/0/0 adjacency. So source address 144.64.21.1 is a spoofed address. uRPF will fail this packet and drop it.

One of uRPF's great advantages is that it dynamically adapts to changes in the FIB caused by changes in the RIB resulting from updates from the various routing protocol databases. uRPF has far lower performance impact as an antispoofing tool compared with the access list approach, has minimal CPU overhead, and operates at a few percent less than the typical CEF switching rates. The use of the MTRIE lookup in CEF allows it to be coded in new, super fast-forwarding ASICs needed to achieve the MPPS rates for OC-12 and higher circuits.

Figure 4-22 *uRPF Dropping Packets that Fail Verification*

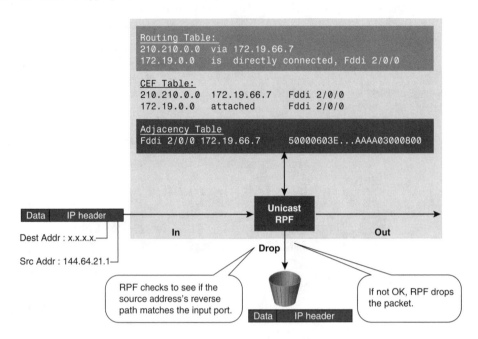

uRPF also requires less operational maintenance than traditional approaches that use IP access or extended access lists. It can be added to the customer's default interface configuration on the ISP's router (remember that this will work only if the router has CEF configured):

```
! Configuration template for customer interfaces
description [enter description of interface]
no ip redirects
no ip direct broadcast
no ip proxy-arp
ip verify unicast reverse-path
bandwidth [bandwidth in kbps]
```

The **ip verify unicast reverse-path** interface command can be added to the same deployment scripts as all the other interface items added when a new customer is installed. Because uRPF dynamically works with the FIB table, the installation engineer has no reason to configure any other access lists. All that needs to be done is to add the customer's route.

uRPF is compatible with other CEF features such as per-packet/per-destination load sharing, CAR/QPPB, WCCPv2, and BGP policy accounting. uRPF was first supported in IOS Software Release 11.1(17)CC CEF images on the RSP 7000, 7200, and 7500 platforms. It is not supported in any IOS Software Release 11.2 or 11.3 images, but it has since been deployed on all releases of IOS Software from 12.0 that support CEF. This includes everything from the largest routers to network access servers (cable, xDSL, and dialup) and the smallest CPE devices.

RPF Configuration Details (as of IOS Software Version 12.0(10)S1)

To use uRPF, enable CEF switching or CEF distributed switching in the router. There is no need to configure the input interface for CEF switching. This is because uRPF has been implemented as a search through the FIB using the source IP address. As long as CEF is running on the router, individual interfaces can be configured with other switching modes. RPF is an input-side function that is enabled on an interface or subinterface supporting any type of encapsulation and that operates on IP packets received by the router.

WARNING   It is very important for CEF to be turned on globally in the router. RPF will not work without CEF.

Configure RPF on the interface using the following interface command syntax:

```
[no] ip verify unicast reverse-path [ACL]
```

For example, do this on a leased-line aggregation router:

```
ip cef
! or "ip cef distributed" for an RSP+VIP based box
!
interface serial 5/0/0
  ip verify unicast reverse-path
```

As another example, the AS 5800 supports CEF in IOS Software Release 12.0. The **interface group-async** command makes it even easier to apply uRPF on all the dialup ports:

```
ip cef
!
interface Group-Async1
  ip verify unicast reverse-path
```

Use the command **show cef interface** *interface* to verify that RPF is operational:

```
Excalabur#sh cef inter serial 2/0/0
Serial2/0/0 is up (if_number 8)

  Internet address is 169.223.10.2/30
  ICMP redirects are never sent
  Per packet loadbalancing is disabled          ┌────────────────────────┐
  IP unicast RPF check is enabled ───────────────│  Unicast RPF Enabled   │
  Inbound access list is not set                 └────────────────────────┘
  Outbound access list is not set
```

```
Interface is marked as point to point interface
Packets switched to this interface on linecard are dropped to next slow path
Hardware idb is Serial2/0/0
Fast switching type 4, interface type 6
IP Distributed CEF switching enabled
IP LES Feature Fast switching turbo vector
IP Feature CEF switching turbo vector
Input fast flags 0x40, Output fast flags 0x0, ifindex 7(7)
Slot 2 Slot unit 0 VC -1
Transmit limit accumulator 0x48001A02 (0x48001A02)
IP MTU 1500
```

Use **show ip interface** *interface* to find specific drops on a interface (as of IOS Software Release 12.0(10)S1):

```
Excalabur#sh ip inter fastEthernet 4/1/0
FastEthernet4/1/0 is up, line protocol is up
  .
  .
  .
Unicast RPF ACL 100
55 unicast RPF drops
0 unicast RPF suppressed drops
```

A counter is maintained to count the number of discards because of RPF. The value of the counter is displayed as part of the output from the command:

```
show ip traffic
```

The RPF drop counter is included in the IP statistics section:

```
ISP-LAB-7505-3#sh ip traffic
IP statistics:
  Rcvd:  1471590 total, 887368 local destination
         0 format errors, 0 checksum errors, 301274 bad hop count
         0 unknown protocol, 0 not a gateway
         0 security failures, 0 bad options, 0 with options
  Opts:  0 end, 0 nop, 0 basic security, 0 loose source route
         0 timestamp, 0 extended security, 0 record route
         0 stream ID, 0 strict source route, 0 alert, 0 other
  Frags: 0 reassembled, 0 timeouts, 0 couldn't reassemble
         0 fragmented, 0 couldn't fragment
  Bcast: 205233 received, 0 sent
  Mcast: 463292 received, 462118 sent
  Sent:  990158 generated, 282938 forwarded
  Drop:  3 encapsulation failed, 0 unresolved, 0 no adjacency
         0 no route, 0 unicast RPF, 0 forced drop
                    ^^^^^^^^^^^^^^
```

ACL Option (added in IOS Software Release 12.0(10)S1)[12]

The optional ACL parameter to the command can be used to control the exact behavior when the received frame fails the source IP address check.

The ACL can be either a standard or an extended IP access list:[13]

```
<1-99>       IP standard access list
<100-199>    IP extended access list
<1300-1999>  IP standard access list (expanded range)
<2000-2699>  IP extended access list (expanded range)
```

If an ACL is specified, when (and only when) a packet fails a uRPF check the ACL is checked to see if the packet should be dropped (using a deny ACL) or forwarded (using a permit ACL). In both cases, the packet is counted as before. ACL logging (**log** and **log-input**) and match counts operate as normal—for example:

```
ip cef distributed
!
interface ethernet 0/1/1
 ip address 192.168.200.1 255.255.255.0
 ip verify unicast reverse-path 197
!
access-list 197 permit ip 192.168.200.0 0.0.0.255 any log-input
```

Frames sourced from 192.168.200.10 arriving at Ethernet 0/1/1 are forwarded (because of **permit**), logged by the ACL, and counted per interface.

Frames sourced from 192.168.201.100 arriving at Ethernet 0/1/1 are dropped (because of **deny**), logged by the ACL, and counted per interface and globally.

Counting is seen per interface:

```
Router> show ip interface ethernet 0/1/1 | include RPF
 Unicast RPF ACL 197
 1 unicast RPF drop
 1 unicast RPF suppressed drop
```

Counting also is seen globally:

```
Router> show ip traffic | include RPF
 0 no route, 1 unicast RPF, 0 forced drop
```

In addition, counting is seen per ACL:

```
Router> show access-lists
Extended IP access list 197
    permit ip 192.168.200.0 0.0.0.255 any log-input (100 match)
```

uRPF's ACL feature has two primary functions. The first and obvious function is to allow for exceptions. Some networks might need to get through the uRPF check, so the ACL allows a bypass technique. The second function is to identify spoof packets. uRPF will not send any notifications of which packets it is dropping. Counters will increment, so the operator will notice excessive uRPF drops. If the operator wants to question what is being dropped, an ACL can be introduced to determine whether the drops are valid (spoofed source addresses) or in error (valid packets being dropped). In the following example, uRPF applies each packet that fails the reverse patch forwarding check to ACL 171. The ACL still drops the packet, but it also logs the packet in the ACL counters and the log file on the processor or VIP/line card.

```
interface ethernet 0/1/1
  ip address 192.168.200.1 255.255.255.0
  ip verify unicast reverse-path 171
  !
access-list 171 deny icmp any any echo log-input
access-list 171 deny icmp any any echo-reply log-input
access-list 171 deny udp any any eq echo log-input
access-list 171 deny udp any eq echo any log-input
access-list 171 deny tcp any any established log-input
access-list 171 deny tcp any any log-input
access-list 171 deny ip any any log-input

Excalabur#sh controllers vip 4 logging
show logging from Slot 4:
  .
  .
4d00h: %SEC-6-IPACCESSLOGNP: list 171 denied 0 20.1.1.1 -> 255.255.255.255, 1 packet
  .
```

uRPF's Debug Options

Dropped uRPF packets can be captured with a **debug ip cef drops rpf** *acl* statement. This debug option was added only into IOS Software Release 12.0S and was not part of the original 11.1CC implementation. The way that this uRPF debug tool is used depends on whether the router is a VIP or non-VIP platform. On Cisco 7500s with VIP cards, debug results do not leave the VIP. To see the results of a debug on a VIP, use an ACL on **debug ip cef drops rpf** with the **log-input** function applied to the ACL. You then can use **show controllers vip** *number* **logging** to see the results of the debug. Example 4-3 provides an example of **show controllers vip 1 logging**, together with the **debug ip cef drops rpf 88** command.

Example 4-3 *Using* **show controller vip1 logging** *on a Cisco 7500 VIP Card*

```
Thundershild#config
Configuring from terminal, memory, or network [terminal]?
Enter configuration commands, one per line.  End with CNTL/Z.
Thundershild(config)#
Thundershild(config)#access-list 88 permit 1.19.1.4 0.0.0.0 log
Thundershild(config)#exit
Thundershild#debug ip cef drops rpf 88
Thundershild#sh controller vip 1 logging

Syslog logging: enabled (0 messages dropped, 0 flushes, 0 overruns)
    Console logging: level debugging, 59 messages logged
    Monitor logging: level debugging, 0 messages logged
    Buffer logging: level debugging, 65 messages logged

Log Buffer (8192 bytes):
smallest_local_pool_entries = 192, global particles = 618
```

Example 4-3 *Using* **show controller vip1 logging** *on a Cisco 7500 VIP Card (Continued)*

```
highest_local_visible_bandwidth = 100000
.
.
.
2d16h: CEF-Drop: Packet from 1.19.1.4 via FastEthernet1/0/0 -- unicast rpf check
2d16h: CEF-Drop: Packet from 1.19.1.4 via FastEthernet1/0/0 -- unicast rpf check
2d16h: CEF-Drop: Packet from 1.19.1.4 via FastEthernet1/0/0 -- unicast rpf check
2d16h: CEF-Drop: Packet from 1.19.1.4 via FastEthernet1/0/0 -- unicast rpf check
2d16h: CEF-Drop: Packet from 1.19.1.4 via FastEthernet1/0/0 -- unicast rpf check
.
.
.
Thundershild#no debug ip cef drops rpf 88
```

WARNING	Care must be taken with any use of the debug feature on a production router. The amount of debug information easily overwhelms the capability of the console and logging functions of a router. This is especially true when the router is handling several tens of megabytes of DoS traffic.

Routing Tables Requirements

uRPF needs accurate information in the FIB to work properly. The fundamental requirement for uRPF to work commonly is stated by Cisco staff in this way: "[A] valid and preferred path must exist in the forwarding table that matches the source address to the input interface."

This does not mean that the router must have the entire Internet Route Table. The amount of routing information needed in the CEF tables depends on where uRPF is configured and what functions the router plays in the ISP's network. For example, a router that is a leased-line aggregation router for customers needs only the information based on the static routes introduced into the IGP or iBGP (depending on which technique is used in the network). uRPF would be configured on the customers' interfaces—hence, the requirement for minimal routing information. In another scenario, a single-homed ISP can place uRPF on the gateway link to the Internet. The full Internet Route Table would be required in this case. This would help protect the ISP from external DoS attacks that use addresses not in the Internet Route Table.

uRPF Exceptions

Some source IP addresses should be allowed through the uRPF filtering (see Example 4-4). uRPF will now allow packets with 0.0.0.0 source and 255.255.255.255 destination to pass so that BOOTP and DHCP still can function. This feature (CSCdk80591) was added from IOS Software Release 12.0(3.05) (but is not in 11.1CC). Also, if the destination address is multicast, uRPF exempts those packets.

Example 4-4 *uRPF Algorithm as of IOS Software 12.0(9)S*

```
lookup source address in forwarding database
if the source address is reachable via the source interface
  pass the packet
else if the source is 0.0.0.0 and destination is a 255.255.255.255
  /* BOOTP and DHCP */
  pass the packet
else if destination is multicast
  pass the packet
else
  drop the packet
```

BCP 38 Implementation with uRPF Strict Mode

uRPF's key BCP 38 implementation principles follow:

- A route must exist in the FIB matching the prefix to the interface. This can be done through a connected interface, a static route, a **network** statement (BGP, OSPF, RIPv2, and so on), or dynamic routing updates.

- Traffic from the interface must match the prefixes for the interface.

- If there are multiple entries for the prefix in the route tables, the prefix local to the router implementing uRPF must be preferred (using BGP weight with multihomed customers).

Given these three implementation principles, uRPF becomes a tool that ISPs can use not only for their customers, but also for their downstream ISPs—even if the downstream ISP has other connections to the Internet.

uRPF Strict Mode with a Single-Homed Leased-Line Customers

Single-homed customers are by far the vast majority of leased-line customers. For these customers, uRPF can be part of the default interface configuration applied when the circuit first is installed. Leased-line customer aggregation routers are ideal with single-homed customers.[14] In this topology, the customer aggregation routers need not have the full Internet Route Table; they simply need the information on the routing prefixes assigned to the customer.[15] Hence, information introduced into the IGP or iBGP (depending on the way you add customer routes into your network) would be enough for uRPF to do its job.

Using Figure 4-23, a typical configuration on the ISP's router would be as follows (assuming that CEF is turned on):

```
interface loopback 0
  description Loopback interface on Gateway Router 2
  ip address 215.17.3.1 255.255.255.255
  no ip redirects
  no ip directed-broadcast
  no ip proxy-arp
!
interface Serial 5/0
  description 128K HDLC link to Galaxy Publications Ltd [galpub1] WT50314E R5-0
  bandwidth 128
  ip unnumbered loopback 0
  ip verify unicast reverse-path  ! Unicast RPF activated here
  no ip redirects
  no ip directed-broadcast
  no ip proxy-arp
!
ip route 215.34.10.0 255.255.252.0 Serial 5/0
```

Figure 4-23 *Single-Homed Customer uRPF for Ingress Filtering*

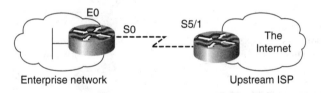

uRPF Strict Mode with Multihomed Leased-Line Customers (One ISP)

uRPF strict mode actually works with multihomed leased-line customers! It works with the asymmetric traffic flows between the customer and the ISP! It is a common myth perpetuated by many people that uRPF does not work when you have multihoming or when you have asymmetric traffic flows.

Engineers who jump to that conclusion tend to not think through the problem or do not have time to think about the problem. There is also some lack of understanding about how the RIB and the FIB interact with today's best-path forwarding routing. uRPF works with best-path forwarding. For uRPF to work correctly, the one path in the FIB must be the path that points back out of the interface closest to the multihomed customer. So, for uRPF to work for multihomed customers where traffic trends to be asymmetric, the FIB must align with how the customer is connected to the router. And that is easier to achieve than is commonly perceived in the industry today.

Details Behind uRPF, Multihomed Customers, and Asymmetrical Routing

Understanding what is happening with routing on the Internet is essential to the configuration of uRPF strict mode on multihomed leased-line customers. For starters, realize that asymmetrical routing is very common for a multihomed leased-line customer (see Figure 4-24). When traffic travels over the Internet asymmetrically, it usually means that packets will take one path to get to the destination and another path to return to the source from the destination. TCP/IP, of course, works perfectly well with asymmetrical routing. If multiple paths are used to get to the destination and cause the packets to arrive out of order, TCP reassembles the packets in their proper order. Asymmetrical traffic flows are normal and happen all the time in the Internet today; in the vast majority of cases, asymmetric flows do not have any perceivable impact on the effectiveness of the client/server communications. Because it is so common, asymmetrical routing has been used as the reason why uRPF will not work on multihomed customer connections.

Figure 4-24 *Typical Asymmetrical Routing Example*

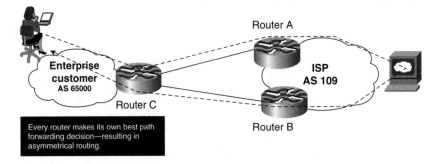

Routing on today's Internet is based on the concept of best-path forwarding. Best-path forwarding starts in the router's RIB. The RIB receives routing updates from the routing protocols running in the router. These, in turn, receive their updates from other routers in the network (their neighbors). With multiple routing updates from multiple routers, the RIB might have a situation in which there are multiple updates on the same prefix. When this happens, the RIB has a means of figuring out which of the multiple entries for this prefix is the best path. This best path is submitted to the FIB for consideration (see Figure 4-25). The result is that the router has selected the best path for forwarding a packet from the inbound interface.

Figure 4-25 *Best-Path Forwarding Is Why We Have Asymmetrical Routing and Impacts on uRPF Deployment*

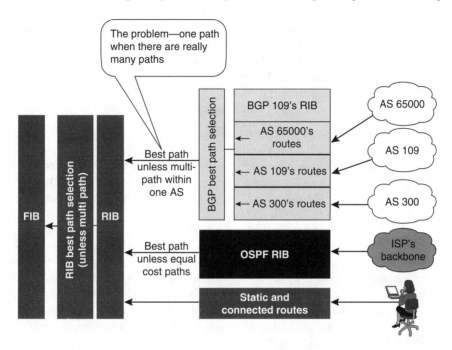

Every router on the Internet makes this best-path decision. Because these decisions are done from a point of view of the router's position in the Internet, the resulting best path might not match what the best path is on other routers. Routing protocols are created with the means to ensure that these independent best-path decisions do not cause routing loops.[10] Although routing loops are not a problem, different best-path decisions might be a problem for a network. As a result, some routing protocols have a means of influencing the best-path decision across a network bounded by an autonomous network. For example, BGP's Local Preference attribute allows values to be placed on prefix updates. These values can be used to ensure that every BGP RIB inside the AS selects the same best path for that prefix. So the best-path results are effective network-wide instead of on just one router.

NOTE   Routing loops occur when two or more routers select the best path back to the other. This causes packets to ping pong back and forth until the packet's TTL times out and drops the packet.

BGP attributes such as Local Preference allow the ISP to control the flow of traffic between its network and other providers' networks. It does not allow them to effectively influence the best-path decisions of other networks. So, in one common form of asymmetrical routing, each ISP makes its own best-path decision. At this time, the tools for one ISP to affect the best-path decisions of another ISP are coarse and are not guaranteed to work.[16] Because each router, and perhaps each ISP, is making its own best-path decision and little can be done to effectively influence this on an Internet-wide scale, asymmetric traffic flow is the result. This affects where uRPF can be applied in the network.

When a router receives a packet from another router, it does not care which interface it came in on. The router examines the destination address, looks up the route in the FIB, and forwards the packet out another interface. With uRPF turned on, the router does need to care which interface the packet was received from. To make this work, the RIB needs to provide information to the FIB to allow uRPF to work. Working through an example is the best way to demonstrate how this applies. Figure 4-26 shows a multihomed customer using a combination of split advertisement and advanced communities to traffic-engineer the network. This is an effective multihoming technique that provides good traffic engineering control to the customer while keeping the ISP's operational overhead for supporting the multihomed customer to a minimum. The RIB on Router A receives the advertisement from Router C for the two prefixes. The route maps used for RFC 1998-style community usage set the local preference for these prefixes in the ISP's network.[17] In this way, the local preference values are use to determine which of the multiple copies of the route—say, 169.21.0.0/17—is sent to the FIB.

Figure 4-26 *BGP Local Preference Affects Traffic Flow with Multihomed Customers*

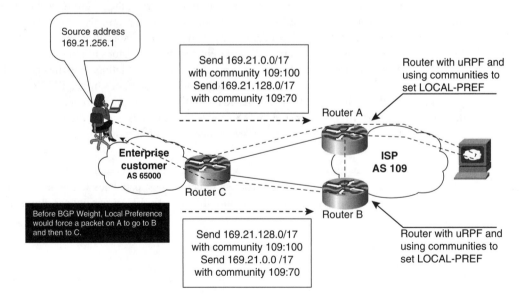

NOTE	In split advertisement, a multihomed customer splits its IPv4 address block into two parts. Each part is advertised out each of the multihomed links with different attributes applied. These attributes could be BGP communities that affect local prefs (RFC 1998 and variants), the BGP community **no-advertise**, AS path prepend, or other BGP-based traffic-engineering techniques. Split advertisement ensures that the entire address block is reachable in case one of the links goes down.

In this example, the customer is using per-prefix load balancing to send traffic to the Internet. So packets arriving on Router A could be from the 169.21.0.0/17 block or the 169.21.128.0/17 block. If a packet bound for 169.21.128.0/17 arrives on Router A, Router A would forward the packet based on the prefix's local preference value, resulting in the packet being sent to Router B and then to Router C. This adds an extra hop but has no perceivable impact on the performance of the packet flow.

However, this will impact uRPF's capability to operate as expected. Because the ISP has no control over the customer's use of per-packet or per-flow load balancing, there can be no effective or scalable way to force all 169.21.0.0/17 packets out one link or 169.21.128.0/17 packets out the other link.[18] So the packets arriving on Router A from Router C could be from any address in the 169.21.0.0/16 address block. Yet uRPF on Router A would see packets in the 169.21.0.0/17 coming from Router C as being valid. Packets from 169.21.128.0/17 would get dropped. A modification to the configuration on Router A is needed to ensure that packets from any address in the /16 would be passed by uRPF.

Figure 4-27 illustrates the solution. The BGP option **weight** overrides the local preference value on the router. It affects only that one router and the route received from the BGP neighbor. Local preference still works as normal in the network. With the BGP **weight** command applied to the BGP session between Router C and Router A, both 169.21.0.0/17 and 169.21.128.0/17 will be submitted to the FIB as their best paths are directly to Router C (versus through Router B for the 169.21.128.0/17 with local preference applied). This will allow any packet from 169.21.0.0/16 to pass through uRPF strict mode as it was turned on Router A's interface that connected to Router C.

The operational impact of using BGP weight on the configuration is minimal. The "extra" hop is eliminated if a packet that should go to Router B arrives on Router A. So the customer might like this added efficiency. The addition to the configuration is minimal because it is one line added to the BGP configuration—easily scripted. The only gotcha is educating the customer and ensuring that he knows how multihoming and this technique work. Of course that is the purpose of this book—helping ISPs and customers to ISPs do the right thing and understand why they are doing it. Chapter 5, "Operational Practices," covers multihoming examples and recommended practices in detail.

Figure 4-27 *BGP Weight Applied to the Customer Peering Allows uRPF to Work*

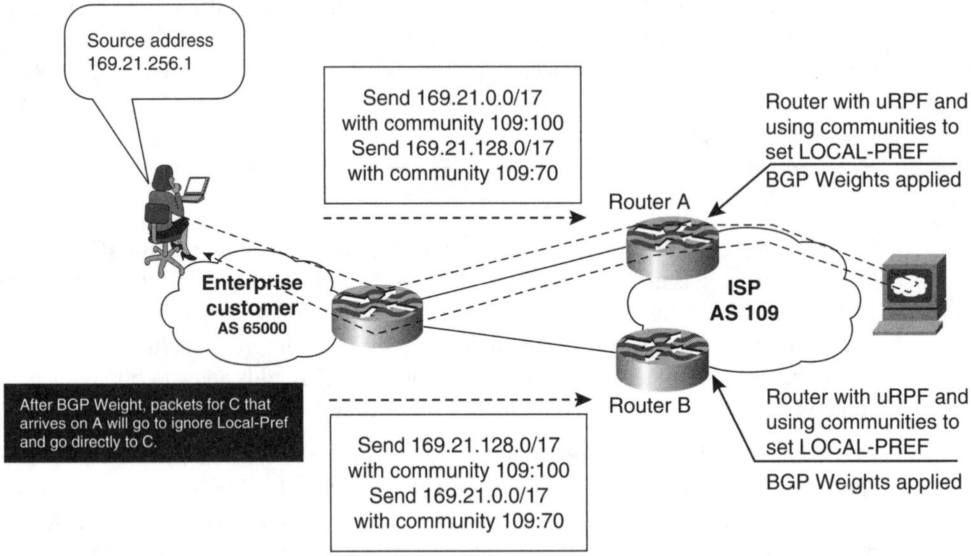

In summary, BGP weight ensures that the route local to the router is the preferred path. BGP weight is local to the router and easily is configured on the BGP neighbor configuration. The BGP weight prefers the local connection even though BGP local preference is pointing the best path to the other multihomed router. Setting the BGP weight has minimal, if any, effect on the traffic flows between the ISP and the multihomed customer. Yet it is enough to align the FIB so that uRPF can accomplish BCP 38 filtering on multihomed customers with asymmetrical routing.

Working Example of uRPF, Multihomed Customers, and Asymmetrical Routing

In this example, depicted in Figure 4-28, the enterprise customer of the ISP is multihomed into two different routers. BGP is used with a private ASN assigned by the ISP. The enterprise's IP address block would be allocated from the ISP or from an IP registry. As the route is advertised into the ISP's routers, an internal BGP weight is applied. This ensures that if there is a tie between two identical prefixes, the one directly from Router C will be preferred on the local router and entered into the FIB.

Figure 4-28 *Multihomed Leased-Line Customer and uRPF*

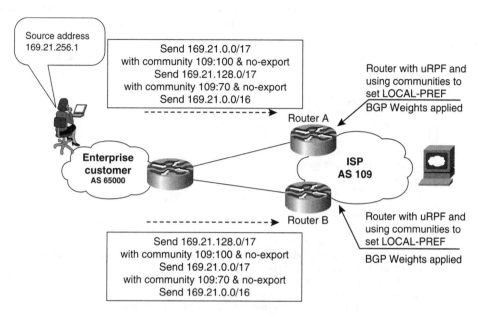

In Example 4-5, the customer divides its allocated /16 address block into two /17s, allowing for some level of traffic engineering. The customer advertises the /16 and two /17s out both links (required to have uRPF work on the ISP's ingress). Preference is communicated to the ISP through BGP communities. The ISP uses the communities advertised from the customer to set the BGP local preference of the /17, making one preferred over the other.[19] Both /17s have the BGP community **no-export** to ensure that they stay inside their upstream ISPs.

Some basic restrictions govern applying uRPF to these multihomed customers:

- Customers should not be multihomed to the same router. This is common sense—it breaks the purpose of building a redundant service for the customer. If the same router is used, the circuits should be configured for parallel paths (using something along the lines of CEF load balancing). uRPF works with parallel path circuits between two routers.

- Customers need to ensure that the packets flowing up the link (out to the Internet) match the prefixes advertised out the link. Otherwise, uRPF will filter those packets. Advertising the same routes out both links is the best way to make sure that this will happen.

- The traffic-engineering trick of splitting the IP address space in half, with each half advertising one link, cannot be used. For example, the enterprise customer cannot advertise 169.23.0.0/17 and 169.23.0.0/16 out one upstream link and 169.23.128.0/17 and 169.23.0.0/16 out the other link. This would break uRPF—unless an ACL is applied to uRPF to allow for this case. The recommended technique is highlighted in Example 4-5 using BGP communities to set local preference.[20]

Example 4-5   *Multihomed uRPF*

```
Router A

interface serial 1/0/1
 description Link to Acme Computer's Router C
 ip address 192.168.3.2 255.255.255.252
 ip verify unicast reverse-path
 no ip redirects
 no ip directed-broadcast
 no ip proxy-arp
 ip route-cache distributed

router bgp 109
 .
 neighbor 192.168.10.3 remote-as 65000
 neighbor 192.168.10.3 description Multihomed Customer - Acme Computers
 neighbor 192.168.10.3 update-source Loopback0
 neighbor 192.168.10.3 send-community
 neighbor 192.168.10.3 soft-reconfiguration inbound
 neighbor 192.168.10.3 route-map set-customer-local-pref in
 neighbor 192.168.10.3 weight 255
 .

ip route 192.168.10.3 255.255.255.255 serial 1/0/1
ip bgp-community new-format


Router B

interface serial 6/1/1
 description Link to Acme Computer's Router C
 ip address 192.168.3.6 255.255.255.252
 ip verify unicast reverse-path
 no ip redirects
 no ip directed-broadcast
 no ip proxy-arp
 ip route-cache distributed

router bgp 109
 .
 neighbor 192.168.10.3 remote-as 65000
 neighbor 192.168.10.3 description Multihomed Customer - Acme Computers
 neighbor 192.168.10.3 update-source Loopback0
 neighbor 192.168.10.3 send-community
 neighbor 192.168.10.3 soft-reconfiguration inbound
```

Example 4-5   *Multihomed uRPF (Continued)*

```
 neighbor 192.168.10.3 route-map set-customer-local-pref in
 neighbor 192.168.10.3 weight 255
 .

 ip route 192.168.10.3 255.255.255.255 serial 6/1/1
 ip bgp-community new-format

Router C
 !
 interface serial 1/0
  description Link to Upstream Router A
  ip address 192.168.3.1 255.255.255.252
  ip verify unicast reverse-path
  no ip redirects
  no ip directed-broadcast
  no ip proxy-arp
  ip load-sharing per-destination
  ip route-cache distributed


 interface serial 1/1
  description Link to Upstream ISP Router B
  ip address 192.168.3.5 255.255.255.252
  ip verify unicast reverse-path
  no ip redirects
  no ip directed-broadcast
  no ip proxy-arp
  ip load-sharing per-destination
  ip route-cache distributed


 router bgp 65000
  no synchronization
  network 169.21.0.0
  network 169.21.0.0 mask 255.255.128.0
  network 169.21.128.0 mask 255.255.128.0
  neighbor 171.70.18.100 remote-as 109
  neighbor 171.70.18.100 description Upstream Connection #1
  neighbor 171.70.18.100 update-source Loopback0
  neighbor 171.70.10.100 send-community
  neighbor 171.70.18.100 soft-reconfiguration inbound
  neighbor 171.70.18.100 route-map Router-A-Community out
  neighbor 171.70.18.200 remote-as 109
  neighbor 171.70.18.200 description Upstream Connection #2
  neighbor 171.70.18.200 update-source Loopback0
  neighbor 171.70.18.200 send-community
  neighbor 171.70.18.200 soft-reconfiguration inbound
  neighbor 171.70.18.200 route-map Router-B-Community out
  maximum-paths 2
  no auto-summary
```

continues

Example 4-5 *Multihomed uRPF (Continued)*

```
!
ip route 169.21.0.0 0.0.255.255 Null 0
ip route 169.21.0.0 0.0.127.255 Null 0
ip route 169.21.128.0 0.0.127.255 Null 0
ip route 171.70.18.100 255.255.255.255 serial 1/0
ip route 171.70.18.200 255.255.255.255 serial 1/1
ip bgp-community new-format
!
access-list 50 permit 169.21.0.0 0.0.127.255
access-list 51 permit 169.21.128.0 0.0.127.255
!
route-map Router-A-Community permit 10
 match ip address 51
 set community 109:70 no-export
!
route-map Router-A-Community permit 20
 match ip address 50
 set community 109:100 no-export
!
route-map Router-A-Community permit 30
!
route-map Router-B-Community permit 10
 match ip address 50
 set community 109:70 no-export
!
route-map Router-B-Community permit 20
 match ip address 51
 set community 109:100 no-export
!
route-map Router-B-Community permit 30
```

Multihomed Leased-Line Customers (Two ISPs)

uRPF also works with a multihomed customer that has a connection to two different ISPs. Figure 4-29 shows how the downstream customer (enterprise or ISP) connects to two upstream ISPs. These two ISPs, Alpha and Beta, interconnect with each other at various places in the world (combining private peering, IXP peering, and transit). Therefore, each ISP will have two BGP entries for the downstream customer's prefix. Yet each ISP would select the shortest-path entry from the BGP table as the best path, enabling uRFP to work.

BGP weight should be used in Routers A and B for all the prefixes being advertised from Router C. This is necessary to provide a safeguard against AS path prepending. It is normal practice for multihomed customers to use the AS path-prepending technique to affect the balance of the incoming traffic flows. In some cases the prepending of ASNs would break the uRPF. For example, the downstream customer prepends enough ASNs to its advertisements to Router A that Router A's best path to Router C would be through Router B. This means that the Router A–C forwarding path actually would select a Router A–B–C forwarding path. uRPF would not have a valid path for source addresses coming up the Router C–A link, effectively blocking the downstream customer's outbound traffic on the Router C–A link. A BGP weight (see Example 4-5) applied on Routers A and B would override the local effects of AS path prepends.

Note that this is a case in which the customer's traffic would be asymmetric through the two upstream connections. Router C would forward traffic based on the shortest-path information provided by Routers A and B. Some traffic flows would exit Router C–A link yet return through the Router C–B link (and vice versa). In both cases of asymmetrical flows, uRPF will block unauthorized traffic from the enterprise customer's network.

Figure 4-29 *Enterprise Customer Multihomed to Two ISPs*

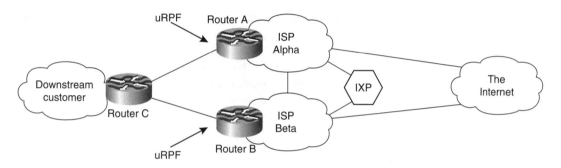

Committed Access Rate to Rate-Limit or Drop Packets[21]

The use of a QoS tool such as CAR as a security tool is a result of the types of recent attacks on the Internet. In 1997, a new generation of attacks was launched on the Internet: the smurf attack. This is a network-level DoS attack named after its exploit program. A smurf attack is built around ICMP echo packets; the other common attack is fraggle, which uses UDP echo packets in the same manner as the ICMP echo packets. Fraggle was a simple rewrite of the smurf program.

The Smurf Attack

The principle behind a smurf attack is surprisingly simple. A perpetrator sends a large amount of ICMP echo (ping) traffic to specific IP broadcast addresses. All the ICMP echo packets have the spoofed source address of a victim. If the routing device delivering traffic to those broadcast addresses performs the IP broadcast–to–Layer 2 translation, the ICMP broadcast function will be forwarded to all hosts on the Layer 2 medium (see Figure 4-30).

Each host on that IP network will take the ICMP echo request and reply to it with an echo reply. This multiplies the inbound traffic by the number of hosts responding. On a multi-access broadcast network, potentially hundreds of machines could be replying to each packet, resulting in what is called an attack from a "smurf amplifier network."

The systems most commonly hit by these types of attacks are Internet Relay Chat (IRC) servers, specific Web sites, and their providers. Two parties are hurt by this attack:

- The intermediary (broadcast) devices, called the amplifiers
- The spoofed address target, the victim

The victim is the target of the large amount of traffic that the amplifiers generate.

Consider a scenario that paints a dramatic picture of the dangerous nature of this attack. Assume a co-location switched network with 100 hosts and an attacker with a T1 circuit available. The attacker sends, say, a 768 Kbps stream of ICMP echo (ping) packets, with a spoofed source address of the victim, to the broadcast address of the bounce or amplifier site. These ping packets hit the bounce site's broadcast network of 100 hosts; each host responds to the packet, creating 100 ping replies outbound. If you multiply the bandwidth, you will see that 76.8 Mbps is generated outbound from the bounce site. Because of the spoofed source address of the originating packets, these reply packets are directed toward the victim (see Figure 4-30.)

Figure 4-30 *How Smurf Uses Amplifiers*

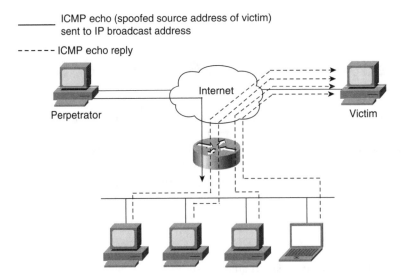

This scenario demonstrates two things:

- The amplifier site loses a large amount of outbound bandwidth to the ICMP packets being used for the smurf attack. If the site does not have 76.8 Mbps of bandwidth, its links will go into saturation and it will be the victim of a very effective DoS attack on its services.

- If the amplifier site has sufficient outbound bandwidth, the victim will be pounded by 76.8 Mbps of inbound traffic. If the victim doesn't have sufficient inbound bandwidth, its link will go into saturation and will become unusable, and its upstream ISP's aggregation router that it connects to will spend a large amount of time trying to deal with the excess traffic that won't fit through the customer's circuit.

This situation can be made worse if the perpetrator has identified more than one smurf amplifier site. This then becomes a distributed DoS attack, which is harder to track and affects more ISPs along the packet path.

Consider the second scenario. The perpetrator has a simple dialup connection available and is going to carry out a DoS attack on a particular Web site. Analog dialups have a maximum of 33.6 Kbps available for outbound bandwidth, so assume that the attacker will use all of this for the attack. The attacker also has identified 20 smurf amplifier networks around the Internet. If each amplifier network has 100 hosts on it, the attacker can multiply his outbound packet flow 2000 times, or convert a 33.6 Kbps ping flood into 67.2 Mbps. Also, because 20 smurf amplifier sites have been identified around the Internet, this becomes much harder for the Web site owner and the host ISP to actually identify. ISPs are multi-homed to the Internet, and it will look as though there are ping attacks coming in through all upstream connections from all over the Internet. The host ISP will see the affect on all its links (depending on its link capacity), but the impact will be most severe where the Web site connects to the ISP's backbone.

This second scenario demonstrates how dangerous the smurf attack can be even from a "simple" dialup user. And with many countries in the world now actively promoting DSL and cable services, the bandwidths available to the "casual" user are becoming ever greater, so the chances of a serious DoS attack from a relatively inexperienced or low-key source is more likely. (Common origins for DoS attacks in the past have included university computer rooms and other networks with public access and less rigid security than typically found in the corporate environment.

These two scenarios demonstrate how critically important it is for ISPs to do the following:

- Implement uRPF on all their customer connections
- Consider rate-limiting ICMP inbound on their networks
- Make sure that direct broadcasts are turned off on all network links

Failure to do any of these simply contributes to the abuse of resources and facilities by many people on the Internet today.

Rate-Limiting with CAR

It is an inevitable consequence of being part of the Internet that every ISP at some point will experience a DoS attack. It is imperative that ISPs have tools and procedures in place to respond to these DoS attacks, preferably before an attack occurs. CAR is one such tool.

CAR is a functionality that works with Cisco Express Forwarding, found in IOS Software Releases 11.1CC and onward from 12.0. It allows network operators to rate-limit certain types of traffic to specific sources or destinations. The main advantage of CAR is that it can work on packets as they arrive on the router's interface, dropping or rate-limiting the DoS flow before any other packet processing.

The following URLs provide details on CAR:

Committed Access Rate (CAR):
http://www.cisco.com/warp/public/732/Tech/car/index.html

Configuring Committed Access Rate:
http://www.cisco.com/univercd/cc/td/doc/product/software/ios122/122cgcr/fqos_c/fqcprt1/qcfcar.htm

The following are two examples that show how CAR can be used to rate-limit particular types of traffic that should not see high volumes in an ISP network. The first example rate-limits ICMP; the second example rate-limits TCP SYN.

Example 1

An ISP has filtered its IRC server from receiving ICMP echo-reply packets to protect it. Now many attackers are going after the customer's devices to fill some network segments.

The ISP chose to use CAR to limit all ICMP echo and echo-reply traffic received at the borders to 256 Kbps. An example follows:

```
! traffic we want to limit
access-list 102 permit icmp any any echo
access-list 102 permit icmp any any echo-reply
! interface configurations for borders
interface Serial3/0/0
 rate-limit input access-group 102 256000 8000 8000 conform-action transmit exceed-
action drop
```

This limits ICMP echo and echo-reply traffic to 256 Kbps, with a maximum burst of 8000 bytes; all packets exceeding this limit are dropped. Multiple rate-limit commands can be added to an interface to control other kinds of traffic as well.

The command **show interface** *interface-name* **rate-limit** shows the statistics for rate-limiting; **clear counters** *interface-name* clears the statistics for a fresh look.

Example 2

You can use CAR to limit TCP SYN floods to particular hosts, without impeding existing connections. Some attackers have started using very high streams of TCP SYN packets to harm systems.

This example limits TCP SYN packets directed at host 10.0.0.1 to 8 Kbps and allows a maximum burst size of 8000 bytes:

```
! We don't want to limit established TCP sessions -- non-SYN packets
!
access-list 103 deny tcp any host 10.0.0.1 established
!
! We do want to limit the rest of TCP (this really only includes SYNs)
!
access-list 103 permit tcp any host 10.0.0.1
!
! interface configurations for network borders
!
interface Serial3/0/0
 rate-limit input access-group 103 8000 8000 8000 conform-action transmit exceed-
action drop
!
```

ISP CAR Configuration Template

It is recommended that ISPs seriously consider installing a CAR configuration on their border routers to deal with ICMP and TCP SYN attacks. There will be a small overhead to handle this, but the small overhead is better than having the network connectivity disrupted or completely disabled because of a DoS attack. The configuration template might be something like the following:

```
! traffic we want to limit
access-list 102 permit icmp any any echo
access-list 102 permit icmp any any echo-reply
!
access-list 103 deny tcp any any established
access-list 103 permit tcp any any
!
! serial interface configuration
interface Serial3/0/0
 description Link to UPSTREAM A
 rate-limit input access-group 102 256000 8000 8000 conform-action transmit exceed-
action drop
 rate-limit input access-group 103 8000 8000 8000 conform-action transmit exceed-
action drop
!
interface Serial 3/1/0
 description Link to UPSTREAM B
 rate-limit input access-group 102 256000 8000 8000 conform-action transmit exceed-
action drop
 rate-limit input access-group 103 8000 8000 8000 conform-action transmit exceed-
action drop
!
```

The template rate-limits ICMP echo and echo-reply to 256 Kbps and TCP SYN to 8 Kbps. Anyone who implements this template should choose values that are appropriate to circuit capacities and the type of traffic normally expected on the network. The example here is taken from a router that has a 2-Mbps uplink circuit to both its upstreams.

For the previous example, the output from the router might look something like the following:

```
gw#show interface serial 3/0/0 rate-limit
Serial3/0/0 "Link to UPSTREAM A"
    Input
    matches: access-group 103
      params:  8000 bps, 8000 limit, 8000 extended limit
      conformed 275702 packets, 14948676 bytes; action: transmit
      exceeded 0 packets, 0 bytes; action: drop
      last packet: 52ms ago, current burst: 4 bytes
      last cleared 03:29:31 ago, conformed 9000 bps, exceeded 0 bps
    matches: access-group 102
      params:  256000 bps, 8000 limit, 8000 extended limit
      conformed 14017 packets, 4390628 bytes; action: transmit
      exceeded 137 packets, 48783 bytes; action: drop
      last packet: 1624ms ago, current burst: 0 bytes
      last cleared 03:29:20 ago, conformed 2000 bps, exceeded 0 bps
  gw#
```

These corresponding access list hits show

```
gw>sh access-list 102
Extended IP access list 102 (Compiled)
    permit icmp any any echo (1464042 matches)
    permit icmp any any echo-reply (3 matches)
gw>sh access-list 103
Extended IP access list 103 (Compiled)
    deny tcp any any established (1426506 matches)
    permit tcp any any (278199 matches)
  gw>
```

This shows all the packets that have matched the access list and to which the rate-limiting parameters would have been applied. The **show interface** excerpt previously showed that 137 packets have exceed the 256 Kbps rate set in the **rate-limit** command, indicating quite a large number of incoming ICMP echoes on the inbound interface.

Smurf Defense Summary

This chapter has discussed several effective tools for minimizing smurf attacks on the Internet. The top three passive tools are listed here. You should review each section for details—each is strongly recommended for consideration in any ISP network.

- Interface services (no IP directed broadcast)
- Egress and ingress filtering (including uRPF)
- CAR

Active defenses are tools, techniques, or procedures executed during attacks. They are used to limit or block the attack in progress. In many instances, these tools will have an effect on other Internet applications and services, yet the trade-off is between no Internet services and limited disruption. It is highly recommended that the ISP document and train staff on the use of these tools. That way, the ISP's NOC can quickly respond to an attack in progress.

Cisco IOS Software has security tools to cover the broad range of networking, and many new security tools are being added as the industry demands them. Many of these tools are situation-specific, with some being written to help enterprise networks and others being more suited for ISP environment. CAR is perhaps the best tool to help as an active smurf defense; examples of CAR configuration in a passive situation have been described already. To use CAR as an active tool, additional instances and access lists can be added as required along the lines of the previous examples.

Reacting to Security Incidents

Based on the evolving security threats in the Internet, what should the ISP's objective be? The ISP has several decisions to make, some short-term, medium-term, and long-term. This section looks at some of the approaches that the ISP should consider.

In all cases, the first policy decision must about what to do in the immediate situation. It can be either to drop it, rate-limit it, or do nothing at all. There is an immediate threat to the network, so the ISP must react immediately to protect the integrity of its own business. Often this decision is made by looking at the nature of the attack, deciding whether there will be an immediate impact on the network, and then reacting by blocking the attack, rate-limiting the packets causing the attack, or simply deciding that the attack won't impact the network.

Approaches

This section describes the approach that all ISPs should consider for their overall security architecture. Most of the tools described in this chapter are passive tools. When configured, they will help prevent security problems from happening and will make it more difficult to cause mischief on the ISP's network.

The distinct phases of dealing with a security incident are the following:

- **Phase 1: Preparation**—The most critical phase covers all the configurations, procedures, data collection, exercises, and other factors that prepare an ISP's operations and security team for handling a security incident.

- **Phase 2: Identification**—This triggers a security incident. Events such as those from monitoring tools that show an increase of activity, a customer calling the NOC, or the identification of an attack are the first step in the incidence response.

- **Phase 3: Classification**—Know thy enemy. Classification digs into what type of attack is being made against a target on the network. This understanding is essential to tracing back and reacting to the incident.

- **Phase 4: Trace back**—Tracing the incident to an entry point into the ISP or across the Internet to the actual source is an essential part of incident response. The reaction phase depends on the results of a traceback through the network.

- **Phase 5: Reaction**—Reaction is what you do to resolve the attack. It could be as simple as choosing not to react or as extreme as unplugging a connection to a network (customer or peer).

These five phases allow for a hierarchy of what an ISP should do to minimize the effects of any security incident.

Some Examples

The first policy decision that an ISP will need to make is what to do with the packets when an attack is identified. When DDoS attacks are identified and classified, the ISP must make a decision. Classification will provide the DDoS flow's source IP addresses—hence, a target for filtering. However, do you filter all the packets from that source address, filter some of the packets from that source address, or just rate-limit the attack from that address?

The source IP addresses from DDoS attacks can have one of four characteristics. The characteristic of the source will be a factor in the decision on coarse packet drops, detailed packet drops, rate limiting, or no action at all.

- **Spoofed RFC 1918 and special-use addresses**—These are the easiest addresses to spot and drop. They are well known, are not in the global Internet Route Table, and easily can be dropped with passive packet-filtering tools. Many networks have ingress/egress packet filters that block these packets from propagating through the Internet. Unfortunately, these passive packet filters are not ubiquitous. So sometimes an ISP will see DDoS attacks with these addresses. The reaction decision is easy: Drop these.

- **Spoofed addresses that are not in the global Internet Route Table**—Cyberpunks have found ways to get around the well-known packet filters that drop well-known RFC 1918 and special-use addresses. The most common technique is to use addresses that have not been allocated to any ISP or added to the global Internet Route Table. RIRs allocate blocks of IP addresses to ISPs and subregistries. These RIR allocations come from delegations of authority from the Internet Assigned Numbers Authority (IANA). The list of IPv4 address blocks that have not been activated is easily accessible at http://www.isi.edu/in-notes/iana/assignments/ipv4-address-space. This makes it easy for someone to create an attack with spoofed addresses based on this list. Because these addresses are not in the global Internet Route Table, a simple check in the forwarding table easily can aid in their identification. Some tools, such as uRPF, make this check straightforward, making it harder for these attacks to be successful. The reaction when faced with these sorts of attacks is to drop the packets.

- **Valid address from a DDoS agent**—Some attackers will sacrifice the DDoS agent that they have penetrated to achieve their objectives. In this case, the source address will be the actual address of the penetrated system. For some attacks (such as TCP SYN and ACK attacks), these are easy to identify and classify. Other attacks, designed to overwhelm the target with valid traffic, are not as easy to identify and classify, especially when the attacks are based on simple HTTP **GET** request. When a particular source address has been classified as a DDoS agent, the ISP needs to decide whether to drop all the packets from that penetrated machine, drop only the attacking traffic flow, or just rate-limit the attack. This is a valid computer with a person behind it. Hence, dropping all packets from this source address might seem extreme. Yet it is a penetrated machine, making it a threat that needs to be resolved. The reaction decision for these sorts of attacks is mixed: Most can be dropped; a few can just be rate-limited.

- **Spoofed address using a valid address from somewhere else on the Internet**—The most difficult source addresses to react to are those that are valid addresses but that are spoofing another site. This is a case in which you will get a reverse DDoS attack. The attacker's actual target is not the target that the DDoS agents send packets to, but the real target is the one whose addresses are being spoofed. For example, the real target is an enterprise with several connections to the Internet. The attacker knows that several connections, redundancy, IDS tools, firewalls, and other tricks make the enterprise a tough target to take down. So, instead of trying to take down the enterprise's network, the attacker works to get others to isolate it from the net. DDoS attacks spoofing the enterprise's source IP range frequently are attempted.

These are just a few examples of techniques used by cyberpunks to implement DoS attacks—there are others based on similar ideas. The more the ISP is aware of the capabilities and opportunities available to these people, the better prepared and protected it will be if any problem occurs on its network.

Summary

This chapter covered router security, routing protocol security, and general network security. It then went into some of the techniques and configuration concepts that ISPs should be considering and implementing in their backbones, especially the significance of BCP 38/RFC 2827. It discussed in depth the great importance of uRPF and gave configuration examples of the different applications and scenarios in which uRPF can be applied. The chapter concluded by discussing the use of CAR as an anti-DoS tool.

The "Technical References and Recommended Reading" section at the end of this book has many references and pointers to further technical documents discussing ISP security issues. This is a very large subject that quite easily could justify a whole book in itself. We hope that this chapter has given you an overview of what is available in IOS Software so that ISPs can protect themselves, their customers, and the Internet.

Endnotes

[1] The Telnet server is disabled on any VTY port that does not have a password or some other authentication configured.

[2] Section enhancements are compliments of Chris M. Lonvick (clonvick@cisco.com).

[3] SSH client and server also was included in IOS Software from 12.1T (and in the mainline 12.2 release).

[4] Experiments with multicast BGP (MBGP) now have begun on some ISP sites. Deployment of MBGP requires a rethink and redesign of the egress and ingress route filters.

[5] Currently, the minimal allocation block for the RIRs consists of /20s.

[6] Because Internet drafts expire six months after publication, it is worth checking whether there is a revised draft or whether an RFC document has replaced the draft before implementing this list.

[7] Thanks to Patrick W. Gilmore of Priori Networks for supplying the list.

[8] NANOG Mailing List—Subject: Re: too many routes. From: Sean M. Doran <smd@clock.org> Date: 10 Sep 1997 20:33:09 –0400 (see www.nanog.org for mailing list archives).

[9] Based on work done by Rakesh Dubey (rdubey@cisco.com) and Steve LeGault (slegault@cisco.com).

[10] Original documentation on uRPF was performed by Bruce R. Babcock (bbabcock@cisco.com).

[11] This technique is used in some multihoming configurations.

[12] This section was taken from the release notes of CSCdp76668 by the engineer who coded this function, Neil Jarvis (njarvis@cisco.com).

[13] There was a bug in IOS Software Release 12.0(10)S. The Help option in IOS Software displays only the standard and extended standard access lists as options. Standard/expanded and extended/expanded ACLs both work.

[14] For multihomed customers, see the section on uRPF limitations.

[15] The customer's assigned IP block (that is, routing prefixes) usually is inserted into the ISP's network in one of several ways. Any of these ways will work as the information is passed to the CEF tables.

[16] At the time of this publication, work has started in the IETF to consider some new options for one ISP to influence the best-path decision of another ISP.

[17] Because local preference is a nontransitive attribute working only inside one AS, many customers are encouraged to include the BGP community **no-export** with their split advertisements along with the advertisement of their entire blocks. That way, they receive the benefits of traffic-engineered multihoming with the ISP while keeping the more specific prefixes from the split-advertisement technique off the rest of the Internet.

[18] Policy-based routing could be used, but it is neither efficient (because of the performance penalty) nor scalable (consider how this would be implemented for thousands of leased-line customers).

[19] RFC 1998, "An Application of the BGP Community Attribute in Multi-home Routing," now is used widely in the ISP community.

[20] Ibid.

[21] This section is an edited version of Craig Huegen's work on smurf and frag protection. For the latest information, refer to Craig's page at http://www.pentics.net/. Craig can be contacted at chuegen@cisco.com.

## CHAPTER 5

Operational Practices

So far this book has given specific and detailed advice about router-configuration best practices for ISP backbones. It is important to see these suggestions in the bigger picture of an actual ISP business. This chapter covers some of the operational issues regarding the establishment of an ISP backbone, the choices made, the positioning of hardware, the configuration of software, and the establishment of external relationships. Aspects of ISP business operations have been covered in other publications, such as *ISP Survival Guide: Strategies for Running a Competitive ISP*, by Geoff Huston, and won't be covered here. The chapter fills the gap between the high-level business strategy and the boxes of equipment that arrive at a brand-new startup's headquarters.

This final chapter guides you through typical point-of-presence (PoP) topologies, PoP design, backbone network design, and the positioning and configuration of ISP services. Defining a workable and scalable addressing plan apparently is a hard task for several newcomers to the Internet, so this topic is covered as well. Two sections deal with routing protocols: The first covers interior routing protocol design, and the second looks at exterior relationships and gives some simple examples for efficient and effective multihoming. Security is an important topic, so some basic considerations are presented. The chapter concludes with a look at areas that most new ISPs forget about: out-of-band management, a test laboratory, and operational standards.

Point-of-Presence Topologies

A PoP is nothing more than a physical location where an ISP has equipment. This can range from a small pile of equipment in the corner of an office to whole floors of large collocation centers, sometimes called carrier hotels, in major cities. Regardless of the shape or implementation of these PoPs, successful ISPs have established a very clear strategy for constructing a smoothly operating PoP. This section covers some of this strategy.

Routers and other equipment are subdivided into clear operating units. These units are typically core, distribution, and access units, often augmented by other units such as border, VPN, broadband, and collocation/hosting units.

Core

The PoP core has devices called core routers. These support high-bandwidth links only, interconnections between similar core devices, connections to other units within the PoP, and connections to other PoPs. It is very common for ISPs to install two core routers—one device implies a single point of failure, something that high-quality and high-availability networks won't tolerate.

The definition of *high bandwidth* depends on the region of the world. In some countries, intracore connections often are made at Gigabit Ethernet, 2.4-Gbps, or 9.6-Gbps speeds. In other countries, 10-Mbps Ethernet is still commonly used. Regardless of the technology or speeds available, the core network clearly is identified—and would look something like the diagram in Figure 5-1.

Figure 5-1 *PoP Core*

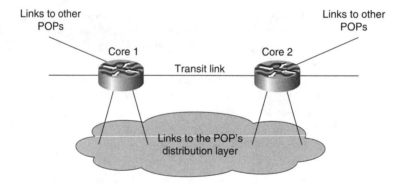

Notice that there are two routers with one high-speed direct interconnect and links outside the PoP to other locations. The direct high-speed interconnect is used so that transit traffic through the PoP has the minimum amount of hardware to traverse. Choosing to place an Ethernet switch as the transit path creates a single point of failure for that PoP because a failure in the switch (or switches) will result in transit no longer being available. The medium used for the high-speed interconnect nowadays is either Ethernet or POS; the latter currently offers higher speeds than Ethernet, but, at the time of this writing, 10-Gbps Ethernet was in development, ready to be a viable competitor to short-reach OC192/STM64 POS connections.

Some ISPs choose to make connections to remote PoPs on one core router only. The advantage is that one less hop is displayed in a route trace, but this makes the router a single point of failure. Of course, if the PoP is connected to three or more PoPs, the ISP could study transit traffic flows to optimize the path for those and to maintain a sensible backup strategy in case of equipment failure.

Distribution

The distribution layer is one step removed from the core and gets its name from its function of acting as a distribution layer between the core routers and the access part of the network. Indeed, many small- to medium-size ISPs don't have any distribution layer; they simply connect the access part of the network to the core. It all depends on the size of the PoP.

The distribution layer can be made up of two or more routers—quite often there could be considerably more. ISPs conscious of providing quality services to their customers often connect premium customers directly to this distribution layer, bypassing any bandwidth aggregation that is taking place at the access layer.

The physical medium used for connecting distribution to core varies. FDDI was very popular in the early to mid-1990s, but since the advent of high-speed connections such as DS3/E3 and Ocx/STMn bandwidth, it has waned in popularity to the extent that it is virtually not used anywhere. Two popular media types are in use today: switched Ethernet and DTP rings. The former type usually is built in the form of Ethernet switches supporting speeds from 10 Mbps to 1 Gbps. The latter type is available from speeds of 622 bps to 2.5 Gbps and using the Spatial Reuse Protocol (SRP) arguably is more efficient and more reliable than using switched Ethernet. (Many ISPs prefer passive technology such as FDDI and DPT to active technology such as switched Ethernet because there is one less hardware or software device in the network to go wrong.)

The other previously popular media type for PoP interconnects was ATM. However, ATM also has fallen by the wayside because the extra items of expensive equipment and ATM's well-known inefficiencies (popularly known as cell tax) when carrying IP have made it quite unpopular in many installations. The relative cheapness of Ethernet switches compared with the cost of ATM to carry out the same function has resulted in Gigabit Ethernet switches replacing ATM switches in ISP cores in many cases.

Figure 5-2 shows a typical PoP with the core and distribution layers drawn in detail. Point-to-point links have been chosen as the core-to-distribution interconnect medium; these either can be back-to-back Ethernet connections or POS interfaces on the routers. Point-to-point links often are chosen over alternative methods because there is only a simple cable joining the devices. As mentioned earlier, inserting extra devices into the ISP network simply means that something else in the packet path could go wrong. This design is very fault tolerant: If the cable fails or one of the core routers fails, the backup path through alternative connections or an alternative core router is available. This design is also very simple, in that no other powered devices are linking the core and distribution layers of the network.

Figure 5-2 *PoP Distribution Layer*

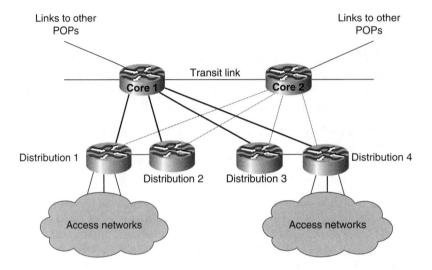

The alternatives designs are to either place Ethernet switches in the core, as shown in Figure 5-3, or use DPT, as shown in Figure 5-4. Installing two large Ethernet switches as the PoP core device is quite a common occurrence for ISPs with medium-size network infrastructures. They save on the expense of installing a large number of high-speed ports on their core routers, but they have the additional expense of purchasing two high-performance Ethernet switches to give them the desired functionality. The common design is to operate the switches as Layer 2 devices, joined by EtherChannel or Gigabit Ethernet and separated into two VLANs. The solid lines in Figure 5-3 indicate the first VLAN; the dotted lines indicate the second VLAN. The routing configuration can be set up so that one VLAN is the primary and the other is backup, or the two VLANs can be load-shared. This design is also very fault-tolerant. If either switch fails or either core router fails, there is a backup path through the other device of the pair. There is additional complexity over the design used in Figure 5-2, but quite often the core switches have many VLANs configured on them to serve other functions in the access layer of the PoP.

Figure 5-3   *PoP Distribution Layer with Ethernet Switches*

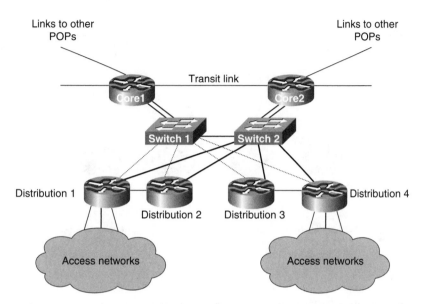

The second alternative is to use Dynamic Packet Transport (DPT), as shown in Figure 5-4. DPT is the commercial name for an optical ring topology developed by Cisco and now recognized as the IEEE 802.17 specification. DPT uses SRP to achieve optimum use of the ring: The more nodes that are added to the ring, the greater the potential throughput of the ring is with good design of the ingress and egress paths. Notice the interleaving of routers in Figure 5-4. To get the best advantage of DPT and SRP, the connections shown are the most efficient. Traffic flows from the distribution layer to the network core. Each distribution router has a direct path to the network core, ensuring maximum utilization of the bandwidth available. Only when the connection from distribution to core breaks in this topology will the bandwidth from distribution routers to core be halved. This type of topology has proven very effective in several ISPs' PoPs in recent years. It is considerably more cost-efficient than using point-to-point POS links or Gigabit Ethernet or using Ethernet switches—and, of course, it is much more reliable because physical failures of the ring are dealt with at the link layer and not at Layer 3.

Figure 5-4   *PoP Distribution Layer Using DPT*

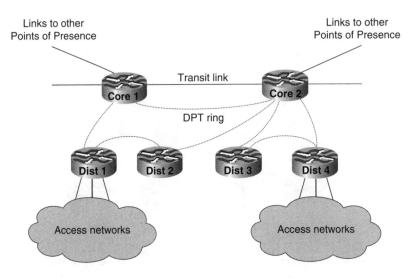

In choosing a PoP design for the distribution layer and its interconnection with the core, bear in mind the principles discussed here. The fewer hardware devices there are in the packet path, the less likely there will be a problem caused by software or hardware failure of those intermediate devices. Each method is commonly used; each method has its strong supporters and opponents. The design in Figure 5-2 is very common, but the one illustrated in Figure 5-3 is also popular because it saves the ISP from deploying many high-speed interfaces for point-to-point connections in the PoP. Likewise, the design in Figure 5-4 is popular with ISPs who have favored the use of FDDI in the past and who recognize the benefits that DPT/SRP can give over both point-to-point links and Ethernet switches.

Access

This is the edge of the ISP network facing the customer. The access layer can be made up of all kinds of devices, from a simple router supporting PSTN modem banks to cable-aggregation devices supporting broadband customers. For this reason, ISPs tend to subdivide their access layers into more manageable units. Larger businesses often have different business units running different access services, and it is useful to give these different units management access to the devices they are servicing. Quite often it is possible to see DIAL (PSTN and ISDN), low-speed permanent line (64 Kbps to 512 Kbps), high-speed permanent line (2 Mbps to 8 Mbps), and broadband (ADSL and cable) located in separate access points. ISPs supporting customers with even greater bandwidth needs will simply add more categories to those listed—in the United States, it is common to see a 45 Mbps access layer, a 155 Mbps access layer, and even higher-bandwidth access layers.

Figure 5-5 gives an example of an access network. It shows two Ethernet switches used to connect several remote access servers (RAS) for dial-in users. RAS servers are generally unsophisticated when it comes to running routing protocols. All they require is an address block assigned to them for providing address space for dial-in users. The distribution routers will inject this prefix into the ISP's iBGP routing protocol running across the backbone.

Most ISPs don't bother too much with the redundancy of the RAS. Several will provision two switches, but it is rare for them to provision two Ethernets out of the RAS. The top-end RAS devices have two Ethernets, so better redundancy can be provided. However, in most cases, ISPs tend to use low-end units—and large numbers of these because failures are actually easier to deal with.

Figure 5-5   *PoP Access Network*

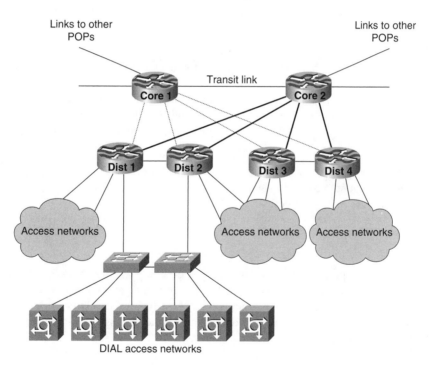

For other types of access networks, there will be other designs. Cable and xDSL access require a much more sophisticated PoP design; details of these are covered later.

Hosting

Another very common service offering is Web hosting. In the early days of the Internet, this was simply the ISP agreeing to allow the customer to bring in some unspecified server and connect it to the ISP's backbone. This was an attractive service offering because the bandwidth needs from the content contained on the server were greater than the customer could afford to supply to its own premises or that the telco easily could provision.

As the Internet has matured, whole businesses have been created dedicated to Web hosting—indeed, the whole network design for such an organization is complex and detailed. For ISPs that simply are interested in hosting a few to a hundred or so servers for customers (the average middle of the road ISP), the following design tips are helpful.

The most important thing to realize is that the ISP knows absolutely nothing about the customer's systems: what software is running, what services are being hosted, and what other things might be offered. In planning such a service, ISPs need to carefully consider what they are offering. Detailed design for a Web hosting network is not covered; only the equipment placement is considered here.

Hosted services should be treated like any other connection to the access part of the ISP network. If hosting is critical to the business, it can be connected directly to the core of the ISP network using high-speed links. Redundancy in routers connecting the hosting LAN to the core is necessary: If one router fails, the other will provide ongoing connectivity. The same is true for any switched Ethernet infrastructure being used on the hosting LAN.

Figure 5-6 shows an example of how the Web hosting network fits into the ISP PoP. Some ISPs connect the hosting layer directly to the PoP core routers. Be aware, however, that this puts a considerable filtering burden on the core routers, something that potentially could compromise rest of the PoP.

Commentary

Figure 5-6 typifies the PoP design that ISPs generally use in their PoPs. The smaller ISPs obviously won't have as much sophistication and segregation of equipment, and the larger ISPs will have a significantly larger layout. Many types of access layers are possible—two have been shown by way of example, although other access layers are very similar in implementation.

Figure 5-6   *PoP Web Hosting Network*

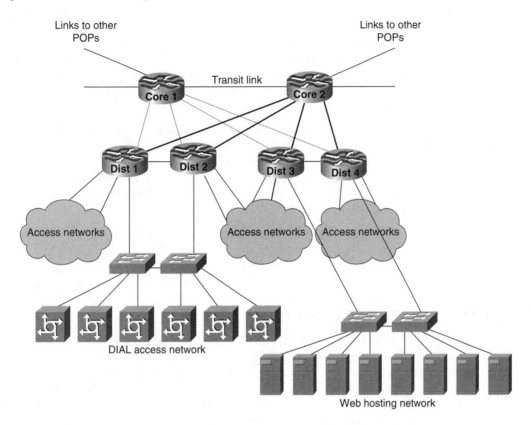

Point-of-Presence Design

Having established the principle of subdividing the PoP into units depending on function and management, the next important principle of PoP design is to establish a basic layout and replicate this across the entire backbone network. Successful ISPs work on the principle of having only three or four different designs for each PoP. This ensures that the network is not too complex, allowing staff training to be given on each design. It also ensures that the engineering and operations staff are aware that the rest of the ISP's backbone will follow one of the few chosen layouts.

The other advantage of having only a few different designs comes at the point of deploying new infrastructure. Instead of having to take time for the senior design engineers to come up with a new design, the ISP operations team simply can instruct the equipment deployment part of the operation to install a PoP in City A using Design B. The new PoP is delivered with a basic configuration ready for the networking team to integrate into the backbone.

The networking team has no surprises because the design conforms to one of the previously agreed-upon standards. In manpower terms, this means that expensive staff members are not tied up with ordering equipment, building racks, or examining collocation space. ISPs tend to choose one design for an average-size PoP—a scaled-down version of this becomes the small PoP, and a scaled-up version becomes the large PoP. There is little benefit to having any further options; as was shown previously, PoPs are made out of core, distribution, and access layers, so having three designs that incorporate this layering is about as much as can be realistically done without the model breaking down.

A further advantage is that the search for collocation space, or room space to install the facility, is actually simplified. If the design specification dictates a particular dimension with particular electrical requirements, particular air-conditioning requirements, and precise security requirements, it becomes significantly easier to work through a checklist to establish a suitable location. Nothing is worse than going halfway through a build to discover some fundamental design flaw about the facility.

These three issues are probably the key components that most ISPs worry about. There are undoubtedly many others, depending on the depth of detail required, but these are fundamental to designing this particular part of the ISP infrastructure.

Backbone Network Design

Typically two styles of backbone design are in use today. The first employs a star-type network, in which the ISP is based in one city and simply installs point-to-point circuits to the other locations. This isn't a wide-area network, as such, but more of a collapsed backbone in the major headquarters hub. The advantage of this style is that management is easier and the network is not complex. Each site has one exit path: to the middle. However, this design is fundamentally flawed when it comes to offering any level of service quality. If any link breaks in the star, the remote site is cut off until the link is restored. If the central node has a problem, the entire network goes down. For this reason, a star network is not used much beyond the initial inception of the ISP business and, in fact, is actively discouraged in some circles these days.

Figure 5-7 shows an example of a network built using a star topology. Notice the single connection from each PoP back to headquarters, where the major facility is. If any circuit fails, the PoP that it connects to the core is disconnected and remains out of service until the link is repaired again. Even more problematic, if the headquarters site has a problem, the entire Internet connection service that this ISP is offering is affected because all external connections from this ISP go through the headquarters. Referring to this figure, it is very easy to see why most ISPs opt for some redundancy in the backbone. This is not a scalable network, nor is it a viable business model.

Figure 5-7   *Star Network Topology*

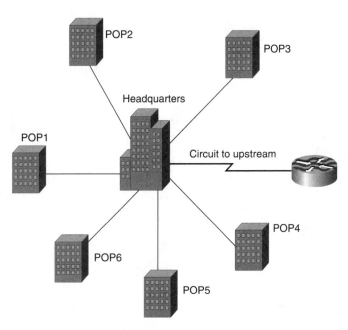

The alternative is the well-tried and very trusted backbone core design. Major locations are selected as the ISP core backbone, and the rest of the network is distributed around that. For example, an ISP might decide that its six major cities will form the core of its backbone and will build high-speed links between these cities. The rest of the network will be built around this core layer. Some people call this a distribution network because it mimics the distribution design used in PoPs, as mentioned previously. Each site in the distribution layer will have redundant links to the core—one primary path will be a high-band link to the core, and one backup path will go to another distribution layer site. If the interdistribution site link goes down, the primary path functions as normal for both sites. If one primary path goes down, the site has backup through the other site and its primary link to the core.

Figure 5-8 shows an example of how the sites in Figure 5-7 could be connected providing redundancy to each site. Notice that each site has two exit paths, and the network itself has two separate connections to the Internet. Three extra domestic circuits are required, and one more upstream circuit is required. However, the major difference is that the network in Figure 5-8 can be run with 99.5 percent guaranteed availability; it is not at the mercy of any one circuit going down, and it is even resilient against complete site failure and upstream circuit failure.

Figure 5-8 *Mesh Backbone*

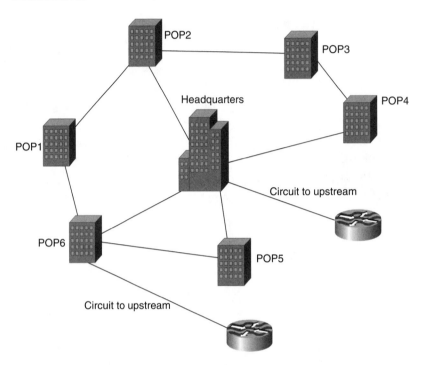

Looking around the many Internet backbones today, it is easy to see that many ISPs have adopted the latter design. Newcomers to the Internet business are still skeptical about it because they see more than the minimum necessary outlay of equipment and resources. There are trade-offs: If there is a desire to have the network 100 percent available, redundancy is required, no matter how good any vendor might claim that its equipment or infrastructure reliability is. If only 80 percent availability is required, building a cheap network will be just fine. In our experience, most newcomers try to do the former using the latter concepts, and finding an acceptable compromise is often the major challenge.

A further point that often is missing in network designs is that many newcomers are completely sold on the possibilities of the new leading-edge technologies being offered. MPLS is perhaps the most recent example: IP backbone providers (usually ISPs) now can compete with the incumbent telcos to provide VPN technologies to customers who previously were the domain of the telcos only. These new-world ISPs would deploy MPLS on top of their existing network infrastructures—or worse, literally throw together the minimum IP infrastructure necessary to support an MPLS backbone. This strategy always is doomed to failure. The most important point when it comes to designing a network is that it must be robust and foolproof enough that any overlay network such as MPLS can operate reliably and transparently.

ISP Services

The art of putting together the system services required to support the Internet infrastructure probably could fill a book in its own right. Our aim here is to try to explain to the network engineer how to properly position and set up the network portion of the various services that an ISP should be offering to its customer base. Meeting network engineers who dismiss services such as the DNS as "Oh, it's the systems engineers problem" is somewhat disconcerting because the positioning and connection of these services to the Internet backbone is actually quite important.

Network engineers need to be aware of several ISP services. The three most important ones today are the DNS, mail, and news services. Although many principles are the same for each service, it is worth covering each in turn.

DNS

The DNS is the public face of the Internet, quite literally. The common complaint from first-time users of the Internet if they can't get to a site is, "The Internet is down." In fact all that could be wrong is that the name isn't in the DNS, or the DNS hasn't been set up properly, or there is some infrastructure problem that renders the DNS unusable. All three scenarios are very common.

The DNS has three important parts: the primary nameserver, the secondary nameserver, and the caching nameserver (or resolver, as some call it). Each attracts a slightly different deployment strategy, and each is really important to deploy properly on an ISP network.

The basic principle for each of these types of servers is redundancy. If one server goes down, the Internet community wants (if not requires) that you have some backup so that name resolution still works. If you have one DNS server and it goes down, the systems using the Internet have no way of mapping any name that you give to an address—nor do they have any way of mapping addresses on Internet infrastructure into names. The former makes the Internet appear down; the latter makes the Internet look like a jumble of numbers rather than the names that we humans can handle more easily.

Primary DNS

Only one primary DNS server exists for each domain name. It is the system that holds the master delegation records of the name from the parent zone. For example, Cisco will have a primary nameserver for the zone cisco.com.

General ISP design is to place the primary DNS server in a very safe part of the network. *Safe* usually equates to *secure*, with ISPs putting their primary DNS behind dedicated firewalls, on secure LANs, and so on. Because there is only one primary DNS server carrying all the records for the zone and any other zones the ISP chooses to host, it is looked after very well. Specifications have been increasing over the years. A key point that we have noticed is that memory and network I/O speed are crucially important, especially for systems carrying a large amount of information.

ISPs often host zones on behalf of their customers or host zones for their peer ISPs as part of the peering agreement they have (more discussion in the following section on secondary DNS). Depending on the size of the files in question, it often is considered good practice to use different physical hardware for local and customer zones files and for peer zone files. The reason is scalability: Two systems will scale better than one, and the ISP's customer zone files don't get any performance impact caused by overloading because of a peer's problem.

Finally, the primary DNS server hosts two types of zone files. The forward zone maps names to addresses so that users can contact remote locations without having to remember the actual addresses (these are harder to remember than names, and addresses tend to change more often than names anyhow). The reverse zone maps addresses to names so that any lookup on an address will reveal the name of the system in question. Reverse zones are used in troubleshooting connection problems as well as for DNS consistency work—some sites will not allow connections to be made unless the forward DNS entry maps to the reverse DNS entry.

Secondary DNS

As the name suggests, the secondary DNS operates in a supporting role to the primary DNS. There can be only one primary DNS for any zone, but there can be several secondaries that hold backup information. The secondary servers get their information from the primaries—any change on the primary automatically is synchronized to the secondary as part of the DNS update process.

ISPs usually can cope with setting up a primary DNS, but when the various name registries tell them that they need two nameservers, the problems begin. The first common mistake is to put the DNS secondary system on the same LAN connected to the same switch as the primary server. If the LAN goes down, the switch breaks, or the gateway routers to the outside world break, both the primary and the secondary DNS are disabled. We return to our "the Internet is down" problem. The solution to this is simple: Put the secondary DNS elsewhere in the network. Some examples are discussed later in this section.

The second common mistake is to simply not bother with a secondary DNS. An IP address is made up for the benefit of the domain registries (which rarely check that it actually responds with correct zone information), and the result is a situation in which 50 percent of all DNS lookups will be aimed at a nonexistent host. This will make all zones served by the primary nameserver look as though they are sluggish because of long delays while 50 percent of them have to time out the nonexistent server.

The third common mistake is to set up only two DNS servers. The first common mistake is avoided by putting the two servers on different parts of the network, but often this is on different LANs in the same PoP; the two systems might be in the same rack and might be fed from the same power source! There is no redundancy here, and it is a waste of time to consider this option.

The minimally correct way of deploying DNS is to have one primary and at least one secondary. Two, three, or four secondaries are even better. Consider this example. An ISP has set up DNS and chooses to have three secondaries. One secondary is located in a remote PoP in the backbone. Another secondary is located in another remote PoP, maybe close to an exchange point or other external link to its backbone. The fourth secondary is located outside the state or country that the ISP is based in. This is the ultimate in redundancy. If the upstream links break, the zones that the ISP is supporting don't disappear, so the ISP and its customers do not disappear from the Internet. The nameserver overseas will respond with addresses, and services such as SMTP will take care of queuing e-mail until the link returns (in the e-mail case, this is far more desirable than having e-mail bounce with Unknown Domain).

The following example is how APNIC, the Regional Internet Registry (RIR) for the Asia Pacific region, handles its DNS setup for the apnic.net zone:

```
$ dig apnic.net ns

;; ANSWER SECTION:
apnic.net.              50m44s IN NS     svc00.apnic.net.
apnic.net.              50m44s IN NS     ns.ripe.net.
apnic.net.              50m44s IN NS     rs.arin.net.
apnic.net.              50m44s IN NS     ns.apnic.net.

;; ADDITIONAL SECTION:
svc00.apnic.net.        1d23h53m25s IN A  202.12.28.131
ns.ripe.net.            1d23h54m46s IN A  193.0.0.193
rs.arin.net.            1d23h53m25s IN A  192.149.252.21
ns.apnic.net.           1d9h29m16s  IN A  203.37.255.97


$
```

The four systems listed here beside the NS records are on different continents! The system svc00.apnic.net is in Tokyo, Japan; ns.ripe.net is in Amsterdam, Netherlands; rs.arin.net is in Washington D.C., U.S.A.; and ns.apnic.net is in Brisbane, Australia. This is probably one of the best examples of DNS redundancy in the Internet today.

Caching DNS

The third type of DNS service is generally a mystery to many of the smaller ISPs because it is hardly discussed outside DNS operator circles and outside larger ISPs. The caching DNS is a system that maintains a cache of DNS information; it doesn't provide a secondary function for any zone files, but it knows where to go to retrieve the information.

Caching nameservers typically are used by the ISP to answer day-to-day DNS queries. End hosts usually ask for a DNS "resolver" when they are being configured. The resolver is the caching nameserver. Note that primary and secondary DNS servers also will answer resolver queries, but as networks scale, this is generally undesirable—the last thing that any ISP wants is for its DNS service to be swamped by miscellaneous DNS queries.

A few good strategies exist for deploying a caching nameserver system in an ISP backbone. One common one is to deploy a caching DNS at each PoP. The hardware requirements aren't significant—a fast processor, large memory, and a fast I/O are the main needs and, at the time of writing, easily could be satisfied by a 1U rack-mount PC available from a number of different vendors. The address of the caching DNS would be distributed to customers at the PoP to use as the DNS resolver so that one system is dedicated to a PoP. If redundancy is required, dedicating two servers per PoP might work: Lookups are done in a round-robin manner, so it doesn't make much sense to put the second resolver at another location—this generates a small amount of extra traffic on the backbone.

A further enhancement of the strategy using two resolvers per PoP is to give two unique addresses to all the resolvers in the ISP backbone. These two addresses are routed as /32 host addresses across the ISP backbone. Each PoP would have two resolvers, so customers connecting to one PoP would use both resolvers there. If these systems both disappeared because of maintenance or an incident, no reconfiguration of the customer systems would be necessary—the ISP's interior routing protocol simply would readjust to point the path to the next nearest systems. An added benefit is that the customer would not observe any downtime in the DNS, improving its perception of the QoS offered.

This is a use of the so-called *anycast address* in IPv4. Many systems share the same IP address. If one system disappears, the interior routing protocol ensures that the next nearest system will receive the traffic. From our own experience, this setup has worked extremely well and has proved itself to be the most reliable way of delivering DNS resolver services to customers. (Notice that each resolver system requires its own unique address also; otherwise, it will be incapable of communicating with other entities in the Internet.)

Mail

Mail is the second most important service on the Internet after Web browsing. Journalists always talk about surfing the Web; most new PC purchases are the result of people wanting to dial up and look at Internet Web sites to find information. Keeping in touch is the second major reason for buying a PC, and e-mail is the popular way of doing so. Also, many companies now use e-mail as the primary method of distributing information to customers and distributing information internally.

So, if e-mail breaks, gets lost, or bounces, the effect is very noticeable. Receiving the bounce message four hours after sending an e-mail is very frustrating and adds to the perception that the Internet is unreliable. In fact, all that might be wrong is that the remote mail host has been disconnected.

Configuring mail servers to fit into an ISP backbone should not be that hard for a network engineer. Yet again, following the rule that two or more of everything is good will ensure that there is a reliable e-mail service. Indeed, some ISPs are almost as diligent with their mail server designs as they are with DNS.

The DNS is helpful in providing redundancy for mail systems using the concept of an MX (or mail exchanger) record. A domain can and should have more than one MX record. A number specifier follows, giving the priority of the mail system—the lower the value is, the higher in priority the mail relay is. The one with the lowest value is the primary MX, the intended destination of the e-mail.

Looking at what some organizations have done to configure their e-mail is helpful. The following example shows PIPEX's arrangement and is a good guide for how it should be done:

```
$ dig pipex.net mx

;; ANSWER SECTION:
pipex.net.              8H IN MX      10 shed.pipex.net.
pipex.net.              8H IN MX      90 lfallback1.lnd.ops.eu.uu.net.
pipex.net.              8H IN MX      99 fallback.mail.pipex.net.

;; ADDITIONAL SECTION:
shed.pipex.net.           8H IN A        158.43.128.176
lfallback1.lnd.ops.eu.uu.net.   57m17s IN A  62.189.34.30
fallback.mail.pipex.net.  1H IN A  158.43.128.81
fallback.mail.pipex.net.  1H IN A  62.189.34.25
fallback.mail.pipex.net.  1H IN A  62.189.34.30

$
```

The primary device has an MX of 10, so mail for user@pipex.net will be delivered to this system if it is available. If the machine does not respond, mail goes to the fallback system with MX of 90. That system has a different IP address than the primary MX and is actually in a different physical location on the ISP's network. If that system also fails, PIPEX has provided a dedicated fallback system with three separate IP addresses.

ISPs that are providing connection services for customers really should offer MX relay services for their customers that are running their own SMTP gateways. Otherwise, the customer has only its own mail host for all e-mail—if the host goes down, e-mail is queued up on the sending system. If the host does not come back on time, the e-mail will be bounced to the sender. A typical setup for all MX records should look like the following:

```
Customer.com            MX 5     mail.customer.com.
Customer.com            MX 10    relay0.isp.net.
Customer.com            MX 20    relay1.isp.net.
```

Mail for the customer is delivered directly to the customer's mail host. If it goes down or the circuit to the customer becomes unavailable, the ISP's relay systems take over in order of priority specified by the MX values. (Note that if an ISP is supplying relaying services for its customers, it must be very careful that its mail software is configured to allow relaying only for its own customers. Open relays are considered extremely bad practice and often result in the perpetrator's network being added to a routing black list.)

News

Usenet News has been around for as long as the Internet has existed in its various forms. Its main popularity centers on the non real-time distribution of information on virtually all possible topics that humankind could be interested in.

Providing a Usenet News (or simply news) service always has been a challenge for ISPs. In our perception, the news heyday was the mid-1990s, with huge volumes of information and materials being distributed around the Internet. A typical full newsfeed was consuming around 20 GB per day, making it both a challenge to store and a challenge to deliver on the typical circuit capacities at the time. It was quite common for customers demanding a full newsfeed to try to sign up to at least a 128-Kbps circuit just to ensure that there was sufficient capacity to deliver news.

Nowadays the newsfeed volume is only marginally larger than it was in the mid-1990s, but typical circuit capacities and hard-disk sizes are one or two orders of magnitude larger. The problem of delivering a newsfeed is not so great, but the lessons of the earlier years are well worth heeding to ensure a scalable and reliable service.

Network Design

Good attention needs to be paid to the design of the news-delivery network. For a network engineer, it should not be something that is simply left to the systems group to work out for themselves because the volume of material that can be delivered often can cause choke points in the backbone. Furthermore, paying close attention to the design will ensure that the customer's experience is a good one and will not add more fuel to the "Internet is slow" perception.

Figure 5-9 shows an example of how an ISP would implement a scalable news-distribution system across its backbone. One system is dedicated to receiving newsfeeds from external ISPs, whether this is peer or upstream or other ISPs that have agreed to provide a newsfeed. This system usually is closed off from the rest of the Internet so that only the permitted hosts get access to the system; this prevents unwanted connections from slowing the system. This single system distributes the received news to the rest of the newsfeeder systems across the backbone. Each PoP could have one or more feeder systems, and a hierarchy could be set up in each PoP if there is sufficient demand for newsfeeds from customers. The newsfeeder systems then distribute the feeds to customers. Depending on the hardware and news software chosen, this could be anything from 10 to more than 100 feeds per server system.

Figure 5-9   *Inbound News Distribution*

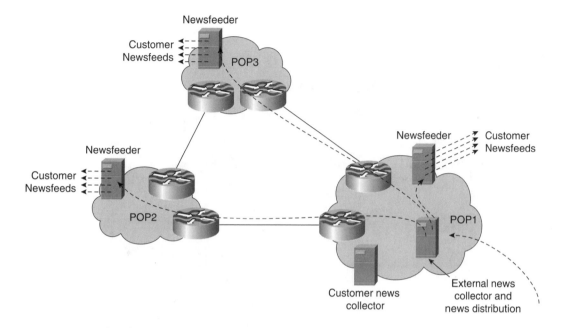

Figure 5-10 shows the reverse cycle. Customer sites that post news items to the Usenet system send their feeds to a dedicated server in the ISP network. One system is shown in the figure, but quite often ISPs will set up one system per PoP simply to receive these feeds. It depends on how much volume there is to handle and how many customers there are. The news-collector system then sends its feed to the news-distribution system, and the cycle continues. If the news is meant to be sent to the Internet, the distribution system sends the items to its external peers.

Commentary

The news-distribution design described in this section is quite simple, with its main advantage being scalability. Computers are relatively cheap these days, so having lots of smaller CPUs and disks is generally better policy for deployment than using one substantial system. Obvious enhancements to this design occur when the ISP provides a system for online browsing of news—again this should be a dedicated system, separate from the systems providing or receiving newsfeeds from customers. Depending on the Usenet news software being used, it should be possible to configure the systems to permit or deny online browsing as appropriate.

Figure 5-10 *Customer News Redistribution*

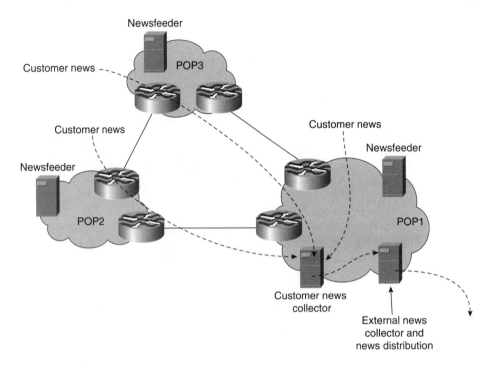

Keeping Software Up-to-Date

A common error made by many ISPs is relying on the server software that is distributed with their UNIX systems rather than keeping the versions current. Mail and DNS are two extremely high-profile services, and the developers and user community continuously are making enhancements and bug fixes.

It's quite common for operations staff to subscribe the ISP to the CERT advisory mailing list—here all advisories about known security problems with software on UNIX- and Windows-based operating systems are announced. Cisco also makes use of the CERT advisory process to announce details of any security problems discovered with the IOS Software. Paying attention to the advisories is a very prudent thing to do: People who want to attack systems or ISP networks also pay attention to the CERT advisory list and often attempt to exploit a newly announced security bug in hopes of gaining access to a system or a network. When a problem is announced on the CERT list, ISPs are strongly encouraged to upgrade the affected software (note that a CERT advisory generally is not made until there is a patch or a workaround from the vendor involved).

For this reason, sticking to vendor-shipped mail and DNS applications is not a good strategy. Operating system releases take a snapshot of the current application status, and interim versions rarely are released (unless a major problem is discovered). Most ISPs take the standard operating system release and then compile or install the current latest version of the server software. Mail (SMTP) and DNS have been listed as the key applications to be aware of, but other critical ones can include news, FTP, Secure Shell, PoP3, and HTTPD. (Any publicly available TCP port needs the latest server software listening on the port to be current at all times.) Because the source has been compiled by the ISP systems engineers, it becomes very simple to patch the version that is in operation, and this generally takes no more than a few minutes of work.

Before deployment, testing of the fix clearly is required, especially if the ISP has any unusual operational requirements or has made some other changes. But the first requirement is always security and integrity of the services supported, so downtime while patching and testing is clearly preferable to having a vulnerable system still in service.

IPv4 Addressing in an ISP Backbone

Designing an IP addressing plan for an ISP backbone is probably one of the more complex issues that an ISP faces when entering the competitive Internet marketplace. Internet growth in recent years has been explosive, and coverage is now well beyond that of academic and government organizations in the United States. Because the finite amount of IPv4 address space available, this growth has resulted in the community's desire to be more careful about how the resource is shared among its users.

The IANA is responsible for the distribution of all IP address space; IANA is now one of the functions of ICANN. To this end, it has delegated the three RIRs (ARIN, RIPE NCC, and APNIC) to carry out its responsibilities in the three regions of the world. The three RIRs and the user community are working to ensure that each user of public address space is efficient with utilization, to be fair to all who require this finite resource. Three RIRs exist at the time of writing; their geographical reach is shown in Figure 5-11. The geographical reach of the two emerging RIRs, LACNIC (Latin American and Caribbean NIC) and AfriNIC (Africa NIC), is shown in the figure as well.

It is hoped that this section will encourage ISPs to consider how to design a scalable addressing plan. Conservation and efficient utilization of address space often are seen as problematic and even undesirable by ISPs trying to minimize the number of prefixes carried around in their network.

This is only an example of the considerations necessary when designing the addressing plan for an ISP network. It does not advise on how to go through the process of applying for address space from the three regional address registries or how to configure the BGP routing protocol.

It is assumed that the reader is familiar with terms such as CIDR, classless addressing, and the /N network mask scheme. Note that antiquated terminology such as Class C is not used here and should not be used in the vocabulary of the Internet.

Figure 5-11 *RIR Areas*

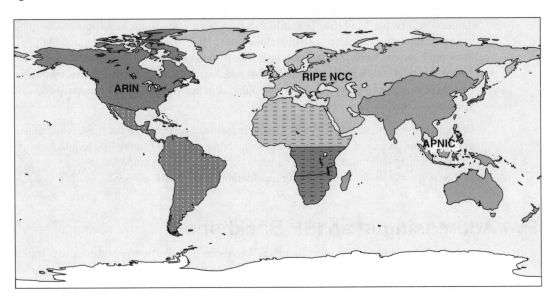

Business Model and IP Address Space

It generally is accepted that to think ahead one and two years when designing an ISP network is reasonable. Beyond that, given the rapid growth of the Internet, it is very difficult to predict what new technologies will be available or which direction the business might be headed.

In the early 1990s, available address space was more limited than it is today. CIDR hadn't yet been deployed on the Internet backbone, and Class B space was rapidly running out. There was real concern about the rate of address space consumption, and the growth of the Internet Route Table was exponential. Some predictions were made that IPv4 space would run out in 1998. This concern spurred on the introduction of CIDR and the classless Internet. Since then, the registries have been making classless network assignments, and DHCP has made addressing and renumbering on the LAN very trivial. What was a problem in 1994 was no longer one in 1996.

An ISP might go into business to service a particular marketplace. However, local operating conditions might change, or new "killer applications" might appear on the Internet. As a result, the ISP's original business objective could change completely. Furthermore, address space requirements usually change when this happens.

The three Internet registries look for an estimate of address requirements for a year or more ahead and make allocations on that basis. They do so because most ISP business plans operate around similar concepts, and this means that ISPs don't have to constantly revisit the registries to get their next allocations.

It is important to sit back for a few minutes and look seriously at the avenues of growth for any ISP business. This isn't easy in a marketplace that is growing exponentially. However, it pays in terms of engineering time to try to get a realistic picture of where the business will lead. Think about whether there likely will be more PoPs or larger PoPs, more backbone links, new services, new equipment with increased port density, and so on. An ISP operation usually has a business plan to guarantee funding from sponsors or shareholders. The existence of a business plan implies that some thought has been given to the direction of growth of the network; the two are interlinked.

Address Plan

It is a constant surprise to many seasoned campaigners how little attention industry newcomers pay to developing a sensible and coherent addressing plan for the backbone. ISPs often spend months of detailed design for their backbone, completely forgetting to put a plan together. A week or few before they go live, they realize that address space is required, and the ensuing panic with applications to the registries results in an inevitable slowing of the deployment plans. Designing a network and thinking of address space requirements are processes that happen at the same time. Documenting requirements at that early stage makes the documentation submission to the RIRs significantly easier, with allocations made in very short time scales.

This section documents a simple example of an address plan for a growing ISP business. Obviously, it is intended only as a guide, but understanding the principles will help in designing most other types of networks. This plan covers only the ISP's infrastructure. Too often, ISPs become bogged down in second-guessing how many customers they will have and how big these customers might be when trying to give their estimates to the registries. The registries are concerned only with the address space that the ISP will use for infrastructure at the first application; they assume that the ISP will apply for address space that it can assign to its customers as well.

Three network plans are presented: the current plan, the plan after six months, and the plan after one year. The addressing schema should take each plan into account because it helps the ISP plan the network growth over the coming 12 months. Notice, however, that each section produces a summary of required address space. When the three plans are developed, they should be documented in a format similar to this text. Another important tenet of an ISP's business is that there can never be too much documentation. Good documentation such as this helps the engineering team working for the ISP to understand the growth plans and helps them engineer the routing protocols as needed. It helps the address registries understand the address space requirements and eases the assignment process.

It has been assumed all along that the ISP is following the essential features of configuring routing protocols; typical examples can be found in Cisco's ISP/IXP Workshop tutorials and were covered in Chapter 3, "Routing Protocols." In general, networks are designed with an IGP (such as OSPF or IS-IS) to carry point-to-point link addresses, loopback interface addresses, and LAN addresses. BGP is used to carry the ISP's customer networks (iBGP) and any externally learned networks (eBGP). (Although BGP probably won't be used until the ISP multihomes [connects to more than one upstream ISP], it pays to follow the design principle in case BGP will be implemented in the future.)

Network Plan: Starting Off

The first stage involves looking at the network design at the start of the ISP's operation. Figure 5-12 gives an example network—it has four routers, three switches with some hosts connected to them, and some customer leased-line connections. There is also a dialup router. Finally, the network has a link to an upstream ISP. This is a simple network with four small PoPs at initial rollout.

Also on the figure are the sizes of the subnets allocated to each portion of the network. In detail, these are as follows:

- WAN point-to-point links have been assigned a /30. There are two hosts on a point-to-point link, so the maximum address space required is a /30. Assigning a larger subnet would result in wasted address space. (If there is trouble calculating how many hosts can fit into a subnet, refer to Table 5-1, which has a few examples of subnetting a /24 address block.)

- LANs have been assigned only the address space that they require.

- One loopback interface is assigned per router.

Figure 5-12 *Network Plan at Deployment*

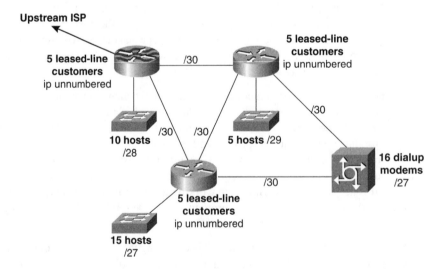

Table 5-1   *Subnet Sizes and Host Counts for a /24 Block*

Network Mask	Subnets	Host Count
/24	1	254
/25	2	126
/26	4	62
/27	8	30
/28	16	14
/29	32	6
/30	64	2
/31	128	None
/32	255	1

The /30 address required for the ISP's upstream link usually is assigned by the upstream ISP and is not required here. It is assumed that IP unnumbered is used to configure the point-to-point links going to a customer site. It also is assumed that one loopback interface is assigned to each of the four routers. Furthermore, it is assumed that each Ethernet switch has been assigned an IP address for administrative access purposes. These assumptions are common practice in most ISPs for these reasons:

- With IP unnumbered, the point-to-point link between the ISP and the customer routers is not assigned an IP address. Non-Cisco equipment will use other conventions but is similarly capable. Using no address means that there is one less network in the ISP's IGP—IGP design always aims to have minimal networks in the interior routing table for efficiency and convergence speed. (Some ISPs have started to use /31s on point-to-point links—this saves a bit more address space but still means that the address has to be carried around in the IGP. See RFC 3021 for more information on 31-bit prefixes.)

- A loopback interface on a router divorces the router's administrative functions from any of its physical interfaces, thereby guaranteeing continued administrative access in case of any physical link failure.

- All LAN equipment is assigned an IP address for administrative access. Although all equipment will have a serial console, often an IP-capable interface is extremely useful as a first line of entry for administration functions (many ISPs reserve console access as a last resort).

At this initial stage, we have five /30s, one /29, one /28, and two /27s, plus a /30 required for the four loopback addresses (loopback interfaces are assigned a /32). You can follow the sums through in detail here:

1 Six /30s make one /28 and one /29.

2 One /28 and one /29 plus the single /29 make two /28s.

3 The two /28s plus the single /28 make one /27 and one /28.

4 One /27 and one /28, together with the two /27s, make one /26, one /27, and one /28.

5 The next usable address boundary from one /26, one /27, and one /28 is a single /25.

In conclusion, this network infrastructure could be numbered out of a single /25 of address space.

NOTE This plan considers only the ISP's infrastructure. Providing address space for the ISP's customers to use is a separate consideration and is covered in more detail in the succeeding sections.

Network Plan: After Six Months

After the first six months of operation, the ISP aims to show moderate growth in its network and estimates that its network infrastructure will show additional equipment and sites. The network is intended to grow to that shown in Figure 5-13. The figure also documents the address plan intended for the network at the end of the first year.

Figure 5-13 *Network Plan at End of Six Months*

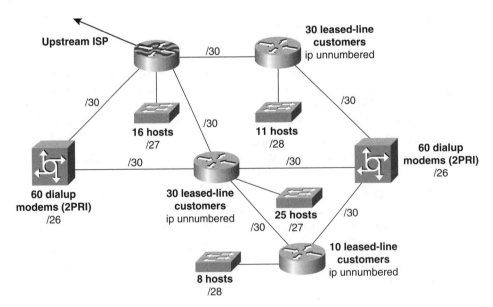

The changes to the network include adding two new sites and upgrading the dialup infrastructure to support more modem lines. There are now six sites, although the ISP still has not planned for any physical redundancy at each site. Notice that the IP addressing for leased-line customers still uses IP unnumbered.

Looking at the utilization at this stage, there are eight /30s for point-to-point links, two /28s, two /27s, and two /26s. There are also two new devices now requiring loopback interfaces (making a requirement for a /29). You can follow the sums through in detail here:

1   Eight /30s make one /27.

2   Two /28s make one /27.

3   Two /27s make one /26

4   Two /26s make one /25.

5   Adding all of these together makes a total of a /24.

6   The extra /29 required for loopback interfaces also should be counted, making the total requirement a /23.

In conclusion, the address space requirement for this projected network at the end of six months is a /23.

Network Plan: End of First Year

The final stage to consider is the plan at the end of the first year of operation. Again, this is a projection on what the business could be like. It is assumed that the ISP has started to do Web hosting for its customers and is investing in a large dialup network (which we shall say that the business plan calls for).

The ISP also plans to deploy two of everything by the end of the first year of operation. This affords increased redundancy and resiliency in the network. (This isn't meant to be a tutorial in network design—these elements simply are included to show how the addressing plan might be done.) The ISP also plans to take on its first BGP customers. Now that it has redundancy in the PoP, in the backbone, and to its upstreams, it feels that it can offer the service at a sufficient quality to be acceptable to customers. This means that it will require address space for point-to-point link addresses.

Figure 5-14 shows how the network has grown and shows the addressing that goes with it. Some values have been omitted for clarity. Each site has dual routers now, and the links between them also require a /30 of address space each. The ISP has two upstream connections now, each coming from different sites. This is also part of the ISP redundancy planning. By the end of the first year, the business is fully functioning and the ISP needs all the hardware and infrastructure redundancy that it can obtain.

Figure 5-14 *Network Plan at End of First Year*

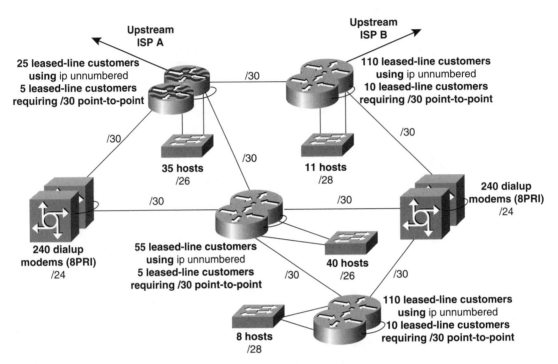

Looking at the utilization now, there are 14 /30s, 2 /28s, 2 /26s, 2 /24s, and 12 /32s for loopback interface addresses (making a requirement for a /28). There are 30 leased-line customers who will need point-to-point link addresses. Also, the switches now are dual-homed to the routers, and the ISP is using the Hot Standby Routing Protocol (HSRP) to create a virtual default gateway for the LAN devices. Using HSRP consumes another /32 per LAN for the virtual gateway address, and ISPs generally configure two standby groups per LAN to load-share between the two routers. This needs to be remembered in the LAN host count. Also, the LAN host count includes the IP address required for the router in every case.

Going through the sums in detail gives the following:

1 For the loopbacks, 14 /30s make 1 /27, 1 /28, and 1 /29.

2 For customer point-to-point links, 30 /30s make 1 /26, 1 /27, 1 /28, and 1 /29.

3 Two /28s make one /27.

4 Two /26s make one /25.

5 Two /24s make one /23.

6 Twelve /32s make one /28.

7 From 1 and 2, the two /29s make one /28.

8 From 1, 2, 6, and 7, the four /28s make one /26.

9 From 1 and 2, the two /27s make one /26.

10 From 8 and 9, the two /26s make one /25.

11 From 4 and 10, the two /25s make one /24.

12 From 2, 3, 4, and 5, this makes a total of one /23, one /24, one /25, one /26, and one /27.

13 The next available address size that this can fit into is a /22.

In conclusion, the address requirements after the first year are a /22. Notice how the network subnets have been packed as efficiently as possible. This is quite a complex network now, yet with judicious use of addressing, it has consumed less than /22 of address space.

Furthermore, because the ISP now has two connections to the Internet, it would have applied for an AS number and used that to multihome to the two upstream ISPs. This allows the layering of the network routing protocols, as will be described later.

Notice also the continued use of IP unnumbered. The ISP should make a reasonable estimate of how many links IP unnumbered can be used for. Sometimes customer routers might not be capable of supporting the concept. Other customers might require use of eBGP to exchange routing information with the ISP and thus will require a /30 address for the point-to-point link. In this case, the ISP has estimated that there will be 30 such customers links. By convention, the links to the upstream ISPs are numbered using address space from the upstream.

Also notice that IP addresses are dynamically assigned on the dialup access servers. Whereas the ISP might be operating at a ratio of 20 users per modem, the requirement is only for one IP address to be available per modem line. Also notice that where a PRI might have 32 channels, generally only 30 are available for use in an ISDN/PSTN service (the other 2 are used for signaling)—quite convenient when it comes to IP addressing.

Putting Together an Address-Deployment Plan

The preceding examples established the address requirements for the sample ISP network that has been the subject of this section. The final thing that needs to be done is to convert it into a reasonable infrastructure-assignment process.

The following sections consider these particular network addressing requirements:

- Loopback interface on the router
- WAN links

- LANs
- Customer networks

Loopback Interfaces

The loopback interface on the router is always the first consideration on an ISP network. It is a helpful general-purpose feature used for many things, including iBGP peering and source address for packets originating from the router (useful for authentication or filtering). The early chapters of this book made many references to the loopback interface, and a whole section was devoted to the benefits of using its address as the source of all IP packets originating from the router.

By the end of the first year, the example ISP estimated that it would have 12 routers in its network, so it is reasonable to assign a /28 to be used for that purpose from the very beginning. It is advisable to assign a single block for this purpose; although some ISPs number loopbacks out of random chunks of address space, the more common practice is to set aside a single block. It becomes very easy to set up filters on the routers and NOC equipment so that only routers and the NOC equipment get access to each other.

The loopback /32s will be carried around only in the IGP, and they pose minimal overhead to the routing protocol chosen.

WAN Links

The second consideration is the WAN links. Unless the network easily can be separated into distinct regions, there is little to be gained by summarizing the WAN /30 address space. Also, because WAN address space grows more slowly than other parts of the network, WAN links should be addressed out of another contiguous block from the allocation (say, the chunk next to the loopback network block).

WAN links and loopbacks address blocks should be contiguous; they generally don't need much optimum routability outside the ISP's backbone because they are used only to connect the backbone. They should be reachable, but they are not significant load-generating destinations as far as the Internet is concerned. This concept will be revisited in the "Multihoming" section later in this chapter.

LANs

Finally we come to the LANs and inter-router links. LANs probably gain hosts faster than other parts of the network, so it is prudent to allow greater headroom here than elsewhere in the network. Again, no benefit can be had from summarization unless the network can be split into a regional layout.

Unless there is a good reason not to do so, DHCP should be used to assign IP addresses. A DHCP server can take care of changing IP addresses and network masks on a LAN, as well as changes in the DNS resolver addresses.

Customer Networks

Customer network assignments have not been covered here because this section concentrates only on infrastructure. However, when an ISP is running BGP within its network, there is no benefit to be had by either aggregating or assigning networks on a regional basis. Customers move and want their connections to move to different parts of the country, so there is little purpose in trying to allocate address space to them regionally. Besides, BGP easily can handle huge numbers of customer-assigned networks.

Naturally, all these customer networks would be aggregated on the edge of the ISP's network. The RIRs will assign blocks of address space to their ISP membership, and the Internet community expects all ISPs to announce these blocks only to other ISPs. Announcing more specific networks from a block generally is frowned upon unless there is a genuine need to do so when aiding situations such as multihoming.

Plan Summary

Following the previous strategy, it should be quite straightforward to consistently number a new ISP backbone. Figure 5-15 shows how this strategy could apply to the scenario described. The ISP can justify a /23 for the infrastructure including loopbacks, so the address distribution looks something like that in Figure 5-15. All three registries make a minimum allocation of a /20 at the time of this writing, so this example assumes that the ISP would receive a /20 with the previously documented plan.

Figure 5-15 *Address-Deployment Plan*

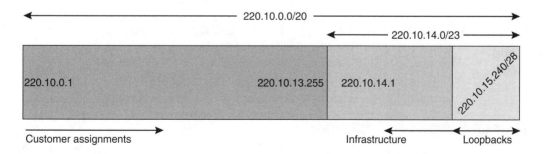

Planning for Future Growth

When the address block in Figure 5-15 has been used up (at the time of this writing, when the 80 percent utilization level has been reached), the ISP should apply for additional address space. If good records have been kept and the documentation has been submitted to the RIR, obtaining the next block should be relatively straightforward. The RIRs generally attempt to allocate enough address space that the ISP makes a yearly request to receive resources. For example, if the ISP has consumed resources faster than documented in the rollout plan, the ISP could make a larger request the second time round and receive the larger allocation.

In the current example, it is assumed that the second allocation made is the same size as the original allocation. The RIRs quite often attempt to allocate contiguous address space—it's not guaranteed, but they usually attempt to do this. The main motivation is to encourage CIDR-ization on behalf of the ISP rather than to make life convenient.

With the second address block being contiguous, as shown in Figure 5-16, the ISP simply can extend the loopback address range for the extra equipment being installed and can keep all the addresses contiguous. The infrastructure can be expanded into the new block as shown, or the ISP can completely renumber the infrastructure into the new address block (it is relatively easy to renumber ISP infrastructure because the vast majority of it is point-to-point links between the routers and because the secondary address support makes this job very simple). Customer assignments also can commence from the top end of the block.

Figure 5-16 *Address-Deployment Plan After Second Allocation*

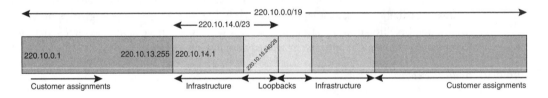

When the 80 percent utilization has been reached, the next application can be made, and so the cycle goes. It might be quite likely that third and future assignments would not be contiguous, so the ISP should not rely on expanding the /19 out into a /18. If it happens, consider it good fortune and take it as encouragement to announce only a /18 to the Internet!

Address Space for Customers

Customers are assigned address space by the ISP according to the policies set out by the RIR of which the ISP is a member. As an approximate guide, ISPs are expected to follow the same procedures with their customers as they have followed with the RIR in obtaining address space. So, when the ISP makes first technical contact with the customer, an assessment of address space requirements is made according to need. *Need* should not be confused with *want*. Staff members from many organizations who have been brought up in the classful IPv4 world still being taught by many academic institutions might believe that an Ethernet can be addressed with only a /24 network (the former Class C). In many documented instances, operations staff of an organization have numbered a backbone using /24s for Ethernets and point-to-point WAN links and become very upset when their requests are turned down by ISPs. In our experience, several potential customers have cancelled service because of refusal to meet the demands for address space.

The best system for assigning address space to customers is to first establish what range of address space customers are likely to need. Will it be anything from /24 to /28, or /18 to /26, or /18 to /28, for example? After the minimum and the maximum have been established, creating a matrix of the different sizes and assigning from the matrix is probably the most efficient way because it maximizes utilization. There are no hard-and-fast rules—the topic has been one of much discussion on many ISP mailing lists.

A simple example might be something like the following:

- Customer 1 needs a /28.
- Customer 2 needs a /26.
- Customer 3 needs a /24.
- Customer 4 needs a /25.
- Customer 5 needs a /27.
- Customer 6 needs a /24.
- Customer 7 needs a /23.
- Customer 8 needs a /28.
- Customer 9 needs a /26.

Assigning these linearly won't work because addresses need to be assigned according to bit boundaries. The schema shown in Figure 5-17 could be one approach to take. The ISP has decided that the largest customer likely to connect to the network will require a /23 of address space. So the ISP partitions the block into /23 chunks and then fills each chunk with the address requirements of the customers as they come in. Notice the attention to bit boundaries: A common mistake is to assign address space across bit boundaries, making the customer static route and iBGP setup on the aggregation routers unjustifiably harder.

Some ISPs have written scripts to do this assignment automatically from their address blocks as part of their customer sign-on and provisioning systems. Others simply maintain a large spreadsheet kept up-to-date with each assignment made. Some of the scripts are available on the Internet. A commonly used example is tree, available by anonymous FTP from ISI.[1]

Figure 5-17 *Example of Customer Assignments*

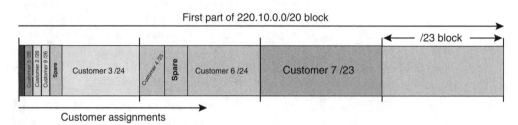

Applying to the RIRs or Upstream ISP for Addresses

The documentation and application process for obtaining address space is different for each of the three RIRs, so it is not covered in this text. However, the actual process should be relatively straightforward.

The first step in making any application for address space is to approach the upstream ISP. Many are members of one of the three RIRs and so can act on behalf of the RIR to assign address space. Some might charge a small fee for the service. When the upstream ISP cannot offer this service or refuses to offer this service, the next step is to approach the RIR serving the region where the new business is based.

The RIR first expects the new ISP to sign up as a member. Membership does not guarantee any allocation of resources, but it is simply the mechanism necessary to set up contact information, billing details, and so forth. The application process comes next. The forms to make the application for resources are kept on the RIR's Web site; joining as a member will help clarify exactly what has to be done next.

It is good practice to allow a few weeks between completing application for membership and actually expecting to receive resources. Setting up membership often requires verification of business status, establishment of billing processes, and so on; this all can take time. The application for resources also can take time because often plans that seem obvious to the designer might not be so obvious to a third party that has to make address-allocation decisions based on them.

If the detail listed previously is followed, there should be sufficient information available for the registry hostmaster team to understand the requirements of the backbone. ISPs should be prepared to disclose network plans (RIRs sign a nondisclosure agreement with membership) and designs, as well as purchase orders or receipts for the equipment requiring address space. All of this information helps the verification process and ensures timely allocation of resources.

Conclusion

This section gave an example of how to work out an addressing scheme for a developing ISP network. This is intended to help the growing ISP business work out how to apply addressing to its network and how to allocate assigned address space to its infrastructure. Indeed, following these processes should aid in the application process for address space from the RIRs.

Interior Routing

One of the hardest questions that a vendor is posed at the time of an RFP is which IGP the new ISP network should choose. As mentioned previously, the choice should be made for technical reasons, not for any others. Furthermore, the choice should be made by the ISP because the engineering and operations staff must run the network after the equipment has been installed. For all intents and purposes, there is little to choose among EIGRP, OSPF, and IS-IS. Because EIGRP is a Cisco-proprietary IGP, its deployment in the ISP world is somewhat less common than the deployment of OSPF and IS-IS. OSPF and IS-IS have a lot in common for most network implementations today, and the choice between the two really comes down to which IGP has the most operational experience with the staff employed. It's quite interesting to observe the spread of IS-IS around the Internet. As engineers leave the established ISPs and move to new jobs, they implement IS-IS as the IGP of choice simply because they are most familiar with it. A similar thing can be seen for OSPF, resulting in interesting debates over which IGP is better.

The ISP IGP Versus BGP Model

Chapter 3 covered the details of setting up the configuration for the three popular IGPs. If those configuration guidelines are followed, there is very little else to say about IGP choice and configuration. The key to a scalable network is simple: Keep the IGP small. BGP is designed to carry a large number of prefixes around the ISP backbone. To that end, iBGP is considered by some network engineers to be the interior routing protocol for their network. The actual model used is quite simple and is best displayed in Figure 5-18:

- The IGP carries infrastructure prefixes, typically backbone point-to-point links and router loopback interface addresses.

- iBGP carries customer-assigned address blocks, access network address pools, and any other prefixes that do not need to be carried in the IGP. iBGP also is used to carry some or all of the Internet Route Table (depending on the ISPs internal policy).

- eBGP is used to carry prefixes between ISPs and to implement routing policy between ISPs.

Figure 5-18 *Routing Protocol Relationships*

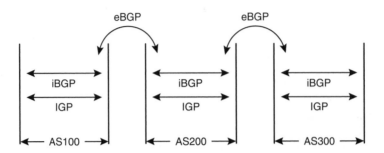

This model is very different from earlier models used in the infancy of the Internet, in which the IGP carried all prefixes in the ISP backbone and BGP was restricted to simply exchanging prefixes between different autonomous systems. The relative lack of scalability of IGPs and the great scalability now available in iBGP through route reflectors and confederations means that iBGP is an excellent tool for carrying prefixes across the ISP's backbone.

When first faced with this model, many network engineers are skeptical about running iBGP to all corners of their backbone. A common misperception in the Internet community is that substantial routers are required before BGP can be run—many engineers forget that several ISP backbones have been built out of nothing more than Cisco 2500 routers that have limited RAM and CPU capabilities. Indeed, the 2500 shares many features with its predecessor, the IGS, which was used in many ISP backbones in the early 1990s. Because iBGP supports routing policy and route filter capabilities, there is no need to carry the full routing table across the entire ISP backbone. It is quite common for ISPs to limit full or large routing table support to the core of their network and simply announce their domestic prefixes to the rest of their backbone. A Cisco 2500 router, for example, is quite happy running BGP with 10,000 prefixes; it will be quite slow at processing updates, but then there are unlikely to be many updates inside an ISP's backbone. Updates are most likely to be generated by new customers being added to the ISP's network, hardly a per-second or even per-minute occurrence in all but the largest of networks.

A typical deployment scenario is the following:

1 An ISP installs all the loopback addresses in the backbone into the IGP. The ISP also installs all the point-to-point link addresses in the backbone into the IGP.

2 All routers in the backbone participate in the IGP. Any that cannot participate in the IGP generally have static default routes pointing to those that can (these are typically dumb access-aggregation devices).

3 The ISP sets up iBGP across the entire ISP backbone using route reflectors (our preferred technique) or confederations. iBGP is configured to peer the routers with the loopback interfaces. As the loopbacks are carried in IGP, the routers can see each other because there is an entry in the forwarding table courtesy of the IGP.

4 The ISP implements a policy for iBGP. All domestic prefixes (the ISP's own prefixes not in the IGP and address space assigned to its customers) are tagged with a certain community.

5 The route reflectors have filters so that the clients receive only the routes that belong to this special community. This way, the ISP ensures that the core routers (the route reflectors) are the only ones carrying the full routing table. The remaining routers in the backbone, the clients in each cluster, carry only the reduced list of prefixes.

6 The clients use a couple of predetermined networks as default networks so that they have an exit path to the backbone core. The two special networks could belong to the ISP itself or, more likely, will belong to the upstream ISPs. If one of these networks disappears, the second will be available as a backup.

This type of deployment makes for a very scalable network and allows the ISP to implement BGP on virtually every router device within its own backbone. This method is much preferred over having an iBGP island in the middle of the network and either pointing static routes or using redistribution from other routing protocols at the edge. The latter has proven itself risky and unreliable in many situations.

Scaling Interior Routing Protocols

This section mostly is concerned with the scaling of iBGP. IGP scalability for the majority of networks is easy to achieve: Keep the number of prefixes small. iBGP is more of a challenge without using two important features, route reflectors and peer groups.

Route Reflectors

The first essential feature is the route reflector. Route reflectors are part of the BGP standard and are described in RFC 2796. It is generally recommended that new ISP network installations today install route reflectors from day one. Failing that, it is also very easy to migrate from using a full iBGP mesh to using route reflectors.

Referring to Figure 5-1, the general design principle is to set up the core routers as the route reflectors and have the remaining routers in the PoP configured as route-reflector clients. Recall from Chapter 3 that it is quite common for ISPs to have two route-reflector clusters per PoP, with each router in the PoP being a client of two route reflectors (instead of setting the cluster ID of the two router reflectors to be the same value). This configuration goes against almost all documented recommendations over the last few years, but it is actually the correct way of configuring route reflectors and almost guarantees avoidance of routing loops.

The two core routers in the PoP should talk standard iBGP with each other and also should be fully meshed with the remaining routers that are not cluster clients in the PoP and the rest of the network. A common network design is to fully mesh the core and border routers in a network, with the remaining routers in the distribution and access layers being clients (as in the example in Figure 5-19). This scales very well for all but the largest networks—and, in those cases, a route-reflector hierarchy provides the solution for distribution of prefixes across the backbone.

Figure 5-19 *Route-Reflector Layout*

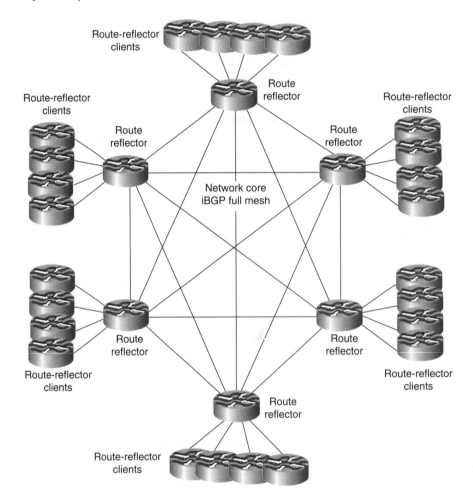

BGP Peer Groups

The second essential feature is the BGP peer group. This groups the BGP peers with the same outbound policy into one group. The normal situation without using peer groups is for the router to calculate the update to be sent to each neighbor individually. For a low number of peers, there is probably not much impact on the router CPU, but as the number of neighbors increases, so does the burden on the CPU—for example, 50 neighbors means that 50 updates have to be computed and sent individually.

When neighbors are grouped according to outbound policy within a peer group, the router calculates the update once per peer group and then sends the update to all members within the group. When peer groups first appeared in IOS Software, there was a very marked increase in iBGP neighbor establishment and iBGP convergence rate on the Motorola CPU-based routers. And with recent enhancements to IOS Software support for peer groups, it is now considered by many engineers standard practice to use peer groups whenever configuring iBGP.

The other advantage of peer groups is a cosmetic one: They improve the readability of the router configuration and make it much less prone to the introduction of errors by the operator or the network engineering staff. This is a considerable advantage, especially in the busy operational environment. It is also quite common for ISPs to create centralized templates with their peer-group configuration. Updates to the peer groups are done centrally, thus ensuring that all routers receive consistent changes to any required iBGP configuration. Compare this to making changes to every iBGP session for every router in the network. A 50-router backbone needs one line changed in a centralized peer group and needs this change to be applied to 50 routers; compare this to 2450 changes required if the ISP was not using peer groups. It is easy to see which is the preferred option.

NOTE   Peer groups also can be used for eBGP neighbors. This is less common because ISPs usually have very specific policies toward each of the external peers, but in principle, peer groups can be used here, too.

Exterior Routing

Connections from one ISP to another take two forms: The ISP either points a static default route to the neighbor or uses BGP.

The use of a static default route is perhaps the most common way that the edge of the Internet connects to the next layer. Enterprises connecting to the Internet often have little more requirement than a static default route to an ISP; the ISP takes care of routing the enterprise's traffic and announcing its prefixes to the rest of the Internet. This is also true for smaller ISPs: They don't require a sophisticated connection and simply rely on their upstream ISP for all their connectivity needs.

When an ISP (and, in some cases, an enterprise) have more sophisticated needs than a static default route can offer them, they can investigate the use of BGP as the exterior routing protocol. BGP allows the network more than one exit point by exchanging routing information with the upstream providers that the network connects to. This then allows the network to be multihomed.

AS Number

Multihoming itself is covered in the next section—a huge number of options are available, and that section covers some of the configuration concepts in more detail. Using BGP to multihome requires the ISP to acquire an AS number (ASN). This can be obtained in the same way in which IPv4 address space can be obtained.

The three regional registries provide ASNs to their membership upon application. The basic requirements are that the organization or ISP have at least two separate connections to the Internet, either to at least two *different* ISPs or to an ISP and an Internet eXchange Point (IXP). The application should list the ASNs that will be connected, allowing the registries to verify the intended connection from the Internet Route Table. ISPs also can apply for ASNs on behalf of their customers—the RIR Web pages should be checked for current information.

At the time of this writing, around 30 percent of the available ASN space has been distributed to organizations connected to the Internet—and around 12,000 of those ASNs actually are being announced to the routing table. The last two years saw a remarkable growth in multihoming as the edge of the Internet required more reliable connections to the core—a sure sign that the Internet is becoming business-critical for many organizations. It is also argued by several that the "middle reaches" of the Internet have shown a marked downturn in service quality and availability, forcing organizations previously content with a single-homed strategy to look for redundancy by connecting to another ISP.

To cater for the growth in ASN usage, an extension to the AS space has been proposed: replacing the 2-byte ASN with a 4-byte ASN. A migration strategy hasn't been worked out fully yet, but several proposals indicate that it shouldn't be too difficult when the time comes for the registries to assign 4-byte ASNs.

Scalable External Peering

Most of the BGP scalability efforts have been applied within the ISP network. eBGP is a point-to-point process between two ISPs, so scaling the protocol here is less complex. However, newcomers to the industry need to consider two commonly used and important techniques for scaling external BGP peering between ISPs.

Route Refresh Capability

The route refresh capability is a long-awaited technique in the operator industry that lets eBGP (and, indeed, iBGP) neighbors apply a new policy to the BGP session without tearing down the whole peering.

For many years, the only technique available when an ISP wanted to apply a new policy to a peering session with a neighbor was to shut down the BGP peering and then bring it up again. Consider what happens in the Internet when this is done:

- Shutting down a peering means that all the prefixes received from the neighboring ISP must be removed from the BGP table and the forwarding table on the local router. For the full routing table, this takes CPU time to achieve.

- The prefixes that have been removed from the local router then have to be removed from all the other routers in the ISP backbone taking part in the full iBGP mesh (subject, of course, to any policy applied between iBGP neighbors). This takes CPU load on all the routers in the backbone.

- If the ISP was providing transit to the Internet, these changes are propagated to the ISP's transit customers. This means more changes and more impact on their router CPUs. And this change propagates through all the neighboring ASNs that relied on the routing information received from this peering that was torn down.

This example simply shows what happens to prefixes received from the peer. The ripple effect is quite pronounced! The same thing happens in the opposite direction:

- Shutting down the peering means that the ISP's prefixes that were announced to the peer are withdrawn from that peer. The local ISP effectively disappears from the neighbor, relying on alternative paths, if they exist, or completely disappearing from the Internet if they don't.

- The neighboring ISP withdraws the prefixes from its BGP and forwarding tables and then withdraws them from all announcements made to neighbors.

Combining the two effects, simply shutting down the BGP peering creates a significant ripple effect through the Internet on both sides of the peering in question. If there were multiple paths from the ISP to the Internet, many routers have to recalculate the best path, affecting traffic flow and apparent Internet "performance" to the end user.

As discussed in the following section, many ISPs also apply route flap damping. If a route flaps, the prefix possibly will be damped (not reannounced by the peer even though it reappears in the BGP table).

To simply apply some new policy on the eBGP peering, the ISP has caused lots of potential problems to hit the Internet:

- A routing prefix withdrawal surge occurs through the local backbone and peers.

- An ISP's prefixes are withdrawn from the Internet.

- The potential of flap damping exists.

- Customers see traffic flow being interrupted for minutes—in the worst case, flow stops altogether

The simple solution to this problem is a new capability introduced into BGP known as route refresh. This capability allows peering routers to reset policy between each other without having to tear down the session. (Cisco had an earlier version of this called soft reconfiguration, which was implemented only on the local router and required potentially double the amount of memory to store the prefixes received from a neighbor.)

When the ISP operator wants to change the policy, the new policy is applied to the router configuration and then the route refresh request is sent to the neighboring router. The neighboring router then simply sends its entire announcement back to its peer, allowing the peer to rebuild its BGP table using the new policy. This is such a simple extension to the BGP functionality, but there is now greater possibility for stability in the Internet Route Table. We would like to see the hard clearing of BGP made as difficult to do as rebooting the router (going through a Q&A session on the router to confirm that the operator is absolutely sure), with the explicit aim of encouraging more ISPs to remember to use the route refresh capability. As covered in the previous chapter, the command to do this is **clear ip bgp** *neighbor* **in|out**, hopefully something that can be "implanted" in all ISP engineers before they touch any operational networks.

BGP Flap Damping

A consequence of the churning in the Internet caused by indiscriminate clearing of BGP sessions, by unstable infrastructure, and by antisocial configuration practices is the request for BGP flap damping to be available in IOS Software. Prefixes that appear and disappear from the Internet Route Table cause a CPU hit on the router: Withdrawing a prefix means that it has to be withdrawn from the BGP and forwarding tables; the prefix also has to be withdrawn from neighbors and so on throughout all the BGP speakers attached to this network.

The mechanics of flap damping were discussed in the previous chapter, and that should be studied in case the mechanism is not clearly understood. Every flap attracts a fixed penalty; the penalty is decayed exponentially. Limits are set for when the prefix is suppressed and when it can be made available to the Internet again.

The purpose of flap damping is to penalize those prefixes that won't remain stable. The more they flap, the more likely they are to disappear from the Internet Route Table. ISPs that implement the Cisco defaults will see their prefixes disappear from the Internet for a maximum of 60 minutes. This is a long time to explain away to customers, so the incentive is there to ensure that stability is guaranteed when making announcements to the Internet.

Flap damping usually is implemented on the ISP's peering and border routers, basically all routers with eBGP sessions. IOS Software does not support flap damping for iBGP, and, in any case, the concept does not make sense. If ISPs are experiencing route flaps caused by the core network, they need to examine their network design and operational practices rather than trying to use an IOS Software feature to fix self-made problems. The eBGP-speaking routers will require slightly more CPU (depending on the number of peers and the number of prefixes received), but the big advantage is that the rest of the network will see a reduction in CPU requirement because the worst flaps are kept out of the core network.

In the mid-1990s, when route flap damping first was implemented in IOS Software, a typical ISP backbone in our experience saw something like 15 percent reduction in CPU requirement for the Motorola CPU–based routers deployed. The border router had the biggest, fastest CPU available at the time, and this took the hit from the instabilities caused by the problems that some of the U.S. backbones were experiencing at the time. The rest of the local backbone was very stable, with route fluctuations reducing noticeably. Most important, the level of customer complaints about strange routing and traffic disappearing reduced as well, although some education was necessary about what route flap damping would actually mean. (An unreachable destination could be caused by a network being disconnected, or that network could be flap-damped. Or it could be caused by the locally originated prefix being suppressed by some ISP somewhere along the path because of flap damping. These particular points need to be remembered by operators, especially customer support centers and network operations centers that deal with customer complaints about unreachabilities in the Internet.)

An ISP can make two choices when implementing flap damping. The first is to use the IOS Software default values; these are considered quite severe by some members of the community, suppressing a prefix after it has flapped three times in the space of a few minutes. The second option is to use the RIPE-229[2] values, which implement progressive flap damping depending on prefix length. Smaller prefixes are hit harder than larger prefixes, based on operational experience gained through the last few years. The RIPE-229 values also allow three flaps before the prefix is suppressed, allowing a little more leeway for software upgrades and other maintenance activities in the ISP network.

Multihoming

In multihoming, a network has more than one connection to another independent network. This can take the form of one ISP having more than one connection to another ISP or having connections to more than one other ISP. For the network engineer, configuring multihoming with BGP poses a challenge that, to many, seems just too hard. Whether it is because BGP has been touted as being difficult or because so many configuration knobs now are available, multihoming has become something of a feared subject for many ISPs.

Writing a definitive text on multihoming is not straightforward—there are so many possible situations and so many different types of interprovider relationships that covering them all is not really feasible. Instead, this section guides you in the basics of establishing a BGP session with other networks and other ISPs, with the principle that once the basics have been established and understood, enhancement of the configuration to deal with more particular or complex scenarios becomes somewhat easier. When faced with a complex multihoming problem, too many engineers try to deal with it without regard to the basic needs. The principle of KISS ("Keep It Simple, Stupid") has been mentioned before and is very applicable to multihoming.

A few configuration scenarios will be covered. These form the basis for virtually all multihoming requirements between ISPs.

- **Multihoming to the same ISP**—This is applicable to the enterprise customer and the smaller ISP that has just started in business. They have one upstream circuit and now require a second one.

- **Multihoming to a different ISP**—As with the previous case, this can apply to both enterprise and ISP customers. It represents the next level in complexity of being part of the Internet.

- **Using communities for multihoming and traffic engineering**—After the ISP has become comfortable with its multihoming configurations, using communities will give it greater control over engineering traffic flows in and out of the network.

- **Multihoming for content providers**—This is a unique situation in which outbound traffic flows are somewhat larger than inbound flows. This requires careful consideration because what might be good practice in the previous examples will not be sufficient in this case.

Basics

Before pushing ahead and installing a new circuit, some of the basics of multihoming must be understood and remembered:

- The new circuit should go to a different PoP of the upstream ISP. If it goes to the same upstream PoP, site redundancy of the upstream is lost. Complete PoP outages can occur because of electrical, operational, or environmental problems.

- If the upstream ISP has only one PoP, request or insist that the new connection be terminated in a different router, one with a different power source and an alternative path out of the network from that of the original connection. This isn't as good as the previous requirement, but it ensures that maintenance of the upstream router doesn't defeat the point of the customer multihoming.

- The new connection should be terminated in a different local router. Terminating a multihomed connection on the same local router creates a single point of failure in that router—and equipment failures (whether software, hardware, or operational) are just as common as infrastructure failures (for example, in circuits). If the network being multihomed is present in more than one location, there is extra benefit to be gained by installing the new connection in a different location: site redundancy.

- If possible, purchase the new circuit from a different circuit provider. We often have seen networks being multihomed at the IP level, but the circuit providing the backup goes through the same telco equipment from the cabinet all the way to the exchange and to the upstream ISP. Some telcos will be happy to guarantee diverse routing (as a paid service), but if a choice of carriers is available, using two makes a lot more sense. One carrier can have a complete outage of the network, resulting in only one of the local network's links being affected.

Likewise, the routing configuration has some basic principles that need to be understood and remembered:

- BGP needs to be used. A lot of multihoming technically can be achieved by using static routes, but that technique is very inflexible, and failover is often not as effective as with BGP.

- Downloading the full routing table is not required. This is a very common misunderstanding in the industry today.

- Cisco IOS Software has sufficient tools available, but their application needs to be understood properly. Provided that the following three "rules" are adhered to, there should be little difficulty understanding the basics of multihoming:

  — IP prefix lists are used for filtering prefixes (don't use access lists because they are harder to understand, are slower to implement in the router, and have been the source of many configuration errors in the past).

  — AS path access lists (or filter lists) are used to filter AS paths. AS path filtering is a very useful tool for many multihoming situations encountered.

  — Route maps are used to implement policy. (Route maps also can be used to apply filtering, but this is recommended only after you fully understand how to use BGP in the context discussed here.)

- Several BGP attributes can and should be used to facilitate proper load balancing when multihoming:

  — Local preference is applied to routing announcements coming from the neighboring AS, to allow the local AS to influence the outbound path that traffic will take. The default local preference is 100; the highest local preference wins.

  — MED (metric) is applied to routing announcements sent to the neighboring AS, to allow the local AS to influence the inbound path that traffic to the network will take. The lowest metric wins. If the metric is not set, Cisco IOS Software assumes that the metric is 0. The MED attribute is used only between locally connected autonomous systems.

  — AS path prepend is used in a similar way to MED, but it has global scope. Applying an AS path prepend to outbound routing announcements sent to the neighboring AS makes the neighboring AS see the path to the local AS as being more AS hops away and, therefore, less preferred than any alternative path that has fewer AS hops in it. The AS (or autonomous systems) prepended should be the local AS; otherwise, unpredictable results could occur. (BGP loop detection might come into play in determining optimum or suitable paths.)

  — Communities are used extensively for transmitting policy options between ISPs. Community values need agreement between neighboring or participating ISPs, as the examples later in this chapter show.

- Announce the RIR-allocated network block. It is very important that the network block (or blocks) that have been allocated by the RIR, or upstream ISP are announced in one piece. For example, if the network 221.10.0.0/19 has been allocated to the local ISP, that network must be announced as a /19. The registries don't make this a requirement, but not doing this will increase the chances that the prefix will be damped or filtered by ISPs elsewhere in the Internet.

- Be prudent with network-block subprefixes that have to be announced. The only requirement to leak subprefixes to the Internet Route Table is for traffic engineering. And traffic engineering is a delicate task, as the examples later in this section show. The unacceptable face of traffic engineering has resulted in a routing table of around 108,000 prefixes, of which a large proportion could be excluded if the origin networks had been more careful with their announcements. (Announcing a /19 network block as 32 /24 networks is like taking a mallet to crack a very small nut—what is more, it rarely works as well as hoped.)

Bearing these points in mind, the rest of the section examines multihoming scenarios and provides some router configuration ideas.

Multihoming Options

Before looking at detailed examples, it's worth considering the different types of multihoming possible and the routing protocols that should be considered for them.

Stub Network

This is where a network is connected to the ISP through a single connection or through multiple parallel circuits between the customer router and the ISP router. In this case, there is no need for BGP—BGP can be used, if desired, but it is simply unnecessary, and often a stub network is easier to configure and manage using static routing protocols and appropriate network equipment (if available or applicable).

The example in Figure 5-20 shows a network connected with two parallel circuits to the upstream ISP. This example does not require BGP (although BGP could be used, if desired). A public AS number will not be assigned to the customer network by the registries for this purpose.

Figure 5-20 *Stub Network*

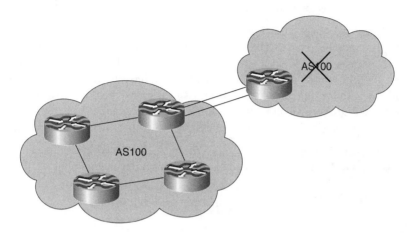

The common solution to this issue is to either use static default routes to load-share on the parallel circuits, or use a hardware device at both ends of the parallel circuits to multiplex the two paths into one higher-bandwidth circuit presented to the routers. The other alternative adopted by some providers is to use Multilink PPP to bond the two circuits together. The first option is the easiest to use because it offers the least complication and has the smallest chance of something going wrong. However, ISPs in regions where high-bandwidth circuits are not available often have to multiplex (MUX) together many lower bandwidth circuits just to fulfill their requirements, and quite often these ISPs purchase T1/E1 MUXs (for example) to join anything up to 16 T1/E1 circuits into a higher-bandwidth pipe. There are several products on the market, and from our experience, using a hardware device often ends up being simpler and more reliable than using the router to do the same thing.

Multihomed Stub Network

If the network in the preceding example is multihomed on to their upstream by connecting to different routers in their upstream's network, BGP will have to be used.

Some ISPs use an IGP for this function (we have seen RIP, EIGRP, and OSPF all being used), but this practice is strongly discouraged because it is a very serious potential source of misconfiguration and problems in the ISP backbone. The chances of having the customer's IGP leaking into the ISP's IGP are very great; such configurations need extremely careful filtering practices on behalf of the ISP. (Some ISPs use a different IGP than the one they use in their backbone, and that can alleviate the problem of cross-pollution.)

The preferred, if not correct, way to do this is to use BGP. When multihoming to the same ISP, it should be noted that only a private ASN is required.[3] There is no need for a public ASN because only the upstream ISP will see the AS. The upstream ISP must strip the private AS from any announcements made to the Internet (using the **remove-private-AS** BGP neighbor command). This saves a visit to the upstream ISP, Local Internet Registry, or the RIR to apply for an ASN (and under RIR policies at the time of this writing, this type of multihoming will not qualify for an ASN).

Figure 5-21 gives an example in which the customer network has three connections to the upstream, with one connection going to a different router/PoP in the upstream's backbone.

Figure 5-21 *Diversely Multihomed Stub Network*

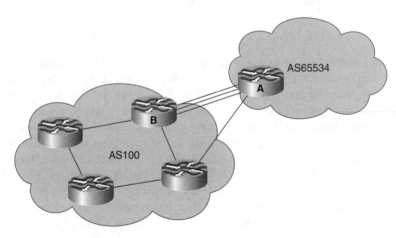

The load sharing on the two parallel connections in Figure 5-21 can be achieved in a variety of ways. Apart from using a hardware MUX or Multilink PPP, the use of BGP is now a possibility. A couple of BGP configuration options are available: The first is eBGP multihop, and the second is BGP multipath.

eBGP Multihop

eBGP multihop is an eBGP peering between the loopback interfaces (or other interface not on the demarcation zone between the two networks) of routers in the two networks. The configuration could be something like the following:

```
Router A:
router bgp 65534
 neighbor 1.1.1.1 remote-as 100
```

```
    neighbor 1.1.1.1 ebgp-multihop 5
   !
   ip route 1.1.1.1 255.255.255.255 serial 1/0
   ip route 1.1.1.1 255.255.255.255 serial 1/1
   ip route 1.1.1.1 255.255.255.255 serial 1/2
   !

   Router B:
   router bgp 100
    neighbor 2.2.2.2 remote-as 65534
    neighbor 2.2.2.2 ebgp-multihop 5
   !
   ip route 2.2.2.2 255.255.255.255 serial 0/0
   ip route 2.2.2.2 255.255.255.255 serial 0/1
   ip route 2.2.2.2 255.255.255.255 serial 0/2
   !
```

The addresses 1.1.1.1 and 2.2.2.2 are the addresses of the loopback interfaces on routers B and A, respectively. Because there is no direct path between the two addresses, a static route needs to be configured on both routers pointing to each other's loopback addresses. Three paths are available, so three static routes need to be installed. If one interface goes down, the static route through the other interface still will be available.

The second essential command is the **ebgp-multihop** statement for BGP. BGP peers normally between addresses on the demarcation zone; the **multihop** statement ensures that BGP will set a higher TTL (the number 5 in the example sets a TTL of 5) so that a BGP peering can be established between routers with several intermediate hops. The number 5 has been used as an example only—some ISPs use 255 as their default value, but we generally recommend not setting the TTL hop much higher than is strictly necessary.

BGP Multipath

The second option available is to use BGP multipath. This should be considered as an alternative to using eBGP multihop and is an option used by several ISPs also. The configuration could be something like the following:

```
   Router A:
   router bgp 65534
    neighbor 1.2.3.1 remote-as 100
    neighbor 1.2.3.5 remote-as 100
    neighbor 1.2.3.9 remote-as 100
    maximum-paths 3
   !

   Router B:
   router bgp 100
    neighbor 1.2.3.2 remote-as 65534
    neighbor 1.2.3.6 remote-as 65534
    neighbor 1.2.3.10 remote-as 65534
    maximum-paths 3
   !
```

Addresses 1.2.3.1, 1.2.3.5, and 1.2.3.9 are the addresses on Router A for the point-to-point link between A and B. Router B has the corresponding /30 addresses. The only extra requirement over a standard BGP configuration is the **maximum-paths 3** directive— this tells the router to install three parallel paths into the FIB.

The downside to the multipath command is that multiple BGP sessions are required. In the rare circumstances in which the full routing table is exchanged between peers, this can require a considerable amount of memory on the router to store many copies of the routing table rather than the one copy that would have been required for the eBGP multihop option.

General Multihoming

The previous two examples are quite specific and offer the solutions to multihoming in those situations. In the Internet at large, multihoming is generally more complex or has more sophisticated requirements. Figure 5-22 shows a more typical example of the type of interconnections that might exist.

Figure 5-22 *General Multihoming*

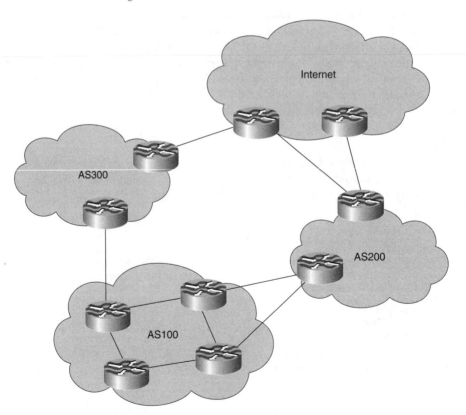

In this case, there is only one solution: Use BGP with a public ASN. The bulk of the rest of this section on multihoming discusses the configuration options and tools that are available.

Before investigating these, it is really important to remember to keep it simple. The simplest way to start off figuring out any multihoming configuration solution is to start with defaults and the minimum configuration, and then build it up into something more complex. Too often network engineers head into the realms of the most sophisticated configurations, full routing tables, and so on, just to solve the simplest of problems. Complexity means greater difficulty in maintaining the configuration, training support staff to handle it, and training operations staff to troubleshoot when there is a major problem and the guru is off on holidays out of mobile phone or e-mail coverage. Because this is probably the hardest part of an interprovider relationship, it is worth spending the time to work out the configuration necessary. Some effort is required; there is no magic solution (although many ISPs and end sites often wish for one).

Multihoming to the Same ISP

This type of multihoming quite often is overlooked in favor of multihoming a network to different ISPs. However, if the upstream ISP is a provider of reasonable quality whose network design, resilience, and redundancy can experience no noticeable service outage, multihoming using a second connection makes a great deal of sense technically because the BGP requirements are somewhat simpler than any other situation. (It often makes a great deal of sense financially because many ISPs offer discounts for second circuits to their backbones.)

In this situation, as mentioned previously, a private AS is all that is required for BGP. The registries will not assign an AS for this case because the AS will not have, or require, a global view. The upstream ISP proxy-aggregates (announces the customer address space from its own AS) for the customer; for all intents and purposes, the Internet sees the customer as a simple statically connected entity. There is no need for detailed local topology information particular to only the ISP and its customer to be announced to the whole Internet.

End Sites

Two types of end sites exist as far as traffic flows are concerned. The first is the ISP that is connecting customers to the Internet. The traffic flow in this case is mostly inbound; a typical volume ratio might be 70 percent inbound and 30 percent outbound. The second is the content provider, and traffic flow levels typically are reversed. This section considers only the first scenario; the later section on "Outbound Traffic Loadsharing" considers the case for the content provider.

Primary and Backup Paths

The first example considered (shown in Figure 5-23) is one with two paths between the networks: One path is used as the primary link, and the other path is used exclusively for backup. This situation is used commonly when the primary path has a high bandwidth and the backup path is of low bandwidth or poor latency and is sufficient only when the main link has failed.

Figure 5-23 *Primary and Backup Paths to the Same ISP*

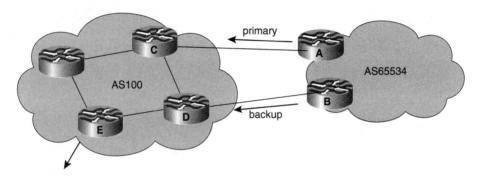

The primary path is between Router A and Router C, with the backup path between Router B and Router D. AS 65534 has an address block of its own—say, 221.10.0.0/19 for this example.

AS 65534 *must* announce its aggregate block to AS 100—it is very important that the aggregate always be announced because the smaller the prefix is, the more likely some ISPs are to filter it (thereby causing reachability problems for the network announcing subprefixes).

The configuration of the various routers follows:

```
Router A:
        router bgp 65534
        network 221.10.0.0 mask 255.255.224.0
        neighbor 222.222.10.2 remote-as 100
        neighbor 222.222.10.2 description RouterC
        neighbor 222.222.10.2 prefix-list aggregate out
        neighbor 222.222.10.2 prefix-list default in
        !
        ip prefix-list aggregate permit 221.10.0.0/19
        ip prefix-list default permit 0.0.0.0/0
        !

Router B:
        router bgp 65534
        network 221.10.0.0 mask 255.255.224.0
        neighbor 222.222.10.6 remote-as 100
        neighbor 222.222.10.6 description RouterD
        neighbor 222.222.10.6 prefix-list aggregate out
        neighbor 222.222.10.6 route-map routerD-out out
```

```
        neighbor 222.222.10.6 prefix-list default in
        neighbor 222.222.10.6 route-map routerD-in in
        !
        ip prefix-list aggregate permit 221.10.0.0/19
        ip prefix-list default permit 0.0.0.0/0
        !
        route-map routerD-out permit 10
          match ip address prefix-list aggregate
          set metric 10
        route-map routerD-out permit 20
        !
        route-map routerD-in permit 10
          set local-preference 90
        !

Router C:
        router bgp 100
         neighbor 222.222.10.1 remote-as 65534
         neighbor 222.222.10.1 default-originate
         neighbor 222.222.10.1 prefix-list Customer in
         neighbor 222.222.10.1 prefix-list default out
        !
        ip prefix-list Customer permit 221.10.0.0/19
        ip prefix-list default permit 0.0.0.0/0
        !


Router D:
        router bgp 100
         neighbor 222.222.10.5 remote-as 65534
         neighbor 222.222.10.5 default-originate
         neighbor 222.222.10.5 prefix-list Customer in
         neighbor 222.222.10.5 prefix-list default out
        !
        ip prefix-list Customer permit 221.10.0.0/19
        ip prefix-list default permit 0.0.0.0/0
        !
```

The configuration on Router A is quite simple. The outbound announcement made is to send the /19 aggregate upstream; inbound, the router accepts only the default route from the upstream. For all intents and purposes, the default route is exactly the same as the full routing table; it says that the ISP announcing the default knows how to get to the whole Internet. One prefix quoting the default is much more preferable than 108,000 prefixes to do the same thing.

Router B is the chosen backup path between the two networks. As mentioned earlier, local preference is used to set a preference on inbound announcements to determine outbound traffic flow. MED is used to set a preference on outbound announcements to influence inbound traffic flow. So the configuration on Router B does just that:

- A local preference of 90 is set on the inbound announcements. As a result, any prefixes learned will have a lower priority than those learned from Router A.

- A MED of 10 is set on outbound announcements. AS 100 sees the prefixes from AS 65534 with an MED of 10, a higher value than heard through the other path and, therefore, less preferred.

Router C and Router D share very similar configurations: The upstream ISP has left all the multihoming options to its customer. The aggregate is allowed in, the default is sent out, and otherwise the configuration is quite simple. It also is easy to maintain—any changes required in the multihoming are left to the customer, reducing the support burden.

If the customer does not want to deal with the complexity of configuring the multihoming, the configuration can be swapped around (so that the MED and local prefs go on AS 100, with the configuration on AS 65534 routers made "simple").

Router E's configuration needs to be set so that it strips the private AS out of any announcements to the Internet. The configuration example follows:

```
Router E:
      router bgp 100
       neighbor 222.222.10.17 remote-as 200
       neighbor 222.222.10.17 remove-private-AS
       neighbor 222.222.10.17 prefix-list Customer out
       !
       ip prefix-list Customer permit 221.10.0.0/19

       !
```

Note the **remove-private-as** directive on the peering with AS 200. This strips the AS 65534 from the /19 aggregate announced by the customer of AS 100 and announces it as though it originated from AS 100.

Load Sharing

The second example, displayed in Figure 5-24, refines the previous one so that both links between the two ISPs can be used to carry traffic at all times. This more commonly is used in the Internet because many long-distance and international circuits are still substantially more expensive per kilometer than those in metropolitan areas.

Figure 5-24 *Load Sharing to the Same ISP*

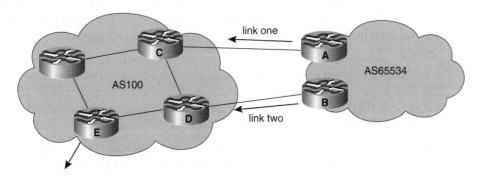

As before, AS 65534 announces its aggregate to the upstream ISP. To achieve the load sharing, the aggregate is also split into two pieces, two /20 networks. One /20 is announced out of one link, and the other /20 is announced out of the other link. The configuration examples are

```
Router A:
      router bgp 65534
       network 221.10.0.0 mask 255.255.224.0
       network 221.10.0.0 mask 255.255.240.0
       neighbor 222.222.10.2 remote-as 100
       neighbor 222.222.10.2 prefix-list routerC out
       neighbor 222.222.10.2 prefix-list default in
       !
       ip prefix-list default permit 0.0.0.0/0
       ip prefix-list routerC permit 221.10.0.0/20
       ip prefix-list routerC permit 221.10.0.0/19
       !
       ip route 221.10.0.0 255.255.240.0 null0
       ip route 221.10.0.0 255.255.224.0 null0
       !

Router C:
      router bgp 100
       neighbor 222.222.10.1 remote-as 65534
       neighbor 222.222.10.1 default-originate
       neighbor 222.222.10.1 prefix-list Customer in
       neighbor 222.222.10.1 prefix-list default out
       !
       ip prefix-list Customer permit 221.10.0.0/19 le 20
       ip prefix-list default permit 0.0.0.0/0
       !
```

Router A inserts the /19 and the first /20 into the BGP process. Notice that the two static routes to place the two prefixes are in the routing table so that the prefixes go into the BGP table. Router A announces the /19 and the first /20 (the prefix list called routerC takes care of this) to Router C. Router B's configuration is almost identical to that of Router A; its configuration uses the other /20.

As before, the upstream ISP configuration has been kept deliberately simple. The upstream ISP simply allows the aggregate and any /20 subprefix from its customer and announces only the default route to its customer.

This is a reasonable first cut at making this type of load sharing work. No local preferences, MEDs, or AS path manipulation is required. If AS 65534 requires further manipulation to balance out traffic patterns, it could try subdividing the /19 into /21 subprefixes and announcing those to the upstream. This would require changes in the BGP configuration and prefix list ranges to suit. Quite often an upstream ISP simply allows the aggregate and a range of subprefix sizes from its customer so that the customer can manipulate the load sharing as required.

Router E configuration is unchanged from the previous example: AS 100 only announces the customer aggregate and removes the private AS from the AS path. There is never any need to announce the customer subprefixes in a situation like this.

Multiple Dual-Homed Customers (RFC 2270)

RFC 2270–based multihoming is an extension of the previous two examples, describing how to scale a situation in which multiple customers are multihoming onto the ISP backbone.

Figure 5-25 shows how multiple customer would multihome onto the backbone of the same upstream ISP. The diagram also shows that the same ASN is used—this is not a drawing error, but it is genuinely all that is required. The configuration will be based on that used in the previous section, so AS 100 routers will be announcing only a default route to customers; there is no other routing information and no routing information from one customer to the other, so there is no chance of BGP loop detection coming into play.

The principles are the same as before: Each customer announces its aggregate to AS 100 and any subprefixes that are necessary to make the load sharing on the dual links work. The configuration examples are

```
Router A1:
      router bgp 65534
        network 221.10.0.0 mask 255.255.224.0
        network 221.10.0.0 mask 255.255.240.0
        neighbor 222.222.10.2 remote-as 100
        neighbor 222.222.10.2 prefix-list routerC out
        neighbor 222.222.10.2 prefix-list default in
        !
        ip prefix-list default permit 0.0.0.0/0
        ip prefix-list routerC permit 221.10.0.0/20
        ip prefix-list routerC permit 221.10.0.0/19
        !
        ip route 221.10.0.0 255.255.240.0 null0
        ip route 221.10.0.0 255.255.224.0 null0
        !

Router C:
      router bgp 100
        neighbor bgp-customers peer-group
        neighbor bgp-customers remote-as 65534
        neighbor bgp-customers default-originate
        neighbor bgp-customers prefix-list default out
        neighbor 222.222.10.1 peer-group bgp-customers
        neighbor 222.222.10.1 description Customer One
        neighbor 222.222.10.1 prefix-list Customer1 in
        neighbor 222.222.10.9 peer-group bgp-customers
        neighbor 222.222.10.9 description Customer Two
        neighbor 222.222.10.9 prefix-list Customer2 in
        neighbor 222.222.10.17 peer-group bgp-customers
        neighbor 222.222.10.17 description Customer Three
        neighbor 222.222.10.17 prefix-list Customer3 in
        ...
        !
        ip prefix-list Customer1 permit 221.10.0.0/19 le 20
        ip prefix-list Customer2 permit 221.16.64.0/19 le 20
        ip prefix-list Customer3 permit 221.14.192.0/19 le 20
        ...
```

```
        ip prefix-list default permit 0.0.0.0/0
        !

Router E:
        router bgp 109
         neighbor 222.222.10.17 remote-as 110
         neighbor 222.222.10.17 remove-private-AS
         neighbor 222.222.10.17 prefix-list Customers out
        !
        ip prefix-list Customers permit 221.10.0.0/19
        ip prefix-list Customers permit 221.16.64.0/19
        ip prefix-list Customers permit 221.14.192.0/19
        !
```

Figure 5-25 *RFC 2270 Multihoming*

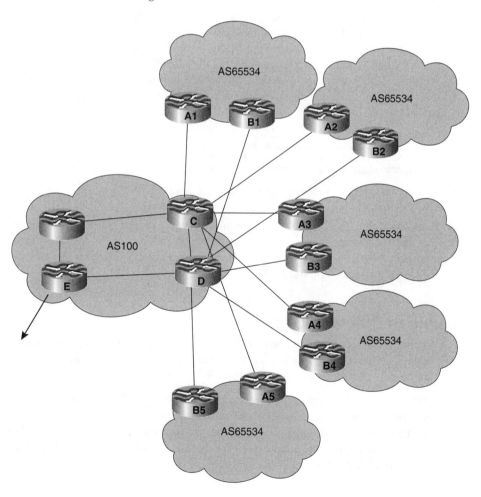

The Router A1 configuration is the template for all the Router A's in the network. The Router B's also all share the same configuration, just using the other /20 from the aggregate block.

The interesting configuration is for Router C. Rather than handcraft an individual configuration for each customer, a peer group is created and applied for each. After all, each customer has the same outbound announcement, a default route, so a peer group can be used easily (it also is more efficient for the router and is much easier to read). Each customer has its own address block that is filtered in the inbound BGP configuration.

Router D configuration is almost identical to that of Router C. Indeed, only the point-to-point link addresses for the BGP peerings are different.

Router E announces just the aggregates to the Internet, stripping out the private AS from the AS path. Note that if the aggregates all come out of AS 100's address space, that address space should be announced to the Internet instead of the individual announcements from the customers. There is no point announcing the subprefixes; even though it does no harm, it is unnecessary information on the routing table and adds to the burden that all the ISPs carrying the full routing table must deal with. A configuration of Router E in this case might be as follows:

```
router bgp 109
 neighbor 222.222.10.17 remote-as 110
 neighbor 222.222.10.17 remove-private-AS
 neighbor 222.222.10.17 prefix-list my-aggregate out
!
ip prefix-list my-aggregate permit 221.8.0.0/13
!
```

Removal of the private AS isn't even required because the subprefixes are stripped out by the prefix list. However, we consider it good practice to include the command in all eBGP configurations, just in case of any configuration errors or any instances in which the prefix list fails to include all prefixes.

Multihoming to Different ISPs

When two connections to an upstream ISP is not sufficient, networks choose to multihome between different ISPs. This is somewhat harder to achieve, and it does need a little more care because the effects are seen over the whole Internet.

It is understood that a public ASN is required for this type of multihoming, although it is perfectly feasible to use a private AS if both upstream parties agree to it. There are several instances of this in the Internet, but by far the more common practice is to use a public ASN. Many of the configuration hints covered in the previous section apply here, but with suitable modification. Several common examples are considered next.

Primary and Backup Paths

The first example considered is on in which there are two paths from the end site to the Internet: One path is used as the primary link, and the other path is used exclusively for backup. This situation is commonly used when the primary path has a high bandwidth, when the backup path is of low bandwidth or poor latency, or when the upstream has a low-quality or expensive transit network and is sufficient only when the main link has failed.

In Figure 5-26 the main link is between Routers A and C; the link between Routers B and D is the backup link. To configure the routers to achieve this traffic flow, an AS path prepend is applied to outbound announcements from Router B—and local preference is applied inbound to announcements received by Router B. Taking an Internet view, if a prepend of one AS is applied on Router B, the path from the Internet through AS 108 to Router B will appear to be one hop longer than the path through AS 109 and Router A. However, traffic from AS 108 to AS 107 should go through AS 109 rather than following the direct path: A prepend of one AS will make the direct path still shorter than the path through the Internet (which might have one or more autonomous systems in the path). A two-AS prepend will look the same length (assuming one AS in the Internet), but a three-AS prepend will make the path through AS 109 look shorter. So this is the value used in the configuration that follows.

Figure 5-26 *Primary/Backup to Different ISPs*

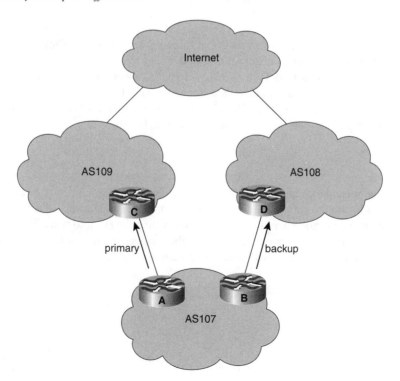

```
Router A:
       router bgp 107
        network 221.10.0.0 mask 255.255.224.0
        neighbor 222.222.10.1 remote-as 109
        neighbor 222.222.10.1 prefix-list aggregate out
        neighbor 222.222.10.1 prefix-list default in
        !
       ip prefix-list aggregate permit 221.10.0.0/19
       ip prefix-list default permit 0.0.0.0/0
        !


Router B:
       router bgp 107
        network 221.10.0.0 mask 255.255.224.0
        neighbor 220.1.5.1 remote-as 108
        neighbor 220.1.5.1 prefix-list aggregate out
        neighbor 220.1.5.1 route-map routerD-out out
        neighbor 220.1.5.1 prefix-list default in
        neighbor 220.1.5.1 route-map routerD-in in
        !
       ip prefix-list aggregate permit 221.10.0.0/19
       ip prefix-list default permit 0.0.0.0/0
        !
       route-map routerD-out permit 10
        set as-path prepend 107 107 107
        !
       route-map routerD-in permit 10
        set local-preference 80
        !
```

The configurations for Router C and Router D are not given: They are not very different from any of the previous examples, in that they should accept the AS 107 aggregate only and announce just a default route to AS 107. As mentioned earlier, when the bulk of traffic flow is into the end site, there is little requirement for outbound load sharing for AS 107 beyond what nearest exit will offer. An example of the IGP configuration for this scenario follows in the case study section later in this chapter.

Load Sharing

The second example refines the previous one so that both links to the two upstream ISPs can be used to carry traffic at all times. Figure 5-27 shows the scenario. The way to implement load sharing here is to start by subdividing the /19 into two /20s—the /19 aggregate still is announced out of each link, but the announcement of a /20 on each link will ensure that traffic for that /20 will follow that path by preference.

Figure 5-27 *Load Sharing*

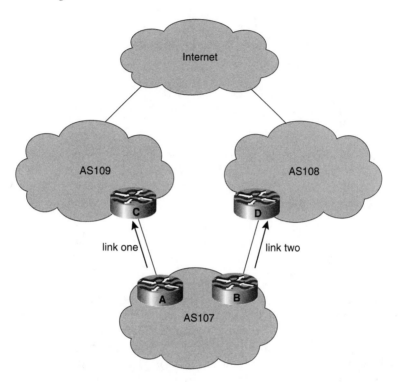

The configurations of the routers are given as follows:

```
Router A:
      router bgp 107
        network 221.10.0.0 mask 255.255.224.0
        network 221.10.0.0 mask 255.255.240.0
        neighbor 222.222.10.1 remote-as 109
        neighbor 222.222.10.1 prefix-list firstblock out
        neighbor 222.222.10.1 prefix-list default in
        !
      ip prefix-list default permit 0.0.0.0/0
        !
      ip prefix-list firstblock permit 221.10.0.0/20
      ip prefix-list firstblock permit 221.10.0.0/19
        !
```

```
Router B:
      router bgp 107
       network 221.10.0.0 mask 255.255.224.0
       network 221.10.16.0 mask 255.255.240.0
       neighbor 220.1.5.1 remote-as 108
       neighbor 220.1.5.1 prefix-list secondblock out
       neighbor 220.1.5.1 prefix-list default in
       !
      ip prefix-list default permit 0.0.0.0/0
       !
      ip prefix-list secondblock permit 221.10.16.0/20
      ip prefix-list secondblock permit 221.10.0.0/19
       !
```

Notice from the Router A configuration that the first /20 is announced out the link to AS 109. All traffic for this /20 will prefer this path, overriding any path from the announcement of the /19. If the link to AS 109 fails, traffic will divert to the path through AS 108 (because of the announcement of the /19 on that path).

A similar situation is true for the path through Router B to AS 108. The announcement of the second /20 through that path ensures that all inbound traffic for that half of the /19 will take this path.

This is a rudimentary first cut at setting up load sharing between two upstream ISPs. It is preferable to start here and slice the address space smaller as needed, rather than chopping the /19 into 32 /24s to try to make something work from there. Simplicity in configuration makes the likelihood of something working somewhat greater. Notice that announcing a subprefix of a /19 quite likely will have less chance of being propagated across the entire Internet than using the /19 would have. This is why it is critical that the /19 always is announced through every path.

If more fine tuning of the load sharing is required, the following example gives an idea of some of the options that might be available. In the previous case, traffic from AS 108 to the first /20 block will take the Internet path to AS 109 rather than going directly over the link to AS 109. This is suboptimal, and ISPs always try to ensure that routing is symmetric and that traffic paths are as short as possible (in the absence of any political requirements). The following example again subdivides the /19 into two /20s, but only one of the /20s is announced outbound, on the link to AS 108. The /19 is announced on this path with an AS path prepend. The link to AS 109 sees only the /19 being announced.

```
Router A:
      router bgp 107
       network 221.10.0.0 mask 255.255.224.0
       neighbor 222.222.10.1 remote-as 109
       neighbor 222.222.10.1 prefix-list default in
       neighbor 222.222.10.1 prefix-list aggregate out
       !
      ip prefix-list aggregate permit 221.10.0.0/19
       !
```

```
Router B:
    router bgp 107
     network 221.10.0.0 mask 255.255.224.0
     network 221.10.16.0 mask 255.255.240.0
     neighbor 220.1.5.1 remote-as 108
     neighbor 220.1.5.1 prefix-list default in
     neighbor 220.1.5.1 prefix-list subblocks out
     neighbor 220.1.5.1 route-map routerD out
    !
    route-map routerD permit 10
     match ip address prefix-list aggregate
     set as-path prepend 107 107
    route-map routerD permit 20
    !
    ip prefix-list subblocks permit 221.10.0.0/19 le 20
    ip prefix-list aggregate permit 221.10.0.0/19
    !
```

Traffic for the /20 will always come into AS 107 through AS 108. If the link to AS 108 fails, traffic will come in through the link to AS 109. Traffic for the rest of the address space will come in through the link to AS 109—the AS path prepend ensures that this happens. Manipulating the size of the prepend allows AS 107 to control which path inbound traffic will take into the network. A single prepend will attract more traffic; whereas, two or three or more will reduce the amount seen for the second /20.

Outbound Traffic Load Sharing

The previous examples dealt with situations in which the customer was trying to deal with load sharing inbound traffic—and paying little attention to dealing with outbound traffic, apart from using the nearest exit. This section goes into how to load-share outbound traffic in more detail; it's more applicable to content providers at the edge of the network or ISPs that are part of the transit path through the Internet core.

ISPs strive to balance traffic on their circuits as much as possible; congestion implies increased latency and poorer performance for customers. They also strive to keep traffic as symmetrical as possible. Although there is no performance downside to having asymmetric traffic, it is generally better to keep flows as symmetric as possible, to make the network easier to scale and easier to manage. Of course, some extreme situations exist in areas of poorer upstream connectivity, where asymmetric flows might be highly undesirable. The case study example in this section illustrates such a case.

The common wisdom regarding the best way to balance outbound traffic for any multi-homed network is to give this network a full view of the Internet Route Table down all the paths to the network. Although this undoubtedly will work, it is far from the most optimal solution. A decade ago, when the routing table had 10,000 prefixes, this might have been viable option. But purchasing a router with huge memory and large CPU simply to process the routing updates and do the best-path selection in a reasonable amount of time is simply not a viable option for many small- to medium-size ISPs. What's more, it is simply unnecessary, as the examples in this section show.

One Upstream ISP and One Local Peer

To start the list of examples, consider perhaps the simplest and most common multihoming that a small ISP will implement, as shown in Figure 5-28. The ISP connects to its upstream ISP, and it needs to connect to its local (competing) ISP so that domestic traffic does not use the expensive upstream connections.

The common way in which this is configured today is for the upstream ISP to send the full routing table to AS 109 and for the local ISP to send all its prefixes to AS 109. But why does AS 109 need to see the full Internet table? There is only one path to the Internet; the peering with the local ISP gives AS 109 access to only local routes, and that is the only information that AS 109 actually needs, beyond a default route to the rest of the Internet.

Figure 5-28 *One Upstream ISP and One Local Peer*

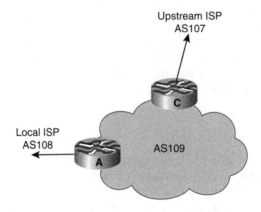

The router configuration for this example is as follows:

```
Router A:
     router bgp 109
      network 221.10.0.0 mask 255.255.224.0
      neighbor 222.222.10.2 remote-as 108
      neighbor 222.222.10.2 prefix-list my-block out
      neighbor 222.222.10.2 prefix-list AS108-peer in
      neighbor 222.222.10.2 filter-list 10 in
      !
     ip prefix-list AS108-peer permit 222.5.16.0/19
     ip prefix-list AS108-peer permit 221.240.0.0/20
     ip prefix-list my-block permit 221.10.0.0/19
      !
```

```
ip route 221.10.0.0 255.255.224.0 null0
!
ip as-path access-list 10 permit ^(108_)+$
!
```

```
Router C:
    router bgp 109
     network 221.10.0.0 mask 255.255.224.0
     neighbor 222.222.10.1 remote-as 107
     neighbor 222.222.10.1 prefix-list default in
     neighbor 222.222.10.1 prefix-list my-block out
    !
    ip prefix-list my-block permit 221.10.0.0/19
    ip prefix-list default permit 0.0.0.0/0
    !
    ip route 221.10.0.0 255.255.224.0 null0
    !
```

The configuration of Router A has both a prefix list and an AS path access list present on the inbound part of the BGP configuration. The prefix list will specifically filter the prefixes coming from AS 108, while the AS path access list will filter the prefixes so that only those originated by AS 108 will be permitted. This is an example of a double application of inbound policy. Strictly, only the prefix list is necessary, but the ISP has chosen to include the AS path filter in case of any configuration problem (such as the prefix list accidentally being erased). Some ISPs include only the AS path filter; however, this is very trusting of the neighboring AS because it simply says that all prefixes originated by the neighboring AS are to be allowed in. This does not provide any safety against the neighboring AS accidentally originating prefixes that it should not be.

The configuration of Router C is very straightforward: The default route is permitted inbound, and only the local address block is permitted out bound.

The result is a very lean routing table within AS 109. This is all that is required to set up multihoming between a neighboring ISP and the upstream ISP.

Two Upstreams ISPs and One Local Peer

The second example adds a second upstream ISP to the previous configuration, as shown in Figure 5-29. This is another common configuration, usually an enhancement of the previous case in which the network wants some resilience for its Internet connection.

Figure 5-29 *Two Upstream ISPs*

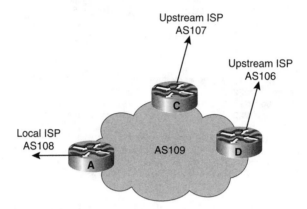

Again, the common solution to this problem is for both upstream ISPs to provide the full routing table to AS 109, as can be shown in the following router configuration examples:

```
Router C:
      router bgp 109
       network 221.10.0.0 mask 255.255.224.0
       neighbor 222.222.10.1 remote-as 107
       neighbor 222.222.10.1 prefix-list rfc1918-deny in
       neighbor 222.222.10.1 prefix-list my-block out
       neighbor 222.222.10.1 route-map AS107-loadshare in
       !
      ip prefix-list my-block permit 221.10.0.0/19
      ! See Appendix B for the RFC1918 list
      !
      ip route 221.10.0.0 255.255.224.0 null0
      !
      ip as-path access-list 10 permit ^(107_)+$
      ip as-path access-list 10 permit ^(107_)+_[0-9]+$
      !
      route-map AS107-loadshare permit 10
       match ip as-path 10
       set local-preference 120
      route-map AS107-loadshare permit 20
       set local-preference 80
       !

Router D:
      router bgp 109
       network 221.10.0.0 mask 255.255.224.0
       neighbor 222.222.10.5 remote-as 106
       neighbor 222.222.10.5 prefix-list rfc1918-deny in
```

```
neighbor 222.222.10.5 prefix-list my-block out
!
ip prefix-list my-block permit 221.10.0.0/19
! See Appendix B for RFC1918 list
!
```

This configuration takes full routes from both upstream ISPs. Router D takes everything and modifies nothing. Router C takes everything, but for all prefixes originated by AS 107 and AS 107's immediately neighboring autonomous systems, it sets a local preference of 120. This is so that all traffic to AS 107 and its immediately neighboring autonomous systems will go out the link to AS 107. The remaining prefixes learned from AS 107 have their local preference set to 80 so that the path through AS 107 is less preferred than the path through AS 106.

Obviously, this won't give perfect load sharing, but it will give you an idea of where to start and what the thought processes should be in achieving a reasonable outbound balance of traffic.

The alternative and much preferred way of configuring BGP for this network is not to use the full routing table. Remember from before that a default route is equivalent to the full routing table, for all intents and purposes; it requires a substantially reduced amount of router memory and CPU time to process. The configuration for the lighter version follows:

```
Router C:
     router bgp 109
      network 221.10.0.0 mask 255.255.224.0
      neighbor 222.222.10.1 remote-as 107
      neighbor 222.222.10.1 prefix-list rfc1918-nodef-deny in
      neighbor 222.222.10.1 prefix-list my-block out
      neighbor 222.222.10.1 filter-list 10 in
      neighbor 222.222.10.1 route-map tag-default-low in
      !
      ip prefix-list my-block permit 221.10.0.0/19
      ip prefix-list default permit 0.0.0.0/0
      !
      ip route 221.10.0.0 255.255.224.0 null0
      !
      ip as-path access-list 10 permit ^(107_)+$
      ip as-path access-list 10 permit ^(107_)+_[0-9]+$
      !

      route-map tag-default-low permit 10
       match ip address prefix-list default
       set local-preference 80
      route-map tag-default-low permit 20
      !
```

```
Router D:
    router bgp 109
     network 221.10.0.0 mask 255.255.224.0
     neighbor 222.222.10.5 remote-as 106
     neighbor 222.222.10.5 prefix-list default in
     neighbor 222.222.10.5 prefix-list my-block out
    !
    ip prefix-list my-block permit 221.10.0.0/19
    ip prefix-list default permit 0.0.0.0/0
    !
    ip route 221.10.0.0 255.255.224.0 null0
    !
```

Router D receives only a default route from AS 106 and sends only the /19 network block originated by AS 109; this is a very straightforward configuration.

Router C is slightly more complex, but again this means carrying a substantially reduced routing table over the version shown earlier. The rfc1918-nodef-deny prefix list allows all prefixes into Router C, apart from the RFC 1918 list documented in the appendixes (the default route also is permitted into Router C). After the prefix list has been applied, the filter list (AS path access list) blocks prefixes that have not been originated by AS 107 or AS 107's immediately neighboring autonomous systems. Finally, the route map is applied to set a low local preference on the default route that AS 107 is announcing to Router C.

The end result of this is that the default route is through Router D, with specific paths being learned from Router C and backup default through Router C. We have seen this type of configuration in action in several smaller ISPs, and it is very effective with small routers, small amounts of memory, and little CPU power. In all tests, the failover occurs more quickly in that the router CPUs have to spend less time processing best paths, less time sending iBGP updates to peers, and so on; this is the preferred and recommended path to multihoming between two upstream ISPs.

Notice that Router A has scarcely been mentioned—nothing changes with its configuration. The path to AS 108 always will be shorter than any alternative path through the upstream ISPs.

Also be aware that some upstream ISPs might be unwilling to announce a default route (usually for fear that a customer will create a configuration error that somehow will damage the network). In this case, the alternative is to use the full table and a prefix that can be used as a default route—a simple workaround. See the case study that follows for another mechanism to get around this problem.

Multiple Upstream ISPs and IXP

The third example adds a little more complication to the network and is probably one of the more extreme cases found on the Internet today, as shown in Figure 5-30.

Figure 5-30 *Multiple Upstream ISPs*

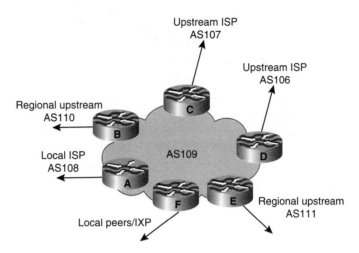

This is an example of a well-connected ISP, present at the local exchange point, with a few private peers, some regional ISP connections providing backup transit, and a couple of upstream/Tier 1 ISPs providing Internet transit.

The configurations for this aren't too hard to generate, either. Following the previous examples, the discussion within the network engineering team to produce the configuration should go like the following:

- **Local peers**—Take all local routes from them, and leave them untouched.

- **Local IXPs**—Take all local routes from them, and leave them untouched. If there is a private peering with an IXP member, we prefer the path over the IXP:

  — Announce the network over the private peering with a longer AS path (prepend of one) or a user a higher MED, if the peer supports MEDs.

  — Tag the prefixes learned over the private peering with a lower local preference.[4] (This keeps the IXP configuration consistent for all peers, allowing you to use peer groups on the IXP routers.)

- **Regional peers**—Take their local routes because they offer better connectivity to these regional networks than the upstream routes will, and this will be cheaper financially. Maybe take their neighboring AS routes as well, if the path is better. Ask for a default route, and tag it with a low local preference—say, 60.

• **Upstream ISPs**—Take only a default route from one upstream ISP and leave it tagged with the default local-preference of 100. For the other upstream ISP, take its originated routes and the originated routes of its immediately neighboring autonomous systems. Also ask for a default route; tag this with a local preference of 80.

In all cases, AS 109 announces its address block to the Internet (if more manipulation of inbound traffic is required, consider the examples earlier in this section).

The summary of this is quite simple: Local traffic stays local, regional traffic stays regional, the primary path is to one upstream ISP, and the backup is to the other upstream ISP. If both upstream ISPs go down, the backup is through the regional peers. All this can be done without taking the full routing table from any of the neighboring autonomous systems. The examples that we have seen in action have a routing table of about 22,000 prefixes, one fifth of the full routing table available at the time of writing. The ISPs in question also have reported no operational or reachability problems so far.

Case Study

The following case study implements the techniques described previously for an ISP that recently needed to multihome to the Internet. The scenario is quite simple, but it covers a situation that causes many newcomers to BGP and the Internet quite a lot of trouble.

The network in Figure 5-31 shows the network layout. AS 5400 is based in Europe, and AS 2516 is based in Japan—this in itself poses a challenge because the multihoming is between entities that are quite literally on opposite sides of the globe. Both circuits are of equal capacity, making the configuration somewhat easier than it might have otherwise been.

The approach taken is quite simple, though, and is based on that has been described already: Keep it simple! Ideally, the two upstream ISPs will send a default route, and one upstream ISP will send a minimal routing table of the prefixes from the network and those originated by local peers. So, in theory, this should all be configurable with a minimal routing table on the AS 17660 network.

Reality is slightly different, though. AS 5400 can offer only the full routing table to any BGP customer, so this must be taken into account in the configuration of Router A. AS 2516 can offer either everything or just the default route, so the option was taken to request just a default route.

Figure 5-31 *Case Study Network*

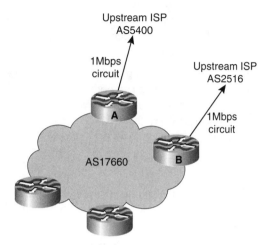

The first cut at producing a working configuration carried out the following tasks:

1   Going to several looking glasses in the center of the Internet gave a good idea of how far AS 2516 and AS 5400 were from the "center." The definition of the "center" is hard, but looking glasses at major U.S. exchange points probably give the most accurate definition of where the center might be—or at least get close. Analysis of the routing table at the looking glasses showed that AS 2516 was, on average, one AS hop closer to the center than AS 5400. The resulting configuration for outbound announcements became the following:

   — To AS 5400, just announce the aggregate block.

   — To AS 2516, announce the aggregate block with a single prepend of AS 17660.

2   The next step was to request AS 2516 to send just a default route. When this was available, the peering with AS 2516 was brought up.

3   AS 5400 could send only the full routing table. Advantage of this was taken to strip away most of the routing table, to leave a sensible number of paths to balance the load sharing of outbound traffic between the two paths.

   — Looking at the many routing table analyses being done on the Internet at the moment, the decision was made to take the top five contributors to the routing table and exclude any prefixes that had those autonomous systems in the path.

— After this, only prefixes originated by AS 5400, its immediately neighboring autonomous systems, and their immediate neighbors were accepted. (AS 5400 is a major transit backbone in Europe, so this allowed paths from peers and peering European networks in.) This produced a routing table of around 30,000 prefixes on Router A.

This wasn't a bad first attempt. Inbound traffic turned out to be almost perfectly balanced, around 500 Kbps on average on both of the circuits. There was some time-of-day variation that seemed a bit unusual, but on the whole, traffic was load-balanced quite well. Outbound traffic was skewed toward the AS 5400 connection, though, and there was clear evidence of severe asymmetric routing, with traffic to the United States outbound on the AS 5400 path but return traffic inbound on the AS 2516 path. To even this out more, the following steps were taken:

1 Going back to the routing analysis data, the next 3 autonomous systems in the list of the top 20 were added to the AS path filter list. This now produced a routing table of around 14,000 prefixes.

2 OSPF was configured to be the conveyor of the default route because it was not possible to hear a default from AS 5400. The primary path was through AS 2516 (low IGP metric), with the backup through AS 5400 (high IGP metric).

The resulting load balancing was almost perfect, with outbound traffic well balanced at about 200 Kbps on each path. Further investigation showed that most traffic to and from Europe was using the AS 5400 path, while most traffic to Asia and the West Coast of the United States was using the AS 2516 path. All in all, this was quite a good result, and all with just 13,000 prefixes in the BGP table on the routers.

The routers used were 2611s with 64 MB of memory. Advice from prospective upstream ISPs to AS 17660 was that they would require a router with a minimum of 128 MB of memory, with the 7204 being the recommended minimum model for any network to multihome.

The final configurations of the routers were as follows:

```
Router A:
router ospf 100
 log-adjacency-changes
 passive-interface default
 no passive-interface Ethernet0/0
 default-information originate metric 20
!
router bgp 17660
 no synchronization
 no bgp fast-external-fallover
 bgp log-neighbor-changes
 bgp deterministic-med
 neighbor core-ibgp peer-group
 neighbor core-ibgp remote-as 17660
 neighbor core-ibgp update-source Loopback0
 neighbor core-ibgp next-hop-self
 neighbor core-ibgp-partial peer-group
```

```
 neighbor core-ibgp-partial remote-as 17660
 neighbor core-ibgp-partial update-source Loopback0
 neighbor core-ibgp-partial next-hop-self
 neighbor core-ibgp-partial send-community
 neighbor core-ibgp-partial prefix-list partial-ibgp out
 neighbor 166.49.165.13 remote-as 5400
 neighbor 166.49.165.13 description eBGP multihop to AS5400
 neighbor 166.49.165.13 ebgp-multihop 5
 neighbor 166.49.165.13 update-source Loopback0
 neighbor 166.49.165.13 prefix-list in-filter in
 neighbor 166.49.165.13 prefix-list out-filter out
 neighbor 166.49.165.13 filter-list 1 in
 neighbor 166.49.165.13 filter-list 3 out
 neighbor 202.144.159.193 peer-group core-ibgp
 neighbor 202.144.159.197 peer-group core-ibgp-partial
 neighbor 202.144.159.198 peer-group core-ibgp-partial
!
 ip prefix-list in-filter  deny rfc1918etc in
 ip prefix-list out-filter permit 202.144.128.0/19
 ip prefix-list partial-ibgp permit 202.144.128.0/19 le 32
!
 ip route 0.0.0.0 0.0.0.0 serial 0/0 254
 ip as-path access-list 1 deny _701_
 ip as-path access-list 1 deny _1_
 ip as-path access-list 1 deny _7018_
 ip as-path access-list 1 deny _1239_
 ip as-path access-list 1 deny _7046_
 ip as-path access-list 1 deny _209_
 ip as-path access-list 1 deny _2914_
 ip as-path access-list 1 deny _3549_
 ip as-path access-list 1 permit _5400$
 ip as-path access-list 1 permit _5400_[0-9]+$
 ip as-path access-list 1 permit _5400_[0-9]+_[0-9]+$
 ip as-path access-list 1 deny .*
 ip as-path access-list 3 permit ^$
!


 Router B:
 router ospf 100
  log-adjacency-changes
  passive-interface default
  no passive-interface Ethernet0/0
  default-information originate
 !
 router bgp 17660
  no synchronization
  no auto-summary
  no bgp fast-external-fallover
  bgp log-neighbor-changes
  bgp deterministic-med
  neighbor core-ibgp peer-group
  neighbor core-ibgp remote-as 17660
  neighbor core-ibgp update-source Loopback0
  neighbor core-ibgp next-hop-self
```

```
neighbor core-ibgp-partial peer-group
neighbor core-ibgp-partial remote-as 17660
neighbor core-ibgp-partial update-source Loopback0
neighbor core-ibgp-partial next-hop-self
neighbor core-ibgp-partial send-community
neighbor core-ibgp-partial prefix-list partial-ibgp out
neighbor 202.144.159.192 peer-group core-ibgp
neighbor 202.144.159.197 peer-group core-ibgp-partial
neighbor 202.144.159.198 peer-group core-ibgp-partial
neighbor 210.132.92.165 remote-as 2516
neighbor 210.132.92.165 description eBGP peering
neighbor 210.132.92.165 soft-reconfiguration inbound
neighbor 210.132.92.165 prefix-list default-route in
neighbor 210.132.92.165 prefix-list out-filter out
neighbor 210.132.92.165 route-map as2516-out out
neighbor 210.132.92.165 maximum-prefix 100
neighbor 210.132.92.165 filter-list 2 in
neighbor 210.132.92.165 filter-list 3 out
!
!
ip prefix-list default-route permit 0.0.0.0/0
ip prefix-list out-filter permit 202.144.128.0/19
ip prefix-list partial-ibgp permit 202.144.128.0/19 le 32
!
ip as-path access-list 2 permit _2516$
ip as-path access-list 2 deny .*
ip as-path access-list 3 permit ^$
!
route-map as2516-out permit 10
 set as-path prepend 17660
!
```

Some comments on the configurations are necessary. For Router A:

- Notice the default route pointing to serial0/0 with distance 254. As long as the serial interface is up (line protocol is up), the static route will be in the routing table, thereby causing the **default-information originate** in the OSPF configuration to announce the default into the network.

- Notice that the OSPF metric has been set to 20.

- eBGP multihop is used as a requirement from AS 5400. Note that five TCP hops have been selected rather than 255, as is used by many ISPs—it's better practice to set the number of hops required rather than just use the largest number possible.

- Notice in the eBGP peering that both an outbound filter list and an outbound prefix list are used. This is double insurance; if one "goes missing," the other one is there as a safety net.

- Note the two peer groups. **core-ibgp** sends the full prefixes to Router B, whereas **core-ibgp-partial** sends only internal prefixes (subprefixes of the aggregate block) to the remaining iBGP speakers in the network. (This network has two route reflectors, hence the border routers talk only iBGP with the route reflectors.)

Some comments are needed for Router B, in addition to those for Router A:

- Note that the default route is heard from AS 2516. The **maximum-prefixes** BGP option has been set in the unlikely event that other parts of the configuration accidentally are removed.

- Note that OSPF originates a default route with metric 10. This is a higher metric than the one from Router A, so it will be the preferred default route through the backbone. As long as the default is heard from AS 2516, there will be a default in the routing table, which means that OSPF will originate its default through the backbone.

- Notice the AS path prepend on the outbound announcement. A single 17660 is included in the outbound announcement to make the inbound traffic flow symmetric on both routers.

Finally, a brief look at the two MRTG graphs for the loading on these two routers' external interfaces shows the relative balance between the two routers. Inbound and outbound loads are reasonably symmetric, although closer examination could reveal that the European path has more inbound traffic later in the day than the Asian path. Reasons for this are unclear at the time of writing—we will have to sit down and look at the NetFlow log information in more detail.

The shaded area in Figure 5-32 and Figure 5-33 represents the inbound traffic load; whereas, the solid line represents the outbound traffic load.

Figure 5-32 *Router A Upstream Link Load*

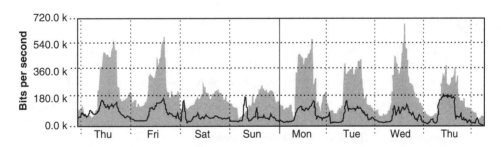

Figure 5-33 *Router B Upstream Link Load*

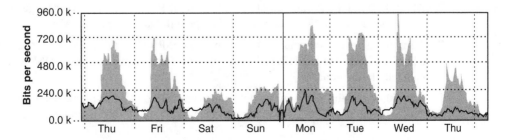

Over time, this configuration will have to be monitored because traffic patterns do change as networks grow and the clientele on the network come and go. But as a case study for good multihoming practice, this is one of the best efforts seen on the Internet today. Unlike the claims from some of the potential upstream ISPs of AS 17660, all this has been achievable with minor router platforms and minimum memory requirements (the two 2600s each still have around 32 MB of memory spare, plenty of room for future growth and refinement of the multihoming needs).

Using Communities

Communities are used extensively in the Internet industry for exchanging and facilitating policy between ISPs. This section only briefly looks at some of the possible uses of communities and gives some pointers on some implementations of communities in the Internet at large.

The first public documentation of community usage in the ISP community was RFC 1998, which documented how the then Internet MCI used communities for customers that multihomed onto its backbone.

Since this RFC appeared, many ISPs have applied the concept and developed community policies for their own network requirements. There isn't really any documentation describing the different policies, but researching ISP operations Web sites and the Internet Routing Registry reveals many of the policies in use today.

RFC 1998

The principle behind RFC 1998 is quite simple: Make life easy for the upstream ISP by standardizing configurations on the backbone aggregation routers, and give the customer more scope to modify its multihoming configuration without involving the upstream ISP.

Four communities are defined; all of them allow the customer to modify the local-preference of prefixes in the upstream ISP network. If the upstream ISP has AS number ASx, then the following communities are defined:

- **ASx:100**—Send this community to the upstream ISP to indicate that this is the preferred path (the default local preference is 100).

- **ASx:90**—Send this community to the upstream ISP so that this prefix is tagged with a local preference of 90. This is the backup path if dual homed onto ASx.

- **ASx:80**—Send this community to the upstream ISP so that this prefix is tagged with a local preference of 80. This is the backup path if multihomed to another ISP and the path lengths are equal.

- **ASx:70**—Send this community to the upstream ISP so that this prefix is tagged with a local preference of 70. This is the backup path if multihomed to another.

A worked example is the easiest way to see these community settings in action. Consider
the diagram in Figure 5-23, a situation in which a small network has a primary path and a
backup path to its upstream ISP. Previously, a configuration was described that used local
preference and MED setting by the local network to achieve the desired configuration. The
same result can be achieved using RFC 1998-style communities; the router configurations
are

```
Router A:
        router bgp 65534
         network 221.10.0.0 mask 255.255.224.0
         neighbor 222.222.10.2 remote-as 109
         neighbor 222.222.10.2 description RouterC
         neighbor 222.222.10.2 prefix-list aggregate out
         neighbor 222.222.10.2 route-map routerC-out out
         neighbor 222.222.10.2 prefix-list default in
         neighbor 222.222.10.2 route-map routerC-in in
         !
        ip prefix-list aggregate permit 221.10.0.0/19
        ip prefix-list default permit 0.0.0.0/0
        !
        route-map routerC-out permit 10
         match ip address prefix-list aggregate
         set community 109:100
        route-map routerC-out permit 20
        !
        route-map routerC-in permit 10
         set local-preference 100
        !


Router B:
        router bgp 65534
         network 221.10.0.0 mask 255.255.224.0
         neighbor 222.222.10.6 remote-as 109
         neighbor 222.222.10.6 description RouterD
         neighbor 222.222.10.6 send-community
         neighbor 222.222.10.6 prefix-list aggregate out
         neighbor 222.222.10.6 route-map routerD-out out
         neighbor 222.222.10.6 prefix-list default in
         neighbor 222.222.10.6 route-map routerD-in in
         !
        ip prefix-list aggregate permit 221.10.0.0/19
        ip prefix-list default permit 0.0.0.0/0
        !
        route-map routerD-out permit 10
         match ip address prefix-list aggregate
         set community 109:90
        route-map routerD-out permit 20
        !
        route-map routerD-in permit 10
         set local-preference 90
        !


Router C:
        router bgp 109
         neighbor 222.222.10.1 remote-as 65534
```

```
      neighbor 222.222.10.1 default-originate
      neighbor 222.222.10.1 prefix-list Customer in
      neighbor 222.222.10.1 route-map bgp-cust-in in
      neighbor 222.222.10.1 prefix-list default out
      !
      ip prefix-list Customer permit 221.10.0.0/19
      ip prefix-list default permit 0.0.0.0/0
      !
      ip community-list 70 permit 109:70
      ip community-list 80 permit 109:80
      ip community-list 90 permit 109:90
      !
      route-map bgp-cust-in permit 10
       match community 70
       set local-preference 70
      route-map bgp-cust-in permit 20
       match community 80
       set local-preference 80
      route-map bgp-cust-in permit 30
       match community 90
       set local-preference 90
      route-map bgp-cust-in permit 40
       set local-preference 100
      !


Router D:
      router bgp 109
       neighbor 222.222.10.5 remote-as 65534
       neighbor 222.222.10.5 default-originate
       neighbor 222.222.10.5 prefix-list Customer in
       neighbor 222.222.10.5 route-map bgp-cust-in in
       neighbor 222.222.10.5 prefix-list default out
      !
      ip prefix-list Customer permit 221.10.0.0/19
      ip prefix-list default permit 0.0.0.0/0
      !
      ip community-list 70 permit 109:70
      ip community-list 80 permit 109:80
      ip community-list 90 permit 109:90
      !
      route-map bgp-cust-in permit 10
       match community 70
       set local-preference 70
      route-map bgp-cust-in permit 20
       match community 80
       set local-preference 80
      route-map bgp-cust-in permit 30
       match community 90
       set local-preference 90
      route-map bgp-cust-in permit 40
       set local-preference 100
      !
```

Notice the similarity between the configurations for Router C and Router D. Apart from the IP addresses on the point-to-point links, they are exactly the same. This is an advantage for the upstream ISP because it has a scalable solution to its different customers' multihoming needs. Its customers can modify which is the primary path and which is the backup path simply by sending different communities: 109:100 means that this is the primary path, and 109:90 means that this is the backup path.

All the configuration work is done on Routers A and B. Router A has the primary path and so sends community 109:100 to Router C. Router C matches this community in the **bgp-cust-in** route map and sets the local preference of the prefix to 100 (which is the default, in any case). Router B has the backup path, so it sends community 109:90 to Router D and sets local preference 90 to any inbound announcements.

If the customer network in AS 65534 wants to change the paths, the engineers there simply need to swap around which communities are sent and which local preferences are set on Routers A and B. The NOC of AS 109 does not need to be involved, thus lowering the support burden of customers, lowering the costs of operating the business, with general benefits to both the business and the customers.

ISP Community Usage

RFC 1998 was written several years ago, and since then, ISPs have refined and enhanced what they use communities for. Many examples exist on the Internet, and a few of them that were publicly visible at the time of this writing are documented here.

The first example is from AS 2764, an Australian-based ISP. The community policies are documented in the AS object stored in the Internet Routing Registry:

```
aut-num:     AS2764
as-name:     ASN-CONNECT-NET
descr:       connect.com.au pty ltd
admin-c:     CC89
tech-c:      MP151
remarks:     Community  Definition
remarks:     ------------------------------------------------
remarks:     2764:1 Announce to "domestic" rate ASes only
remarks:     2764:2 Don't announce outside local PoP
remarks:     2764:3 Lower local preference by 25
remarks:     2764:4 Lower local preference by 15
remarks:     2764:5 Lower local preference by 5
remarks:     2764:6 Announce to non customers with "no-export"
remarks:     2764:7 Only announce route to customers
remarks:     2764:8 Announce route over satellite link
notify:      routing@connect.com.au
mnt-by:      CONNECT-AU
changed:     mrp@connect.com.au 19990506
source:      CCAIR
```

The remarks section describes the communities supported. For example, if a customer of AS 2764 sends a prefix with community of 2764:2 set, AS 2764 will announce the prefix only within the local PoP. If a customer sends a prefix with community 2764:8 set, the prefix will be announced only over AS 2764's satellite connection to the United States, and so on.

The second example is from AS 702, a European-based ISP. Its community policies also are documented in its AS object, stored in the Internet Routing Registry:

```
aut-num: AS702
as-name: AS702
descr:   UUNET - Commercial IP service provider in Europe
remarks: ----------------------------------------------------------
remarks: UUNET uses the following communities with its customers:
remarks: 702:80  Set Local Pref 80 within AS702
remarks: 702:120 Set Local Pref 120 within AS702
remarks: 702:20  Announce only to UUNET ASes and UUNET customers
remarks: 702:30  Keep within Europe, don't announce to other UUNET ASs
remarks: 702:1   Prepend AS702 once at edges of UUNET to Peers
remarks: 702:2   Prepend AS702 twice at edges of UUNET to Peers
remarks: 702:3   Prepend AS702 thrice at edges of UUNET to Peers
remarks: Details of UUNET's peering policy and how to get in touch
remarks: with UUNET regarding peering policy matters can be found at:
remarks: http://www.uu.net/peering/
remarks: ----------------------------------------------------------
mnt-by:  UUNET-MNT
changed: eric-apps@eu.uu.net 20010928
source:  RIPE
```

Notice that AS 702 supports one of the RFC 1998 values: 702:80. If that community is attached to a prefix sent to AS 702 by a customer, AS 702 will set the local preference to 80. 702:20 and 702:30 are interesting because they determine boundaries about how far a prefix will be announced within the AS 702 network. Finally, the 702:1, 702:2, and 702:3 communities determine the number of autonomous systems prepended in any announcements that AS 702 makes of customer prefixes to AS 702's peers. This gives customers the option of a primary path to and from AS 702, but they possibly have a backup path through another ISP when they multihome. Or they can use this community to help fine-tune their multi-homing load sharing between AS 702 and their other upstream ISPs.

The third example is one of the most comprehensive seen in use in the Internet at this time. An excerpt is given in the following:

```
aut-num:    AS5400
as-name:    CIPCORE
descr:      Concert European Core Network
remarks:    Communities scheme:
remarks:    The following BGP communities can be set by Concert BGP
remarks:    customers to affect announcements to major peerings.
remarks:
remarks:    Community to                        Community to
remarks:    Not announce      To peer:          AS prepend 5400
remarks:
remarks:    5400:1000         European peers     5400:2000
remarks:    5400:1001         Ebone (AS1755)     5400:2001
remarks:    5400:1002         Eunet (AS286)      5400:2002
remarks:    5400:1003         Unisource (AS3300) 5400:2003
remarks:    5400:1005         UUnet (AS702)      5400:2005
remarks:    5400:1006         Carrier1 (AS8918)  5400:2006
remarks:    5400:1007         SupportNet (8582)  5400:2007
remarks:    5400:1008         AT&T (AS2686)      5400:2008
```

```
remarks:      5400:1009       Level 3 (AS9057)    5400:2009
remarks:      5400:1010       RIPE (AS3333)       5400:2010

...

remarks:      5400:1100         US peers          5400:2100
notify:       peertech@concert.net
mnt-by:       CIP-MNT
source:       RIPE
```

Customers of AS 5400 have a large variety of communities available to them, allowing prefix announcements to be made to all of AS 5400's peers and to multihoming load balancing to be determined between AS 5400 and their other upstream ISPs. This model is based on that used by AS 3257, whose detailed community policy is listed at http://www.as3257.net/html/communities.htm. Although implementing this might seem unduly complicated (it is not that hard, just a very large route map), the benefits for the networks that use this sort of scheme is that their customers have a great deal of liberty when it comes to configuring their multihoming needs.

Communities Conclusion

These examples hopefully have shown some of the benefits of using communities in ISP networks. A large number of options are possible, not just for multihoming, as has been covered here. Communities have been used to color different prefixes for announcement within an ISP's own backbone, to replace complex external filters on border routers, and to remove the generation of filters from the border routers to the aggregation routers where the customers first connect to the backbone. All these benefits significantly reduce the complexity of operating an ISP backbone and, from our experience, significantly simplify the whole customer-provisioning process within an ISP operation. You are strongly encouraged to study the use of communities further—the Cisco.com site has a considerable range of materials, and the Consulting Engineering pages on the Cisco.com site have more examples of ISP applications.

Security

Chapter 4, "Security," covered in considerable detail the considerations that an ISP must make, and the tools available, to protect the ISP's portion of the Internet from problems that can affect the network's performance and security, and the security of its customers. However, this book has not specifically covered the security considerations that an ISP needs to make at the basic level of connecting customers and servers to the backbone.

This section covers some of the better security practices and includes sample templates that can be used as a basis for the security provisions on the network. This is not intended to be the last word in security (many texts cover network security in considerable depth), but it is intended to be the absolute minimum that an ISP must install on its backbone and for its customers.

ISP Border Packet Filters

The decision of whether to install packet filters on the network border usually depends on the size of the ISP operation and whether the design and operations team feels that such filters can serve any useful purpose to protect the backbone.

There is no hard-and-fast rule, but we have found that smaller ISPs tend to implement quite severe filters on their network edges, while the largest ISPs probably implement only one or two key filters to prevent DOS attacks on their networks.

Much of any ISP filtering is installed on the aggregation router where the customers connect to the backbone. The rest of an ISP's infrastructure is core network equipment, and that is protected by its own set of access filters. ISPs that put weak filtering on aggregation routers (no one should be putting anything weak on this part of the network) tend to need much more carefully thought-out filtering on their border routers. Appendix C, "Example Configurations," provides a typical configuration example of an "ISP Essentials" application in a small ISP: The border router there has detailed filtering so that unwanted packets are not permitted into the ISP backbone.

Assuming that the ISP has network block 221.19.0.0/19, a minimum inbound access list on an external-facing peering interface might be something like the following:

```
!
access-list 100 deny ip 221.19.0.0 0.0.31.255 any
access-list 100 deny ip 0.0.0.0 0.255.255.255 any
access-list 100 deny ip 10.0.0.0 0.255.255.255 any
access-list 100 deny ip 127.0.0.0 0.255.255.255 any
access-list 100 deny ip 169.254.0.0 0.0.255.255 any
access-list 100 deny ip 172.16.0.0 0.15.255.255 any
access-list 100 deny ip 192.0.2.0 0.0.0.255 any
access-list 100 deny ip 192.168.0.0 0.0.255.255 any
access-list 100 permit ip any any
!
```

This blocks all outside packets a with source address from the local network address space (to block DOS attacks), blocks all RFC 1918 address space, and blocks other address space, such as the loopback network and the autoconfiguration network.

The outbound filter actually is quite similar to this, again filtering special-use address space and the RFC 1918 blocks. Traffic with those addresses as source addresses should not be leaked out into the Internet:

```
!
access-list 101 deny ip 10.0.0.0 0.255.255.255 any
access-list 101 deny ip 127.0.0.0 0.255.255.255 any
access-list 101 deny ip 169.254.0.0 0.0.255.255 any
access-list 101 deny ip 172.16.0.0 0.15.255.255 any
access-list 101 deny ip 192.168.0.0 0.0.255.255 any
access-list 101 deny ip 192.0.2.0.0.0.0.255.255 any
access-list 101 permit ip any any
!
```

The configuration might be applied to the router like the following:

```
!
interface hssi 5/0
 description 34Mbps link to Galactic Internet
 ip address 221.1.2.1 255.255.255.252
 ip access-group 100 in                  ! inbound filter
 ip access-group 101 out                 ! outbound filter
 no ip directed-broadcast
!
access-list compiled                     ! compile access-lists
!
```

Chapter 4 covered a range of other filtering options available to ISPs and the hardware support available in different platforms to deal with DOS attacks. The preceding list is probably sufficient for most ISPs and, when used as a compiled access list on higher-end platforms, does not pose much of a performance penalty on the routers.

Aggregation Router Filters

The minimum inbound filter that any ISP should be applying to the customer-facing interfaces on its aggregation routers is the unicast RPF check. This ensures that all packets coming from the customer are checked to make sure that their origin address comes out of the address block assigned to the customer. This check is much more efficient than applying any inbound filters on the aggregation router, and it is a recommended best practice throughout this book. If the customer has address space 221.4.0.0/22, the interface configuration to achieve inbound filtering is as follows:

```
!
interface serial 1/0
 description 2Mbps link to Planet Toyshop
 ip unnumbered Loopback0
 ip verify unicast reverse-path             ! inbound filter
 no ip direct-broadcast
!
ip route 221.4.0.0 255.255.252.0 serial 1/0
!
```

The ISP optionally could install an outbound filter as well (if the customer router is incapable of doing filtering), but most ISPs generally supply templates or sample filters for their customers' use. The typical outbound filter would look like the inbound filter discussed in the next section.

Notice that if the customer uses BGP and is multihomed, the uRPF check configuration needs a little more planning—this was discussed in much more detail in the previous chapter. But for the vast majority of ISPs and customer connections, this configuration is all that is sufficient. If every connected end site had an RPF check applied on unicast traffic, there would be a marked reduction in the amount of spoofed content on the Internet today.

Customer Router Filters

As a service to their customers, all ISPs should be supplying sample filters for routers that are used to connect permanently connected networks to the Internet. If the customers are using routers that are incapable of filtering, to quote an ISP overheard recently, "that device should be replaced with a real router." It is an unfortunate fact today that too many people equate security with firewalls and completely fail to remember that a router is a very sophisticated first-line security device in its own right.

A typical customer template might look like the following:

```
interface ethernet 0
 description backbone LAN
 ip address 221.4.3.254 255.255.252.0
 no ip directed-broadcast
 no ip proxy-arp
 no ip redirects
!
interface serial 0
 description Connection to Planet ISP
 ip unnumbered Ethernet 0
 ip access-group 100 in
 ip access-group 101 out
 no ip directed-broadcast
!
access-list 100 permit icmp any any
access-list 100 permit tcp any any established
access-list 100 permit tcp any any eq 22
access-list 100 permit tcp any host 221.4.0.1 eq www
access-list 100 permit tcp any host 221.4.0.2 eq smtp
access-list 100 permit udp any host 221.4.0.3 eq domain
access-list 100 permit tcp any host 221.4.0.3 eq domain
access-list 100 permit udp any any eq ntp
access-list 100 deny   udp any any eq 2049
access-list 100 permit udp any any gt 1023
access-list 100 deny   ip any any log
!
access-list 101 permit ip 221.4.0.0 0.0.3.255 any
access-list 101 deny   ip any any log
!
```

List 100 is a very tight list, allowing only a limited number of connections:

- Permit ICMP
- Permit any established TCP sessions (sessions that have been initiated from inside the customer network)
- Permit Secure Shell
- Permit WWW to the appointed Web server (and make sure that the Web server is secured and running the latest software)
- Permit SMTP to the appointed mail host (and make sure that the mail system is not running as a relay, is secured, and is running the latest software)

- Permit DNS lookups and zone transfers to the appointed DNS server (and make sure that the nameserver is running the most recent software and is secured)
- Permit NTP
- Block UDP port 2049 (NFS port)
- Permit UDP on unprivileged ports (this could be a security risk, but most ISPs and customers are content with this)
- Block everything else, and log it

List 101 is the basic list, ensuring that only traffic from legitimate address ranges is permitted out into the Internet. Don't fall into the trap of assuming that the upstream ISP will filter "illegal" traffic.

This is the absolute minimum necessary configuration for any end-site router connecting any site to the Internet. Obviously, it is not the last word in high security, but we consider it to be mandatory for any new Internet-connected site. Firewalls and other internal filtering also should be considered and implemented within the network.

ISP Server Considerations

Servers within the ISP or customer network need to be properly set up and secured before they are plugged into any LAN—or even connected to the Internet.

ISP servers should be connected behind a router with strong filters, never plugged into the core of the backbone, as has been mentioned previously. Using a router gives the ISP a chance to install strong filters to protect the servers. For example, if the server is a Web server, only port 80 should be visible to the outside world, and so on.

The actual servers themselves require, at minimum, TCP wrappers to be installed and all nonessential services to be switched off. At the time of this writing, the most recent release of Red Hat Linux included a default firewall installation in the install process. This is very significant because now operating system vendors are taking security more seriously. A sample of an ipchains configuration is given here:

```
:input ACCEPT
:forward ACCEPT
:output ACCEPT
-A input -s 0/0 -d 0/0 -i lo -j ACCEPT
-A input -p tcp -s 0/0 -d 0/0 ssh -y -j ACCEPT
-A input -p tcp -s 0/0 -d 0/0 http -y -j ACCEPT
-A input -p tcp -s 0/0 -d 0/0 smtp -y -j ACCEPT
-A input -p udp -s 0/0 -d 0/0 ntp -j ACCEPT
-A input -p udp -s 0/0 -d 0/0 domain -j ACCEPT
-A input -p tcp -s 0/0 -d 0/0 0:1023 -y -j REJECT
-A input -p tcp -s 0/0 -d 0/0 2049 -y -j REJECT
-A input -p udp -s 0/0 -d 0/0 0:1023 -j REJECT
-A input -p udp -s 0/0 -d 0/0 2049 -j REJECT
-A input -p tcp -s 0/0 -d 0/0 6000:6009 -y -j REJECT
-A input -p tcp -s 0/0 -d 0/0 7100 -y -j REJECT
```

The following list describes the actions of each line of the ipchains configuration:

- Accept all packets from the loopback interface.
- Accept incoming Secure Shell connections.
- Accept incoming Web connections (because I'm a Web server).
- Accept incoming SMTP connections (because I'm a mail host).
- Accept incoming NTP connections (for time synchronization).
- Accept incoming DNS connections.
- Block TCP connections to privileged TCP ports.
- Block TCP connections to port 2049 (Sun NFS).
- Block UDP connections to privileged UDP ports.
- Block UDP connections to port 2049 (Sun NFS).
- Block TCP connections to ports 6000 to 6009 (X Windows).
- Block TCP connections to port 7100.
- Notice the **–y** on all the TCP connections. This allows only new TCP connections to be made (SYN bit set, ACQ and FIN bits cleared).

If the ipchains/iptables firewall software is not part of the Linux distribution, it is easy enough to download from many of the Internet mirror sites. For commercial UNIX systems, the TCP wrapper software is freely downloadable from the Internet. Installation instructions and examples aren't given here—there are sufficient examples on the Internet, as a simple search on Google shows.

If non-UNIX–based operating systems are being used, security needs to be considered even more carefully—those operating systems tend to be aimed at the mass market, where convenience of the desktop is considered almost at the exclusion of any semblance of security. The same rules apply here. Any systems being connected to the public Internet need sufficient filters; purchasing firewall software for these systems is an excellent choice.

Firewalls

Firewalls have their place within the Internet backbone, more generally for protecting end-site networks than for use within ISP backbones. Some ISPs install firewalls between their networks and the Internet, but these are rare and have very particular reasons for doing so. Most ISPs rely on the type of packet filtering described previously.

However, for end sites, a firewall has become almost the de facto requirement in the Internet today. In the early to mid-1990s, firewalls were for the security-obsessed, but today, with the large number of attacks on networks, exploited hosts, altered Web sites, and so on, the firewall has become necessary for the largest corporation down to the home user sitting at end of a dialup or ADSL link. The personal firewalls available with Linux have been mentioned already, and an example of the configuration for ipchains was given previously.

Firewalls take all forms, from dedicated hardware such as the Cisco PIX device, to software such as ipchains running on Linux systems. Whatever turns out to be the most appropriate solution, its use is strongly recommended for any edge site connecting to the Internet.

Remote Access

For ISP engineers, the best way of accessing a network in recent years has to be use Secure Shell. In the early days of the Internet, Telnet was quite popular, but it now has largely been abandoned in the developed Internet as being far too insecure and risky to use. Communication between host and client is unencrypted; passwords to log in are unencrypted. Anyone sniffing packets or snooping on a network has immediate access to the network, a risk that is too big for most ISPs.

The preferred method is to set up the Secure Shell server on a chosen host (or two) inside the network. The traveling engineer then can dial up and has secure access to the core backbone through these servers. Routers now have Secure Shell server and client support on them, so Telnet can be disabled on routers for access purposes.

Secure Shell software is freely available: OpenSSH is downloadable from many mirror sites on the Internet and is an example of one of the many packages available on the Internet. Of course, many commercial implementations of Secure Shell exist as well, but it is really up to the ISP operator to decide what to use. In the spirit of the Internet, many ISP engineers prefer to use Open Source public-domain software.

Some organizations are looking at using IPSec-based solutions for remote access. Although these work very well, there seems to be a preference to use simpler, less complicated software for remote access. IPSec solutions provide a dedicated tunnel between ISP engineer laptop and the home site; whereas, SSH can tunnel the selected TCP ports, leaving direct access to the Internet for the rest of the engineer's needs. (This isn't meant to be a comparison or discussion of the capabilities of SSH and IPSec; it's more a reality comparison of what ISP engineers are doing today.)

Likewise, Secure Shell clients are commercially available or freely downloadable from the Internet, and they support most operating systems available today. Telnet, RSH, and similar insecure remote access protocols can be consigned to history for good.

Out-of-Band Management

The out-of-band management network is the most necessary part of the ISP's operation, yet it is so rarely found outside the largest operations. *Out of band* quite simply means that the ISP operations staff has a means of getting access to the network infrastructure when the main links to the site are down.

When ISPs without an out-of-band network are asked what their strategy is when they can't get in-band access to their equipment, the response is often along the lines of sending someone with a laptop to connect to the console port of the router. Although this might work for a centrally managed site, it is a ludicrous concept for any ISP that has more than one location. As mentioned earlier in this chapter, the goal of any ISP is to provide as close to 100 percent availability of the network as is feasible. Putting an engineer in a car or an airplane to fix a problem can means hours of downtime, irritated customers, and loss of revenue. But it is quite amazing that so many ISPs rely on this strategy while claiming four or five 9s (99.99 percent or 99.999 percent) of network availability.

Modem

The out-of-band network can take many forms. The simplest is installing a modem on the console port of the equipment in the remote site and then cascading the auxiliary ports to the console ports of the remaining equipment. This works as a useful last resort, but it gets very unwieldy with more than two or three items of equipment. Putting two or three modems in the PoP can help with this, but the solution generally is not very scalable.

At least the principle of out-of-band connection is there, though. If all the connections to the site go down, the ISP engineers still can dial into the PoP, connect to a router, and maybe try to diagnose what the problems might be. Also, if they are working remotely on a piece of equipment, making a mistake that cuts off access easily can be repaired with a simple connection through the dialup lines.

Indeed, one of the best ways of establishing whether there has been a complete site failure is determining that the dialup modem isn't responding. Then there is probably little point in dispatching an engineer; time then is better spent contacting the site management team to restore power or correcting whatever failure might have happened.

Console Server

The next logical step from using one modem or multiple modems is to install a console server. This is a device to which all the equipment consoles are connected. The most popular console server in recent years has been the Cisco 2511 router—it has 1 Ethernet, 2 WANs, and 16 asynchronous serial ports. Originally intended as a dialup router, it has long since been retired from that function in most ISPs and now is used as a console server throughout many ISP backbones.

The configuration is actually quite simple. The Ethernet port of the router is connected to the management LAN in the PoP, providing access to for the NOC engineers when the network is fully functional. When the PoP is disconnected from the backbone, the modem attached to the auxiliary port allows dialup connections to be made to the router, providing full access to each piece of equipment in the PoP.

A sample configuration for the console server follows:

```
!
ip alias 221.1.0.1 2001
ip alias 221.1.0.2 2002
ip alias 221.1.0.3 2003
ip alias 221.1.0.4 2004
ip alias 221.1.0.5 2005
ip alias 221.1.0.6 2006
ip alias 221.1.0.7 2007
ip alias 221.1.0.8 2008
ip alias 221.1.0.9 2009
ip alias 221.1.0.10 2010
ip alias 221.1.0.11 2011
ip alias 221.1.0.12 2012
ip alias 221.1.0.13 2013
ip alias 221.1.0.14 2014
ip alias 221.1.0.15 2015
ip alias 221.1.0.16 2016
!
line 1
 location Console of PoP-cr1
 no exec
 transport preferred none
 transport input telnet
line 2
 location Console of PoP-cr2
 no exec
 transport preferred none
 transport input telnet
line 3
 location Console of PoP-br1
 no exec
 transport preferred none
 transport input telnet
line 4
 location Console of PoP-gw1
 no exec
 transport preferred none
 transport input telnet
line 5
 location Console of PoP-gw2
 no exec
 transport preferred none
 transport input telnet
line 6 16
 location Spare
 no exec
 transport preferred none
 transport input telnet
!
```

Note the use of the **ip alias** commands in the configuration. This allows the ISP to insert a mapping of the console port name to the address and port so that the NOC operations staff can access the console port in question without having to remember addresses or port numbers. For example, the name console.pop-cr1.isp.net could be mapped to the address 221.0.1.1 in the ISP's DNS.

Out-of-Band ISDN

Some ISPs use ISDN as the means of accessing their out-of-band management system. ISDN is readily available in many countries, often at a cost not too dissimilar to PSTN, but without the need for an external modem attached to the router. Experience has shown that modems can become faulty, so having the enhanced reliability available through ISDN is an advantage for some. An added advantage is that ISDN supports 128 Kbps, making real-time upgrades of router or switch images that much more practical than over a V.34 modem link.

Out-of-Band Circuits

The terminal server usually is connected to the management LAN in the PoP. But if access to the PoP is completely disconnected from the outside world because the ISP's equipment completely fails or all the telco circuits fail, the ISP still will need access to the equipment to aid in restoring the service. (For example, the two core routers might have crashed, causing all external access to be disconnected. Regaining access to these routers gives the NOC some chance of restoring connectivity to the PoP.)

This is where ISPs will install a separate WAN backbone on a different telco infrastructure simply to service the out-of-band management network. (Of course, when the entire telco infrastructure fails into the site, there is little that anyone can do and little advantage to having an out-of-band network provision that can work around this problem.)

The serial ports on the 2511 router are connected to the remote sites in whatever efficient pattern is required and are connected directly to the NOC for immediate access to the routers. Redundancy also can be built into the network, and an IGP can be used to carry routing information for this network.

Testing Out of Band

It goes without saying that the out-of-band provisioning at each ISP PoP should be tested on a regular basis. Although the regular access to the out-of-band network might be over the ISP's backbone through its management network, it is really important that the backup paths are tested as well.

This is especially true when a modem or ISDN is used as the backup path. External modems can be notoriously unreliable when they are needed most, so doing a daily check to ensure that the out-of-band phone line and modem work is an essential part of any NOC's activities. Likewise, checking that the ISDN link is working is good practice. In some countries, the telco has been known to "retire" an ISDN line that has not been used for some time, so when the ISP requires it, a "service unobtainable" message is received rather than the connection that was hoped for. A daily check makes sense here, too.

Commentary

Given how straightforward it is to install out-of-band management for a network, it is continuously surprising that so many ISPs try to manage without it. Using the expense of a terminal server as an excuse for not doing it is quite unjustified, considering the expense difference between the equipment for the rest of the network and the out-of-band device compared to the revenue generated by the business. Most ISPs actually wonder how they managed without the out-of-band facility after this has been demonstrated to them and the capability has been installed on the network.

Test Laboratory

As with out-of-band management, the other essential part of an ISP's operation is the test laboratory. A large number of ISPs make one a core requirement of their business, yet it is very surprising how many newcomers to the industry seem to think that they can manage fine without one.

The test laboratory is used for several purposes:

- To test new hardware before it is deployed in the field
- To test new software before it is deployed in the field
- To test failure scenarios, workarounds, and so on, to avoid having to do these tests on the live network
- To test new products, especially connection services before they are deployed
- To run pilots or beta versions of services, future software, and future hardware products

No doubt other possibilities exist, too, but these are the main ones considered by ISPs.

Anything new being developed for the ISP business has the potential to impact existing services. As mentioned earlier in the chapter, if the ISP's goal is to operate a business with as close to 100 percent uptime as possible, doing anything to affect this goal will result in angry customers and loss of business. Having a location to test concepts without impacting on the day-to-day business is crucial to the operational future of the company.

Testing New Hardware and Software

With the constant development of new technology, connection and backbone devices (routers, switches, and so on) are becoming ever more sophisticated and faster. New interfaces are being developed, new WAN technologies are deployed, and powerful new features are being added to operating system software.

An ISP without a test laboratory has little choice but to connect new products (potentially running new software) directly to its network backbone. Many major trouble spots in

Internet history have been caused by such introductions into live running networks. Whether it was bugs in router software or bugs in equipment such as ATM or Frame Relay switches, all have resulted in downtime extending to several days and affecting more than just the ISP that implemented a change without any testing.

Performing the correct test procedure before anything new is introduced to the live operational network involves a considerable amount of time in the test lab before careful deployment to the backbone. The following list is typical of many networks:

Step 1 Install hardware/software in the test lab.

Step 2 Run for one week and observe performance. Work with the vendor to resolve any issues. If there are software bugs, obtain a fixed version of the software and repeat this step.

Step 3 After a successful run for a week, implement some load on the test lab network. The best way of doing this is through a traffic generator. Again, if there are performance issues under load, revert to Step 2 and carry on until the load test can run successfully for a week.

Step 4 Deploy the new hardware/software on a less critical part of the backbone. For example, install software at a PoP with fewer customers or a lower revenue-generating rate. If there are live problems, the revenue impact is minimized in time of failure. If there are problems within a week of this test, revert to Step 2 after resolving problems with the vendor.

Step 5 Engineering approval follows. The software or hardware is deemed suitable for wider deployment in the backbone, so a phased installation over a few weeks can be planned. Again, caution is necessary.

— If new router software is being deployed, PoPs designed with hardware redundancy should have only one of the pair of routers upgraded. If there is a major failure, the other router in the pair can take over the load and provided continued service until the problem is fixed.

— If new hardware is being deployed, the hardware redundancy advantage in the PoP should be used. For example, if two core routers are to receive new WAN interface cards, install one card one week and the other card the following week. This ensures that if there is a field problem with the card or the software drivers, the other router will be in a stable, known state.

Step 6 Continue this process until the whole network has been deployed with the new hardware/software.

The test lab is a critical part of this deployment phase. For every step in which a problem has been observed, the test lab is used to try to work out what the problem is. The main network receives minimal impact, and the customers connected to it are minimally affected.

Designing a Test Lab

From the description of the previous test scenario, it should be quite clear what components make up an ISP's test lab. Some ISPs build a replica of one of their PoPs; others simply have a few of the major devices used on their backbone connected in a simple network.

Preference usually is given to the PoP replica design because it becomes very simple to replicate problems that occur on the live network. Several ISPs even have this test lab as part of their backbones—the lab won't take an active part in the IGP or the iBGP, but it is close enough that this could be done, if necessary. Furthermore, this test lab can be added to the ISP's operational procedures so that staff training on new network designs and operational practices can take place on "live" network equipment that looks like the real network.

A major issue with some ISPs is justifying funding for a test network. For experienced Internet engineers, this is an extraordinary issue to have. Providing an "always on" service with a technology that is developing rapidly means that having spare equipment around to test things on has always been part of their tool set. To find newcomers naively assuming that they will never test anything is quite hard to understand—and this is not particularly helped by equipment vendors who do not actively support the need for such a test component in new backbones.

However the funding model is designed in any business, the engineers responsible for the network need to be creative in arranging for their test network requirements.

- Rapidly growing networks could purchase equipment in advance of requirements and install it in the test lab. When the equipment is needed in the backbone, new test equipment can be purchased and the old test equipment can be moved from the lab to the live network. The other advantage of this technique is that equipment has had "burn-in" time—if it has been working for three months in the lab, it is known to work and there are unlikely to be surprises.

- Many ISPs maintain a stock of spares, whether they are spare parts or whole routers/switches. They opt for break/fix maintenance contracts from their vendors (which means that they can send faulty parts back to base for replacement) and replace faulty hardware from their stock. Instead of having the stock sitting in a cupboard or store room, many ISPs opt to have "hot spares," with the equipment powered up and operating as the test lab. This does mean that the test lab is raided when a backbone component fails, but raiding a noncritical part of the live network is preferable to an outage.

- Vendors such as Cisco offer heavily discounted prices on equipment that will only ever be used in a test laboratory. The ISP must undertake that the equipment will be used only for testing purposes, but that is a small price to pay for allowing the business to ensure that it can test new products, software, services without the major financial burden of buying standard-price equipment purely for testing purposes.

Commentary

Given the suggestions in this section, it is quite easy to justify the installation of a test lab. A test lab should be considered as essential to the ISP network as the major part of the backbone, and it contributes substantially to the operational reliability of the network.

Operational Considerations

Why design the world's best network when good operational practices have not been considered?

This might be such an innocent question, but it is surprising how many new ISPs completely forget about any operational practices for their networks. The best-designed network can work only as well as the operators who are running it. Likewise, good operational practices often can make up for a lot of deficiencies in the physical layout of networks.

This section highlights some of the issues that need to be considered for the operational part of an ISP network.

Maintenance

Changes should never ever be made on the live running network—period. Operators who make configuration changes on the live running network during peak traffic periods cause most problems, accidents, and disasters on ISP backbones.

A new ISP should establish when maintenance will be carried out on the network— anywhere on the network. These times should be published on the operations Web pages. Customers also should be told quite clearly and specifically when the at-risk periods are in the backbone so that expectations are set and there are no surprises.

When should maintenance periods be set? First, the time of day must be established. This is done by looking at traffic profiles—the period of lowest traffic is the time when the maintenance should be carried out. For most typical networks, this is between 4 a.m. and 7 a.m.

Next, the day of the week needs to be established:

- Doing maintenance on a Monday makes little sense unless the operations team wants to work all weekend preparing for it. Besides, for smaller ISPs without a 24-hour operations team on site, getting up and going to the site at 4 a.m. on a Monday morning is psychologically hard to do.

- Doing maintenance on a Friday makes little sense, too. Apart from the well-known IP engineer maximum of never touching anything on Friday, doing work on Friday invariably means spending all weekend clearing up any problems that might have occurred during the maintenance work.

- So, this leaves Tuesday, Wednesday, and Thursday. Two periods per week make more sense than just one. A Tuesday maintenance followed by a Thursday maintenance allows for spillover of Tuesday's work to Thursday. Indeed, a Tuesday/Thursday option is the popular option for many ISPs in the industry today. Tuesday maintenance allows a Tuesday/Wednesday cleanup, and Thursday maintenance allows a Thursday/Friday cleanup, not impinging on the weekend.

Here's the summary of this: All maintenance should be carried out on Tuesday and Thursday, between the hours of 4 a.m. and 7 a.m. If this makes sense for the network, publicize it and don't do any work, not matter how trivial, on the backbone equipment outside these hours.

Network Operations Versus Customer Support

Network operations are very different from customer support. Trying to support the network with the same team that is supporting customers means that the network will become neglected in the face of customer demands. And in times of network failure, customer support will spend all its time dealing with phone calls rather than fixing the breakage in the network.

As they grow from being more than a few-person operation, most ISPs very quickly split customer support from the network operations team. NetOps or the NOC have a different contact number (or different entry in the call-management system) and generally cannot be contacted by customers. Customer support is usually answerable to the sales organization within the ISP; whereas, the NOC is answerable to the network engineering or operations division. They have different priorities, focuses, and responsibilities. All this means that the network will be fixed in the time of crisis, without customers getting in the way of staff trying to solve the problems.

Escalation from customer support can be to the NOC, if it is clear that the problem that a customer is experiencing is caused by a misconfiguration on the backbone, external connections, or a problem somewhere within the backbone. This escalation path should be made clear within the ISP operation.

Escalation from the NOC can be to the network operations and network engineering teams. It is unusual, and should be discouraged, for the customer support team to escalate directly to engineering because the NOC is the team trained to deal with the first-level problems within the network.

If an ISP cannot afford to have a NOC (because it is too early in the start up process), arming engineers with a pager or a mobile phone and operating an on-call rotation is the best alternative. This is antisocial for the engineers who are on the rotation (due to the potential frequency of calls and serious disruption to sleep and non-work activities), so this should be considered only as a last resort or should be done only during the initial startup stages in any network.

Engineering

The final team required within an ISP is the engineering team. This team designs the network, plans the next phase, and fixes any operational problems that cannot be handled by the NOC. Quite often, larger ISPs divide engineering into systems and network engineering, and they often divide this further between engineering and operations. This leaves a well-focused team for each part of the ISP network, with no conflict of interest and a good operational process.

Change Management

Change management is about documenting what work will be done in the network, what the impact will be, what the backout path will be, and how long it will take. Documenting changes ensures that the network is fully documented, that there is a case history of changes made, and that the origin of new problems that arise can be traced back more easily.

Background

When a change-management process is introduced into an ISP business, it often is seen as a restriction to progress, stopping changes and putting added bureaucracy in the path of good business and growth. However, with more people operating the network, it becomes harder to track the changes being made in the network, even if a strict maintenance period had been established. ISPs are not the only organizations with a change-management process—even medium to large corporate networks have such a system. Examples of a change-management system can be found at these locations:

http://www.cisco.com/warp/customer/432/change-mgmt.html
http://www.cisco.com/warp/public/126/chmgmt.html

Both document the necessary qualities of a change-management system and the processes and best practices that should be implemented.

ISP Practices

Change-management meetings take place the day before the maintenance is due to happen, with the network manager being able to assess whether one proposed change would collide or conflict with any other proposed changes. Documenting the change process and the backout process, ensures that remote hands can do the work, that no part of the process is missed or overlooked, and that there is a higher likelihood of the change actually working as proposed.

When the work is actually due to take place during the maintenance periods, the operations staff members responsible for implementing changes follow the detailed list of tasks as documented in the change-management process. Quite often the engineer who described the changes necessary also is present, either leading the team or serving as part of the team of engineers making the changes. Although it is recommended to include every conceivable detail, more than likely some oversight has been made in the more complicated tasks, and it is often easier for the instigator of the changes to be involved from the start rather than having to be raised from sleep in the small hours of the morning.

After the work has been completed, documenting the work done in the change-management form is recommended. For example, if something goes wrong or there are particular oversights, a future work plan can review past experiences to ensure that the issues faced previously do not recur.

It is our experience that a network can function properly only when a change-management process has been established. If one engineer is running everything, such a process is probably overkill, but a business with even half a dozen engineers in operations responsible for different parts of the network means that such a system is necessary. A network has so many complex interactions that only a review of proposed work can fully establish whether one change will have an impact anywhere else on the backbone.

Summary

This chapter provided an overview of many of the facets of designing and operating an ISP backbone. This included PoP topologies and design, backbone design, ISP services, and the development of IPv4 addressing plans. The chapter also covered interior and exterior routing protocols, introduced simple techniques for multihoming, and touched on some of the basic requirements for security on an ISP backbone. The remaining parts of the chapter considered out-of-band management for the network and the importance of a test lab, before finishing with a brief look at some of the key operational requirements in the network.

Considerably more detail is possible in these topics—this chapter has simply been an overview to aid newcomers to the ISP industry in getting the best start for their business, to help them be aware of needs, and to offer a fast track into the world that is the Internet.

Endnotes

[1] The exact URL is ftp://ftp.isi.edi/tools/ra. The version at the time of this writing was tree-2.1.5.tar.Z.

[2] RIPE-229 documents the recommended coordinated route flap damping parameters (ftp://ftp.ripe.net/ripe/docs/ripe-229.txt). The technical background of route-flap damping is discussed in Chapter 3.

[3] The private AS range is 64512 to 65534. AS 65535 is reserved.

[4] Note that some ISPs prefer to send traffic over private peerings rather than their IXP peerings. This case is only an example, and policies between the local AS and its private peers should be set up according to local conditions and requirements. For example, an ISP might want to send all traffic over the IX apart from delay-sensitive traffic or traffic from special customers that goes over the private peering link.

Access Lists and Regular Expressions

This appendix provides a handy reference for the access list types supported in Cisco IOS Software at the time of this writing. It also provides some examples of BGP path-filtering regular expressions in common use. As always, refer to the online documentation for the most up-to-date information.

Access List Types

<1-99>	IP standard access list
<100-199>	IP extended access list
<200-299>	Protocol type-code access list
<700-799>	48-bit MAC address access list
<1100-1199>	Extended 48-bit MAC address access list
<1300-1999>	IP standard access list (expanded range)
<2000-2699>	IP extended access list (expanded range)
compiled	Enables IP access-list compilation (new from 12.0(6)S)
rate-limit	Simple rate limit–specific access list
permit	Specifies packets to forward
deny	Specifies packets to reject
dynamic	Specifies a dynamic list of permits or denies
<0-255>	An IP protocol number
ahp	Authentication Header Protocol
eigrp	Cisco's EIGRP routing protocol
esp	Encapsulation Security Payload
gre	Cisco's GRE tunneling

continues

icmp	Internet Control Message Protocol
igmp	Internet Gateway Message Protocol
igrp	Cisco's IGRP routing protocol
ip	Any Internet protocol
ipinip	IP in IP tunneling
nos	KA9Q NOS–compatible IP over IP tunneling
ospf	OSPF routing protocol
pcp	Payload Compression Protocol
pim	Protocol Independent Multicast
tcp	Transmission Control Protocol
udp	User Datagram Protocol
a.b.c.d	Source or destination address
any	Any source host
host	A single source host (equivalent to a.b.c.d 255.255.255.255)
log	Log matches against this entry
log-input	Log matches against this entry, including input interface
precedence	Matches packets with given precedence value
tos	Matches packets with given TOS value

Other options exist, depending on which upper-layer protocol (TCP or UDP) has been chosen. For example, TCP has these further options for configuring an access list: ack, eq, established, fin, gt, log, log-input, lt, neq, precedence, psh, range, rst, syn, tos, and urg.

IOS Software Regular Expressions

Here are some examples of regular expressions used for BGP peerings on ISP routers today. Refer to the documentation for more in-depth discussion and detailed examples.

^200$	Matches AS200 only
.*	Matches anything
.+	Matches at least one character
^*	Matches all paths, including the local AS
^$	Matches the local AS only
^200_	Matches all autonomous systems received from AS200

_200_	Matches all paths containing AS200
_200$	Matches all paths with AS200 as the origin
^200_210$	Matches AS210 origin and received from AS200 only
_200_210_	Matches all paths that have been through AS200 and AS210 link
^(200_)+$	Matches at least one of AS200 (or multiple occurrences of one AS) (usually from AS_PATH stuffing[1])
^(_[0-9]+)$	Matches at least one AS (or multiple occurrences of one AS)
_\(65350\)_	Matches all paths having confederation sub-AS 65350 in the path
^[0-9]+$	Matches AS_PATH length of 1
^[0-9]+_[0-9]+$	Matches AS_PATH length of 2
^[0-9]*_[0-9]+$	Matches AS_PATH length of 1 or 2
^[0-9]*_[0-9]*$	Matches AS_PATH length of 1 or 2 (or 0)[2]
^[0-9]+_[0-9]+_[0-9]+$	Matches AS_PATH length of 3
_(701|1800)_	Matches anything that has gone through AS701 or AS1800
_1849(_.+_)12163$	Matches anything of origin AS12163 and transited through AS1849

ISPs that are using utilities such as the RAToolSet (see Appendix E, "Traffic Engineering Tools") to generate their BGP configurations will see substantially more sophisticated regular expressions—it is unusual for anyone to generate by hand anything more sophisticated than what has been listed previously.

Endnotes

[1]AS path stuffing means seeing an AS path such as 200_200_200 for a network announcement. This is commonly used when defining particular routing policy, such as with load sharing.

[2]Zero is in brackets because announcements received from a neighboring AS will include an AS in the path. But if the filter is used for iBGP path filtering, it will also match the local AS.

Cut-and-Paste Templates

The following are some cut-and-paste templates that you can modify to configure your routers. Make sure that you change any sample IP addresses or AS numbers used in the templates to match your own addressing! *Do not use the addresses in the examples because they are invalid.*

As described in the main text, it is considered good practice to set up a configuration template for each class of router running in the network. Use these templates, taken from running configurations in ISP backbones today, to construct your own templates suitable for your needs.

General System Template

Note the inclusion of Cisco Express Forwarding (CEF) in this template (see Example B-1). CEF gives access to important features such as Unicast RPF. The 7500 series routers support the distributed CEF option—if CEF is required, don't forget the **distributed** keyword. Some routers have CEF enabled by default, so the **ip cef** directive probably is not required in the template. (It's good practice to include it anyway, just in case any future defaults change or CEF accidentally has been switched off.)

Example B-1 *General System Template*

```
!
! General stuff we don't want
!
no service finger            ! replaced with ip finger from 12.0
no service pad
no service udp-small-servers
no service tcp-small-servers
no ip finger
no ip bootp server
no ip source-route
no cdp run
```

continues

Example B-1 *General System Template (Continued)*

```
!
! Nagle
!
service nagle
!
! Full timestamping
!
service timestamps debug datetime localtime show-timezone msec
service timestamps log datetime localtime show-timezone msec
!
! Keepalives
!
service tcp-keepalives-in
!
! All routers need a loopback
!
interface loopback 0
 description Loopback interface for router XY
 ip address y.y.y.y 255.255.255.255
!
! Enable logging with two loghosts using facility local4
!
no logging console
logging buffered 16384
logging trap debugging
logging source-interface loopback 0
logging facility local4
logging x.x.x.A
logging x.x.x.B
!
! Make sure we are classless
! - these commands are default from 12.0 - best included anyway
!
ip subnet-zero
ip classless
!
!!!! Enable Cisco Express Forwarding !!!!
!
ip cef
!
```

General Interface Template

Many ISPs now make sure that CEF is running on their routers by default, and they specify **ip verify unicast reverse-path** on all their customer-facing interfaces. Example B-2 includes the configuration. If CEF is not enabled on the router, the command parser will not accept the **Unicast RPF check** command.

Example B-2 *General Interface Template*

```
!
! Customer Facing Interfaces
!
interface serial 0/0
 description BW Connection to XYZ, Circuit ID, Cable ID.
 bandwidth BW
 ip verify unicast reverse-path
 no ip redirects
 no ip directed-broadcast
 no ip proxy-arp
 no cdp enable
!
interface hssi 1/0
 description BW Connection to ABC, Circuit ID, Cable ID.
 bandwidth BW
 ip verify unicast reverse-path
 no ip redirects
 no ip directed-broadcast
 no ip proxy-arp
 no cdp enable
!
! Core Network Interfaces
!
interface fastethernet 2/0
 description Core link to Router2, X-over Ethernet
 no ip redirects
 no ip directed-broadcast
 no ip proxy-arp
 no cdp enable
!
```

General Security Template

Notice that TACACS+ is included in the template in Example B-3. Using a centralized authentication system is strongly recommended. Such a system scales and is moderately secure, unlike storing individual or shared passwords on every router in the backbone.

Example B-3 *General Security Template*

```
!
! General stuff
!
service password-encryption
enable secret <removed>
no enable password
!
! Enable AAA and TACACS+
!
aaa new-model
aaa authentication login default tacacs+ enable
aaa authentication enable default tacacs+ enable
!
! And set up the TACACS+ authentication - two servers
!
ip tacacs source-interface loopback 0
tacacs-server host z.z.z.A
tacacs-server host z.z.z.B
tacacs-server key <removed>
!
! Enable Secure Shell
! - need to run "crypto key generate rsa" before applying this template
!
ip ssh time-out 120
ip ssh authentication-retries 3
!
! Protect the console ports - list NOC and other permitted addresses in acl 198
!
access-list 198 permit ip n.n.n.n m.m.m.m any
access-list 198 deny ip any any log
!
line con 0
 location Router Console - use as last resort
 exec-timeout 1 0
 transport preferred none
 tracsport input none
line aux 0
 location Connected to XY-BR router Console - access through reverse telnet
 no exec
 transport preferred none
 transport input telnet
```

Example B-3 *General Security Template (Continued)*

```
line vty 0 4
 location Router VTY ports - only telnet and SSH permitted
 access-class 198 in
 transport preferred none
 transport input telnet ssh
 transport output telnet ssh
!
```

General iBGP Template

This generic template (see Example B-4) should be used for configuring iBGP on a router. It also includes a sample configuration for a peer group. Notice the configuration of the BGP version (which some consider being ultraparanoid and others consider good practice) and also the use of **next-hop-self** for iBGP peerings.

Example B-4 *General iBGP Template*

```
!
! Set up our AS
!
router bgp 65280
!
! Defaults we need to fix
!
 no synchronization
 no auto-summary
!
! Catch all logs
!
 bgp log-neighbor-changes
!
! Set up peer-group
!
 neighbor ibgp-peer peer-group
 neighbor ibgp-peer description Internal BGP peers
 neighbor ibgp-peer remote-as 65280
 neighbor ibgp-peer update-source loopback 0
 neighbor ibgp-peer next-hop-self
 neighbor ibgp-peer version 4                 ! ultra paranoid
 neighbor ibgp-peer send-community            ! send communities internally
 neighbor ibgp-peer password <removed>        ! use password on peering
!
```

General eBGP Template

This generic template should be used for configuring eBGP on a router. It also includes a sample configuration for an external BGP peer-group. The eBGP template will differ depending on whether the router is a border router or a customer aggregation router, so it is a good idea to set up a template for each scenario encountered.

Notice the introduction of route flap damping—using the RIPE-229 parameters is considered by many to be better than using the Cisco defaults because they are less aggressive. See Appendix D, "Route Flap Damping," for the detailed flap-damping configuration. The route maps and prefix lists mentioned in Example B-5 are for applying policy and route filtering as appropriate.

Example B-5 *General eBGP Template*

```
!
! Set up our AS
!
router bgp 65280
!
! Use BGP damping, preferably using RIPE-210 values
!
 bgp dampening graded-flap-damp
!
! Defaults we need to fix
!
 no synchronization
 no auto-summary
!
! Catch all logs
!
 bgp log-neighbor-changes
!
! enable deterministic MED
!
 bgp deterministic-med
!
! Set up peer-group
!
 neighbor ebgp-peer peer-group
 neighbor ebgp-peer description Generic eBGP peergroup
 neighbor ebgp-peer remove-private-AS
 neighbor ebgp-peer version 4
 neighbor ebgp-peer prefix-list isp-out out
 neighbor ebgp-peer prefix-list isp-in in
 neighbor ebgp-peer route-map out-policy out
 neighbor ebgp-peer route-map in-policy in
 neighbor ebgp-peer password <removed>
 neighbor ebgp-peer maximum-prefix 150000
!
```

Martian and RFC 1918 Networks Template

This list represents the common filtering practice of several ISPs. It includes default, multicast, and RFC 1918 networks, as well as the so-called Martian networks. The list was documented in the Internet draft by Bill Manning, which, at the time of writing, was found at www.ietf.org/internet-drafts/draft-manning-dsua-07.txt. The use of these filters on inbound and outbound interfaces of border routers is recommended. It is also recommended that these prefixes be used on BGP peerings where the ISP is receiving or sending full prefixes to a neighboring autonomous system.

The recommended list of filters will change over time—the list is quoted at the time of this writing, mid-2001. You are encouraged to check the companion web site (www.ispbook.com) and whitepaper supplements to this book for any updates before implementing any of these filters. Two examples of the filters are given (see Examples B-6 and B-7): The first example uses access lists, now considered deprecated for BGP route filtering; the other example uses prefix lists, which are easier to understand and much more efficient for the router to process.

IP Access List Example

Example B-6 *Access List to Deny RFC 1918 and Martian Networks*

```
!
access-list 150 deny    ip 0.0.0.0 0.255.255.255 255.0.0.0 0.255.255.255
access-list 150 deny    ip 10.0.0.0 0.255.255.255 255.0.0.0 0.255.255.255
access-list 150 deny    ip 127.0.0.0 0.255.255.255 255.0.0.0 0.255.255.255
access-list 150 deny    ip 169.254.0.0 0.0.255.255 255.255.0.0 0.0.255.255
access-list 150 deny    ip 172.16.0.0 0.15.255.255 255.240.0.0 0.15.255.255
access-list 150 deny    ip 192.0.2.0 0.0.0.255 255.255.255.0 0.0.0.255
access-list 150 deny    ip 192.168.0.0 0.0.255.255 255.255.0.0 0.0.255.255
access-list 150 deny    ip 224.0.0.0 31.255.255.255 224.0.0.0 31.255.255.255
access-list 150 deny    ip any 255.255.255.128 0.0.0.127
access-list 150 permit ip any any
!
```

IP Prefix List Example

Example B-7 *Prefix List to Deny RFC 1918 and Martian Networks*

```
!
ip prefix-list rfc1918-sua description Networks which shouldn't be announced
ip prefix-list rfc1918-sua deny 0.0.0.0/8 le 32
ip prefix-list rfc1918-sua deny 10.0.0.0/8 le 32
ip prefix-list rfc1918-sua deny 127.0.0.0/8 le 32
ip prefix-list rfc1918-sua deny 169.254.0.0/16 le 32
ip prefix-list rfc1918-sua deny 172.16.0.0/12 le 32
ip prefix-list rfc1918-sua deny 192.0.2.0/24 le 32
ip prefix-list rfc1918-sua deny 192.168.0.0/16 le 32
ip prefix-list rfc1918-sua deny 224.0.0.0/3 le 32
ip prefix-list rfc1918-sua deny 0.0.0.0/0 ge 25
ip prefix-list rfc1918-sua permit 0.0.0.0/0 le 32
!
```

Example Configurations

This appendix aims to give ISPs learning about the art of constructing an ISP caliber backbone a little guidance on some of the configuration steps and design hints that have been covered throughout the "IOS Essentials" whitepaper and this book. The common elements of an ISP's network have all been included, including border, aggregation, and dial access routers. Clearly it is almost impossible to give sample configurations suitable for all ISPs. The following aims to give guidance to small or medium ISPs that have not been in operations long so that they gain the general principles of what is required for the network routers.

Simple Network Plan

Figure C-1 shows a simple network diagram of a basic ISP point of presence (PoP), which will be used in these examples. It has the key elements of an ISP PoP: a border router, two core routers, aggregation routers (for leased-line or permanently connected customers), two service routers (for web hosting and the ISP's own services), a dial aggregation router, and a router that connects to the network operations center. Obviously, as ISPs grow, their network will be more sophisticated than this, and their configuration needs likewise will grow to match. However, this example should serve as a good grounding for future growth.

An important element to which you should pay attention throughout these examples is the very rigorous filtering that has been applied throughout the network. Filtering at the right places ensures security for the ISP, as well as a reliably performing network.

Figure C-1 *Network Used for Configuration and Filtering Sample*

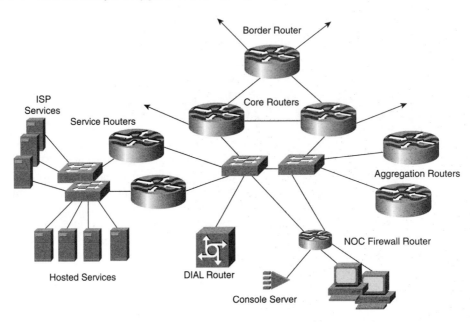

Configurations

The following Cisco IOS Software configurations work and have been tested in a lab environment. They are based heavily on known current configurations used in the field today, with additions/modifications to include as many recommendations from the main text of this book as is feasible.

The configurations have been annotated using IOS Software comments (with !) where more explanation is required. This should make it easier to cut and paste configurations into your own test environment. But remember the golden rule: "Never cut and paste into a live network, and don't implement any configuration until you have extensively tested it in your own environment."

NOTE   You can find a companion web site for this book with the configurations in this appendix at www.ispbook.com.

The IP addresses and AS numbers used are completely fictitious and, at the time of writing, still belong to IANA reserved address space. At some time in the future, these addresses or address spaces will become allocated to an ISP and assigned to an end customer. It is very important that you do not use these addresses in your own backbone or announce them to the Internet. Address space should be obtained from your upstream ISP or from one of the regional Internet registries.

ISP Addressing Plan

For reference purposes, the following addressing plan has been used for this ISP backbone. The address block is 220.144.128.0/19.

220.144.159.192/26	Router loopbacks
220.144.159.128/26	ISP network operations center
220.144.159.64/26	Point-to-point links and VLANs
220.144.159.0/26	ISP services LAN
220.144.158.0/24	Customer-hosting LAN
220.144.157.0/24	DIAL pool
:	
:	

220.144.128.0 and upwards to be used for customer assignments

NOC Hosts

220.144.159.129	loghost, TACACS+, FTP, TFTP
220.144.159.130	Network management workstation
220.144.159.131	Secure Shell gateway
220.144.159.132	RADIUS server for DIAL
220.144.159.160	.160 through .175: Host range for terminal server console port access
220.144.159.180	Primary DNS
220.144.159.189	Out-of-band management terminal server
220.144.159.190	NOC firewall router

ISP Services LAN

220.144.159.1	Secondary DNS, NTP server
220.144.159.2	Secondary MX, caching DNS server
220.144.159.3	Primary MX, FTP, WWW
220.144.159.4	PoP3, SMTP relay for DIAL only
220.144.159.5	Newsreading system for DIAL only
220.144.159.59	Service–Router1
220.144.159.60	Service–Router2
220.144.159.61	HSRP gateway 1
220.144.159.62	HSRP gateway 2

Border Router

The border router is perhaps the most important router in an ISP's backbone network operation. It provides connectivity to the rest of the Internet for the ISP and also protects the ISP's network and customers from the ravages of the Internet. In ISP workshop presentations, we use the analogy of the front door of your house or the garden gate protecting you from the world out there. The configuration of the border router is critical to the correct and reliable operation of the rest of the ISP's business. The configuration in Example C-1 is similar to some of those that are deployed on live networks today.

Example C-1 *Border Router Configuration Example*

```
version 12.0
service nagle
no service pad
service tcp-keepalives-in
service timestamps debug datetime msec localtime show-timezone
service timestamps log datetime msec localtime show-timezone
service password-encryption
!
hostname border-router
!
boot system flash c7200-k4p-mz.120-10.S2
boot system flash
!
logging buffered 16384 debugging
aaa new-model
aaa authentication login default tacacs+ enable
aaa authentication enable default tacacs+ enable
aaa accounting exec default start-stop tacacs+
aaa accounting commands 15 default start-stop tacacs+
!
enable secret shhhhhthisisasecret
!
clock timezone GMT 0
ip subnet-zero
ip cef
no ip source-route
no ip finger
ip telnet source-interface Loopback0
ip tftp source-interface Loopback0
ip ftp source-interface Loopback0
ip ftp username cisco
ip ftp password shhhhsecret
no ip bootp server
!
! Set up DNS - note that one secondary NS is hosted by my upstream ISP
ip domain-name net.galaxy
ip name-server 220.144.159.1
ip name-server 220.144.159.2
ip name-server 219.10.2.1
!
! SSH support
```

Example C-1 *Border Router Configuration Example (Continued)*

```
ip ssh time-out 120
ip ssh authentication-retries 3
!
interface Loopback0
 description Loopback interface on border-router
 ip address 220.144.159.192 255.255.255.255
 no ip directed-broadcast
!
interface FastEthernet0/0
 description Ethernet to Core1 (x-over ethernet)
 ip address 220.144.159.65 255.255.255.252
 no ip redirects
 no ip directed-broadcast
 no ip proxy-arp
 ip route-cache flow
!
interface Serial1/0
 description 256Kb HDLC link to Buzz Internet
 bandwidth 256
 ip address 219.10.1.2 255.255.255.252
 ip access-group 100 in
 ip access-group 101 out
 no ip redirects
 no ip directed-broadcast
 ip route-cache flow
 no fair-queue
!
interface Serial1/1
description 512Kb HDLC link to Whoosh Internet
 bandwidth 512
 ip address 219.50.10.2 255.255.255.252
 ip access-group 100 in
 ip access-group 101 out
 no ip redirects
 no ip directed-broadcast
 ip route-cache flow
 no fair-queue
!
interface FastEthernet2/0
 description Ethernet to Core2 (x-over ethernet)
 ip address 220.144.159.69 255.255.255.252
 no ip redirects
 no ip directed-broadcast
 no ip proxy-arp
 ip route-cache flow
!
router ospf 100
 network 219.50.10.0 0.0.0.3 area 0
 network 219.10.1.0 0.0.0.3 area 0
 network 220.144.159.64 0.0.0.7 area 0
 network 220.144 159.192 0.0.0.0 area 0
 passive-interface Serial1/0
```

continues

Example C-1 *Border Router Configuration Example (Continued)*

```
 passive-interface Serial1/1
 passive-interface Loopback0
 log-adjacency-changes
!
router bgp 64511
 no synchronization
 bgp log-neighbor-changes
 ! Use peer-groups - more efficient
 neighbor core-ibgp peer-group
 neighbor core-ibgp remote-as 64511
 neighbor core-ibgp update-source Loopback0
 neighbor core-ibgp password BGPsecretPW
 neighbor core-ibgp send-community
 ! Get full routing table from both upstreams - block RFC1918+ address space inbound
 ! only announce my address block outbound
 neighbor 219.10.1.2 remote-as 64400
 neighbor 219.10.1.2 description Connection to Buzz Internet
 neighbor 219.10.1.2 prefix-list infilter in
 neighbor 219.10.1.2 prefix-list outfilter out
 neighbor 219.10.1.2 password BuzzSecretPW
 neighbor 219.50.10.1 remote-as 64500
 neighbor 219.50.10.1 description Connection to Whoosh Internet
 neighbor 219.50.10.1 prefix-list infilter in
 neighbor 219.50.10.1 prefix-list outfilter out
 neighbor 219.50.10.1 password WhooshSecretPW
 ! iBGP with core routers - using route reflectors
 neighbor 220.144.159.193 peer-group core-ibgp
 neighbor 220.144.159.193 description Core1
 neighbor 220.144.159.194 peer-group core-ibgp
 neighbor 220.144.159.194 description Core2
 no auto-summary
!
ip classless
ip route 10.0.0.0 255.0.0.0 Null0
ip route 172.16.0.0 255.240.0.0 Null0
ip route 192.168.0.0 255.255.0.0 Null0
ip route 220.144.128.0 255.255.224.0 Null0
ip tacacs source-interface Loopback0
ip bgp-community new-format
!
no logging console
logging trap debugging
logging source-interface Loopback0
logging 220.144.159.129
! SNMP access-list
access-list 1 permit 220.144.159.129
access-list 1 permit 220.144.159.130
access-list 1 deny   any log
! INBOUND access-list on external interfaces
! BLOCK THE MARTIANS
access-list 100 deny   ip 10.0.0.0 0.255.255.255 any
access-list 100 deny   ip 127.0.0.0 0.255.255.255 any
```

Example C-1 *Border Router Configuration Example (Continued)*

```
access-list 100 deny    ip 172.16.0.0 0.15.255.255 any
access-list 100 deny    ip 192.168.0.0 0.0.255.255 any
access-list 100 deny    ip 220.144.128.0 0.0.31.255 any
access-list 100 deny    ip any 0.0.0.255 255.255.255.0
access-list 100 deny    ip any 0.0.0.0 255.255.255.0
! ACCESS TO SERIAL PORTS
access-list 100 permit icmp any host 219.10.1.2
access-list 100 permit icmp any host 219.50.10.2
access-list 100 permit icmp any 220.144.128.0 0.0.31.255
access-list 100 permit udp any host 219.10.1.2 eq ntp
access-list 100 permit udp any host 219.50.10.2 eq ntp
access-list 100 deny    ip any host 219.10.1.2 log
access-list 100 deny    ip any host 219.50.10.2 log
access-list 100 permit tcp any 220.144.128.0 0.0.31.255 established
! SSH
access-list 100 permit tcp any 220.144.128.0 0.0.31.255 eq 22
access-list 100 permit tcp any 220.144.128.0 0.0.31.255 eq ftp
access-list 100 permit tcp any 220.144.128.0 0.0.31.255 eq ftp-data
! For web
access-list 100 permit tcp any 220.144.128.0 0.0.31.255 eq ident
access-list 100 permit udp any 220.144.128.0 0.0.31.255 eq ntp
access-list 100 permit tcp any 220.144.128.0 0.0.31.255 eq smtp
access-list 100 permit tcp any 220.144.128.0 0.0.31.255 eq www
access-list 100 permit tcp any 220.144.128.0 0.0.31.255 eq pop3
! IMAP
access-list 100 permit tcp any 220.144.128.0 0.0.31.255 eq 143
! LDAP
access-list 100 permit tcp any 220.144.128.0 0.0.31.255 eq 389
! HTTPS
access-list 100 permit tcp any 220.144.128.0 0.0.31.255 eq 443
! NFS
access-list 100 deny    tcp any 220.144.128.0 0.0.31.255 eq 2049 log
! NFS
access-list 100 deny    udp any 220.144.128.0 0.0.31.255 eq 2049 log
! X
access-list 100 deny    tcp any 220.144.128.0 0.0.31.255 eq 6000 log
access-list 100 permit tcp any 220.144.128.0 0.0.31.255 gt 1023
access-list 100 permit udp any 220.144.128.0 0.0.31.255 gt 1023
access-list 100 deny    ip any any log
! OUTBOUND access-list on external interfaces
! My address block
access-list 101 permit ip 220.144.128.0 0.0.31.255 any
! and external facing interfaces
access-list 101 permit ip host 219.10.1.2 any
access-list 101 permit ip host 219.50.10.2 any
access-list 101 deny    ip any any log
! VTY access-list
access-list 198 permit ip 220.144.159.128 0.0.0.63 any    ! NOC systems
access-list 198 permit ip 220.144.159.192 0.0.0.63 any    ! Router loopbacks
access-list 198 deny    ip any any log
```

continues

Example C-1 *Border Router Configuration Example (Continued)*

```
! Industry convention is that acl 199 blocks everything
access-list 199 deny    ip any any log
!
! BGP INBOUND filters
ip prefix-list infilter description Networks which shouldn't be accepted
ip prefix-list infilter deny 0.0.0.0/8 le 32
ip prefix-list infilter deny 10.0.0.0/8 le 32
ip prefix-list infilter deny 127.0.0.0/8 le 32
ip prefix-list infilter deny 169.254.0.0/16 le 32
ip prefix-list infilter deny 172.16.0.0/12 le 32
ip prefix-list infilter deny 192.0.2.0/24 le 32
ip prefix-list infilter deny 192.168.0.0/16 le 32
ip prefix-list infilter deny 220.144.128.0/19 le 32
ip prefix-list infilter deny 224.0.0.0/3 le 32
ip prefix-list infilter deny 0.0.0.0/0 ge 25
ip prefix-list infilter permit 0.0.0.0/0 le 32
!
! BGP OUTBOUND filters
ip prefix-list outfilter description Networks which should be announced to upstreams
ip prefix-list outfilter permit 220.144.128.0/19
!
tacacs-server host 220.144.159.129
tacacs-server key SecretToo
snmp-server community NotTelling RO 1
snmp-server location Somewhere
snmp-server contact Network Operations Center <noc@net.galaxy>
snmp-server enable traps snmp
snmp-server host 220.144.159.130 SecretToo
banner login ^
Authorized Access Only

This system is the property of Galaxy Internet

Disconnect IMMEDIATELY if you are not an authorized user!

Contact noc@net.galaxy +98 765 4321 for help.
^
!
line con 0
 exec-timeout 3 0
 transport preferred none
 transport input none
 transport output telnet
line aux 0
 transport preferred none
 transport input none
 transport output telnet
line vty 0 4
 access-class 198 in
 exec-timeout 0 0
 transport preferred none
```

Example C-1 *Border Router Configuration Example (Continued)*

```
 transport input telnet ssh
 transport output telnet
!
! Where Router core-dumps go
exception protocol ftp
exception dump 220.144.159.129
! NTP configuration
ntp authentication-key 1 md5 secretAlso
ntp authenticate
ntp trusted-key 1
ntp source Loopback0
ntp server 219.10.1.1
ntp peer 220.144.159.1 key 1
ntp server 219.50.10.1
end
```

Core Router

Two core routers were given in the example in Figure C-1. However, only one configuration is given here—the configuration for Core-router2 is almost identical. Notice that the core router has a simpler configuration than the routers at the edge of the ISP's network. Core routers tend not to do packet filtering or routing policy; the design goal is more reliability and a configuration that requires no change in the short to medium terms. Example C-2 assumes that the core router is a Cisco 7206.

Example C-2 *Core Router Configuration Example*

```
version 12.0
service nagle
no service pad
service tcp-keepalives-in
service timestamps debug datetime msec localtime show-timezone
service timestamps log datetime msec localtime show-timezone
service password-encryption
!
hostname Core-router1
!
boot system flash slot0:c7200-k4p-mz.120-10.S2
boot system flash
!
logging buffered 16384 debugging
aaa new-model
aaa authentication login default tacacs+ enable
aaa authentication enable default tacacs+ enable
aaa accounting exec default start-stop tacacs+
aaa accounting commands 15 default start-stop tacacs+
enable secret shhhhthisisasecret
```

continues

Example C-2 *Core Router Configuration Example (Continued)*

```
!
ip cef
clock timezone GMT 0
ip subnet-zero
no ip source-route
no ip finger
ip telnet source-interface Loopback0
ip tftp source-interface Loopback0
ip ftp source-interface Loopback0
ip ftp username cisco
ip ftp password shhhhsecret
no ip bootp server
!
ip domain-name net.galaxy
ip name-server 220.144.159.1
ip name-server 220.144.159.2
ip name-server 219.10.2.1
!
! SSH support
ip ssh time-out 120
ip ssh authentication-retries 3
!
interface Loopback0
 description Loopback interface on Core-router1
 ip address 220.144.159.193 255.255.255.255
 no ip directed-broadcast
!
interface FastEthernet0/0
 description Ethernet to Border (x-over ethernet)
 ip address 220.144.159.66 255.255.255.252
 no ip redirects
 no ip directed-broadcast
 no ip proxy-arp
!
interface Serial1/0
 description E1 HDLC link to Smalltown PoP
 bandwidth 2048
 ip address 220.144.159.77 255.255.255.252
 no ip redirects
 no ip directed-broadcast
 no fair-queue
!
interface FastEthernet2/0
 description Ethernet to Core2 (x-over ethernet)
 ip address 220.144.159.73 255.255.255.252
 delay 9
 no ip redirects
 no ip directed-broadcast
 no ip proxy-arp
!
interface FastEthernet3/0
 description Core Ethernet (SW1 port 1)
```

Example C-2 *Core Router Configuration Example (Continued)*

```
  ip address 220.144.159.97 255.255.255.240
  no ip redirects
  no ip directed-broadcast
  no ip proxy-arp
 !
 interface FastEthernet4/0
  description Core Ethernet (SW2 port 1)
  ip address 220.144.159.113 255.255.255.240
  no ip redirects
  no ip directed-broadcast
  no ip proxy-arp
 !
 router ospf 100
  network 220.144.159.64 0.0.0.3 area 0
  network 220.144.159.72 0.0.0.3 area 0
  network 220.144.159.76 0.0.0.3 area 0
  network 220.144.159.96 0.0.0.15 area 0
  network 220.144.159.112 0.0.0.15 area 0
  network 220.144 159.193 0.0.0.0 area 0
  passive-interface Loopback0
  log-adjacency-changes
 !
 router bgp 64511
  network 220.144.128.0 mask 255.255.224.0
  no synchronization
  bgp log-neighbor-changes
 ! Two peergroups, one for the CORE iBGP,
 ! the other for Route Reflector Cluster
  neighbor core-ibgp peer-group
  neighbor core-ibgp remote-as 64511
  neighbor core-ibgp update-source Loopback0
  neighbor core-ibgp password BGPsecretPW
  neighbor core-ibgp send-community
  neighbor rr-client peer-group
  neighbor rr-client remote-as 64511
  neighbor rr-client update-source Loopback0
  neighbor rr-client password BGPsecretPW
  neighbor rr-client send-community
  neighbor rr-client route-reflector-client
  neighbor 220.144.159.192 peer-group core-ibgp
  neighbor 220.144.159.192 description Border
  neighbor 220.144.159.194 peer-group core-ibgp
  neighbor 220.144.159.194 description Core2
  neighbor 220.144.159.195 peer-group rr-client
  neighbor 220.144.159.195 description Gateway1
  neighbor 220.144.159.196 peer-group rr-client
  neighbor 220.144.159.196 description Gateway2
  neighbor 220.144.159.197 peer-group rr-client
  neighbor 220.144.159.197 description Service1
  neighbor 220.144.159.198 peer-group rr-client
```

continues

Example C-2 *Core Router Configuration Example (Continued)*

```
 neighbor 220.144.159.198 description Service2
 neighbor 220.144.159.200 peer-group rr-client
 neighbor 220.144.159.200 description DIAL Access Router
 no auto-summary
!
ip classless
ip route 10.0.0.0 255.0.0.0 Null0
ip route 172.16.0.0 255.240.0.0 Null0
ip route 192.168.0.0 255.255.0.0 Null0
ip route 220.144.128.0 255.255.224.0 Null0
ip tacacs source-interface Loopback0
ip bgp-community new-format
!
no logging console
logging trap debugging
logging source-interface Loopback0
logging 220.144.159.129
access-list 1 permit 220.144.159.129
access-list 1 permit 220.144.159.130
access-list 1 deny   any log
! VTY access-list - NOC
access-list 198 permit ip 220.144.159.128 0.0.0.63 any
! Router loopbacks
access-list 198 permit ip 220.144.159.192 0.0.0.63 any
access-list 198 deny   ip any any log
access-list 199 deny   ip any any log
!
tacacs-server host 220.144.159.129
tacacs-server key SecretToo
snmp-server community NotTelling RO 1
snmp-server location Somewhere
snmp-server contact Network Operations Center <noc@net.galaxy>
snmp-server enable traps snmp
snmp-server host 220.144.159.130 SecretToo
banner login ^
Authorized Access Only

This system is the property of Galaxy Internet

Disconnect IMMEDIATELY if you are not an authorized user!

Contact noc@net.galaxy +98 765 4321 for help.
^
!
line con 0
 exec-timeout 3 0
 transport preferred none
 transport input none
 transport output telnet
line aux 0
 transport preferred none
```

Example C-2 *Core Router Configuration Example (Continued)*

```
 transport input none
 transport output telnet
line vty 0 4
 access-class 198 in
 exec-timeout 0 0
 transport preferred none
 transport input telnet ssh
 transport output telnet
!
exception protocol ftp
exception dump 220.144.159.129
ntp authentication-key 1 md5 secretAlso
ntp authenticate
ntp trusted-key 1
ntp source Loopback0
ntp server 220.144.159.192 key 1
ntp server 220.144.159.1 key 1
ntp peer 220.144.159.194 key 1
end
```

Aggregation Router

The aggregation or gateway routers are used for connecting fixed-link customers to the ISP's backbone. As in previous sections, only one example will be given. The second aggregation router will use a very similar configuration. The aggregation router in Example C-3 is assumed to be a 3640.

Example C-3 *Aggregation Router Configuration Example*

```
version 12.0
service nagle
no service pad
service tcp-keepalives-in
service timestamps debug datetime msec localtime show-timezone
service timestamps log datetime msec localtime show-timezone
service password-encryption
!
hostname Gateway-router1
!
boot system flash
logging buffered 16384 debugging
aaa new-model
aaa authentication login default tacacs+ enable
aaa authentication enable default tacacs+ enable
aaa accounting exec default start-stop tacacs+
aaa accounting commands 15 default start-stop tacacs+
enable secret shhhhhthisisasecret
```

continues

Example C-3 *Aggregation Router Configuration Example (Continued)*

```
!
ip cef
clock timezone GMT 0
ip subnet-zero
no ip source-route
no ip finger
ip telnet source-interface Loopback0
ip tftp source-interface Loopback0
ip ftp source-interface Loopback0
ip ftp username cisco
ip ftp password shhhhsecret
no ip bootp server
ip domain-name net.galaxy
ip name-server 220.144.159.1
ip name-server 220.144.159.2
ip name-server 219.10.2.1
!
! SSH support
ip ssh time-out 120
ip ssh authentication-retries 3
!
partition flash 2 8 8
!
interface Loopback0
 description Loopback interface on GW1
 ip address 220.144.159.195 255.255.255.255
 no ip directed-broadcast
!
interface FastEthernet0/0
 description Core Ethernet (SW1 port 3)
 ip address 220.144.159.99 255.255.255.240
 no ip redirects
 no ip directed-broadcast
 no ip proxy-arp
!
interface FastEthernet0/1
 description Core Ethernet (SW2 port 3)
 ip address 220.144.159.115 255.255.255.240
 no ip redirects
 no ip directed-broadcast
 no ip proxy-arp
!
interface Serial1/0
 description HDLC 64K link to Cust1 CT1
 bandwidth 64
 ip verify unicast reverse-path
 ip unnumbered Loopback0
 no ip redirects
 no ip directed-broadcast
 no ip proxy-arp
!
interface Serial1/1
```

Example C-3 *Aggregation Router Configuration Example (Continued)*

```
  description 64K HDLC link to Cust2 CT2
  bandwidth 64
  ip unnumbered Loopback0
  no ip redirects
  no ip directed-broadcast
  no ip proxy-arp
!
interface Serial1/2
  description 64K HDLC link to Cust 3 CT3
  bandwidth 64
  ip verify unicast reverse-path
  ip unnumbered Loopback0
  no ip redirects
  no ip directed-broadcast
  no ip proxy-arp
!
interface Serial1/3
  description 64k HDLC link to Cust 4 CT4
  bandwidth 64
  ip verify unicast reverse-path
  ip unnumbered Loopback0
  no ip redirects
  no ip directed-broadcast
  no ip proxy-arp
!
router ospf 100
  network 220.144.159.64 0.0.0.3 area 0
  network 220.144.159.72 0.0.0.3 area 0
  network 220.144.159.76 0.0.0.3 area 0
  network 220.144.159.96 0.0.0.15 area 0
  network 220.144.159.112 0.0.0.15 area 0
  network 220.144 159.193 0.0.0.0 area 0
  passive-interface Loopback0
  log-adjacency-changes
!
router bgp 64511
  network 220.144.128.0
  network 220.144.129.0 mask 255.255.255.224
  network 220.144.129.32 mask 255.255.255.224
  network 220.144.129.64 mask 255.255.255.192
  no synchronization
  bgp log-neighbor-changes
  neighbor rr peer-group
  neighbor rr remote-as 64511
  neighbor rr update-source Loopback0
  neighbor rr password BGPsecretPW
  neighbor rr send-community
  neighbor 220.144.159.193 peer-group rr
  neighbor 220.144.159.193 description Core1
  neighbor 220.144.159.194 peer-group rr
```

continues

Example C-3 *Aggregation Router Configuration Example (Continued)*

```
 neighbor 220.144.159.194 description Core2
 no auto-summary
!
ip classless
ip route 10.0.0.0 255.0.0.0 Null0
ip route 172.16.0.0 255.240.0.0 Null0
ip route 192.168.0.0 255.255.0.0 Null0
ip route 220.144.128.0 255.255.224.0 Null0
ip route 220.144.128.0 255.255.255.0 Serial1/0 permanent
ip route 220.144.129.0 255.255.255.224 Serial1/1 permanent
ip route 220.144.129.32 255.255.255.224 Serial1/2 permanent
ip route 220.144.129.64 255.255.255.192 Serial1/3 permanent
ip tacacs source-interface Loopback0
ip bgp-community new-format
!
no logging console
logging trap debugging
logging source-interface Loopback0
logging 220.144.159.129
access-list 1 permit 220.144.159.129
access-list 1 permit 220.144.159.130
access-list 1 deny   any log
! VTY access-list - NOC
access-list 198 permit ip 220.144.159.128 0.0.0.63 any
! Router loopbacks
access-list 198 permit ip 220.144.159.192 0.0.0.63 any
access-list 198 deny   ip any any log
access-list 199 deny   ip any any log
!
tacacs-server host 220.144.159.129
tacacs-server key SecretToo
snmp-server community NotTelling RO 1
snmp-server location Somewhere
snmp-server contact Network Operations Center <noc@net.galaxy>
snmp-server enable traps snmp
snmp-server host 220.144.159.130 SecretToo
banner login ^
Authorized Access Only

This system is the property of Galaxy Internet

Disconnect IMMEDIATELY if you are not an authorized user!

Contact noc@net.galaxy +98 765 4321 for help.
 ^
!
line con 0
 exec-timeout 3 0
 transport preferred none
 transport input none
 transport output telnet
```

Example C-3 *Aggregation Router Configuration Example (Continued)*

```
line aux 0
 transport preferred none
 transport input telnet
 transport output telnet
line vty 0 4
 access-class 198 in
 exec-timeout 0 0
 transport preferred none
 transport input telnet ssh
 transport output telnet
 !
exception protocol ftp
exception dump 220.144.159.129
ntp authentication-key 1 md5 secretAlso
ntp authenticate
ntp trusted-key 1
ntp source Loopback0
ntp server 220.144.159.193 key 1
ntp server 220.144.159.194 key 1
ntp peer 220.144.159.196 key 1
ntp peer 220.144.159.197 key 1
ntp peer 220.144.159.198 key 1
end
```

Service Router

The service routers are used for connecting the hosted services (for example, content provider systems) and the ISP's own services (mail, news, DNS) to the ISP's backbone. Only one example is provided. The second aggregation router will use a very similar configuration. The router in Example C-4 is assumed to be a 2620 with four Fast Ethernet ports.

Example C-4 *Service Router Configuration Example*

```
version 12.0
service nagle
no service pad
service tcp-keepalives-in
service timestamps debug datetime msec localtime show-timezone
service timestamps log datetime msec localtime show-timezone
service password-encryption
!
hostname Service-router1
!
boot system flash
logging buffered 16384 debugging
aaa new-model
aaa authentication login default tacacs+ enable
```

continues

Example C-4 *Service Router Configuration Example (Continued)*

```
aaa authentication enable default tacacs+ enable
aaa accounting exec default start-stop tacacs+
aaa accounting commands 15 default start-stop tacacs+
enable secret shhhhhthisisasecret
!
clock timezone GMT 0
ip subnet-zero
no ip source-route
no ip finger
ip telnet source-interface Loopback0
ip tftp source-interface Loopback0
ip ftp source-interface Loopback0
ip ftp username cisco
ip ftp password shhhhsecret
no ip bootp server
ip domain-name net.galaxy
ip name-server 220.144.159.1
ip name-server 220.144.159.2
ip name-server 219.10.2.1
!
! SSH support
ip ssh time-out 120
ip ssh authentication-retries 3
!
partition flash 2 8 8
!
interface Loopback0
 description Loopback interface on SR1
 ip address 220.144.159.197 255.255.255.255
 no ip directed-broadcast
!
interface FastEthernet0/0
 description Core Ethernet (SW1 vlan1 port 4)
 ip address 220.144.159.101 255.255.255.240
 no ip redirects
 no ip directed-broadcast
 no ip proxy-arp
!
interface FastEthernet0/1
 description Core Ethernet (SW2 vlan2 port 13)
 ip address 220.144.159.117 255.255.255.240
 no ip redirects
 no ip directed-broadcast
 no ip proxy-arp
!
interface FastEthernet1/0
 description Hosted Server Ethernet (SW3 vlan1 port 1)
 ip address 220.144.158.1 255.255.255.0
 ip access-group 140 in
 ip access-group 141 out
 standby 10 priority 150
 standby 10 preempt
```

Example C-4 *Service Router Configuration Example (Continued)*

```
 standby 10 ip 220.144.158.253
 standby 20 ip 220.144.158.254
 no ip redirects
 no ip directed-broadcast
 no ip proxy-arp
!
interface FastEthernet1/1
 description Galaxy ISP Server Ethernet (SW3 vlan2 port 8)
 ip address 220.144.159.59 255.255.255.192
 ip access-group 150 in
 ip access-group 151 out
 standby 30 priority 150
 standby 30 preempt
 standby 30 ip 220.144.159.61
 standby 40 ip 220.144.159.62
 no ip redirects
 no ip directed-broadcast
 no ip proxy-arp
!
router ospf 100
 network 220.144.159.96 0.0.0.15 area 0
 network 220.144.159.112 0.0.0.15 area 0
 network 220.144 159.197 0.0.0.0 area 0
 network 220.144.159.0 0.0.0.63 area 0
 passive-interface FastEthernet1/1
 passive-interface Loopback0
 log-adjacency-changes
!
router bgp 64511
 network 220.144.158.0
 no synchronization
 bgp log-neighbor-changes
 neighbor rr peer-group
 neighbor rr remote-as 64511
 neighbor rr update-source Loopback0
 neighbor rr password BGPsecretPW
 neighbor rr send-community
 neighbor 220.144.159.193 peer-group rr
 neighbor 220.144.159.193 description Core1
 neighbor 220.144.159.194 peer-group rr
 neighbor 220.144.159.194 description Core2
 no auto-summary
!
ip classless
ip route 10.0.0.0 255.0.0.0 Null0
ip route 172.16.0.0 255.240.0.0 Null0
ip route 192.168.0.0 255.255.0.0 Null0
ip route 220.144.128.0 255.255.224.0 Null0
ip tacacs source-interface Loopback0
ip bgp-community new-format
```

continues

Example C-4 *Service Router Configuration Example (Continued)*

```
!
no logging console
logging trap debugging
logging source-interface Loopback0
logging 220.144.159.129
access-list 1 permit 220.144.159.129
access-list 1 permit 220.144.159.130
access-list 1 deny   any log
! WHAT GETS OUT
access-list 140 permit ip 220.144.158.0 0.0.0.255 any
access-list 140 deny   ip any any log
! WHAT GETS IN
access-list 141 permit ip host 220.144.158.1 host 220.144.158.2
access-list 141 permit ip host 220.144.158.2 host 220.144.158.1
access-list 141 permit ip 220.144.159.128 0.0.0.63 220.144.158.0 0.0.0.255
access-list 141 permit icmp any 220.144.158.0 0.0.0.255
access-list 141 permit tcp any 220.144.158.0 0.0.0.255 established
access-list 141 permit tcp any 220.144.158.0 0.0.0.255 eq ident
! SSH
access-list 141 permit tcp any 220.144.158.0 0.0.0.255 eq 22
access-list 141 permit tcp any 220.144.158.0 0.0.0.255 eq www
access-list 141 permit udp any 220.144.158.0 0.0.0.255 gt 1023
access-list 141 deny   ip any any log
! WHAT GETS OUT
access-list 150 permit ip 220.144.159.0 0.0.0.63 any
access-list 150 deny ip any any log
! WHAT GETS IN
access-list 151 permit ip host 220.144.159.1 host 220.144.159.2
access-list 151 permit ip host 220.144.159.2 host 220.144.159.1
access-list 151 permit ip 220.144.159.128 0.0.0.63 220.144.159.0 0.0.0.63
access-list 151 permit icmp any 220.144.159.0 0.0.0.63
access-list 151 permit tcp any 220.144.159.0 0.0.0.63 established
access-list 151 permit tcp any 220.144.159.0 0.0.0.63 eq ident
access-list 151 permit udp any 220.144.159.0 0.0.0.63 gt 1023
! 220.144.159.1 is 2ary DNS, NTP
access-list 151 permit tcp any host 220.144.159.1 eq domain
access-list 151 permit udp any host 220.144.159.1 eq domain
access-list 151 permit udp any host 220.144.159.1 eq ntp
! 220.144.159.2 is 2ary MX, DNS cache
access-list 151 permit tcp any host 220.144.159.2 eq smtp
access-list 151 permit tcp any host 220.144.159.2 eq domain
access-list 151 permit udp any host 220.144.159.2 eq domain
! 220.144.159.3 is 1ary MX, FTP & WWW
access-list 151 permit tcp any host 220.144.159.3 eq smtp
access-list 151 permit tcp any host 220.144.159.3 eq ftp
access-list 151 permit tcp any host 220.144.159.3 eq ftp-data
access-list 151 permit tcp any host 220.144.159.3 eq www
! 220.144.159.4 is PoP3 server and SMTP relay for DIAL only
access-list 151 permit tcp any host 220.144.159.4 eq pop3
access-list 151 permit tcp 220.144.157.0 0.0.0.255 host
    220.144.159.4 eq smtp
```

Example C-4 *Service Router Configuration Example (Continued)*

```
! 220.144.159.5 is News reader for DIAL only
access-list 151 permit tcp 220.144.157.0 0.0.0.255 host
    220.144.159.5 eq nntp
access-list 151 deny ip any any log
! VTY access-list - NOC
access-list 198 permit ip 220.144.159.128 0.0.0.63 any
! Router loopbacks
access-list 198 permit ip 220.144.159.192 0.0.0.63 any
access-list 198 deny   ip any any log
access-list 199 deny   ip any any log
!
tacacs-server host 220.144.159.129
tacacs-server key SecretToo
snmp-server community NotTelling RO 1
snmp-server location Somewhere
snmp-server contact Network Operations Center <noc@net.galaxy>
snmp-server enable traps snmp
snmp-server host 220.144.159.130 SecretToo
banner login ^
Authorized Access Only

This system is the property of Galaxy Internet

Disconnect IMMEDIATELY if you are not an authorized user!

Contact noc@net.galaxy +98 765 4321 for help.
^
!
line con 0
 exec-timeout 3 0
 transport preferred none
 transport input none
 transport output telnet
line aux 0
 transport preferred none
 transport input telnet
 transport output telnet
line vty 0 4
 access-class 198 in
 exec-timeout 0 0
 transport preferred none
 transport input telnet ssh
 transport output telnet
!
exception protocol ftp
exception dump 220.144.159.129
ntp authentication-key 1 md5 secretAlso
ntp authenticate
ntp trusted-key 1
ntp source Loopback0
```

continues

Example C-4 *Service Router Configuration Example (Continued)*

```
ntp server 220.144.159.193 key 1
ntp server 220.144.159.194 key 1
ntp peer 220.144.159.196 key 1
ntp peer 220.144.159.197 key 1
ntp peer 220.144.159.198 key 1
end
```

NOC Router

The NOC router is used to connect the ISP's essential services (such as SYSLOG, TACACS+, and primary DNS) and the operations engineers' workstations to the ISP's backbone. The router in Example C-5 is assumed to be a 2620 with three Fast Ethernet ports.

Example C-5 *NOC Router Configuration Example*

```
version 12.0
service nagle
no service pad
service tcp-keepalives-in
service timestamps debug datetime msec localtime show-timezone
service timestamps log datetime msec localtime show-timezone
service password-encryption
!
hostname NOC-router
!
boot system flash
logging buffered 16384 debugging
aaa new-model
aaa authentication login default tacacs+ enable
aaa authentication enable default tacacs+ enable
aaa accounting exec default start-stop tacacs+
aaa accounting commands 15 default start-stop tacacs+
enable secret shhhhthisisasecret
!
clock timezone GMT 0
ip subnet-zero
no ip source-route
no ip finger
ip telnet source-interface Loopback0
ip tftp source-interface Loopback0
ip ftp source-interface Loopback0
ip ftp username cisco
ip ftp password shhhhsecret
no ip bootp server
ip domain-name net.galaxy
ip name-server 220.144.159.1
ip name-server 220.144.159.2
ip name-server 219.10.2.1
```

Example C-5 *NOC Router Configuration Example (Continued)*

```
!
! SSH support
ip ssh time-out 120
ip ssh authentication-retries 3
!
partition flash 2 8 8
!
interface Loopback0
 description Loopback interface on NOC
 ip address 220.144.159.199 255.255.255.255
 no ip directed-broadcast
!
interface FastEthernet0/0
 description Core Ethernet (SW1 vlan1 port 6)
 ip address 220.144.159.103 255.255.255.240
 no ip redirects
 no ip directed-broadcast
 no ip proxy-arp
!
interface FastEthernet0/1
 description Core Ethernet (SW2 vlan2 port 15)
 ip address 220.144.159.119 255.255.255.240
 no ip redirects
 no ip directed-broadcast
 no ip proxy-arp
!
interface FastEthernet1/0
 description NOC Ethernet
 ip address 220.144.159.190 255.255.255.192
 ip access-group 130 in
 ip access-group 131 out
 no ip redirects
 no ip directed-broadcast
 no ip proxy-arp
!
router ospf 100
 network 220.144.159.96 0.0.0.15 area 0
 network 220.144.159.112 0.0.0.15 area 0
 network 220.144 159.199 0.0.0.0 area 0
 network 220.144.159.128 0.0.0.63 area 0
 passive-interface FastEthernet1/0
 passive-interface Loopback0
 log-adjacency-changes
!
ip classless
ip route 10.0.0.0 255.0.0.0 Null0
ip route 172.16.0.0 255.240.0.0 Null0
ip route 192.168.0.0 255.255.0.0 Null0
ip route 220.144.128.0 255.255.224.0 Null0
```

continues

Example C-5 *NOC Router Configuration Example (Continued)*

```
ip tacacs source-interface Loopback0
ip bgp-community new-format
!
no logging console
logging trap debugging
logging source-interface Loopback0
logging 220.144.159.129
access-list 1 permit 220.144.159.129
access-list 1 permit 220.144.159.130
access-list 1 deny   any log
access-list 130 permit ip 220.144.159.128 0.0.0.63 any      ! WHAT GETS OUT
access-list 130 deny   ip any any log
access-list 131 permit icmp any 220.144.159.128 0.0.0.63    ! WHAT GETS IN
access-list 131 permit tcp any 220.144.159.128 0.0.0.63 eq ident
access-list 131 permit tcp any 220.144.159.128 0.0.0.63 established
! 220.144.159.129 is LOGHOST, TACACS+, FTP-dumps, TFTP
access-list 131 permit udp 220.144.159.192 0.0.0.63 host
    220.144.159.129 eq syslog
access-list 131 permit udp 220.144.159.192 0.0.0.63 host
    220.144.159.129 eq tftp
access-list 131 permit tcp 220.144.159.192 0.0.0.63 host
    220.144.159.129 eq ftp
access-list 131 permit tcp 220.144.159.192 0.0.0.63 host
    220.144.159.129 eq ftp-data
access-list 131 permit tcp 220.144.159.192 0.0.0.63 host
    220.144.159.129 eq tacacs
! 220.144.159.130 is NOC MGMT Workstation
access-list 131 permit udp 220.144.159.192 0.0.0.63 host
    220.144.159.130 eq snmp
access-list 131 permit udp 220.144.159.192 0.0.0.63 host
    220.144.159.130 eq snmptrap
! 220.144.159.131 is SSH gateway
access-list 131 permit tcp any host 220.144.159.131 eq 22
! 220.144.159.132 is DIAL Radius server (NT running Cisco Secure)
access-list 131 permit udp host 220.144.159.200 host 220.144.159.132 eq 1645
access-list 131 permit udp host 220.144.159.200 host 220.144.159.132 eq 1646
! 220.144.159.180 is Primary DNS
access-list 131 permit udp any host 220.144.159.180 eq domain
access-list 131 permit tcp any host 220.144.159.180 eq domain
access-list 131 deny ip any any log
! VTY access-list - NOC
access-list 198 permit ip 220.144.159.128 0.0.0.63 any
access-list 198 permit ip 220.144.159.192 0.0.0.63 any    ! Router loopbacks
access-list 198 deny   ip any any log
access-list 199 deny   ip any any log
!
tacacs-server host 220.144.159.129
tacacs-server key SecretToo
snmp-server community NotTelling RO 1
snmp-server location Somewhere
snmp-server contact Network Operations Center <noc@net.galaxy>
snmp-server enable traps snmp
```

Example C-5 *NOC Router Configuration Example (Continued)*

```
snmp-server host 220.144.159.130 SecretToo
banner login ^
Authorized Access Only

This system is the property of Galaxy Internet

Disconnect IMMEDIATELY if you are not an authorized user!

Contact noc@net.galaxy +98 765 4321 for help.
^
!
line con 0
 exec-timeout 3 0
 transport preferred none
 transport input none
 transport output telnet
line aux 0
 transport preferred none
 transport input telnet
 transport output telnet
line vty 0 4
 access-class 198 in
 exec-timeout 0 0
 transport preferred none
 transport input telnet ssh
 transport output telnet
!
exception protocol ftp
exception dump 220.144.159.129
ntp authentication-key 1 md5 secretAlso
ntp authenticate
ntp trusted-key 1
ntp source Loopback0
ntp server 220.144.159.193 key 1
ntp server 220.144.159.194 key 1
end
```

Access Server

This is the typical configuration of an access server with a connected modem bank. The router in Example C-6 is assumed to be a 3640 with 64 asynchronous ports.

Example C-6 *Access Server Configuration Example*

```
version 12.0
service nagle
no service pad
service tcp-keepalives-in
```

continues

Example C-6 *Access Server Configuration Example (Continued)*

```
service timestamps debug datetime msec localtime show-timezone
service timestamps log datetime msec localtime show-timezone
service password-encryption
!
hostname Access-router
!
boot system flash
logging buffered 16384 debugging
aaa new-model
aaa new-model
aaa authentication login default group tacacs+ enable
aaa authentication login radius-login group radius
aaa authentication enable default group tacacs+ enable
aaa authentication ppp default none
aaa authentication ppp ppp-auth if-needed group radius
aaa authorization network radius-auth group radius
aaa accounting network default stop-only group radius
enable secret shhhhhthisisasecret
!
clock timezone GMT 0
ip subnet-zero
no ip source-route
no ip finger
ip telnet source-interface Loopback0
ip tftp source-interface Loopback0
ip ftp source-interface Loopback0
ip ftp username cisco
ip ftp password shhhhsecret
no ip bootp server
ip domain-name net.galaxy
ip name-server 220.144.159.1
ip name-server 220.144.159.2
ip name-server 219.10.2.1
!
! SSH support
ip ssh time-out 120
ip ssh authentication-retries 3
!
partition flash 2 8 8
!
interface Loopback0
 description Loopback interface on Access-Router
 ip address 220.144.159.200 255.255.255.255
 no ip directed-broadcast
!
interface FastEthernet0/0
 description Core Ethernet (SW1 port 6)
 ip address 220.144.159.104 255.255.255.240
 no ip redirects
 no ip directed-broadcast
 no ip proxy-arp
```

Example C-6 *Access Server Configuration Example (Continued)*

```
!
interface FastEthernet0/1
 description Core Ethernet (SW2 port 6)
 ip address 220.144.159.120 255.255.255.240
 no ip redirects
 no ip directed-broadcast
 no ip proxy-arp
!
interface Group-Async1
 ip unnumbered Loopback0
 no ip directed-broadcast
 encapsulation ppp
 ip tcp header-compression passive
 async mode interactive
 peer default ip address pool ppp-dialin
 no cdp enable
 ppp max-bad-auth 3
 ppp reliable-link
 ppp authentication chap ms-chap pap ppp-auth
 ppp authorization radius-auth
 group-range 65 128
!
router ospf 100
 log-adjacency-changes
 network 220.144.159.200 0.0.0.0 area 0
 network 220.144.159.96 0.0.0.15 area 0
 network 220.144.159.112 0.0.0.15 area 0
 passive-interface Loopback0
!
router bgp 64511
 network 220.144.157.0 mask 255.255.255.128
 no synchronization
 bgp log-neighbor-changes
 neighbor rr peer-group
 neighbor rr remote-as 64511
 neighbor rr update-source Loopback0
 neighbor rr password BGPsecretPW
 neighbor rr send-community
 neighbor 220.144.159.193 peer-group rr
 neighbor 220.144.159.193 description Core1
 neighbor 220.144.159.194 peer-group rr
 neighbor 220.144.159.194 description Core2
 no auto-summary
!
ip local pool ppp-dialin 220.144.157.1 220.144.157.64
!
ip classless
ip route 10.0.0.0 255.0.0.0 Null0
ip route 172.16.0.0 255.240.0.0 Null0
ip route 192.168.0.0 255.255.0.0 Null0
```

continues

Example C-6 *Access Server Configuration Example (Continued)*

```
ip route 220.144.128.0 255.255.224.0 Null0
ip route 220.144.157.0 255.255.255.128 Null0
ip tacacs source-interface Loopback0
no ip http server
ip bgp-community new-format
!
ip radius source-interface Loopback0
no logging console
logging trap debugging
logging facility local5
logging source-interface Loopback0
logging 220.144.159.129
access-list 1 permit 220.144.159.129
access-list 1 permit 220.144.159.130
access-list 1 deny   any log
!
! Access-list 155 is a dynamic access used to restrict e-mail only clients
! to the PoP3 and MAIL relay servers
access-list 155 permit tcp any host 220.144.159.4 eq pop3
access-list 155 permit tcp any host 220.144.159.4 eq smtp
access-list 155 deny   ip any any
!
! Access-list 156 is a dynamic access list used to restrict
! clients with expired subscriptions to the billing server
! so they can renew their subscription - it is the default unless
! clients have paid up :-)
access-list 156 permit tcp any host 220.144.129.36 eq www
access-list 156 deny   ip any any
! VTY  access-list - NOC
access-list 198 permit ip 220.144.159.128 0.0.0.63 any
access-list 198 permit ip 220.144.159.192 0.0.0.63 any   ! Router loopbacks
access-list 198 deny   ip any any log
access-list 199 deny   ip any any log
!
dialer-list 1 protocol ip permit
!
tacacs-server host 220.144.159.129
tacacs-server key SecretToo
snmp-server community NotTelling RO 1
snmp-server location Somewhere
snmp-server contact Network Operations Center <noc@net.galaxy>
snmp-server enable traps snmp
snmp-server host 220.144.159.130 SecretToo
radius-server host 220.144.159.132 auth-port 1645 acct-port 1646
radius-server key AlsoSecret
radius-server vsa send accounting
radius-server vsa send authentication
banner login ^
Authorized Access Only
```

Example C-6 *Access Server Configuration Example (Continued)*

```
This system is the property of Galaxy Internet

Disconnect IMMEDIATELY if you are not an authorized user!

Contact noc@net.galaxy +98 765 4321 for help.
^
!
line con 0
 exec-timeout 3 0
 transport preferred none
 transport input none
 transport output telnet
line 65 128
 session-timeout 5  output
 exec-timeout 1 0
 autoselect during-login
 autoselect ppp
 login authentication radius-login
 modem Dialin
 autocommand ppp
 length 25
 transport input all
 escape-character NONE
 autohangup
 stopbits 1
 flowcontrol hardware
line aux 0
 transport preferred none
 transport input telnet
 transport output telnet
line vty 0 4
 access-class 198 in
 exec-timeout 0 0
 transport preferred none
 transport input telnet ssh
 transport output telnet
!
exception protocol ftp
exception dump 220.144.159.129
ntp authentication-key 1 md5 secretAlso
ntp authenticate
ntp trusted-key 1
ntp source Loopback0
ntp server 220.144.159.193 key 1
ntp server 220.144.159.194 key 1
ntp peer 220.144.159.196 key 1
ntp peer 220.144.159.197 key 1
ntp peer 220.144.159.198 key 1
end
```

Out-of-Band Console Server

This is the typical configuration of an access server that has been configured as an out-of-band management device (refer to Example C-7). The router in this case is a 2611 router with 32 asynchronous ports that have been wired to the consoles of the equipment used in Figure C-1 and described in the preceding configurations.

Example C-7 *Out-of-Band Console Server Configuration Example*

```
version 12.1
service nagle
no service pad
service tcp-keepalives-in
service timestamps debug datetime msec localtime show-timezone
service timestamps log datetime msec localtime show-timezone
service password-encryption
!
hostname cs2611
!
logging buffered 16384 debugging
aaa new-model
aaa authentication login default tacacs+ enable
aaa authentication enable default tacacs+ enable
aaa accounting exec default start-stop tacacs+
aaa accounting commands 15 default start-stop tacacs+
enable secret shhhhhthisisasecret
!
clock timezone GMT 0
ip subnet-zero
no ip source-route
no ip finger
ip rcmd source-interface Loopback0
ip telnet source-interface Loopback0
ip tftp source-interface Loopback0
ip ftp source-interface Loopback0
ip ftp username cisco
ip ftp password shhhhsecret
no ip bootp server
ip domain-name net.galaxy
ip name-server 220.144.159.1
ip name-server 220.144.159.2
ip name-server 219.10.2.1
!
!
interface Ethernet0/0
description Galaxy Net Core LAN
 ip address 220.144.159.189 255.255.255.192
 no ip route-cache
 no ip mroute-cache
!
ip classless
ip route 0.0.0.0 0.0.0.0 220.144.159.190
ip tacacs source-interface Ethernet0/0
```

Example C-7 *Out-of-Band Console Server Configuration Example (Continued)*

```
!
! map IP addresses to reverse telnet ports - easier for humans to deal with
! than trying to remember port numbers
ip alias 220.144.159.160 2065
ip alias 220.144.159.161 2066
ip alias 220.144.159.162 2067
ip alias 220.144.159.163 2068
ip alias 220.144.159.164 2069
ip alias 220.144.159.165 2070
ip alias 220.144.159.166 2071
ip alias 220.144.159.167 2072
ip alias 220.144.159.168 2073
ip alias 220.144.159.169 2074
ip alias 220.144.159.170 2075
ip alias 220.144.159.171 2076
ip alias 220.144.159.172 2077
ip alias 220.144.159.173 2078
ip alias 220.144.159.174 2079
ip alias 220.144.159.175 2080
ip alias 220.144.159.176 2081
ip alias 220.144.159.177 2082
ip alias 220.144.159.178 2083
ip alias 220.144.159.179 2084
!
no ip http server
!
no logging console
logging trap debugging
logging source-interface Loopback0
logging 220.144.159.129
access-list 1 permit 220.144.159.129
access-list 1 permit 220.144.159.130
access-list 1 deny   any log
! VTY access-list - NOC
access-list 198 permit ip 220.144.159.128 0.0.0.63 any
access-list 198 permit ip 220.144.159.192 0.0.0.63 any   ! Router loopbacks
access-list 198 deny   ip any any log
access-list 199 deny   ip any any log
!
tacacs-server host 220.144.159.129
tacacs-server key SecretToo
snmp-server community NotTelling RO 1
snmp-server location Somewhere
snmp-server contact Network Operations Center <noc@net.galaxy>
snmp-server enable traps snmp
snmp-server host 220.144.159.130 SecretToo
banner login ^
Authorized Access Only
```

continues

Example C-7 *Out-of-Band Console Server Configuration Example (Continued)*

```
This system is the property of Galaxy Internet

Disconnect IMMEDIATELY if you are not an authorized user!

Contact noc@net.galaxy +98 765 4321 for help.
 ^
!
line con 0
 exec-timeout 3 0
 transport preferred none
 transport input none
 transport output telnet
line aux 0
 transport preferred none
 transport input telnet
 transport output telnet
line 65
 location Console of SW1
 no exec
 transport preferred none
 transport input telnet
line 66
 location Console of SW2
 no exec
 transport preferred none
 transport input telnet
line 67
 location Console of Border-router
 no exec
 transport preferred none
 transport input telnet
line 68
 location Console of Core1
 no exec
 transport preferred none
 transport input telnet
line 69
 location Console of Core2
 no exec
 transport preferred none
 transport input telnet
line 70
 location Console of Gateway1
 no exec
 transport preferred none
 transport input telnet
line 71
 location Console of Gateway2
 no exec
 transport preferred none
 transport input telnet
```

Example C-7 *Out-of-Band Console Server Configuration Example (Continued)*

```
line 72
 location Console of Service1
 no exec
 transport preferred none
 transport input telnet
line 73
 location Console of Service 2
 no exec
 transport preferred none
 transport input telnet
line 74
 location Console of NOC router
 no exec
 transport preferred none
 transport input telnet
line 75
 location Console of SSH Gateway
 no exec
 transport preferred none
 transport input telnet
line 76
 location Console of LOGHOST/TACACS+/NOC Workstation
 no exec
 transport preferred none
 transport input telnet
line 77
 location Console of Network Management Workstation
 no exec
 transport preferred none
 transport input telnet
line 78
 location Console of RADIUS server
 no exec
 transport preferred none
 transport input telnet
line 79
 location Console of Primary DNS
 no exec
 transport preferred none
 transport input telnet
line 80
 location Console of Secondary DNS
 no exec
 transport preferred none
 transport input telnet
line 81
 location Console of Secondary MX
 no exec
 transport preferred none
 transport input telnet
```

continues

Example C-7 *Out-of-Band Console Server Configuration Example (Continued)*

```
line 82
 location Console of Primary MX, ftp, www
 no exec
 transport preferred none
 transport input telnet
line 83
 location Console of PoP3 server
 no exec
 transport preferred none
 transport input telnet
line 84
 location Console of DIAL News
 no exec
 transport preferred none
 transport input telnet
line 85 96
 location Spare
 no exec
 transport preferred none
 transport input telnet
line vty 0 4
 access-class 198 in
 exec-timeout 0 0
 transport preferred none
 transport input telnet ssh
 transport output telnet
!
exception protocol ftp
exception dump 220.144.159.129
ntp authentication-key 1 md5 secretAlso
ntp authenticate
ntp trusted-key 1
ntp source Loopback0
ntp server 220.144.159.193 key 1
ntp server 220.144.159.194 key 1
end
```

Summary

This appendix offered a simple example of the configurations used in a medium-size ISP. The preceding examples are known to work at the time of this writing, and they should be useful in helping new ISP businesses get a foot on the ladder to success.

OSPF has been used as the IGP here simply because the candidate sample network implemented OSPF. Implementing the network using IS-IS or EIGRP would also be quite feasible.

Route Flap Damping

BGP Flap Damping Configuration

Recommended route flap-damping parameters for use by ISPs were composed into a document by the RIPE Routing Working Group and are available at www.ripe.net/docs/ ripe-229.html. These values are used by many European and U.S. ISPs, and they are based on the operational experienced gained in the industry.

The configuration examples are reproduced here for convenience—the values have been updated to include recent changes in the locations of the root nameservers. The current address list is documented at www.golden-networks.net—this site should be consulted prior to implementing RIPE-229 flap damping.

IP Access List Example

This is a configuration example using the IP access list, similar to what is quoted in the RIPE-229 document. We don't recommend this method any longer—IP prefix lists have long superseded access lists for prefix filtering. See the next section for the prefix-list configuration.

Note that access-list 180 covering the root nameserver and access-list 184 covering the global top-level domain nameserver networks have been updated with the most recent values. It is strongly recommended that you check these addresses and network prefixes announced to the Internet before implementing the filters. (You can use the UNIX command **dig . ns** to find the nameserver addresses and then use **sh ip bgp x.x.x.x** on a router to find the size of the prefix being advertised in the Internet routing table.)

```
router bgp 65280
 bgp dampening route-map RIPE229-flap-damp

! no flap dampening for special user defined networks defined in access-list 183
route-map RIPE229-flap-damp deny 10
 match ip address 183
! no flap dampening for root nameserver networks in access-list 180
route-map RIPE229-flap-damp deny 20
 match ip address 180
```

```
! no flap dampening for gtld nameserver networks in access-list 184
route-map RIPE229-flap-damp deny 30
 match ip address 184
! flap dampening for all the /24 and longer prefixes
route-map RIPE229-flap-damp permit 30
 match ip address 181
 set dampening 30 820 3000 60
! flap dampening for all /22 and /23 prefixes
route-map RIPE229-flap-damp permit 40
 match ip address 182
 set dampening 15 750 3000 45
! flap dampening for all remaining prefixes
route-map RIPE229-flap-damp permit 50
 set dampening 10 1500 3000 30
!

! Access Lists for route flap dampening as per RIPE-229 definition
! with updated root server networks
access-list 180 permit ip host 198.41.0.0 host 255.255.255.0     ! A J
access-list 180 permit ip host 128.9.0.0 host 255.255.0.0        ! B
access-list 180 permit ip host 192.33.4.0 host 255.255.255.0     ! C
access-list 180 permit ip host 128.8.0.0 host 255.255.0.0        ! D
access-list 180 permit ip host 192.203.230.0 host 255.255.255.0  ! E
access-list 180 permit ip host 192.5.4.0 host 255.255.254.0      ! F
access-list 180 permit ip host 192.112.36.0 host 255.255.255.0   ! G
access-list 180 permit ip host 128.63.0.0 host 255.255.0.0       ! H
access-list 180 permit ip host 192.36.148.0 host 255.255.255.0   ! I
access-list 180 permit ip host 193.0.14.0 host 255.255.255.0     ! K
access-list 180 permit ip host 198.32.64.0 host 255.255.255.0    ! L
access-list 180 permit ip host 202.12.27.0 host 255.255.255.0    ! M
access-list 180 deny    ip any any
! match /24 prefixes
access-list 181 permit ip any 255.255.255.0 0.0.0.255
access-list 181 deny    ip any any
! match /22 and /23 prefixes
access-list 182 permit ip any 255.255.252.0 0.0.3.255
access-list 182 deny    ip any any
! match special prefixes
access-list 183 permit ip host 169.223.0.0 host 255.255.0.0
access-list 183 deny    ip any any
! updated gtld name server networks
access-list 184 permit ip host 192.5.6.0 host 255.255.255.0       ! A
access-list 184 permit ip host 192.33.14.0 host 255.255.255.0     ! B
access-list 184 permit ip host 192.26.92.0 host 255.255.255.0     ! C
access-list 184 permit ip host 192.31.80.0 host 255.255.255.0     ! D
access-list 184 permit ip host 192.12.94.0 host 255.255.255.0     ! E
access-list 184 permit ip host 192.35.51.0 host 255.255.255.0     ! F
access-list 184 permit ip host 192.42.93.0 host 255.255.255.0     ! G
access-list 184 permit ip host 192.54.112.0 host 255.255.255.0    ! H
access-list 184 permit ip host 192.36.144.0 host 255.255.255.0    ! I
access-list 184 permit ip host 210.132.96.0 host 255.255.224.0    ! J
access-list 184 permit ip host 213.177.192.0 host 255.255.248.0   ! K
access-list 184 permit ip host 192.41.162.0 host 255.255.255.0    ! L
access-list 184 permit ip host 202.153.112.0 host 255.255.240.0   ! M
access-list 184 deny ip any any
!
```

IP Prefix List Example

Prefix lists also can be used and, indeed, should be used. The preceding example was rewritten using the **ip prefix-list** commands available in Cisco IOS Software versions 11.1CC and 12.0 and later software releases. This makes the configuration more readable, if not more intuitive. Again, remember to check the root nameserver networks for any changes before implementing these. It is also worth checking the BGP routing table to ensure that these networks still are announced with the following prefix lengths:

```
router bgp 65280
 bgp dampening route-map RIPE229-flap-damp
!
ip prefix-list my-nets description Networks we don't suppress
ip prefix-list my-nets seq 5 permit 169.223.0.0/16
!
ip prefix-list suppress22 description Dampening of /22 and /23 prefixes
ip prefix-list suppress22 seq 5 permit 0.0.0.0/0 ge 22 le 23
!
ip prefix-list suppress24 description Dampening of /24 and longer prefixes
ip prefix-list suppress24 seq 5 permit 0.0.0.0/0 ge 24
!
ip prefix-list rootns description Root-nameserver networks
ip prefix-list rootns permit 198.41.0.0/24       ! A & J
ip prefix-list rootns permit 128.9.0.0/16        ! B
ip prefix-list rootns permit 192.33.4.0/24       ! C
ip prefix-list rootns permit 128.8.0.0/16        ! D
ip prefix-list rootns permit 192.203.230.0/24    ! E
ip prefix-list rootns permit 192.5.4.0/23        ! F
ip prefix-list rootns permit 192.112.36.0/24     ! G
ip prefix-list rootns permit 128.63.0.0/16       ! H
ip prefix-list rootns permit 192.36.148.0/24     ! I
ip prefix-list rootns permit 193.0.14.0/24       ! K
ip prefix-list rootns permit 198.32.64.0/24      ! L
ip prefix-list rootns permit 202.12.27.0/24      ! M
!
ip prefix-list gtldns description Global Top Level Domain Servers
ip prefix-list gtldns permit 192.5.6.0/24        ! A
ip prefix-list gtldns permit 192.33.14.0/24      ! B
ip prefix-list gtldns permit 192.26.92.0/24      ! C
ip prefix-list gtldns permit 192.31.80.0/24      ! D
ip prefix-list gtldns permit 192.12.94.0/24      ! E
ip prefix-list gtldns permit 192.35.51.0/24      ! F
ip prefix-list gtldns permit 192.42.93.0/24      ! G
ip prefix-list gtldns permit 192.54.112.0/24     ! H
ip prefix-list gtldns permit 192.36.144.0/24     ! I
ip prefix-list gtldns permit 210.132.96.0/19     ! J
ip prefix-list gtldns permit 213.177.192.0/21    ! K
ip prefix-list gtldns permit 192.41.162.0/24     ! L
ip prefix-list gtldns permit 202.153.112.0/20    ! M
!
route-map RIPE229-flap-damp deny 10
 match ip address prefix-list my-nets
!
route-map RIPE229-flap-damp deny 20
 match ip address prefix-list rootns
```

```
!
route-map RIPE229-flap-damp deny 30
 match ip address prefix-list gtldns
!
route-map RIPE229-flap-damp permit 40
 match ip address prefix-list suppress24
 set dampening 30 820 3000 60
!
route-map RIPE229-flap-damp permit 50
 match ip address prefix-list suppress22
 set dampening 15 750 3000 45
!
route-map RIPE229-flap-damp permit 60
 set dampening 10 1500 3000 30
!
```

Traffic Engineering Tools

As a follow-up on how to track where your customers are going on the Internet, this appendix provides a list of publicly available tools that can be used to pull in statistics from your network. Most ISPs do not use things like HP OpenView, Sun NetManager, CiscoWorks, or Spectrum to manage their networks. These network management packages are great for the enterprise LANs, but they do not have the simple scaleable tools needed for ISP networks. Instead, ISPs pull together different, mostly public-domain, tools and use UNIX scripts to generate charts and reports (with GNUplot or RRDTool) for traffic engineering and quality of service (QoS) management.

Note that one Cisco-specific solution is to use NetFlow. NetFlow first was made available on 75*xx*, 72*xx*, and 7000/RSP running the 11.1CC. The introduction of release 12.0 meant that NetFlow became available on the 3600 series and higher platforms from 12.0(1), and became available on the smaller Cisco IOS Software platforms from 12.0(2)T. It is also available in the form of Sampled NetFlow on the GSR. There are a few whitepapers on the Cisco web pages—searching using the Cisco.com search engine will reveal several of those quite readily.

Internet Traffic and Network Engineering Tools

This section lists just some of the many Internet traffic and network engineering tools available. These are the tools that ISPs use to monitor their networks, help monitor traffic flows, and determine many business-critical functions such as peering policies, QoS, and so on.

Stan Barber presented a talk at the February 1998 NANOG titled "Monitoring Your Network with Freely Available Statistics Reporting Tools." The slides for this presentation are available at http://www.academ.com/nanog/feb1998/nettools.html and are recommended reading for all ISPs wondering how to monitor their new infrastructure.

CAIDA

The Cooperative Association for Internet Data Analysis (CAIDA) has a very comprehensive web site listing a lot of tools and pointers. This CAIDA effort is supported through sponsorship provided by the United States National Science Foundation (NSF), Cisco Systems, and other organizations.

CAIDA: http://www.caida.org

CAIDA Internet Tools Taxonomy: http://www.caida.org/tools/taxonomy.html

Scion/NetScarf

This was a project by Merit Network, Inc., to get a picture of what is happening on the Internet. Apart from versions that run on most UNIX platforms and their variants, there is a version that runs on Windows NT. The most recent version of the software was released in June 1997. The project has now ceased because funding has run out, but the web site and software are still available: http://www.merit.edu/~netscarf/.

NeTraMet/NetFlowMet

NeTraMet is one of the original and better tools for TCP/IP flow analysis. SingNet used NeTraMet on an Intel PC with BSD UNIX and a Digital FDDI card. The results were dumped onto a system that did all the flow analysis, and the results were posted to an internal web server. More recently, a capability has been added to analyze Cisco NetFlow records—NetFlowMet is part of this package now. (See http://www.auckland.ac.nz/net/NeTraMet/.)

cflowd

One of the most popular public-domain tools being used for NetFlow analysis is cflowd. It is hosted by CAIDA and can be found at http://www.caida.org/tools/measurement/cflowd/.

The key Cisco documents on NetFlow are constantly being updated (because Cisco is adding new features and functionality all the time). It's best to do a keyword search on Cisco.com to find all the documentation on NetFlow.

NetFlow tools (flowdata.h, fdrecorder.c, fdplayback.c, and fdg.c) that were used to build cflowd are located on Cisco's FTP site: ftp://ftp-eng.cisco.com/ftp/NetFlow/fde/README.

MRTG

Multi Router Traffic Grapher (MRTG) is a Perl script-based package to create graphics of interface loading on the routers. It saves you from having to create UNIX scripts to do the same thing. MRTG works on UNIX (requiring the more recent versions of Perl 5), and there is a version for Windows NT/2000, too. The package also contains contributed tools enabling you to monitor CPU loads, disk space, temperature, and many other functions that an ISP can use to watch a network. Indeed, virtually anything can be monitored and graphed with MRTG, which makes it a very powerful and extremely popular tool for ISPs. Everything to do with MRTG can be found at http://www.mrtg.org.

RRDTool

RRDTool comes from the author of MRTG and is designed to be a more powerful and flexible system for graphing collected statistics. It is not meant to be a full replacement for MRTG, and future versions of MRTG are planned to sit on top of RRDTool.

RRDTool is gaining popularity with ISPs that want greater variety and flexibility in the graphing that they can do with their MRTG captured data. It can be found at its home site, http://www.rrdtool.org.

Linux Network Management Tools

This site provides a comprehensive list of many of the current Internet network management tools. It includes many of the tools listed in this appendix—for reference purposes, consult http://linas.org/linux/NMS.html.

Vulture

SNMP Vulture is a tool to do long-term SNMP data collection and analysis of routers and other similar devices. Vulture has a number of features that make it suitable for various tasks:

- Per-interface configuration. Different data can be collected on each defined interface.
- Template-based configuration. Different sorts of interfaces might require recording different information; whoever heard of collisions on a serial interface?
- Configurable per-router community strings.
- Web-based graphical browsing of stored data.
- Built-in data-archival mechanism for stale data.

Vulture is written in Perl version 5 and uses the CMU version 2 libraries to do the low-level SNMP access. The Vulture distribution includes both the CMU libraries and a small module to connect the libraries to Perl. The browser interface also requires the generally available Gnuplot and PBMPlus utilities to generate graphical output. See http://www.vix.com/vix/vulture/ for more details.

Net SNMP

The CMU SNMP project was taken over by UCD, briefly called UCD-SNMP and more recently renamed and moved over to SourceForge. The software has been extensively modified and updated and is now considered quite a useable, extensible, and configurable system. Even better, it is freely available at http://net-snmp.sourceforge.net/.

SysMon

Sysmon is a network-monitoring tool designed by Jared Mauch to provide high performance and accurate network monitoring. Currently supported protocols include SMTP, IMAP, HTTP, TCP, UDP, NNTP, and PING tests. More information and the latest version can be found at http://www.sysmon.org/.

Treno

Treno is a tool to develop end-to-end performance information. It can be tried out from PSC from this WWW form interface: http://www.psc.edu/~pscnoc/treno.html. For more information about Treno, go to http://www.psc.edu/~pscnoc/treno_info.html.

Scotty—Tcl Extensions for Network Management Applications

Scotty is the name of a software package that allows implementation of site-specific network management software using high-level, string-based APIs. The software is based on the Tool Command Language (Tcl), the latest source for which can be found at http://www.scriptics.com/, and it is now part of most Linux distributions. Tcl simplifies the development of portable network management scripts.

The Scotty source distribution includes two major components. The first is the Tnm Tcl Extension, which provides access to network management information sources. The second component is the Tkined network editor that provides a framework for an extensible network management system. This tool used to be called Tkined. For more information, see http://wwwhome.cs.utwente.nl/~schoenw/scotty/.

NetSaint

NetSaint is a web-based network-monitoring tool used by several ISPs. It can monitor servers and the network and send e-mail or pages if there are problems. It's written in C and designed to run on Linux. See http://netsaint.sourceforge.net/ for more information.

Big Brother

Another useful tool, similar to NetSaint, is Big Brother. Source code is available for UNIX and Linux. Clients include NT, Novell, and Mac. Visit http://www.bb4.com/ for details.

NOTE	With all of this software available, it is *not* expensive or difficult to collect and analyze data on your network. You can create your own tools and run them on the many Intel-based UNIX systems (for example, Linux, BSDI, and so on).

Other Useful Tools to Manage Your Network

A variety of other tools are available to help with the configuration and management of the network. Most ISPs are well aware of these, but it is worth making a list of the most useful ones to assist newer entrants to the industry in getting a good feel for what is currently in use.

traceroute

The standard UNIX **traceroute** command is probably the most basic tool available for fault detection and diagnosis in the Internet today. The utility also has spawned several enhancements, such as prtraceroute from the PRIDE project and the more advanced traceroute that comes with Linux. Cisco IOS Software, of course, has its own traceroute command, using the routing table in the router to provide detailed information. The source for traceroute can be found at ftp://ftp.ripe.net/tools/traceroute.tar.Z.

For those without access to any of these, or if you require a traceroute from another part of the Internet, an excellent public traceroute facility is located at http://www.traceroute.org, a catalog of traceroute "looking glasses" around the world.

Looking Glasses

A looking glass isn't really a UNIX tool as such; it's more a facility that has been made available by a large number of ISPs and other organizations around the globe. It provides a web interface to users, allowing them to check conditions of the Internet routing table at that site. A complete list of looking glass sites can be found at http://www.traceroute.org.

The most well known and one of the first looking glasses was the one set up by Ed Kern at Digex. It can be found at http://nitrous.digex.net. The source code for Ed's Looking Glass is also there—it builds on any UNIX system.

ISPs that want to make a looking glass available should do so with due consideration of any security issues and, of course, loading on the router. Ideally, looking glass–supporting routers should do just that and should not be part of any critical infrastructure.

whois

Another standard UNIX command that is invaluable for use on the Internet is whois. Many enhancements have been made to whois itself by the PRIDE project in the early 1990s and then by the RIPE NCC, to optimize it to support lookups on Internet databases that were based on the RIPE database software. It is recommended that you replace the shipping whois client on UNIX systems with the RIPE version, available at ftp://ftp.ripe.net/tools/ripe-whois-tools-2.4.tar.gz.

Gnuplot

Gnuplot is a useful public-domain graphing tool. If configuring MRTG is too much, or if you need to graph something else quickly, this is probably the way to do it. See http://www.gnuplot.org/ or http://sourceforge.net/projects/gnuplot/ for details.

RTRMon—A Tool for Router Monitoring and Manipulation

The RTR system currently comes with three programs, rtrmon, rtrpass, and rtrlogin. rtrmon (for "router monitor") is the core of the system. It uses predefined actions to log into routers, issue commands, process the output, archive the results, and possibly mail reports. It is designed to provide the framework for a variety of potential monitoring tasks and to be readily extensible with new reporting code if the built-in methods are insufficient for complex analysis. rtrmon can even update router configurations, despite its monitor moniker.

The rtrpass program is meant to provide an easy interface to a more secure method of storing passwords. Because rtrmon needs to be capable of providing passwords to routers to log into them and to gain enable privileges, routers must be accessible to the hosts on which rtrmon is running. To reduce the risks associated with this, rtrpass manages a PGP-encrypted file for each rtrmon user that contains his own password and his enable password, if the user has enable access. Passwords can be controlled on a per-router basis, if desired.

rtrlogin is used to log into routers, to automatically log in using a username and password, to get enable privileges, to set the terminal length and width to the size of your window, and to run any commands that you have saved in your personal login file. The session then can be used interactively. See http://www.vix.com/vix/rtrmon/ for more information.

RAToolSet/IRRToolSet

The RAToolSet is a suite of tools that enable ISPs to simplify and streamline the implementation of BGP policies in their peerings with other ISPs. The software suite runs on most UNIX systems and was built by Cengiz Alaettinoglu while working at ISI in California.

The RAToolSet requires the existence of a routing registry from which to derive its configurations—this routing registry can be part of the Internet Routing Registry (IRR), or it can be a private routing registry run by the ISP. The registry contains policy descriptions of routes that appear in the Internet, policy descriptions of autonomous systems used in the Internet, and other valuable information. The three regional Internet registries are part of the Internet Routing Registry—other members of the IRR include the RADB (run by Merit Network) and several provider-run routing registries.

The RAToolSet now is maintained by the RIPE NCC and has been renamed the IRRToolSet to reflect its function in today's Internet. More information can be found on the RIPE NCC's web site at http://www.ripe.net/ripencc/pub-services/db/irrtoolset/index.html—this includes information about the origin and requirements to use the toolset, as well as a mailing list of users and participants. The software can be downloaded from ftp://ftp.ripe.net/tools/IRRToolSet.

Features that are part of the IRRToolSet include RtConfig (a router configuration generator), AOE (AS Object Editor), and ROE (Route Object Editor). These three tools are perhaps the most widely used components of the toolset, and many ISPs make use of them to simplify and automate the generation of eBGP configurations.

Cisco's MIBs

All the Cisco SNMP MIBs are publicly available. If you have commercial SNMP management packets or shareware-freeware packets, you might need to grab the MIB. Here is the FTP site: ftp://ftp.cisco.com/pub/mibs/.

Replacement Syslog Daemons

Some ISPs are not satisfied with the standard syslog function bundled with most UNIX systems. Hence, there have been some efforts to provide an enhanced capability. Two examples are given here.

syslog-ng

syslog-ng is a replacement for the standard syslog found on most UNIX systems. It is supported on Linux, BSD, AIX, HP-UX, and Solaris. It gives a much enhanced configuration scheme that enables the filtering of messages based not only on priority/facility pairs, but also on message content. Regular expressions also can be used to direct log streams to different destinations. syslog-ng also supports forwarding logs on TCP, with hash-protected log files planned for a future release. See http://www.balabit.hu/en/products/syslog-ng/ for more information.

Modular Syslog (msyslog)

Until quite recently, secure syslog (ssyslog) was available for UNIX systems. Designed to replace the syslog daemon, ssyslog implements a cryptographic protocol called PEO-1 that allows the remote auditing of system logs. Auditing remains possible even if an intruder gains superuser privileges in the system. The protocol guarantees that the information logged before and during the intrusion process cannot be modified without the auditor (on a remote, trusted host) noticing.

However, the project now has been superceded by Modular Syslog (msyslog), which uses many of the features of ssyslog—msyslog can be obtained from www.corest.com.

Overall Internet Status and Performance Tools

Many people are asking just how well the Internet is performing. Ever since the NSFnet was decommissioned, there has been no one place to understand the performance and traffic profiles on the Internet. Yet people trying to figure out how to do this. The following lists are sites, projects, and software attempting to get a true big picture of what is happening on the Internet. ISPs can elect to join one or more of these programs to add more data to these projects.

NetStat

This tool pings various parts of the Internet from various locations on the Internet, collects the data, and provides an average response time on the major U.S. backbone. It is based on ping. For more information, visit http://www.netstatsys.com/.

What Other ISPs Are Doing

Here are just a few examples of what ISPs from all over the Internet are using to manage their network. Randy Bush (randy@psg.com) asked major ISPs in the United States on the NANOG mailing list what they used for traffic analysis. His summary follows. Notice especially the number of UNIX script-based tools. Readers can find more information by looking at the NANOG mailing list archives at www.nanog.org.

We do SNMP polling every 15 minutes at SESQUINET on every line over which we have administrative control and over every peering point. We produce a daily report on errors and usage. We are getting ready to switch to Vulture or NetScarf (or some combo) to give us more interactive information.

We perform measurement of certain basic network parameters, such as usage (bandwidth used/total bandwidth) and line error rates on all of our noncustomer links. We perform CPU usage, memory usage, and environmental monitoring of all our routers. We also perform the line usage and error rate on all customer lines. We monitor all of our customers' routers unless they say otherwise and notify them of any problems. Finally, we monitor select points throughout the Internet (root name servers and so on) on a four-times-an-hour basis using pings. We accomplish this monitoring using the following items: an in-house built package that uses SNMP, traceroute, and ping to provide graphs and tabular statistical information. We use Cabletron's Spectrum for a quick network overview.

We do SNMP MIB-II stuff, plus the cflowd stuff and something we call mxd (which measures round-trip times, packet loss and potential reason, and so on, from a whole bunch of different points in our network to a bunch of other points in our network. We use it to create delay matrices, packet loss reports, and other reports. There are some other things, but these are the biggies.

The mxd thing was originally just sort of a toy for neat reports, but in the last year, it has become a critical tool for measuring delay variance for one of our VPDN customers that does real-time video stuff (and is, to some extent, helping us figure out where we have delay jitter and why; however, it's also raising more questions).

Because most of my professional career has been in the enterprise world, I can offer you what we used to measure availability to our mail servers, Web servers, DNS servers, and so on at one of my previous employers.

We employed several application tests, along with network performance tests. Our primary link was via UUnet, a burstable T1. We purchased an ISDN account from another local provider who wasn't directly connected to UUnet. Probably a good example of a joe-average-user out there.

Every five minutes, we measured round-trip response times to each of the servers and gateway router (via **ping**) and recorded it. We also had application tests, such as DNS lookups on our servers, timing **sendmail** test mails to a /dev/null account and time to retrieve the whole home page.

This wasn't meant to be a really great performance-monitoring system; it was actually meant to 1. check how our availability looked from a "joe user" perspective on the Net (granted, reachability/availability wasn't perfect because it was only one point in the net), and 2. look at response time trends/application trends to see if our hardware/software was cutting it.

We use a traffic flow monitoring system from Kaspia Systems (www.kaspia.com). The Kaspia product collects all sorts of data from router ports and RMON probes, stores the data, and performs various trend analysis. We collect traffic flow, router CPU usage, and router memory information plus various errors. There is a data-reduction process that runs once a day and a very nifty Web interface. The product is not cheap, but the system definitely fills a void here.

Maybe I should organize a talk on what we are doing with it for an upcoming NANOG. As an old instrumentation engineer, I think the basis of our use of the tool is pretty solid. Plus, I actually developed a means for calibration of the accuracy of the flow data. I have not had time yet to work out a validation for the trends, but I'll get to it one of these decades.

Also, the Kaspia people will give you a 30-day trial on their product at no charge.

For nonintrusive stuff, we keep a log of all interface status changes on our routers, and we pull five-minute byte-counts inbound and outbound on each interface, which we graph against port speed. Watching the graphs for any sort of clipping of peaks gives a pretty good indication of problems, and watching for shifts of traffic between ports on parallel paths does likewise.

As for intrusive testing, we do a three-packet min-length **ping** to the LAN-side port of each of our customers' routers once each five minutes, and we follow that up with additional attempts if those three are lost. We log latency, and if we have to follow up with a burst, we log loss rate from the burst. **Ping**ing through to the LAN port obviously lets us know when CPE routers konk out; occasionally we see hung routers that still have operational WAN ports talking to us. Likewise, simply watching VC-state isn't a reliable enough indicator of the status of the remote router. Plus, it tells you if the customer has kicked the Ethernet transceiver off their equipment, for instance. It wouldn't matter to you probably, but our demarc is all the way out at the WAN port because we own and operate our customers' CPE.

I think a bit about what more we could be doing; flows analysis and whatnot. . .. It's nice to think about, and eventually we'll get around to it, but programmer time is relatively precious and other things have higher priority because the current system works and tends to tell us most of what we seem to need to know to provide decent service.

We place quite a bit of emphasis on network stats. Currently we have about three years of stats online, and we are working on converting our in-house engine to an rdbms so we can more easily perform trend analysis. Besides Kaspia, other commercial packages include trendsnmp (www.desktalk.com) and concord's packages (www.concord.com). Our in-house stuff is located at http://netop.cc.buffalo.edu/, if you are curious about what we do.

We are Neanderthals right now—we use a hacked rcisco to feed data to nocol. We watch bandwidth (separately as well) on key links—and also watch input errors and interface transitions (for nocol)—all done with Perl and expect-like routines, parsing "sho int's" every few minutes.

Emergency stuff goes through nocol; bandwidth summaries are mailed to interested parties overnight.

We have running here now the MRTG package that generates some fancy graphics, but, in my opinion, these graphics are useless, and looking in detail to some of the reports, they are not accurate. Several of our clients request the raw data, but this package only maintains raw data just to generate the graphs.

In the past we used to have a kind of ASCII report (Vikas wrote some of the scripts and programs) generated from information obtained using the old SNMP tool set developed by nysernet, but I guess that nobody maintained the config files and I believe that the SNMP library routines used aren't working.

We have been using the MRTG package, which is basically a special SNMP agent that queries the routers for stats and then does some nice graphing of the data on the Web.

SNMP queries with a heavily modified version of MRTG from the nice guy in Germany. It works very nicely. We have recently installed NetScarf 2.0, and are contemplating merging NetScarf 3.0 with the MRTG front end.

I'm researching whether I can rewrite Steve Corbato's fastpoll program using the fastsnmp library from the NetScarf people. I think this will allow fastpoll to scale better. I've successfully written a quick C program that uses the library to collect the required data for a router—now I've just got to make it so that we can manage it easily (in other words, autogenerated config files from our databases).

My goal is to be able to collect 1- to 2-minute period data on all links that are greater than 10 Mbps—15 minutes of data for everything else. The two-minute collection period will allow the bandwidth to scale up to 280 Mbps before experiencing two counter rollovers within a polling interval. Hopefully that will hold us over until the interface counters are available as Counter64 objects with SNMPv2 (if that ever happens).

What fastpoll collects now is ifInOctets, ifOutOctets, ifInUcastPkts, ifOutUcastPkts, ifInErrors, and ifOutDiscards. Rather than storing the raw counters, it calculates the rate by dividing the delta by the period. Getting the accurate period is actually the hard part—I am having SNMP send me the uptime of the router in each query and using that to calculate the interval between polls and to detect counter resets due to reboots. The other trick to handle is the fact that, although IOS Software updates the SNMP counters for process-switched packets as they are routed, it looks like the counter for SSE switched packets on C70X0 routers get updated only once every 10 seconds.

Summary

As you can see, there are many ways of monitoring information from the ISP network. That most ISPs use their own custom scripts perhaps shows the lack of commercial software available in this area and that each ISP operation has its own unique conditions and ways of going about things.

One day a forward-looking organization will produce a combined software tool with the usability of all these features and yet is lightweight enough to operate scaleably and flexibly in an ISP's backbone network. Even those ISPs that have implemented commercial packages seem to require a fair amount of Perl scripting to provide coverage or support for features or services in their network.

This appendix naturally lists only a snapshot of what is available. You are encouraged to check updates and ask on the various operator forums what the current trends and practices are.

Example ISP Access Security Migration Plan

This appendix gives one example of how an ISP could migrate its network equipment (routers, switches, and NAS) from a state in which Telnet access is open to the outside world to the point at which only specific authorized workstations are allowed access to the Telnet prompt.

Unfortunately, at the time this text was written, most ISPs were not taking these simple precautions to help secure their networks. This section is designed to help those ISPs put in the minimum necessary precautions. This is a simple procedure that draws a security circle around an ISP's network and then slowly narrows the circle until just the authorized IP addresses are included in the VTY's ACL.

Use this appendix in conjunction with the security template recommended in Appendix B, "Cut and Paste Templates." ISPs starting with a new network deployment should be using the templates discussed earlier—to fix a problem highlighted by reading this book, follow the three-phase plan listed in this appendix.

Phase 1—Close Off Access to Everyone Outside the CIDR Block

The theme in Phase 1 is to get the ball rolling by limiting access to just those IP addresses inside the ISP's CIDR block. A standard ACL is created to permit Telnet only from the IP addresses in the CIDR block. This ACL is used with the VTY's **access-class** command to ensure that the source IP address of any Telnet packet coming to the VTY port matches the ACL.

Why just the ISP's CIDR block? First, it's an easy-to-implement technique for an ISP that has no filters. The ISP does not have to worry about locking out staff members who need access to the router from different parts of the network. Hence, it can be done with the least worry that it will affect the ISP's operations. Second, it limits the threat from the entire Internet to just IP addresses inside the ISP's CIDR block. Minimizing risk is one of the fundamental requirements of security. Finally, because the ISP is beginning with no protection, this incremental step ensures that everything is working before deepening the security configurations on the network.

Figure F-1 is an example of an ISP's network. The allocated CIDR blocks are 169.223.0.0/16 and 211.255.0.0/19[1]. Phase 1 involves creating an ACL that can be used with the VTY's **access-class** command to restrict Telnet to IP addresses with the CIDR block.

Figure F-1 *ISP Network Example*

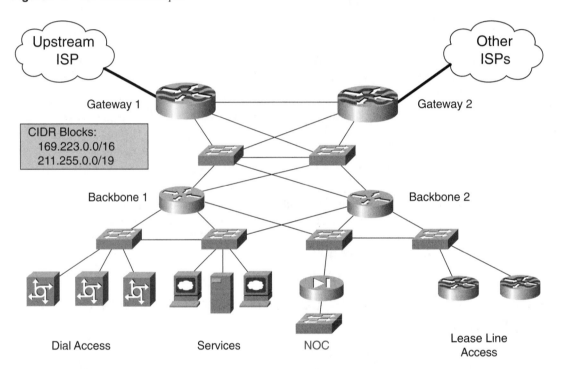

The configuration in Example F-1 is used on all routers in the network. Notice that the AAA authentication used is simplistic—it normally would not be recommended for an ISP backbone. Similar configurations should be used on the switches in the network. Any staff workstations/servers also should use appropriate tools to limit Telnet access to the workstations/server's resources[2].

Example F-1 *Simple VTY Configuration to Limit Access to Just the ISP's CIDR Block*

```
aaa new-model
aaa authentication login ISP local
!
username Cisco1 password 7 11041811051B13
!
access-list 3 permit 211.255.0.0 0.0.31.255
access-list 3 permit 169.223.0.0 0.0.255.255
access-list 3 deny   any
!
line vty 0 4
 access-class 3 in
 exec-timeout 5 0
 transport preferred none
 transport input telnet
 login authentication ISP
 history size 256
```

Phase 2—Add Antispoofing Filters to Your Peers

Limiting the security risk through restricted Telnet access is only the first step. This just stops the rest of the world from logging into the ISP's routers—they still are open to your customers and any other location that is using address space (legitimately or otherwise) from ISP's CIDR block.

The next step is to ensure that parties outside the ISP's network cannot *spoof* source addresses from the ISP's CIDR block. Several forms of source address spoofing and Telnet sequence number hijacking attacks can penetrate the VTY's access class protections. To minimize the risk of these sorts of attacks, an ISP can place antispoofing filters at the edges of its network.

As highlighted in Chapter 4, "Security," antispoofing filters are used to ensure that any address coming from the Internet into the ISP's network does not contain a source address from the ISP's network. For example, if a packet from the Internet with a source address of 211.255.1.1 comes into the ISP in Figure F-2, the antispoofing filter would drop the packet.

WARNING   Remember, no one from the general Internet should be sending you packets with a source address from your own network!

Few ISPs implement antispoofing packet filters. The key reason given is possible performance impact. Yes, applying packet filters to any router might cause a performance impact, but, as has been demonstrated in Chapter 4, tools such as Unicast RPF have minimal CPU impact at multimegabit-per-second speeds. An essential tenet of security is balancing the trade-offs. Sacrificing some performance to minimize the security risk to valuable network resources[3] is a logical trade-off, made less of a trade-off these days especially with the new improvements in packet per second (PPS) that the more recent Cisco IOS Software offers ISPs.[4]

Where to Place the Antispoofing Packet Filters

Place antispoofing filters at the edge of an ISP's network. This usually means the router(s) that interconnects with other ISPs. Routers Gateway1 and Gateway2 are examples in Figure F-2. Any attempt to spoof from the core of the Internet (in other words, the upstream ISP) or an ISP peer connection would be dropped on the inbound interface.

Figure F-2   *Applying Antispoofing Filters*

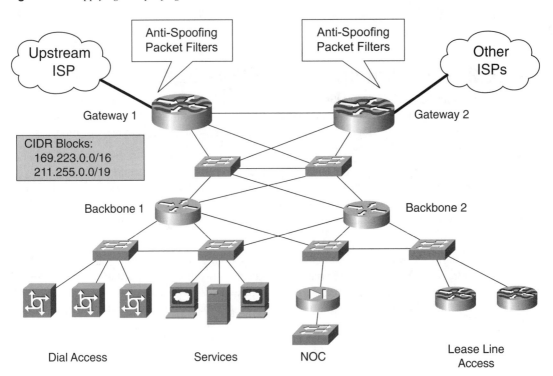

Example F-2 highlights a typical antispoofing filter. Notice that two CIDR blocks are used in the example—169.223.0.0/16 and 211.255.0.0/19—two lines of seven in the ACL 111. Here is what the other lines do:

- deny ip 127.0.0.0 0.255.255.255—This is the loopback address for TCP workstations, PCs, and servers. It should not be transmitted over the Internet. If it is, then it is either a broken TCP stack or an indication that someone is trying to break into a resource.

- deny ip 10.0.0.0 0.255.255.255—RFC 1918 private address space. Cisco advocates RFC 1918 private address space use in enterprise networks in conjunction with Network Address Translation (NAT). Any packets with RFC 1918 addresses in their source either are from a broken NAT implementation or are part of a spoofing attack.

- deny ip 172.16.0.0 0.15.255.255—RFC 1918 private address space.

- deny ip 192.168.0.0 0.0.255.255—RFC 1918 private address space.

- deny ip 169.223.0.0 0.0.255.255—One of the example ISP's CIDR blocks.

- deny ip 211.255.0.0 0.0.31.255—The other CIDR block.

- permit ip any any—Permit normal packets.

Each line with a **deny** has a **log** option turned on. This includes any matches in the internal log buffer and output to syslog (if the router has it configured). The **log** option is not used on the last **permit**. Good packets do not need to be logged. Note that enabling logging will take a more significant CPU hit because logged packets need to be sent to the process level in the router to be recorded and sent to the loghost. Logging generally is enabled only when the ISP wants to monitor potential or apparent attacks happening on its network.

Example F-2 *Antispoofing Configuration Example*

```
Router Gateway1
!
interface hssi 0/1
 description 16Mbps link to our upstream provider
 bandwidth 16384
 ip access-group 111 in
 no ip redirects
 no ip directed-broadcast
 no ip proxy-arp
!
access-list 111 deny ip 127.0.0.0 0.255.255.255 any log
access-list 111 deny ip 10.0.0.0 0.255.255.255 any log
access-list 111 deny ip 172.16.0.0 0.15.255.255 any log
access-list 111 deny ip 192.168.0.0 0.0.255.255 any log
access-list 111 deny ip 169.223.0.0 0.0.255.255 any log
access-list 111 deny ip 211.255.0.0 0.0.31.255 any log
access-list 111 permit ip any any
```

continues

Example F-2 *Antispoofing Configuration Example (Continued)*

```
Router Gateway2
!
interface serial 0/1
 description Compressed 2Mbps bi-lateral peer to our neighboring country
 bandwidth 2048
 ip access-group 111 in
 no ip redirects
 no ip directed-broadcast
 no ip proxy-arp
!
access-list 111 deny ip 127.0.0.0 0.255.255.255 any log
access-list 111 deny ip 10.0.0.0 0.255.255.255 any log
access-list 111 deny ip 172.16.0.0 0.15.255.255 any log
access-list 111 deny ip 192.168.0.0 0.0.255.255 any log
access-list 111 deny ip 169.223.0.0 0.0.255.255 any log
access-list 111 deny ip 211.255.0.0 0.0.31.255 any log
access-list 111 permit ip any any
```

Phase Three—Close Off Network Equipment to Unauthorized Access

When Phase 1 and Phase 2 are completed, work can begin on Phase 3—closing off access to everyone except the NOC staff. The speed an ISP moves from the first two phases to the third phase is dependent on the confidence of the ISP's engineers. Some might want to monitor the operational impact of the first two phases before incrementing another layer of security. Others might bypass Phase 1 and immediately restrict access only to the NOC staff. Either way works. Each ISP needs to develop plans that suit its environment. The most important thing is to implement the security measures.

Two basic steps are necessary to close Telnet access to just the NOC staff. First, identify the IP address block for the NOC's network. Figure F-3 shows the NOC's network behind a firewall using IP block 211.255.1.0/24. Second, modify the ACLs for the VTY's access class with the addresses assigned to the NOC. Example F-3 highlights this modification.

Figure F-3   *Closing Off Access to Everyone Except the NOC Staff*

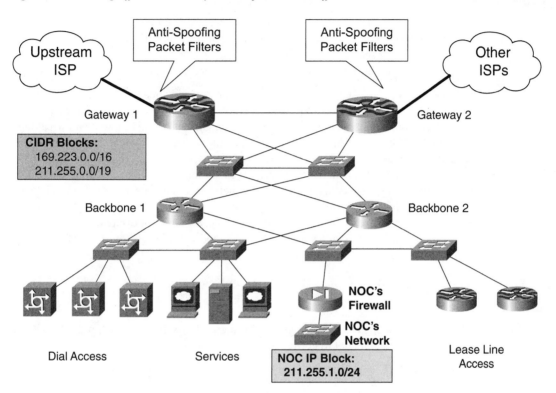

Example F-3   *ACLs with Telnet Access Closed to All but the NOC's Network*

```
aaa new-model
aaa authentication login ISP local
!
username Cisco1 password 7 11041811051B13
!
access-list 3 permit 211.255.1.0 0.0.0.255
access-list 3 deny    any
!
line vty 0 4
 access-class 3 in
 exec-timeout 5 0
 transport preferred none
 transport input telnet
 login authentication ISP
 history size 256
```

Summary

The three simple phases in this appendix are all that are required to convert a wide-open, insecure ISP backbone into one with moderate security. It is quite possible to wrap up the network even more securely, and you are encouraged to consult the main body of the book, especially Chapter 4, to find recommendations of what to do next.

The downsides of an insecure backbone have been covered already in the main text. But it is worth reiterating that if some unauthorized person can get a login prompt for an ISP's network equipment, that person has a very good chance of breaking into it and wreaking havoc in that backbone. Worse, the unauthorized individual could plant "time bombs" that the ISP is unaware of until they take effect. Security is a mandatory requirement for an ISP backbone—if it isn't there at the moment, you are strongly encouraged to drop everything, even pause reading this book, and protect your network immediately. It's never too late. As more ISPs tighten up security, those that previously relied on obscurity for their security will become targets, resulting in operational misery and angry or disappointed customers. Because customers are usually a business's livelihood, avoiding customer dissatisfaction is usually a high priority.

Endnotes

[1] These networks do not represent a real allocation. They were pulled from the APNIC blocks as an example, not to portray any real, live network.

[2] Tools such as TCP Wrapper are well known and have a role in an ISP's overall security architecture.

[3] Spoofing attacks are more likely to target workstation and server resources. These resources likely would depend on tools such as TCP Wrapper—these wrappers also can be bypassed by spoofing attacks. So placement of antispoofing filters protects the entire network, not just the routers.

[4] This includes distributed switching (FIB), Cisco Express Forwarding (CEF), Distributed NetFlow, and other improvements in the 11.1CC and 12.0S code trains.

GLOSSARY

ACE	access control entry (single line in an ACL)
ACL	access control list
AFRINIC	African Regional Network Information Center
APNIC	Asia Pacific Network Information Center
APOPS	Asia Pacific Operators
APRICOT	Asia Pacific Rim Internet Conference on Operational Technologies
ARIN	American Registry for Internet Numbers
ARPANET	Advanced Research Projects Agency Network
AS	autonomous system
ASIC	application-specific integrated circuit
ATM	Asynchronous Transfer Mode
BCP	best current practice
BGP	Border Gateway Protocol
BOOTP	Boot Protocol
CAR	Committed Access Rate
CEF	Cisco Express Forwarding
CIDR	classless interdomain routing
CLI	command-line interface
CPU	central processing unit
dCEF	Distributed Cisco Express Forwarding
DHCP	Dynamic Host Configuration Protocol
DLL	dynamic link library

DNS	Domain Name System
DoS	denial of service
EGP	exterior gateway protocol
EOF	European Operators Forum
FIB	Forwarding Information Base
FTP	File Transfer Protocol
GPS	global positioning system
HSRP	Hot Standby Routing Protocol
IANA	Internet Assigned Numbers Authority
IEPG	Internet Engineering and Planning Group
IETF	Internet Engineering Task Force
IGP	interior gateway protocol
INET	Internet Society's annual conference
InterNIC	Internet Network Information Center
IOS	Internet Operating System (Cisco IOS)
IRR	Internet Routing Registry
IS-IS	Intermediate System-to-Intermediate System
ISP	Internet service provider
LACNIC	Latin American and Caribbean Network Information Center
LIR	Local Internet Registry
MED	multiexit discriminator
MIB	Management Information Base
MIT	maintenance-induced trouble
MPLS	Multiprotocol Label Switching
NANOG	North American Network Operators Group
NAS	network access server
NOC	network operations center
NSAP	network service access point
NSP	network services provider
NTP	Network Time Protocol
ORF	outbound route filter
OSPF	Open Shortest Path First

PGP	pretty good privacy
PoP	point of presence
PoP3	Post Office Protocol version 3
PPP	Point-to-Point Protocol
PPS	packets per second
QoS	quality of service
RADB	Routing Arbiter Database
RAM	random-access memory
RFC	Request For Comments (IETF document)
RIB	Routing Information Base
RIP	Routing Information Protocol
RIPE	Réseaux IP Européens
RIPE NCC	RIPE Network Coordination Center
RIR	Regional Internet Registry
RR	route reflector
RPC	remote-procedure call
RPF	reverse path forwarding
SMTP	Simple Mail Transfer Protocol
SNMP	Simple Network Management Protocol
SPD	selective packet discard
STD	Internet standard—status of IETF document
TAC	Technical Assistance Center
TCAM	ternary content addressable memory
TCP	Transmission Control Protocol
TFTP	Trivial File Transfer Protocol
TLD	top-level domain
uRPF	unicast reverse path forwarding
VIP	Versatile Interface Processor (found on 7500 family)
VPN	virtual private network
WWW	World Wide Web

Technical References and Recommended Reading

This appendix lists the technical references and further reading pertinent to this book. You are encouraged to review the references quoted. The references from each section of *Cisco ISP Essentials* have been listed separately.

Software and Router Management

Cisco product bulletins

http://www.cisco.com/warp/public/cc/general/bulletin/index.shtml

Cisco IOS Software Release 12.0S new features

http://www.cisco.com/warp/public/cc/pd/iosw/iore/iomjre12/prodlit/934_pb.htm

Cisco IOS Software Release 12.0S ordering procedures and platform hardware support

http://www.cisco.com/warp/public/cc/pd/iosw/iore/iomjre12/prodlit/935_pb.htm

Cisco IOS Software release notes for Release 12.0S

http://www.cisco.com/univercd/cc/td/doc/product/software/ios120/relnote/7000fam/rn120s.htm

Cisco IOS Software Release 12.0S migration guide

http://www.cisco.com/warp/public/cc/pd/iosw/iore/iomjre12/prodlit/940_pb.htm

Cisco IOS Releases

http://www.cisco.com/warp/public/732/Releases/

Types of Cisco IOS Software releases

http://www.cisco.com/warp/public/cc/pd/iosw/iore/prodlit/537_pp.htm

Cisco IOS Software release designations defined—"Software Lifecycle Definitions"

http://www.cisco.com/warp/public/417/109.html

Software naming conventions for Cisco IOS

http://www.cisco.com/warp/customer/432/7.html

Cisco IOS reference guide

http://www.cisco.com/warp/public/620/1.html

Cisco IOS roadmap

http://www.cisco.com/warp/public/620/roadmap.shtml

Cisco Resource Manager

http://www.cisco.com/warp/public/cc/pd/wr2k/rsmn/index.shtml

Private I

http://www.opensystems.com/index.asp

Crystal Reports

http://www.seagatesoftware.com/crystalreports/

Netforensics

http://www.netforensics.com/

NTP RFCs

RFC 1128, RFC 1129, RFC 1165, and RFC 1305, all available at http://www.ietf.org/rfc

Cisco IOS Software NTP architecture

http://www.cisco.com/univercd/cc/td/doc/product/iaabu/cddm/cddm111/adguide/ntp.htm

Network Time Protocol (NTP) master clock for the United States

http://tycho.usno.navy.mil/

Datum Inc., Bancomm Timing Division

http://www.datum.com/

True Time, Inc.

http://www.truetime.com

The Time Web Server (Time Sync), by Dave Mills

http://www.eecis.udel.edu/~ntp/

Coetanian Systems Time Synchronization Server 100

http://www.coetanian.com/tss/tss100.htm

UCD-SNMP project home page

http://net-snmp.sourceforge.net/

Creating core dumps in Cisco IOS Software

http://www.cisco.com/univercd/cc/td/doc/cisintwk/itg_v1/tr19aa.htm

General Features

Cisco IOS command-line interface

http://www.cisco.com/univercd/cc/td/doc/product/software/ios120/12cgcr/fun_r/index.htm

CEF whitepaper

http://www.cisco.com/warp/public/cc/pd/iosw/iore/tech/cef_wp.htm

Cisco Express Forwarding overview (12.0 docs)

http://www.cisco.com/univercd/cc/td/doc/product/software/ios120/12cgcr/switch_c/xcprt2/xccef.htm

Cisco Express Forwarding configuration task list

http://www.cisco.com/univercd/cc/td/doc/product/software/ios120/12cgcr/switch_c/xcprt2/xccefc.htm

Phil Harris's *Packet Magazine* article on CEF (more of a CEF FAQ)

http://www.cisco.com/warp/public/784/packet/oct99/router.html

Security

Increasing security on IP networks. An old but very important document on some of the security essentials in IP-based networks.

http://www.cisco.com/univercd/cc/td/doc/cisintwk/ics/cs003.htm

Cisco's Internet security advisories. An online list of all of Cisco's security advisories. It includes tutorials and details on how to protect yourself from some of the ugliness on the Internet today.

http://www.cisco.com/warp/customer/707/advisory.html

Cisco's IOS Software documentation—"12.2 Security Configuration Guide." The documentation with IOS Software Release 12.2 release reorganizes many of the security features of IOS into their own chapter. Available on the Cisco Documentation CD or publicly online at Cisco.com:

http://www.cisco.com/univercd/cc/td/doc/product/software/ios122/122cgcr/fsecur_c/f

Cisco IOS password-encryption tips

http://www.cisco.com/warp/public/701/64.html

Defining strategies to protect against UDP diagnostic port denial-of-service attacks

http://www.cisco.com/warp/public/707/3.html

Cisco public domain TACACS+ server for UNIX

ftp://ftp-eng.cisco.com/pub/tacacs/tac_plus.F4.0.4.alpha.tar.Z

Neighboring router authentication: overview and guidelines

http://www.cisco.com/univercd/cc/td/doc/product/software/ios112/122cgcr/fsecur_c/fothers/scfroutr.htm

Cisco IOS TurboACL documentation

http://www.cisco.com/univercd/cc/td/doc/product/software/ios120/120newft/120limit/120s/120s6/turboacl.htm

Committed Access Rate (CAR)

http://www.cisco.com/warp/public/732/Tech/car/index.html

Configuring Committed Access Rate

http://www.cisco.com/univercd/cc/td/doc/product/software/ios122/122cgcr/fqos_c/fqcprt1/qcfcar.htm

RFC 1812. "Requirements for IP Version 4 Routers." F. Baker (ed). June 1995. (Status: Proposed standard.) Also see the update, RFC 2644.

http://www.ietf.org/rfc/rfc1812.txt

RFC 2196/FYI8. "Site Security Handbook." B. Fraser. September 1997. (Obsoletes RFC 1244) (Status: Informational.) One of the most useful starting places for Internet security.

http://www.ietf.org/rfc/rfc2196.txt

RFC 2827/BCP 38. "Network Ingress Filtering: Defeating Denial-of-Service Attacks Which Employ IP Source Address Spoofing." P. Ferguson and D. Senie. May 2000. (Status: Best current practice.)

http://www.ietf.org/rfc/rfc2827.txt

RFC 2350/BCP 21. "Expectations for Computer Security Incident Response."
N. Brownlee and E. Guttman, June 1998. (Status: Best current practice.)

http://www.ietf.org/rfc/rfc2350.txt

RFC 2644/BCP 34. "Changing the Default for Directed Broadcasts on Routers."
D. Senie. August 1999. (Supplement to RFC 1812.) (Status: Best current practice.)

http://www.ietf.org/rfc/rfc2644.txt

RFC 3013/BCP 46. "Security Expectations for Internet Service Providers." T. Killalea.
November 2000. (Status: Best current practice.)

http://www.ietf.org/rfc/rfc3013.txt

"Security Checklist for Internet Service Provider (ISP) Consumers." draft-ietf-grip-user-02.txt. (Now expired.) T. Hansen. June 1999.

Not an IETF web site any more, but you can still find it by searching various online archives.

"Site Security Handbook Addendum for ISPs." draft-ietf-grip-ssh-add-00.txt. (Now expired.) T. Debeaupuis, August 1999.

Not an IETF web site any more, but you can still find it by searching various online archives.

Craig Huegen's Smurf Page. A very useful resource for ISPs to learn how to protect themselves from the many flavors of denial-of-service attacks.

http://www.pentics.net/

Denial-of-Service Attacks Information Pages. By Paul Ferguson and Daniel Senie. Another very useful resource for ISPs to learn how to protect themselves from the many flavors of denial-of-service attacks.

http://www.denialinfo.com/

Jared Mauch's Smurf Sweep Results Page. (jared@puck.nether.net) Jared has scanned large sections of the Internet looking for networks that could be used as smurf amplifiers. This page lists his results and provides a way to check IP prefixes and AS numbers.

http://puck.nether.net/smurf-check/

Routing

Internet Routing Architectures, **Second Edition.** Cisco Press.
(http://www.ciscopress.com) ISBN 1-57870-0233-X. Authors: Sam Halabi with Danny McPherson.

RFC 2281. "Cisco Hot Standby Routing Protocol." March 1998 (Status: Informational.)

http://www.ietf.org/rfc/rfc2281.txt

"Using the Border Gateway Protocol for Interdomain Routing." Available on the Cisco Documentation CD or publicly online at Cisco.com:

http://www.cisco.com/univercd/cc/td/doc/cisintwk/ics/icsbgp4.htm

"Internetworking Technology Overview." Online whitepapers and tutorials on the essentials of routing and switching. Available on the Cisco Documentation CD or publicly online at Cisco.com:

http://www.cisco.com/univercd/cc/td/doc/cisintwk/ito_doc/index.htm

Technology information and whitepapers. Key references and practical internetworking examples. Available on the Cisco Documentation CD or publicly online at Cisco.com:

http://www.cisco.com/univercd/cc/td/doc/cisintwk/index.htm

Other References and Recommended Reading

Cisco ISP Essentials **online version**

http://www.cisco.com/public/cons/isp/essentials

Cisco ISP Essentials supporting web site: http://www.ispbook.com.

Computer Networks, Third Edition, by Andrew Tannenbaum (ISBN: 0-13349-945-6).

Interconnections: Bridges and Routers, Second Edition, by Radia Perlman
(ISBN: 0-20163-448-1).

Internetworking with TCP/IP, Volume 1: Principles, Protocols, and Architecture, by Douglas Comer (ISBN: 0-13216-987-8).

IP Routing Fundamentals, by Mark Sportack (ISBN: 1-57870-071-x).

IP Routing Primer, by Robert Wright (ISBN: 1-57870-108-2).

Routing in the Internet, by Christian Huitema (ISBN: 0-13132-192-7).

OSPF Network Design Solutions, by Thomas M. Thomas (ISBN: 1-57870-046-9).

ISP Survival Guide: Strategies for Running a Competitive ISP, by Geoff Huston
(ISBN: 0-47131-499-4).

"Documenting Special Use IPv4 Address Blocks That Have Been Registered with IANA," Internet draft by Bill Manning.

http://www.ietf.org/internet-drafts/draft-manning-dsua-07.txt

INDEX

Symbols

| (vertical bar), string searches, 19–20

A

AAA (Authorization, Authentication, and Accounting)
    command auditing, 156–158
    controlling router access, 154–155
access, out-of-band management
    console servers, 310–311
    modems, 310
    out-of-band circuits, 312
    out-of-band ISDN, 312
access layer, PoP topologies, 228–229
access lists
    route flap-dampening, 373–374
    templates, 333
    types of, 323–324
access network prefixes, 75
access servers, sample configuration, 361–365
ACE depth limit, ASIC-based ACLs, 184
ACLs, 179
    ASIC-based, 183–184
    black-hole routing, 189, 191
    effect on CPU utilization, 179–180
    egress packet filtering, 185
    ingress packet filtering, 187–189
    ISP migration strategies, 391–392
        antispoofing filters, 393–396
    on VTY ports, 149–150
    PSA, 185
    Turbo ACLs, 181–183
activate command, 128
active configurations, storing on NVRAM, 15–17
active NTP modes, 26–27
adding prefixes
    to IGPs, 70–72
    to OSPF, 77
address families, 125
    activate style commands, 128
    network style commands, 129

address space
    applying for, 256
    assigning to customers, 254–255
addressing, sample configuration, 339
adjacency change logging, IGPs, 72–73
advertisements, route filtering, 170–173
    CIDR, 174–178
aggregates, 62
    comparing old and address family style, 133
aggregation routers
    configuring BGP next-hop-self, 95
    packet filtering, 305
    sample configuration, 349–353
analyzing syslog data, 23–24
anti-spoofing filters, peer configuration, 393–396
applications
    BigBrother, 383
    CAIDA, 380
    cflowd, 380
    Gnuplot, 384
    looking glasses, 383–384
    MIBs, 385
    MRTG, 381
    NeTraMet, 380
    NetSaint, 382
    RAToolSet, 385
    RRDTool, 381
    RTRMon, 384
    Scion/NetScarf, 380
    Scotty, 382
    syslog daemons, 385–386
    SysMon, 382
    traceroute, 383
    Treno, 382
    updating, 242
    Vulture, 381
    whois, 384
applying for address space, 256
architecture, NTP, 25
    client/server models, 26–27
AS number, 262
AS path, length restrictions, 105
ASIC-based ACLs, 183–184
assigning address space to customers, 254–255
association modes, NTP, 26–27

U

Train with authorized Cisco Learning Partners.

Discover all that's possible on the Internet.

One of the biggest challenges facing networking professionals is how to stay current with today's ever-changing technologies in the global Internet economy. Nobody understands this better than Cisco Learning Partners, the only companies that deliver training developed by Cisco Systems.

Just go to **www.cisco.com/go/training_ad**. You'll find more than 120 Cisco Learning Partners in over 90 countries worldwide.* Only Cisco Learning Partners have instructors that are certified by Cisco to provide recommended training on Cisco networks and to prepare you for certifications.

To get ahead in this world, you first have to be able to keep up. Insist on training that is developed and authorized by Cisco, as indicated by the Cisco Learning Partner or Cisco Learning Solutions Partner logo.

Visit **www.cisco.com/go/training_ad** today.

CISCO SYSTEMS

EMPOWERING THE
INTERNET GENERATION™

CISCO SYSTEMS
®

IF YOU'RE USING

CISCO PRODUCTS,

YOU'RE QUALIFIED

TO RECEIVE A

FREE SUBSCRIPTION

TO CISCO'S

PREMIER PUBLICATION,

PACKET™ MAGAZINE.

Packet delivers complete coverage of cutting-edge networking trends and innovations, as well as current product updates. A magazine for technical, hands-on Cisco users, it delivers valuable information for enterprises, service providers, and small and midsized businesses.

Packet is a quarterly publication. To start your free subscription, click on the URL and follow the prompts:
www.cisco.com/go/packet/subscribe

☐ **YES!** I'm requesting a **free** subscription to *Packet*™ magazine.

☐ No. I'm not interested at this time.

☐ Mr.
☐ Ms.

First Name (Please Print)   Last Name

Title/Position (Required)

Company (Required)

Address

City   State/Province

Zip/Postal Code   Country

Telephone (Include country and area codes)   Fax

E-mail

Signature (Required)   Date

☐ I would like to receive additional information on Cisco's services and products by e-mail.

1. Do you or your company:
A ☐ Use Cisco products   C ☐ Both
B ☐ Resell Cisco products   D ☐ Neither

2. Your organization's relationship to Cisco Systems:
A ☐ Customer/End User   E ☐ Integrator   J ☐ Consultant
B ☐ Prospective Customer   F ☐ Non-Authorized Reseller   K ☐ Other (specify):
C ☐ Cisco Reseller   G ☐ Cisco Training Partner
D ☐ Cisco Distributor   I ☐ Cisco OEM

3. How many people does your entire company employ?
A ☐ More than 10,000   D ☐ 500 to 999   G ☐ Fewer than 100
B ☐ 5,000 to 9,999   E ☐ 250 to 499
C ☐ 1,000 to 4,999   F ☐ 100 to 249

4. Is your company a Service Provider?
A ☐ Yes   B ☐ No

5. Your involvement in network equipment purchases:
A ☐ Recommend   B ☐ Approve   C ☐ Neither

6. Your personal involvement in networking:
A ☐ Entire enterprise at all sites   F ☐ Public network
B ☐ Departments or network segments at more than one site   D ☐ No involvement
C ☐ Single department or network segment   E ☐ Other (specify):

7. Your Industry:
A ☐ Aerospace   G ☐ Education (K–12)   K ☐ Health Care
B ☐ Agriculture/Mining/Construction   U ☐ Education (College/Univ.)   L ☐ Telecommunications
C ☐ Banking/Finance   H ☐ Government—Federal   M ☐ Utilities/Transportation
D ☐ Chemical/Pharmaceutical   I ☐ Government—State   N ☐ Other (specify):
E ☐ Consultant   J ☐ Government—Local
F ☐ Computer/Systems/Electronics

CPRESS

PACKET

Packet magazine serves as the premier publication linking customers to Cisco Systems, Inc. Delivering complete coverage of cutting-edge networking trends and innovations, *Packet* is a magazine for technical, hands-on users. It delivers industry-specific information for enterprise, service provider, and small and midsized business market segments. A toolchest for planners and decision makers, *Packet* contains a vast array of practical information, boasting sample configurations, real-life customer examples, and tips on getting the most from your Cisco Systems' investments. Simply put, *Packet* magazine is straight talk straight from the worldwide leader in networking for the Internet, Cisco Systems, Inc.

We hope you'll take advantage of this useful resource. I look forward to hearing from you!

Cecelia Glover
Packet Circulation Manager
packet@external.cisco.com
www.cisco.com/go/packet

PACKET